The Early Modern in South Asia

Did modernity arrive in South Asia with British colonialism? Or was South Asia already modern by then? What might have that modernity looked like?

The Early Modern in South Asia engages with these questions. It brings together ten chapters, which collectively trace the contours of South Asia's early modernity between the sixteenth and eighteenth centuries. They do this by examining the nature of historical change in various domains, including philosophy, warfare, law, environment, politics, violence, religion, and society. The chapters argue that in all these fields, there were noticeable developments during this period, marking a shift from the medieval to the early modern. The introductory chapter contextualizes this by analysing the politics of periodization in history-writing across the world. It discusses the meanings of the relatively new concept of early modernity and the implications of its use for how we understand historical change and continuity in South Asia.

Meena Bhargava teaches history at Indraprastha College for Women, University of Delhi, India. She is a historian of medieval and early modern South Asia. The areas of her research include Mughal history, environmental history, history of narcotics and drugs, agrarian history, and land rights in eighteenth- and nineteenth-century India. Her most recent publication is *Understanding Mughal India: Sixteenth to Eighteenth Centuries* (2019).

Pratyay Nath teaches history at Ashoka University, Sonipat, India. He is a historian of early-modern South Asia. The areas of his research include military history, environmental history, imperial history, and history of the historical discipline. His most recent publication is *Climate of Conquest: War, Environment, and Empire in Mughal North India* (2019).

The Early Modern in South Asia

Querying Modernity, Periodization, and History

Edited by
Meena Bhargava
Pratyay Nath

CAMBRIDGE
UNIVERSITY PRESS

University Printing House, Cambridge CB2 8BS, United Kingdom

One Liberty Plaza, 20th Floor, New York, NY 10006, USA

477 Williamstown Road, Port Melbourne, vic 3207, Australia

314 to 321, 3rd Floor, Plot No.3, Splendor Forum, Jasola District Centre, New Delhi 110025, India

103 Penang Road, #05–06/07, Visioncrest Commercial, Singapore 238467

Cambridge University Press is part of the University of Cambridge.

It furthers the University's mission by disseminating knowledge in the pursuit of education, learning and research at the highest international levels of excellence.

www.cambridge.org

Information on this title: www.cambridge.org/9781009215374

© Cambridge University Press 2022

This publication is in copyright. Subject to statutory exception and to the provisions of relevant collective licensing agreements, no reproduction of any part may take place without the written permission of Cambridge University Press.

First published 2022

Printed in India by Avantika Printers Pvt. Ltd.

A catalogue record for this publication is available from the British Library

ISBN 978-1-009-21537-4 Hardback

Cambridge University Press has no responsibility for the persistence or accuracy of URLs for external or third-party internet websites referred to in this publication, and does not guarantee that any content on such websites is, or will remain, accurate or appropriate.

*In memory of
Professor Rajat Datta
1956–2021*

Contents

Acknowledgements ix

1. Introduction: History and the Politics of Periodization 1
   Meena Bhargava and Pratyay Nath

I. Religion, Ideology, Identity

2. Locating the Early Modern in South Asian Sufism 43
   Kashshaf Ghani

3. Beginnings of Modernity in South Asia: Natural Philosophy in Persianate Islam 64
   Charles Ramsey

4. Contestations and Negotiations: Early Modern Individualism in Jain Heterodoxy, *c.* 1470–*c.* 1770 83
   Shalin Jain

II. Economy, Environment, Society

5. Early Modernity and South Asian Economic History: Problematic, Periodization, Processes, and Possibilities 103
   Rajat Datta

6. Markers of the Early Modern: Ecology, State, and Society in Rajasthan 124
   Mayank Kumar

7. Through the Prism of Environmental History: Defining the Early Modern in South Asia 141
   Meena Bhargava

8. The Early Modern Conundrum: Peninsular India and the Idea of
   Periodization in a 'Regional' Perspective 161
   Ranjeeta Dutta

III. Politics, Law, War

9. *Fidalgos, Soldados, Arrenegados*: Portuguese Adventurers in
   Hugli and Early Modern Politics 183
   Radhika Chadha

10. Law, Empire, and the New Julfan Armenians: The Early Modern
    in the Indian Ocean World 203
    Santanu Sengupta

11. Was Mughal Warfare Early Modern? 224
    Pratyay Nath

About the Contributors 247

Index 250

Acknowledgements

In November 2015, Rajat Datta co-organized a two-day conference titled 'Configuring Early Modern South Asia' at the Institute of Advanced Studies, Jawaharlal Nehru University, New Delhi. This was probably the first conference held in India to unpack some of the theoretical aspects of the category of early modernity. It initiated conversations that challenged some of the long-established and jealously guarded methodological orthodoxies of South Asian history-writing. The continuation of these conversations eventually precipitated another conference. Titled 'Debating the Early Modern in South Asian History', this was held at Ashoka University, Sonipat, in February 2018. Most of the chapters of the present volume were initially presented there. As one of the most vocal advocates of the category of early modernity among academics based in India, Datta delivered the keynote address at this conference. He also agreed to co-edit the proceedings afterwards; however, his busy schedule did not allow that. Nevertheless, he continued to be actively involved in the preparation of this volume. But just as we were about to submit the final manuscript to the press, he suddenly passed away on 30 October 2021. Published in this volume, his keynote address from the conference is one of his last publications. It serves as a constant reminder of his absence in a project that he had helped germinate. This volume is dedicated to his memory.

The conference at Ashoka University was supported by the funds generously granted by the then Vice Chancellor, Pratap Bhanu Mehta, and the then Dean of Faculty and Research, Malabika Sarkar. The conference was hosted by the Department of History. Aside from the authors of the chapters this volume carries, we are also thankful to Anubhuti Maurya, Aparna Vaidik, Mahesh Gopalan, Nayanjot Lahiri, Pankaj Jha, Priyanka Khanna, Ranabir Chakravarti, Rudrangshu Mukherjee, Shivangini Tandon, Sraman Mukherjee, and Tanuja Kothiyal for participating in this conference in various capacities. Tanika Sarkar delivered the plenary address. Finally, the staff and students at Ashoka University made sure that the conference ran smoothly. We extend our heartfelt gratitude to each one of these individuals for their contribution in making the conference a success. We only wish that all the papers presented there could be accommodated in this volume.

Soon after this second conference, the process of converting some of the ideas presented there into something more durable began. Here, we were fortunate to have a remarkable group of contributors who supported us through an arduous journey of four years. We are thankful to them for submitting their drafts on time, putting up with our numerous requests for alterations and revisions, and participating in the two workshops we arranged. The volume would not have been possible without their active and wholehearted involvement. We are also grateful to Tanika Sarkar, Shinjini Das, and Akash Bhattacharya, who read an early draft of the introduction and gave us their valuable feedback. Finally, we would like to thank the staff of Cambridge University Press, whose patience, efficiency, and guidance brought this volume to fruition.

Meena Bhargava and Pratyay Nath

1

Introduction

History and the Politics of Periodization

Meena Bhargava and Pratyay Nath

In concluding the second volume of *The History of Bengal*, the doyen of Indian historians, Sir Jadunath Sarkar, lyrically wrote about the demise of the independent Nawabi of Bengal and the emergence of Company rule. As the final episode of Mughal rule in the province, Nawabi rule had brought only misery all around, he argued. As the ruling class indulged in debauchery, factionalism, sadism, and the pursuit of self-interest, the common people had been plunged into 'deepest poverty, ignorance and moral degradation'.[1] Articulating textbook pro-British sentiments, he went on to say that the victory of the English East India Company had released 'the rational progressive spirit of Europe' upon this 'hopelessly decadent society'.[2] Through the gradual establishment of British civil administration, military power, economic structures, and general stabilization of law and order, the region had begun to flourish. This had ushered in an era of rejuvenation of every sphere of social, cultural, and political life. Sarkar argued:

> It was truly a Renaissance, wider, deeper, and more revolutionary than that of Europe after the fall of Constantinople ... under the impact of the British civilization it [Bengal] became a pathfinder and a light-bringer to the rest of India.... In this new Bengal originated every good and great thing of the modern world that passed on to the other provinces of India.[3]

Published in 1948, these lines echoed what another historian Susobhan Sarkar had put down just two years back in a political pamphlet for leftist activists operating in Bengal against the backdrop of the impending partition of India. Here he had outlined his thesis about the 'Bengal Renaissance' – a term he had used to designate what he saw as a religious, intellectual, cultural, and political reawakening in nineteenth-century Bengal. For him, it had been produced by the 'impact of British rule, bourgeois economy and modern western culture' and had heralded the advent of modernity in and the beginning of modernization of India.[4] What Susobhan Sarkar wrote for a non-academic readership, Jadunath Sarkar articulated for an academic one. Together, their arguments represent some of the early interpretations of a set of historical processes that had engulfed Bengal for most of the nineteenth century. These arguments eventually became something of a canon as the idea of this Renaissance as the harbinger of Indian modernity grew roots in academic circles and broader society alike, especially in the decades immediately following India's independence.

Since the 1970s, however, this idea of the Bengal Renaissance came to be fiercely critiqued, mainly by Marxist historians. For instance, Sumit Sarkar criticized its strong elitist orientation. He argued that as a part of the Hindu social elite seeking in British colonial government its deliverance from the ostensible tyranny of Muslim rule, they had facilitated the transformation of South Asia's pre-capitalist society towards a weak and distorted version of colonial, bourgeois modernity in course of the nineteenth century. Patronized by this social group, the scope of the so-called Bengal Renaissance had remained limited to a small elite Hindu social circle and a colonial intellectual framework, and it had failed to make any enduring contribution towards genuine social transformation.[5]

By the beginning of the 1990s, scholars informed by postcolonial theory started analysing the nature of colonial power and the meanings of nationalism. In turn, this led to the problematization of the very idea of the modernity that the Bengal Renaissance was supposed to have inaugurated. Moving away from the Enlightenment optimism about modernity, alternate perspectives about the rise of modernity in South Asia began to emerge around this time. Partha Chatterjee's work from these years, for example, focuses on how the emergent Indian elite of the early nineteenth century started fashioning a new modern self for the nation, one that was modern and non-Western at the same time. They did this by bifurcating the sociocultural world into two realms – the 'material' and the 'spiritual'. While the former related to the public domain where Indian political, military, and economic institutions had already yielded to Western superiority, the latter comprised a private sanctum where traditional forms of Indian culture and spirituality thrived in isolation from Western influence.[6] Chatterjee developed these ideas further subsequently to argue against the idea of there being one universal modernity; instead, he suggested that it is more historically accurate to think in terms of multiple modernities, themselves produced by the geographical, political, and cultural specificities of different societies.[7]

These new histories of colonial India problematized the earlier notion of modernity as a progressive, beneficial, civilizational advancement that had arrived in South Asia through British colonialism. As a result, the haloed idea of the Bengal Renaissance heralding a new age of rationality and modernization also ended up being sharply critiqued. Yet what went unchallenged in these revisionist histories of modernity in the Indian subcontinent is the temporal association of the emergence of modernity in this part of the world with the onset of British colonialism – something that itself is an inheritance of the colonial discourse. This association was finally broken in the late 1990s with the introduction of the category of early modernity, not by historians of colonial South Asia, but by those researching an earlier period.

In two articles published separately in 1997, John Richards and Sanjay Subrahmanyam redefined the idea of South Asian modernity by introducing a new category – early modern – to designate roughly the sixteenth through the eighteenth centuries. Richards argued that in keeping with the tendencies visible in other parts of the world, the Indian subcontinent too experienced an increase in the pace and magnitude of historical change during this period. The category of the early modern, he argued, represents and captures the materiality of the speedy and colossal changes in the way humans organized themselves and interacted with other humans and the natural world.[8] Subrahmanyam, on the other hand, focused more on ideological, religious, and cultural processes that manifested across the world during this period. South Asia, he argued, was an integral part of these global processes.[9] We will have an opportunity to discuss these ideas in greater detail soon.

For several years following these interventions, historians of South Asia – especially those employed in universities within the subcontinent – remained sceptical about the category of early modernity. The sixteenth through eighteenth centuries, after all, had long been considered an integral part – the pinnacle even – of the South Asian medieval. However, the last decade has seen an explosion of research that deploys this category to study this segment of South Asian history. In part, this has been a response to global historical scholarship, where the category of the early modern has become firmly established in course of the last three decades and has opened entirely new analytical pathways. It also has to do with the transformation of our understanding of the idea of modernity itself in the last few decades as well as when and how exactly it emerged in South Asia and, indeed, the whole world. Finally, it also emanates from a postcolonial critique of the meanings of modernity, colonialism, and the discipline of history, in particular the politics of periodization.

This recent intellectual ferment makes this an opportune moment to pause and reflect on the meanings and implication of the category of early modernity. Many of the works that have used it in studying South Asian history have done so merely as a convenient shorthand to refer to a particular time period; few have gone into teasing out the theoretical aspects of the nature of the early modern condition itself. What did early modernity mean and entail exactly? What was the nature of the historical processes that set this period of South Asian history apart from the times before or after so as to justify the use of this new category? If modernity emerged in South Asia in the sixteenth century as early modernity, then how was this modernity different from what was ushered in by colonial rule in the nineteenth century? The present volume is one of the first collaborative ventures to directly address these theoretical questions. It brings together 10 chapters that investigate various spheres of the South Asian historical experience roughly between the sixteenth and eighteenth centuries. The themes range from religion to law, warfare to economy, environment to violence, and philosophy to politics. The chapters are bound together by their common quest to define the meanings of early modernity in the individual fields they investigate.

In this introduction, we chart out the wider historiographical context of this intervention and set a new intellectual agenda for South Asian historiography, one that contributes to the process of decolonizing historical periodization and rewriting the history of this part of the world. Since the sixteenth through the eighteenth centuries have traditionally formed a part of the South Asian medieval, exploring the meanings of early modernity must begin by unpacking the category of the medieval itself and by analysing what all it means in this historical context. This is what the first three sections are dedicated to. The first explores the origins of the category in European historical thinking, the second studies its myriad uses in other parts of the world, and the third focuses on the career of the category in South Asian historiography. Next, we turn to the question of modernity in the fourth section, since this is an issue the category of early modernity directly connects with. In the fifth and sixth sections, we shift our focus to the category of early modernity, explore in some detail its various meanings in different contexts, and address some of the scepticisms surrounding it. The final section lays down the structure of the volume, introduces the 10 chapters, and outlines the broader intellectual agenda. Overall, this introduction is a journey to understand the idea of early modernity in relation to questions of historical periodization and the changing politics of history-writing.

European Origins of the Medieval

In the introduction to a special issue of the *Journal of Medieval and Early Modern Studies*, John Dagenais and Margaret Greer explore the relation between the rise of the category of the Middle Ages and the development of western European modernity.[10] Focusing on the writings of Francesco Petrarca (1304–1374), the authors argue that the category of the medieval emerged in the fourteenth century as a by-product of the rise of a new modern consciousness. They argue that it was Petrarca who introduced the basics of the idea of the medieval, which were expounded by other scholars subsequently – a dark and depressed period that occupied a linear stretch of time between Roman Antiquity and his own times.[11] This can be seen as the beginning of the process of 'temporalization (Verzeitlichung) of history' that Reinhart Koselleck argues comprised a key intellectual process that heralded modernity.[12] It was at this moment of the emergence of Humanism in western Europe in the fourteenth and fifteenth centuries that the tripartite division of European history was conceptualized for the first time.[13] Between the glorious Classical Age and a so-called modern reawakening, a thousand years of 'darkness', 'squalor', 'barbarism', and 'primitiveness' were identified.[14] Incidentally – as Dagenais and Greer point out – these adjectives were similar to those used to characterize the indigenes of the various lands western European armies started making forays into since the late fifteenth century.[15] This is revealing of how the colonized other was perceived as being similar to people living in a different temporality – the non-modern or pre-modern – and were hence relegated by the white man to the status of the primitive. At the same time, the association of the category of the medieval with all similar sorts of negative attributes meant that for western Europe, this time period gradually emerged as what Carol Symes calls a 'penal colony', where all things that did not fit within the mainstream idea of the emergent modern would be relegated.[16] The medieval thus became a temporal and cultural other that contained everything that new-age Europeans found repugnant, regressive, and backward – 'systemic persecution, witch-hunts, irrationality, torture, "radical" Islam'.[17] The subsequent colonization of territory across the world by Europe – a process that unfolded rapidly since the early sixteenth century – was accompanied by this simultaneous colonization of the past.[18]

In the fifteenth century, various humanist scholars contributed to this idea of a dark Middle Age. Leonardo Bruni (1370–1444) and Flavio Biondo (1392–1463), for instance, portrayed it as a dark era that followed the demise of the Western Roman Empire at the hands of barbarian invasions.[19] However, as Timothy Reuter points out, the idea of the medieval was initially more a part of passing cultural and aesthetic judgement on the preceding centuries than a device of periodization of history. It was in course of the sixteenth through eighteenth centuries that this idea of a dark age, separating a glorious ancient past and a revived modern era, gradually crystallized into a schema of periodization that was increasingly favoured in the writing of academic history, which itself gradually emerged as a distinct intellectual field during this period. The key figure there was the German scholar Christoph Cellarius (1638–1707), who articulated this schema in his *Historia Medii Aevi* in 1688.[20] Drawing upon several already existing ideas, Cellarius conceptualized history in terms of an ancient (*historia antiqua*) that stretched up to the fourth century, a modern (*historia nova*) that commenced at the fall of Constantinople in 1453, and a medieval (*historia mediii aevi*) that separated the two.[21] According to Koselleck, it was around this time, or shortly afterwards, that a second decisive intellectual shift occurred in conceptualizing historical time. He argues that by this juncture (late seventeenth century), scholars had started gaining some distance and perspective on the first moment of rupture in thinking about historical time – symbolized by the reflections of Petrarca in the fourteenth century on the novelty of his own times and the backwardness of the medieval. The whole process between these two historical moments comprised what Koselleck calls the 'temporalization of history'.[22] 'Since then,' he writes, 'one has lived in Modernity and been conscious of so doing.'[23]

Over the eighteenth and nineteenth centuries, this tripartite schema of periodization emerged as the dominant one in historical thinking in much of western Europe.[24] Scholars who played key roles in the process include Edward Gibbon (1737–1794) in the eighteenth century and Jacob Burckhardt (1818–1897), Jules Michelet (1798–1874), and Lord Acton (1834–1902) in the nineteenth.[25] However, something else of enormous significance happened around this time. In his *Civilization of the Renaissance in Italy*, Burckhardt propounded the thesis of the Renaissance as a revolutionary cultural movement that first unfolded in Italy in the fifteenth century and then spread northward from there to other parts of western Europe. Within such a framework, the historical processes designated as the Renaissance were recognized to bring about a decisive break between the medieval and the modern.[26] In effect, this argument by Burckhardt signified the arrival of the modern man of the nineteenth century – well after the era of Koselleck's 'temporalization' – who looked back at the time of Petrarca and interpreted that now-distant moment of early humanism as the point of commencement of his own time. This idea of the Renaissance was the final step in the conceptualization of the medieval in the context of the history of western Europe.

Writing the Medieval outside Europe

As modern academic history-writing was coming of its own from older discourses about the past in western Europe during the eighteenth and nineteenth centuries, European nation-states were also founding new colonies across the world. It was through the violent process of European colonization that the discipline of history as well as the notion of the medieval reached most non-European parts of the world. Along with territory, western European civilization thus also came to colonize the pasts of these regions and their peoples. Since then, the dissemination of the idea of the medieval has produced curious results in different places. In China, for instance, the concept failed to take roots. Timothy Brook and T. H. Barrett argue that the idea of the medieval as a dark intermediate phase of the past has simply not worked in case of Chinese history.[27]

In contrast, the tripartite division of history as well as the equivalence of the medieval with a dark age struck roots quickly in Japan, although the country was never colonized by Europeans. Yet, as Thomas Keirstead points out, the imagery of the gloom of the medieval being followed by the light of modern civilization was used by Japanese historians of the early twentieth century in the service of Japanese nationalism. Faced by the racial disdain of the Europeans, Japanese nationalist historians used history-writing as a means of proclaiming their national glory and a status equal to that of the Europeans.[28] In the process, they discovered multiple parallels between aspects of the European and Japanese medievals, including foreign invasions, an ostensible loss of masculinity of a society, and the subsequent emergence of a class of warriors. Not unlike Europe, in Japan too, the medieval emerged as the 'penal colony' Symes talks about; everything that did not fit the nationalist narrative of the rise of a modern Japanese nation was dumped there. By discursively producing a Japanese medieval that neatly matched the European medieval, these histories claimed that if Europe could proceed from its dark Middle Ages to the dawn of modernity and progress, then so could Japan.[29]

Iran presents yet another interesting case. Here, some chroniclers and historians appropriated the idea of the 'medieval' to a limited degree to argue a case for a pre-Islamic 'golden age' in Iran, one that was brought to a close by Arab Muslim conquest in the seventh century. The middling period in such a formulation occupied the position between the fall of the Sassanid dynasty to the Arab armies in the seventh century on the one hand and the recent times on the other. Although not exactly a dark age, this intermediate phase has been sometimes portrayed as one where the glorious pre-Islamic ancient civilization of Iran was subverted to the will of the barbaric Arabs. The meanings associated with this phase once again finds remarkable similarity with the European idea of the medieval – foreign invasions and domination, suppression of indigenous culture and values, and the loss of a golden era. In recent times, such an interpretation of Iranian history has fuelled certain nationalist sentiments and has sometimes inspired a push towards a de-Arabization of the Iranian language and culture. Yet, since it was the Arab conquerors who brought Islam to Iran and since the country continues to be an Islamic republic at present, it finds it impossible to completely disavow of its Islamic past or vilify the post-Sassanid period as an unqualified dark age. The result, as Mohamad Tavakoli-Targhi argues, is a cultural and historical schizophrenia in thinking about the so-called medieval past of Iran.[30]

In the case of South Asia, the idea of the medieval has been a loaded and contested one. The first academic histories of the subcontinent were written by Orientalists, British scholars, and colonial officials since the early nineteenth century. Their work reflected a prejudice against the pre-colonial period. Here, periodization remained garbed in a religious-civilizational framework, which divided the historical time of South Asia between a Hindu classical antiquity and a Mohammedan dark age that preceded the British period – divided by civilizational boundaries that are statist, essentialist, and rigid in nature. The tripartite division time was expounded first by the Scottish historian James Mill (1773–1836) in his *The History of British India* (1817). He interpreted the South Asian past as per the interests of British imperialism. The glorious golden age of South Asian antiquity, he maintained, had been interrupted by Muslim invasions. Mill defined the pre-colonial period of the Indian sub-continent not simply in terms of the religion of the ruling dynasties but also in terms of a new idiom for imperial control – oriental despotism. Implicit in this was a denial of any sense of history, rationality, and modernity for South Asia. For him, it was only the civilizing mission of the British that could liberate and modernize the Indian subcontinent.[31] Thus, in the early nineteenth century itself, the so-called Mohammedan period of the South Asian past – middling as it was between the so-called Hindu and British periods – was conceptualized as a dark age. It was imbued with the familiar tropes – foreign invasions, subjugation of indigenous society, and cultural, intellectual, and moral decay – that have characterized the medieval not only in Europe but also in several other parts of the world. In the garb of the Mohammedan period, the creation of the idea of a dark medieval period in South Asian history prepared the perfect stage for justifying British imperialism and for projecting colonial rule as the harbinger of modernity.

Politics of the Medieval in Twentieth-Century South Asia

Following its uses within the colonialist-imperialist intellectual framework of the nineteenth century, the category of the medieval yielded itself to new historiographical and political approaches in the twentieth. This section explores three of them.

Around the beginning of the twentieth century, British historians like Stanley Lane-Poole started using the terms 'ancient', 'medieval', and 'modern' to revise the nomenclature of the nineteenth-century tripartite schema of periodization as Hindu, Mohammedan, and British, respectively. This was one more step in using the European prism of history-writing to study the South Asian past. By the early twentieth century, the first generation of professional Indian historians embraced this new terminology of periodization.[32] While politically they moved away from the early British historians, these Indian historians – despite their best intentions – were not able to undo the colonization of the South Asian past that had started a century back. Even as they gradually moved away from the Hindu–Mohammedan–British nomenclature in favour of the ostensibly more secular ancient–medieval–modern format, the original cultural and political baggage associated with each of three temporal categories remained.

To be fair, there was hardly any escape in sight. By this time, the modern western European discourse of History had delegitimized all the other forms of historical traditions and had established itself as the sole legitimate, scientific discourse about the past. As practitioners of the discipline, Indian nationalist historians bought into this colonial discourse and operated within it. The first generations of nationalist historians dedicated their lives to revising the racist colonial interpretation of South Asia's past. In their writings, the medieval emerged as a site for a liberal nationalist struggle to reclaim South Asia's past from colonial hegemony. For the nationalists, the medieval was not a time when Muslim rule forced Hindu civilization into a dark age, but rather one where enlightened Muslim rulers like Akbar brought various communities together to forge something like a united nation. By locating the birth of the nation in the pre-colonial period, the nationalists thus denied their colonial masters the agency they claimed in creating a nation out of the South Asians through their administrative measures and technological innovations.

A second major shift in the understanding of the South Asian medieval unfolded over the 1950s through the 1970s. Under the influence of the Marxian framework of analysis, the medieval emerged as a site of heated scholarly debates over how well it fit the scheme of Karl Marx's historical materialism. The thrust of historical inquiries in these debates remained squarely on the nature of political economy. One major topic of the heated arguments was whether or not medieval South Asia had experienced feudalism.[33] The other main intervention was to go beyond the debates about the regressive or progressive nature of Muslim rule and understand the dynamics of medieval South Asia in terms of the surplus-extraction by agrarian-bureaucratic states, the exploitation of the peasantry by a revenue-hungry parasitical class of warrior-aristocrats, and the class struggle – in the form of insurgencies – waged by peasants against their politico-economic oppressors.[34] Through their writings, Marxist historians like Irfan Habib, R. S. Sharma, and Harbans Mukhia challenged the cultural stereotype of an unchanging, static pre-colonial South Asian society subservient to autocratic despots – ideas that were as much enshrined in colonial ideologies of power as Marx's idea of the Asiatic mode of production and Karl Wittfogel's notion of oriental despotism. Collectively, the social and economic histories produced by these Marxist scholars and some of their non-Marxist colleagues changed many of the basic assumptions about the South Asian medieval and recast the period by introducing entirely new questions and categories of historical analysis.

Since the 1980s, a third interpretation of the medieval increasingly emerged in India's public domain, largely outside the realm of professional history-writing. The politically ascendant Hindu right in India went back to the colonial discourse of the association of the medieval with the notion of Muslim rulers oppressing the Hindu majority of the Indian nation. Resurrecting colonial discursive tropes, this political rhetoric focused on identifying Muslims – and to a lesser degree the British – as foreign invaders of the subcontinent. Similar to the Iranian idea of reviving the lost pre-Islamic golden age by a national movement and de-Arabization of Iranian culture, the political right in India started advocating a national awakening and empowerment of the Hindus as a means for restoring the ancient golden era and ending the dark times they believe to have set in with the so-called Muslim invasions during the medieval period.[35]

Emanating from radically different political positions, these three major approaches to the South Asian past have revised the colonial imagination of the Mohammedan or medieval period in many ways. Yet, at the end of the day, there is an element of commonality among all these positions towards the idea of the medieval – they all find the category useful in pursuing their presentist goals. For the liberal-nationalists, the medieval signifies the site where the modern harmonious nation of Hindus and Muslims – something they want to see in the present India – was forged through the benevolent, tolerant, and inclusive reign of Muslim sovereigns like Akbar. Marxist historians put the South Asian medieval to the litmus test of historical materialism at a juncture of the twentieth century when leftist politicians and intellectuals were debating the nature of the dominant mode of production of postcolonial India and the prospects of transforming its society and economy through political action. Finally, for the Hindu right, the medieval conjures an image of a dark age of oppression of the Hindus by tyrannical Muslim rulers. While these three positions represent radically different political orientations and hence offer very different interpretations of the medieval, the fact that they all use the category validates and perpetuates the colonization of the Indian past. At the end of the day, all these different versions of the South Asian medieval are little more than what Partha Chatterjee calls 'derivative discourse', the terms of which were set by the colonial order of knowledge.[36]

Introduction

It is true that as long as we write academically about the South Asian past within the modern European discipline of History, we too perpetuate the colonization of this past. No escape from this is in sight. Especially at a time when across the world, authoritarian states are seeking to rewrite the histories of their nations to promote their intolerant regimes, historians seem to have no choice but to uphold their disciplinary rigour more vocally than ever. But at the same time, the editors of this volume also see some merit in continuing to engage with and revise certain historical categories of the discipline that were introduced by the colonial order of knowledge.

The decolonization of the medieval offers one such prospect. The first step towards this, as John Dagenais and Margaret Greer put it, is to recognize that European colonial powers not only colonized the space of the colonized but also their time; we ought to realize that the 'Middle Ages is a colonised region within the history of Modernity'.[37] Next, we must look for elements of dynamism and change to demolish the stereotypical image of the 'medieval' as a stagnant and primitive space of the pre-modern.[38] Much of this has already been achieved for South Asia by generations of historians, especially since the mid-twentieth century. Their work has taught us much about the dynamics of the British colonization of the Indian past. We have also known for a while now that contrary to the interpretation of British imperialist histories, the so-called medieval period of South Asian history was a time of vibrant commerce, technological innovation, tolerant political regimes, cultural cosmopolitanism, religious heterodoxy, intimate contacts with the outside world, as well as the constant circulation of people, objects, and knowledge.[39]

In the last three decades, the idea of the medieval in South Asia has been challenged in one more way – by redefining the temporal and historical associations of the category itself. This involves rethinking the long-standing association of the medieval with the political dominance of South Asia by Islamicate polities – itself a product of the early twentieth-century rechristening of Mill's Mohammedan period as medieval. There have been two main episodes in this process of the redefinition of the medieval, both of which showed alternate conceptual possibilities of history-writing.

The first unravelled during the 1960s through the 1980s, as historians of various shades fervently debated the nature of political economy in the period between the fragmentation of the Gupta Empire in the sixth century and the rise of the Delhi Sultanate in the thirteenth. What emerged out of these debates was the category of the early medieval, which was canonized by Brajadulal Chattopadhyaya in his *The Making of Early Medieval India* (1994). Eschewing arguments in favour of viewing this period as an extended part of the ancient period, he persuasively reasoned in favour of recognizing this as a separate historical period in its own right, one that anticipated some historical tendencies of the medieval period.[40] Chattopadhyaya's arguments ended the enduring association of the category of medieval with the period of Islamicate political dominance of South Asia; through the category of the early medieval, he extended the scope of the medieval backward in time to include around six centuries prior to the invasion of North India by Islamicate powers.

The second episode of rethinking the category of the medieval started shortly after the publication of Chattopadhyaya's book. As mentioned earlier, the articles of Richards and Subrahmanyam from 1997 recast a big portion of the so-called medieval period as early modern. Looking back at this moment today, one cannot fail to recognize it as yet another important step towards decolonizing the South Asian Middle Ages. As Daud Ali points out, several trends in history-writing since the 1980s led to the development of this new category. These include new histories of the Mughals that sought to situate the empire in a broader global context, new research on South India and the Indian Ocean that generated fresh studies about coastal societies and their interactions with European traders, and, finally, a systematic revision of the image of the eighteenth century as an era of decline and ruin.[41] Starting from the close of the twentieth century, historians increasingly started locating the emergence of some forms of modernity in South Asia as early as the sixteenth century. This effectively limited the scope of the medieval to the thirteenth through fifteenth centuries, alarming South Asianists who had long played self-assigned custodians of medieval Indian history and its Islamicate heritage.

Alongside this, a set of essays published in the *Medieval History Journal* in 1998 unpacked and problematized the category of the medieval itself, not only for South Asia but also for other parts of the world. All this engendered a serious rethinking of the meanings of the medieval in South Asian history. Yet it is not only the idea of the medieval has com came to be revised through this intellectual churning of the last two decades of the twentieth century; the introduction of the category of early modernity also has serious implications for our understanding of the emergence of modernity. However, in order for us to approach that subject, we have to first consider what historians understand by modernity itself, both in general and in the context of South Asian history.

The Idea of Modernity

What is modernity? Is it something specifically European or essentially global? Is there only one modernity or many? These are ideologically laden and politically charged questions. As Dorothy Ross points out, interpretations of modernity could be radically different from one commentator to another, depending on one's politics and worldview. For the liberals, it is something good, marked by the benefits of parliamentary democracy, capitalist development, individual liberty, and technological progress. But at the same time, Ross points out that 'there were numerous fellow travellers on the road of historical advance – republican, romantic, modernist, and socialist – who deplored many of its consequences and formed alternative models'.[42] Given the vast range and the diversity of interpretations of modernity, we touch upon only a few ideas here and focus on the arguments we find most relevant for our discussion about South Asian history.

Let us start with Jack Goldstone. He is of particular importance to us for being one of the fiercest critics of the category of early modernity. Goldstone points out that modernity carries different meanings in different fields. In art and architecture, for instance, modern refers to a specific stylistic break with older times: 'departing from classically-inspired [sic] representational art in painting and sculpture, and from traditional proportions, ornamentation, and concealment of functional structures in architecture'.[43] In this form, it comprises a period of a little less than a hundred years, stretching from the late nineteenth century to the 1970s.[44] Sociologically, it stands for a period commencing in the late eighteenth century, one of the weakening of religion as a sociocultural force, dominance of scientific and rational thinking, widespread use of fossil fuel and electricity, large-scale production and consumption of consumer goods, driving of transport by mechanical engines, and democratic forms of government. Essentially, such an approach is similar to the conceptualization of modernity as progress or improvement of human civilizational conditions.[45] The Marxian paradigm takes a more materialist approach, where the advent of modernity is equated with the replacement of the feudal mode of production with a capitalist one and the emergence of labour as a commodity.[46]

Commentators who have written after Goldstone have expanded the ambit of the category further. Sudipta Kaviraj, for instance, lays down the following list of interrelated processes: capitalist industrialization, increasing centrality of the state in the social order (Michel Foucault's 'governmentality'), urbanization, sociological individuation, secularization in politics and ethics, creation of a new order of knowledge, vast changes in the organization of family and intimacy, and changes in the fields of artistic and literary culture.[47] In formulations like this, what gets emphasized are not only the elements of tangible socio-economic and political change but – informed by the critique of modernity by scholars like Foucault – also the rise of disciplinary and classificatory mechanisms, regimes of surveillance, as well as new systems of the formation and accumulation of knowledge through which novel forms of power operate and govern citizen bodies. On these lines, Chatterjee adds:

> The regime of power in the modern societies prefers to work not through the commands of a supreme sovereign but through the disciplinary practices that each individual imposes on his or her own behavior on the basis of the dictates of reason.... The burden of reason, dreams of freedom; the desire for power, resistance to power: all these are elements of modernity. There is no promised land of modernity outside the networks of power.[48]

From a slightly different perspective, Dipesh Chakrabarty breaks the list of the various processes thought to comprise modernity into two broad heads. In the first category, he puts the advent of changes in the outside world – 'the institutions (from parliamentary and legal institution to roads, capitalist businesses, and factories)'.[49] This he terms as 'modernization'. This is accompanied by what he calls 'modernity' – ferments in the intellectual realm, involving 'the development of a degree of reflective, judgmental thinking about these processes [of modernization]'.[50]

In recent years, this intellectual dimension of modernity has received a lot of attention. Wolfgang Reinhard, for instance, discusses it by focusing on the figure of René Descartes. Reinhard argues that Descartes's *The Discourse on the Method* (1637) marked a work of scholarship that was nothing like intellectual contributions by the humanists or Christian reformists of the fifteenth or sixteenth centuries. Reinhard further suggests that while these people essentially wanted to revive the scholarship of older times, Descartes did not want to revive anything. Instead, he wanted to begin from scratch by establishing the basics of a new scientific method. This eventually ushered in a new era of human well-being through scientific application and innovation. Discussing the role of other scientists and philosophers, Reinhard concludes that 'it was this alliance of philosophy and science that initiated that permanent change which became our fate up to the present day. And the modernity of the "modern period" consists in nothing else but the consistent acceptance of this change'.[51]

Several scholars have challenged such conceptualizations of modernity. Björn Wittrock, for instance, points out that many of the categories through which the idea of modernity is often understood – 'broad notions as the nation-state or the constitutional republic, and of such mediating concepts as the public sphere and civil society' – are overwhelmingly derived from the European historical experience.[52] Within such a framework, modernity is conceptualized as something that emerged in Europe and then disseminated to the rest of the world. Admittedly, recent scholars have moved far away from the nineteenth-century understanding of this dissemination as a glorious outward march of progress and civilization from Europe. Many scholars have highlighted how the 'spread of modernity' transpired through extremely violent processes of conquest, colonization, genocide, and cultural hegemony. Yet the conviction in the European origins of 'modernity' remains strong among many social scientists.

Japanologist Carol Gluck is one of the scholars who have critiqued this Eurocentrism very sharply. She points out that given the nature of the world around us, the standard characteristics drawn from the European experience – 'rationality, secularization, democracy' – can no longer be seen as strict attributes of modernity.[53] She forwards a revised list of attributes that includes the dominance of the nation-state as the unit of political or territorial organization, large-scale political participation of nations, economic dominance of capital and industry, co-option into the global geopolitical framework of power, and social transformations in urban spaces.[54] She asserts that under these circumstances, no rhetoric of a march towards progress can reinforce the idea that one day modernity will arrive and usher in an irreversible process of civilizational improvement.[55] As the workings of power gives rise to new regimes of violence and exploitation as well as social and national inequalities, different places in the same modern world continue to be considerably heterogeneous in terms of politics, society, and economy.[56]

This resonates with Kaviraj's arguments, who also suggests that the production of a huge body of knowledge about the histories of different non-European societies has created a crisis of social theory in recent years. This, he points out, is because the major premises, instances, and arguments of mainstream social theory conventionally derive from the historical specificities of Europe.[57] Fitting all the new empirical evidence from non-European societies into this overwhelmingly Eurocentric theoretical framework has proved to be extremely challenging. Kaviraj suggests that the only way around this is to nuance existing social theory by moving away from its European origins and informing it with the experiences of other societies. This, he argues, will help us understand the diverse and heterogeneous development of modernity in different parts of the world.[58]

Following these arguments, if we agree to eschew the idea of modernity as something that developed exclusively in Europe and spread outward from there, then the next question is how else we can think of this category. How do we explain the multiplicity of forms in which we find modernity all around us today? Once again, responses to such questions vary. Given the paucity of space, we consider two. In order to make sense of this complex history of the modern world, Gluck propounds the concept of 'blended modernities'. She explains that 'according to the metaphor of historical blending, no version of the modern is merely imitative of or inferior to another one, because by definition each inflection of modernity emerged as a new blend in a separate (metaphorical) space'.[59] She argues that the merit of this metaphor is that it frees the various modernities across the world from the shackles of being judged and understood against the standards of modern Europe.[60] She adds that the metaphor also enables us to comprehend the shared features of our modern societies while allowing us to appreciate the absence of any absolute and universal qualities, since the blends are different by definition.[61] She concludes by stressing that '[H]istory, in short, offers no abstract model of the modern, only embedded real modernities produced by creative blending that never reaches an end'.[62]

Kaviraj makes a slightly different case. He argues that the different processes that comprise modernity did not experience a 'symmetrical' simultaneous development over time. Instead, he suggests, they went through a phase of 'sequential' 'braiding', where each process shaped the subsequent processes. He explains that the nature of modernity in a particular society depends on the 'precise sequence in which constituent processes of [its] modernity appears'.[63] In such a framework, the ways in which modernity evolves in a particular society is moulded by the original conditions within which modern processes and institutions emerge. The principal merit of such an argument, Kaviraj points out, is that it allows us to understand modernity as a highly contingent process deriving from the historical specificities of a particular region and not as a uniform condition that developed in the same way everywhere.[64]

Such a way of thinking about modernity resonates with Subrahmanyam's argument about it being a 'global and conjunctural phenomenon, not a virus that spreads from one place to another'.[65] Charting a broader context for the historical emergence of modernity, he locates it in myriad processes that fostered increasing contact between different parts of the world. For him, these processes comprise 'the Mongol dream of world conquest, European voyages of exploration, activities of Indian textile traders in the diaspora, the "globalization of microbes" that historians of the 1960s were fond of discussing, and so on'.[66] He explains that precisely because these processes were uneven over time and space as well as were deeply rooted in local historical contexts, modernity also evolved as a heterogeneous and conjunctural global condition.[67]

The editors of this volume find merit in conceptualizing modernity in these ways. We agree that modernity is not something that developed only in Europe; it is rather a global phenomenon that appeared in an increasingly connected world and was generated by what Kaviraj looks upon as a sequential braiding of different historical processes. Drawing upon Chatterjee, one can argue that there have been at least three different forms of modernity in our immediate context of South Asia. First, there were certain processes and experiences that emerged from the fifteenth century onwards and that bore strong trans-continental connections with other contemporary societies, while being deeply rooted in the South Asian historical experience. This is what Chatterjee calls early modernity. Next, he argues that the 1830s onwards, this early modernity – at once indigenous and shared – was derailed by the arrival and growing hegemony of colonial modernity. This is when indigenous forms of modernity were increasingly transformed through a violent process of war and conquest in favour of the colonization of the economy, transformation of the political system with Britain acquiring a paramount position, and the dissemination of colonial education that created both servile clerks and ardent nationalists.[68] Finally, starting in the mid-twentieth century, we find a postcolonial modernity following the independence and partition of South Asia. This postcolonial modernity has been shaped not only by the enduring legacies of early modernity and colonial modernity, but also by the forces, impulses, and imperatives of postcolonial nation-building and global politics.[69]

What Is Early Modernity?

Finally, we arrive at the question that lies at the heart of this volume – what is early modernity? Justus Nipperdey points out that the initial use of the category of early modernity occurred in North American universities during the interwar period. At that time, the mainstream idea in the Anglophone academia was that modernity had emerged around the time of the Renaissance and had continued unabated ever since. As a critique of this understanding, some American historians started using the category of early modernity for the sixteenth through eighteenth centuries more in the sense of a non-modern time than the early phase of modernity – a meaning it would eventually assume. By projecting the early modern period as a phase divorced from modernity, these historians pushed the origins of modernity closer to their own times – between the mid-seventeenth and late eighteenth centuries. At the same time, there were others who looked upon the sixteenth through eighteenth centuries as indeed being imbued with a form of modernity, albeit one that was only the preliminary form of what would appear after the eighteenth century.[70] Both the groups, in their own different ways, reconceptualized a part of history that had conventionally been considered to be an integral part of European modernity in the Anglophone academia. The category spread to the other side of the Atlantic by the 1950s.[71] Moshe Sluhovsky points out that it saw widespread currency during the 1960s and 1970s, when it emerged as a way for historians to bridge the gap between the medieval and the modern periods of European history, one that advocated a gradual transition to the later stages of the medieval to early forms of modernity without any dramatic breaks.[72]

One of the most important interventions around this time came from Koselleck. He propounded the notion of the 'temporalization of history' – a process that unfolded roughly between the sixteenth and eighteenth centuries, and decisively created a discursive modernity in Europe. Koselleck mainly explores the transformations in the domain of ideas while tracing this history. Focusing on two historical figures – Martin Luther (1483–1546) and Maximilien Robespierre (1758–1794), he argues that between the times of these two men, there came about a profound change in the way Europeans thought about time and, more specifically, the future. In the seventeenth century, Koselleck argues, strategic and political considerations of emergent nation-states replaced Christian eschatology as the dominant ideology shaping these thoughts.[73] However, in the following century, one more change came about – ideas of temporal change and progress became imbued with ideas of 'rational prediction and salvational expectation'.[74] For Koselleck, this moment in the eighteenth century marked the decisive shift into modernity. However, he firmly emphasizes that it was the changes over the past three centuries that made this final shift possible.[75]

Sluhovsky suggests that this understanding changed since the 1980s; instead of an early yet distinct phase of modernity, early modernity increasingly came to be seen as an extension of the medieval. This was done by a new tendency of ascribing to the sixteenth and the first half of the seventeenth centuries certain negative attributes conventionally associated with the medieval and by locating the inception of modernity in the mid-seventeenth century or later.[76] On the one hand, some scholars conceptualized this inception in terms of a major shift in the realm of science and philosophy, where the medieval tendency of understanding the world through similarities was replaced by a new ontological paradigm of classifications that privileged the idea of difference. On the other hand, some others imagined the same process in terms of the emergence of the self-conscious and self-reflexive modern individual and bourgeois subjectivity, which replaced the medieval notion of selfhood that centred on community, kin, and religion. In both cases, the cultural, social, and intellectual reverberations of the Protestant reformation were considered to have played a central role in facilitating these processes.[77] Together, they led to the new conceptualization of modernity that, according to Sluhovsky, was 'masculine, both Protestant and secular at the same time, rational, stable, cerebral, and introspective, as opposed to premodernity that was Catholic, exterior, irrational, unstable, feminine, and corporeal'.[78] It was in this process, dominant especially during the 1980s and 1990s, that the conceptualization of early modernity as a preliminary form of modernity in Europe – epitomized in some writings of Koselleck – got jeopardized.

Yet, around the same time, the global turn in history-writing breathed new life into this category. By the 1990s, it started gaining increasing currency in histories of non-European parts of the world. This process helped the category break out of the European context, where it had remained trapped for almost a century as a part of what Luke Clossey calls the 'deductive approach' of tracing the prehistory of European modernity. Instead, what now emerged with the globalization of the category revealed an 'inductive approach', whereby scholars started exploring the new historical tendencies that engulfed different parts of the world during the sixteenth through eighteenth centuries.[79] We will discuss this expanding body of literature mainly with reference to the case of South Asia.

Here, we must return to the interventions by Richards and Subrahmanyam, whose articles from 1997 set the ball rolling for the historiography of this part of the world. Richards argues that six major processes defined the world in the sixteenth through eighteenth centuries and hence can be seen to be the main characteristics of early modernity. These were the establishment of global oceanic routes, emergence of the first global economy, rise of large and stable states and empires, steady growth of population across the world, agrarian expansion, and dissemination of new technologies and biological species. Having delineated these processes, Richards argues that each of these processes characterized the South Asian past during this period as well. He thus makes a strong case for using this category rather than phrases like 'Mughal India' or 'Late Medieval India' or 'Late Pre-Colonial India' while writing South Asian history.[80] Subrahmanyam adds that this was also the time of geographical explorations redefining the frontiers of the known world, heightened struggle between sedentary and pastoral societies, spectacular proclamations of universal sovereignty by a large numbers of monarchs, and the widespread currency of millenarian beliefs.[81]

More recently, Rosalind O'Hanlon has added to the list of features of early modernity. She highlights the tendency of big empires across the globe to promote the circulation and migration of elite personnel – bureaucrats, ambassadors, military professionals, artisans, and men of letters. This was accompanied by the rise of a scribal culture and the emergence of new scribal elites. This, in turn, triggered the emergence of novel and transformative discourses in various intellectual and technological fields. It was accompanied by disenchantment about and distancing from earlier forms of knowledge. There was also a strong emergence of vernacular languages and cultures, in turn bolstering the process of the rise of strong regional identities. Artistic genres produced distinct and self-conscious voices of the individual, be it in fiction, autobiographies, or travelogues. Helped by the large-scale adoption of new technologies like print and paper, these fostered the growth of thriving public spheres.[82]

In the last few years, other scholars have shed further light on the dynamics of historical processes in South Asia between the sixteenth and eighteenth centuries, and have thereby added substantially to our understanding of the meanings of early modernity in this part of the world. For Velcheru Narayana Rao, David Shulman, and Subrahmanyam, early modernity in South India stands for brilliant literary expressions of historical consciousness across various genres and languages. They argue that unlike the evolution of history in western Europe as a distinct intellectual domain with a formal style, method, and structure, early modernity in South Indian historical consciousness was marked by fluidity, flexibility, and multiplicity in terms of form, content, and genre. Thus, they point out that while both Europe and South India shared one characteristic of early modernity – the heightening of historical consciousness – the contours of this consciousness were different owing to the cultural specificities of the individual sociocultural milieus.[83]

In more recent years, these scholars have carried forward their ideas about the sixteenth century marking the dawn of a new era in South Asia. Shulman, for instance, argues that in South India, the sixteenth century inaugurated a new paradigm of cultural sensibilities, oriented more than ever towards realism and empiricism. Through a study of various texts in Sanskrit as well as South Indian vernaculars like Malayalam, Tamil, and Telugu, Shulman shows how the literary imagination of the time got entangled with emerging scientific discourses like plant sciences, chemical sciences, and medical sciences. In the process, contemporary authors harnessed the knowledge provided by their predecessors, but they also created radically original forms of knowledge in response to the rapidly changing sociocultural conditions around them.[84]

Elaine Fisher highlights another important difference between South Asia and western Europe – unlike the latter, the former did not witness any major public figure rejecting devotion and advocating atheism. For Fisher, the essence of South Asian early modernity lay in an opposite tendency – 'an embrace rather than a rejection of religion in public space'.[85] This took the form of intense theological debates leading to the sharpening of sectarian religious identities. According to Fisher, all of this played out in the emergence of 'public theologies' – a pluralistic public sphere marked by intense publicization of religious ideas and dialogues.[86]

Jonardon Ganeri similarly argues that although philosophical thought in South Asia underwent a paradigmatic change in the sixteenth and seventeenth centuries, once again its trajectories were very different in comparison with what transpired in western Europe. He sees South Asian philosophical early modernity as being squarely based in 'logical form and linguistic practice' rather than the close association with observations about the natural world that characterized the early modern philosophical developments in western Europe.[87] Yet, he argues, the early modernities in both the regions shared a common trait – in both cases, philosophers increasingly developed a keen criticality towards ancient texts, whereby rather than being deferential and subservient to them like their predecessors, they engaged with them meaningfully based on the new knowledge and experience they had gathered in their present.[88]

For Shankar Nair, early modernity in South Asia refers to intellectual exuberance in Sanskrit, Arabic, and Persian philosophical domains. Nair points out that traditionally, the practitioners of the Islamic or Arabic and the Hindu or Sanskritic traditions had treaded parallel intellectual pathways and rarely had the intellectual and linguistic resources to engage each other directly in informed intellectual dialogue. Under such circumstances, a new paradigm emerged in course of the sixteenth and seventeenth centuries, as Mughal patronage of a group of Hindu and Muslim scholars for the translation of Sanskrit texts led to the emergence of Persian as some sort of an intellectual *lingua franca*. Its merit lay in its accessibility for both the philosophical communities and its amenability for facilitating cross-cultural philosophical dialogue.[89]

Nile Green locates early modernity in an epistemological shift at the close of the sixteenth century, whereby the documentation and transmission of knowledge underwent a profound transformation because of an expansion in cultures of record-keeping and historiography, accompanied by the emergence of robust bureaucratic and scribal cultures. Green argues that while this tendency resonated with the experience in other parts of the world, in South Asia this ascendancy of texts as the new 'conceptual and practical locations of knowledge' transpired even without the proliferation of print culture during this period, quite in contrast to the picture in regions like western Europe or Japan.[90]

Based on the scholarship on other parts of the world, it is possible to add more points to this already detailed and rather lengthy list. Shared historical processes and long-term currents that accelerated in this period had a deep impact on the rapidly moving anthropogenic change – human-induced environmental change or the collective human action on the world's ecosystems – during the nineteenth and twentieth centuries. Trends that began to gather fundamental constituents of modern agrarian environments were perceptible in the sixteenth century. Early modernity can be associated with increasing engagements with firearms, a growing preoccupation with cartography to aid increasingly intrusive and bureaucratic states govern and project their power beyond their immediate realms, a vigorous pursuit and circulation of 'exotic' items as a part of an expanding gift-economy, the increasing politicization of the oceanic space and the rise of European naval power therein, and the development of a new strategic consciousness among empires and nation-states. Empirical research has firmly established that these various processes characterized most parts of the world – including South Asia – during the sixteenth through eighteenth centuries. Together, they also characterized the early modern condition.

Within a specific region, the way these processes unfolded remained strictly contingent on the historical specificities and context of that region. As such, it was entirely possible that some of the processes of one region did not appear in another. For instance, while most powerful states and empires invested in charting the realms through cartography since the sixteenth century, the rise of Mughal power in South Asia was not accompanied by any imperial venture to visually map its territories.[91] In fact, the first major cartographic initiative was undertaken only in 1647 at a sub-imperial level.[92] Similarly, while many states imposed an increasing monopoly over the means of violence in many parts of the world, the specificities of social, military, and environmental conditions ensured that nothing of the sort occurred in the Mughal Empire. A large part of the subject population of the empire, in fact, remained perpetually armed and belligerent. Finally, the gradual separation of the church and the state – one of the defining historical processes of Europe of this period – never occurred in South Asia; religion and statecraft remained fairly intertwined. This shows that while a particular region could share many common global processes, there was no one-to-one correspondence between different regions because of their historical specificities.

Among the various processes, some – like engagements with firearms, circulation of elite personnel, global commerce, and the rise of the vernaculars – continued well after the eighteenth century. Hence, in regions like South Asia, they also contributed to the making of colonial modernity. But some – like the political ideology of universal sovereignty and circulation of millenarian belief – did not. They remained specifically early modern tendencies. In such a conceptualization, the early modern no longer remains a chronological category that simply designates a period of time before the advent of colonial modernity. By virtue of recognizing multiple modernities in the world and at least three successive varieties of modernity in South Asia, early modernity can be seen as a form of modernity in its own right, one that was at once shared and indigenous, one which was derailed in a large measure by the emergence of colonial modernity in the nineteenth century. As such, the term early modernity attains the status of a descriptive category, signifying specific local as well as global processes that happened to be rampant in a certain period of time.

In Defence of the Early Modern

Having described the contours of early modernity, it is now time to consider some of the criticisms against this category. The most detailed critique comes from Goldstone. His allegations are primarily twofold. He writes: '"Early Modern" derives from a particular sociological theory of history that privileges modes of production in characterizing and powering history, not from any "natural" historical periodization.'[93] He argues that it primarily serves to fill up the historical void between the demise of feudalism – a process complete by the early sixteenth century – and the rise of industrial capitalism in the late eighteenth. The other objection is that by virtue of being the time-filler following the end of the feudal mode of production, the category of early modernity is based squarely on the European historical experience, since there was no socio-economic formation similar to feudalism anywhere else in the world.[94]

Goldstone says that given this context, one of two things happen when we apply the category of early modernity to a non-European society. The first possibility is that we empty out the category of all historical meaning and use it simply as a signifier for the period between 1500 and 1800, irrespective of whether or not these particular years or the entire period have any historical significance in these different societies.[95] The second possibility is that we imbue the category with meaning drawn from the European historical experience and then apply it to the rest of the world. This is disastrous, argues Goldstone, because it is Eurocentric and does not reflect the reality of historical change and continuity in various parts of the non-European world.[96]

These are substantial criticisms. We would like to club our responses in two principal points. First, it is true that in many instances, the initial ideas of early modernity were developed to explain the shift from feudalism to capitalism. However, we have come a long way from that. In recent times, the idea has become greatly nuanced and eclectic. In Koselleck's formulation of early modernity in terms of the 'temporalization of history', for instance, the sociological definition of modernity takes a back seat. Here, the period is explained in terms of an ideological and cultural shift in how societies looked at their past. In such a formulation, the idea of early modernity no longer remains intertwined with the institution of feudalism. Hence, there does not remain any problem in applying the category to non-European historical contexts, whether or not they experienced feudalism.

Second, in the recent historical research that uses the category of the early modern, neither is the category expunged of all meaning and rendered a hollow chronological marker nor is it filled with meaning derived from the European historical experience. As we have argued earlier, one way of delinking the category from its European origins has been to stop thinking of modernity itself in terms of something that originated only in Europe. As Subrahmanyam, Richards, O'Hanlon, and Chatterjee argue, modernity needs to be conceptualized as a global condition that emerged in different parts of the world from very different circumstances. What we see in the period between the sixteenth and eighteenth centuries is the near-simultaneous rise of various forms of indigenous modernities that shared many global characteristics, but were also rooted in their diverse historical contexts and, consequently, had their own peculiarities. In such an approach, the early modern condition refers to all these various forms of modernity. However, in course of the nineteenth and twentieth centuries, one of these multiple forms of modernity – one that had developed in north-western Europe – emerged as the dominant form of modernity throughout the world through the violent processes of war, diplomacy, and colonization. This form of western modernity unfolded in constant negotiation with indigenous forms of modernity. Eventually, in parts of the world like South Asia, decolonization began at one point, and the new liberated nation-states took these negotiations in new directions and moulded them further with the imperatives of the postcolonial condition. The result is the kind of 'blended modernities' of today's world that Gluck has explained.

Randolph Starn has argued that the early modern period has no standard timeline.[97] This is, however, nothing new for historical periods. Initially conceptualized to study the European past, standard historical periodization has always displayed variation when applied to a non-European context. However, this does not mean that they needed to be immediately discarded or that their use has not enabled any comparative study or academic dialogue across regions. In fact, compared to the categories of ancient and medieval, there seems to be more surety among historians about the temporal span of the early modern – the sixteenth through eighteenth centuries. Obviously, there are some variations in terms of a specific process or region, but there is a growing consensus among scholars about these centuries being associated with the category. There are not many voices that have extended it too far beyond this in either direction of the timeline.

Starn has also asserted that early modern is a teleological category because it anticipates the advent of modernity.[98] In response, it is possible to refer to some arguments made by Sheldon Pollock. He argues that though the notion of early modern has been a matter of dispute among scholars both regionalists and generalists with regard to its teleological connotation, it needs to be urged that the period between 1500 and 1800 cannot be assigned any shared structure or content *a priori* 'let alone to insist on finding in it western modernity in embryonic form'.[99] He reiterates the importance of historical synchronicity, in which there is no space for definitional consistency or conceptual symmetry. The period, he stipulates, constituted an entirely reasonable periodization for intellectual history and can be called early modern in the sense of a 'threshold, where potentially different futures may have been arrested or retained only as *masala* for that dominant form'.[100] He further writes that the category is teleological in the sense that we are familiar with the modern world of today and we wish to know how human societies ended up here.[101] Furthermore, we know that the emergence of colonial modernity in the nineteenth century jeopardized previously existing forms of modernity in South Asia, and we wish to explore the nature of these pre-colonial forms of modernity. But precisely because the indigenous early modernity was short-circuited – and in a large measure discontinued – by the advent of colonial modernity, early modernity does not represent the initial phase of an uninterrupted journey of modernity. In other words, much of the forms of indigenous early modernity did not lead anywhere after the close of the eighteenth century; they were mostly derailed. Hence, the idea of teleology does not hold beyond allowing us a glimpse into what lay before that derailment occurred.

Chakrabarty has critiqued the idea of early modernity by suggesting that when we find evidence of historical processes similar to those that unfolded in Europe in the sixteenth through eighteenth centuries and move to use the category of the early modern to analyse this evidence, we express certain conscious choices. He suggests that this is triggered by a revolt against the earlier tendency of looking at the West as the harbinger of modernity and a desire to see different parts of the world as equals in terms of their historical trajectories.[102] He argues that while this displays a presentist political commitment towards the principle of 'equal opportunity', it does not do justice to the real processes of the past.[103] 'The sentiment is entirely laudable,' he concludes, 'but it speaks mainly of the moral preferences that most historians share today. But they are, after all, preferences – axioms of our age.'[104]

Chakrabarty's critique is valid to some extent. After all, our use of the category of the early modern for South Asian history is partially informed by our politics of decolonizing the Middle Ages and reviewing the origins of modernity. However, one wonders if there is anything at all in the historical profession that is not ideologically laden and not a product of the historian's politics or preferences.

Starting from formulating research questions, selecting which sources to consult, negotiating the sources while trying to answer the questions, framing a narrative on the basis of the findings, and making arguments about the past – is every single action among these not a product of the historian's preferences, not deeply shaped by the 'axioms of our age'? Of course, using the category of the early modern to study a part of the past of South Asia – and, in fact, the whole world – is an ideological project. The entire framework of historical periodization, in fact, is an act of power and a product of ideology. Right now, we do not see an escape from it.

Chakrabarty voices one more concern. As mentioned previously, he divides the idea of the modern into two components – 'modernization' in the outer world and 'modernity' in the intellectual realm. He implies that sometimes historians label a particular period of South Asian history early modern simply because they find elements of 'modernization' there. According to Chakrabarty, this is problematic. He urges historians to go a step further and find out if the region also experienced an advent of modernity in the intellectual domain – one of the fundamental assumptions about what defined the advent of modernity in Europe.[105] Contrary to the allegation levied by others that the category of early modernity is Eurocentric, Chakrabarty's argument thus implies the opposite – in its failure to demonstrate that what characterized the inception of modernity in western Europe also appeared in other parts of the world, the uses of the category does not uphold European standards to a satisfactory extent. As we have already argued, the premise of this entire line of argument too is the assumption that modernity is something essentially European. By arguing in favour of a different way of thinking about modernity, it is possible to be free from judging the rest of the world in terms of European standards. Hence, while historians must look for whether South Asia participated in various global processes, they have no liability to try to investigate if something that transpired in Europe happened there too.

In comparison to the possible shortfalls, the benefits of the category of early modernity seem vastly greater.[106] O'Hanlon points out that while thinking in terms of the traditional equivalence between modernity and colonial rule for South Asia, one difficulty that emerges is the nature of transition from a pre-modern society to a modern one. Any idea of an abrupt transformation with the onset of colonial rule betrays a lack of appreciation for the capability of change and dynamism within South Asian society. O'Hanlon argues that thinking in terms of an early modern period is helpful in this respect, because it allows us to see how South Asia responded to and participated in new shared global tendencies much before the age of colonialism. She stresses that recognizing the pre-colonial forms of modernity in South Asia helps us problematize traditional binaries between pre-modern or pre-colonial one the one hand and the false equivalence between modern and colonial on the other.[107]

Pollock argues that designating the three centuries leading up to the violent global spread of European modernity in the nineteenth century as early modern makes it possible to comprehend the history of a world where societies 'began to participate in a world economy, to live in vaster and more complex states, to confront a demographic explosion, a diffusion of unprecedented technology, and larger movements of people in a newly unified or at least unifying world'.[108] Doing so, it liberates modernity from the monopoly of Europe and thereby nullifies the European imperialist claim of bringing modernity to the rest of the world. As O'Hanlon points out, it recognizes that different forms of shared modernity arose in different corners of the world independent of Europe's agency.[109] It helps us acknowledge the existence of a connected, dynamic, and changing modern world much before the nineteenth century.

Finally, recognizing the sixteenth through eighteenth centuries as early modern has another importance for South Asian historiography. By taking out the entire history of the rise and fall of the Mughal Empire – the most powerful and enduring Islamicate polity of South Asia – from the domain of the medieval, the colonial association of the medieval with the political dominance of South Asia by Islamicate states can be negated.[110] This complements the work of the proponents of the category of early medieval, which had a similar effect on the conceptualization of the medieval period for South Asia. In the process, we contribute towards the efforts to the decolonization of the South Asian Middle Ages.

The Intellectual Project of This Volume

Against the backdrop of this discussion, let us spell out in a little more detail what exactly this volume does. The main question that it addresses is around the meanings and forms of early modernity in various domains of the South Asian history between the sixteenth and eighteenth centuries vis-à-vis historical tendencies of change and continuity. Already during the last decade there has been an explosion of books – both monographs and edited volumes – on South Asia that focus on the sixteenth through eighteenth centuries and use the phrase 'early modern' in their titles to designate this period.[111] Many of these volumes are collections of essays, representing collective efforts by groups of scholars to shed light on the nature of historical processes that constituted early modernity in South Asia.[112] Most of these volumes set specific tasks for themselves. For Thomas de Bruijn and Allison Busch, for instance, the point of departure is the argument that the South Asian early modernity comprised heightened forms of mobility and circulation. They argue that this has been usually understood in terms of the mobility of material objects – commercial traffic, transregional trade, better communication, and transmission of technologies. In contrast, they bring together a group of essays to explore the nature of cross-fertilization of literary texts and traditions, and the mobility of ideas and languages.[113] In another volume, O'Hanlon and David Washbrook begin by highlighting the familiar ideas about early modernity engendering heightened interactions of South Asia with the outside world, increasing volume of all sorts of mobility, and the emergence of paper regimes of documentation. Against this backdrop, they bring together a collection of articles to argue that the changing nature of religious culture and intellectual exchanges in South Asia between the sixteenth and eighteenth centuries marked a critical stage in the transition of the medieval to the modern.[114]

Over the last decade or so, such works have contributed immensely to our understanding of what early modernity comprised in different spheres of the South Asian historical experience. In a sense, the current volume represents a maturation of many of the arguments and theorizations offered by these earlier works. Taking forward some of the earlier investigations and branching out into new directions, our work signifies yet another step in the increasing expansion and consolidation of the field. We do this by addressing two main areas of lacuna that characterizes the existing corpus literature on the subject.

First, most existing works engage with the meanings of the conceptual category of early modernity only cursorily. They mostly focus on the dynamics of historical processes between the sixteenth and the eighteenth centuries, having assumed that this is the period that comprised the early modern era. What remains largely unaddressed is any exploration about the nature of continuity and discontinuity of South Asian historical processes and the intellectual need to identify a specific period as early modern. The question of what changes between medieval and early modern on the one hand as well as between early modern and colonial modern on the other often remains implicit in these writings. In contrast, the chapters of the current volume foreground the nature of such changes. Instead of taking early modernity as a given category, they probe into why this category needs to be used at all in different fields. In doing this, they dedicate themselves specifically to understanding the nature of historical continuity and discontinuity – something that is at the heart of the exercise of periodization – in these fields.

At the same time, this volume contributes to our understanding of the precise characteristics of historical processes across the board that we designate as early modern. In contrast to the fact that most existing monographs and edited volumes are built around specific themes – religious practices, textual traditions, or literary cultures – the present volume addresses a wide range of themes. In fact, a noticeable feature of the existing literature on the dynamics of early modernity in South Asia is a strong orientation towards textual and cultural analysis – itself reflective of the current dominance of field by historians trained or employed in the United States academia and that of a culturalist perspective among them. This orientation has resulted in an overwhelming focus on literary tendencies, textual traditions, scribal cultures, philosophical ideas, and religious interactions. In the process, this has resulted in the marginalization of themes like economy, infrastructure, statecraft, warfare, or environment. In contrast, the fact that the present volume is built around a general question rather than a specific theme enables it to offer analysis of a range of themes, both cultural and material.

The volume has three parts. With three chapters, the first part explores the realm of religion, ideology, and identity. Here, Kashshaf Ghani's chapter focuses on the specific developments in the domain of South Asian Sufism between the early sixteenth and early nineteenth centuries. He argues that three specific dimensions set Sufi processes of this period away from the times before or after – a redefinition of the relationship between mystical Islam and political Islam, new forms of philosophical expression including the increasing use of vernacular languages, and the emergence of reformist movements. This discussion of the early modern condition in terms of the history of Sufism is complemented by Charles Ramsey's chapter on new tendencies that appeared in Islamic natural philosophy mainly during the seventeenth century. It focuses on the ideas of two individuals – Mulla Sadra of Persia and Shaykh Sirhindi of India, whose intellectual interventions signified fresh engagements with theological questions in the Persianate world. Ramsey interprets the rise of these new intellectual tendencies in the context of the larger millenarian religious climate of the times. Shalin Jain's chapter enriches this discussion on the changing intellectual landscape of South Asia by extending the investigation into the Jain community. Like Ramsey, Jain's study too is based on an analysis of two individuals – in this case a fifteenth-century lay preacher named Lonka Shah and a seventeenth-century merchant named Banarsidas. Through a critical analysis of their ideas, he argues that what marked the emergence of early modernity in Jainism was the rise and proliferation of a humanistic rationality and new notions of individual agency, alongside a tendency of challenging established social norms and an irreverent scepticism towards religious orthodoxy.

The second part of the book comprises four chapters. Here, we move from issues of the intellectual realm to more material questions of economy, society, and ecology. Rajat Datta's chapter deals with the field of political economy within a comparative global historical framework. For him, early modernity raises the notion of multipolar and convergent modernities. In the field of economy, he defines early modernity in terms of heightening of production processes, rise of military-fiscalism in states, diversification of trading enterprises, increasing sophistication of primary and secondary production, a thriving cash nexus, and tremendous overall economic growth in South Asia. The next two chapters, by Mayank Kumar and Meena Bhargava, engage with the nature of the early modern condition in terms of human engagements with the natural environment. Kumar defines the category for Rajasthan in the seventeenth through eighteenth centuries in terms of heightened efforts by the state to document and control environmental resources. To this end, the state deployed new officials, invested in creating irrigational infrastructure, sought to bypass intermediaries in interacting with rural communities, imposed taxes on community uses of natural resources, and tried to control the domestic realm through social and legal means. In contrast to Kumar's focused study of Rajasthan, Bhargava provides a more holistic analysis of the changing relationships between humans and the environment in South Asia. She argues that here the features of early modernity comprised a steep rise in human population, leading to the expansion of the agrarian frontier and the heightening of anthropogenic impact on the environment, the ripples of which were felt in land-use patterns, engagements with non-agricultural lands, and management of ecological resources. Finally, Ranjeeta Dutta's chapter highlights the usefulness of the category of early modernity in fostering new forms of historical inquiry about peninsular idea, in taking historiographical treatment of the region beyond the conventional analytical frames that are derived largely from the historical experience of North India. Against this backdrop, Dutta characterizes the early modern condition in South India in terms of heightened interactions between fertile wet zones and dry upland areas, the emergence of new warrior groups and agrarian aristocracy, and greater transregional migration by professional and religious groups.

The third part of the book presents three chapters that explore political processes, legal procedures, and military violence. Radhika Chadha focuses on the Portuguese traders, pirates, renegades, and freebooters on the Bengal coast in eastern India in the sixteenth and seventeenth centuries to search for a typology of early modern politics. She argues in favour of a new, expanding, fluid political spectrum where both settled empires and enterprising, independent political actors could negotiate each other, exploiting the myriad overlaps of political spheres. This is followed by a chapter on maritime law by Santanu Sengupta. It looks at the changing legal culture of the Indian Ocean during the seventeenth through early nineteenth centuries. Sengupta argues that the early modern legal world of maritime commerce was marked by legal plurality and hybridity, something that allowed a diasporic mercantile community like the Armenians to deftly negotiate and adapt to a variety of circumstances. He points out that although the early colonial government accommodated itself within this heterogeneous early modern legal world, by the second quarter of the nineteenth century, this hybridity was increasingly replaced by the legal hegemony of British colonial power. The final chapter by Pratyay Nath takes us into the world of war, by asking what qualifies Mughal warfare to be designated as early modern. Nath argues that the answer lies in four major tendencies – an enhanced ability of armies to adapt to myriad fighting conditions, a centralizing military organization, a heightened efficiency in the management of war, and a culture of war centred on the imperial cult and the legitimation of violence in terms of justice. It were these tendencies that characterized military early modernity for South Asia, something that was jettisoned since the mid-eighteenth century by the rise of European military techniques, administration, and culture.

An important argument that runs through almost all these chapters is that the tendencies that marked the early modern condition roughly between the sixteenth through eighteenth centuries did not emerge overnight. Rather, most of these tendencies themselves signified the maturation of historical processes of earlier times. Ramsey, for instance, explains that the new questions that were raised by Sirhindi and Mulla Sadra in the seventeenth century were rooted in the criticality that had characterized Islamic natural philosophy in the earlier centuries. Similarly, Nath points out that Akbar's centralizing reforms in Mughal military administration drew upon earlier traditions prevalent in the armies of the Delhi Sultanate as well as Turko-Mongol polities. In this outlook, the preceding centuries – especially the medieval period – does not remain Symes' 'penal colony of history', the other of everything that the modern represents; rather, it emerges as the period that bore the roots of modernity itself, from which early modernity emerged organically without any dramatic historical breaks.

At the other end of the spectrum, several of our contributors indicate that fresh tendencies that appeared in the sixteenth through seventeenth centuries sometimes stretched right into the nineteenth century. This was true, for example, of the reformist ideas that Ghani argues characterized Sufi Islam in the seventeenth and eighteenth centuries as well as the increasing state-control that Kumar argues the kingdoms of modern Rajasthan began asserting on the natural environment since the sixteenth century. This indicates that as much as we do not envision early modernity simply as the introductory phase of South Asian modernity, we also do not envision early modernity as something completely divorced from colonial modernity. Rather, in our perspective, colonial modernity itself was something hybrid, built on the derailment of some of the historical characteristics of South Asian early modernity, the appropriation, reformulation, and continuation of some others, and, finally, the import of many tendencies of western European modernity.

Yet, these historical continuities notwithstanding, the image of early modernity that emerges from our chapters is that of a distinct historical period of the evolution of South Asian society, one that engendered new developments across almost all domains of human activity. As a historical condition, it was at once local and global, a product of both indigenous developments and transregional processes, and as much peculiar to this region in some ways as shared across the world in others. This kind of a conceptualization of early modernity – itself a maturation of the intellectual contributions of several scholars who have written before us – is subversive, creative, and liberative at the same time. On the first count, it subverts the conventional periodization of South Asian history and contributes to the decolonization of the South Asian past. In doing so, we join forces with historians advocating similar revisionist schemes of periodization like the early medieval, and invite others to rethink more of the categories that have framed the writing of South Asian history till now. Second, this conceptualization of early modernity creates increasing possibilities for comparative historical studies that can help us understand the historical experience through its comparison with that of various other parts of the world that were undergoing similar churnings. It is perhaps for this reason that out of the various historical periods, it is the early modern period has seen the greatest explosion of transregional histories in its various forms – comparative history, connected history, and global history – in the last two decades. We hope that by facilitating the writing of more such histories in years to come, the category of early modernity will contribute towards the breaking of the isolation in which South Asian history was mostly written till the close of the twentieth century. Finally, this conceptualization of early modernity liberates modernity from what Terence Cave calls 'Eurocentric claustrophobia'.[115] Instead, it envisions the early forms of modernity as a hybrid, shared historical condition, produced in various parts of the world around the same time through a conjuncture of shared and specific processes. In doing so, we wish to engage in dialogue other scholars who are interested in unpacking the meanings, politics, and violences of the idea of modernity. For us, that is the essence of inhabiting the modern and attempting to go beyond it.

Notes

1. Jadunath Sarkar (ed.), *The History of Bengal*, vol. 2: *Muslim Period 1200–1757* (Dacca: University of Dacca, 2006 [1948]), 497.
2. J. Sarkar, *History of Bengal*, 497.
3. J. Sarkar, *History of Bengal*, 498.
4. Susobhan Sarkar, 'Notes on the Bengal Renaissance', in Susobhan Sarkar, *On the Bengal Renaissance*, 13–68 (Calcutta: Papyrus, 1979), see 13.
5. Sumit Sarkar, 'Rammohun Roy and the Break with the Past', in *Rammohun Roy and the Process of Modernization in India*, ed. V. C. Joshi, 46–68 (New Delhi: Vikas, 1975).
6. Partha Chatterjee, *The Nation and Its Fragments: Colonial and Postcolonial Histories* (Delhi: Oxford University Press, 1995 [1993]), 3–13.
7. Partha Chatterjee, *Our Modernity* (Rotterdam and Dakar: SEPHIS CODESRIA, 1997), 9.
8. John F. Richards, 'Early Modern India and World History', *Journal of World History* 8, no. 2 (1997): 197–209.
9. Sanjay Subrahmanyam, 'Connected Histories: Notes towards a Reconfiguration of Early Modern Eurasia', *Modern Asian Studies* 31, no. 2 (1997): 735–762.
10. John Dagenais and Margaret R. Greer, 'Decolonizing the Middle Ages: Introduction', *Journal of Medieval and Early Modern Studies* 30, no. 3 (2000): 431–448.
11. Dagenais and Greer, 'Decolonizing the Middle Ages', 432–434.
12. Reinhart Koselleck, *Futures Past: On the Semantics of Historical Time*, translated and with an introduction by Keith Tribe (New York: Columbia University Press, 2004 [1979]), 9–25. For a brief history of the emergence of the category of the medieval, see Timothy Reuter, 'Medieval: Another Tyrannous Construct?' *Medieval History Journal* 1, no. 1 (1998): 25–45.
13. Koselleck, *Futures Past*, 17.
14. Dagenais and Greer, 'Decolonizing the Middle Ages', 434.
15. Dagenais and Greer, 'Decolonizing the Middle Ages', 434–435.
16. Dagenais and Greer, 'Decolonizing the Middle Ages'.
17. Carol Symes, 'When We Talk about Modernity', *American Historical Review*, 116, no. 3 (2011): 715–726, see 721.
18. Dagenais and Greer, 'Decolonizing the Middle Ages'.
19. William A. Green, 'Periodization in European and World History', *Journal of World History* 3, no. 1 (1992): 13–53, see 19.
20. Reuter, 'Medieval', 26–27.
21. Harbans Mukhia, '"Medieval India": An Alien Conceptual Hegemony?', *Medieval History Journal* 1, no. 1 (1998): 91–105, see 99.
22. Koselleck, *Futures Past*, 11.

23. Koselleck, *Futures Past*, 17.
24. During the nineteenth and twentieth centuries, there emerged in France and then other romance-language countries an alternate fourfold division of time into the ancient, medieval, modern, and contemporary periods, with 1789 as the division between the last two. The tripartite division remained mainstream in English, German, and North American academia.
25. Green, 'Periodization', 23–29.
26. Green, 'Periodization', 25. Merry Wiesner-Hanks points out that the term 'Renaissance' was first used by Giorgio Vasari (1511–1574) to refer to the rebirth of Classical art in fifteenth- and sixteenth-century western Europe. This marks a contrast with Burckhardt, who used it in a civilizational and temporal sense, as a bridge between the medieval and the modern. Merry E. Wiesner-Hanks, *What Is Early Modern History?* (Cambridge and Malden: Polity Press, 2021).
27. Timothy Brook, 'Medievality and the Chinese Sense of History', *Medieval History Journal* 1, no. 1 (1998): 145–164; T. H. Barrett, 'China and the Redundancy of the Medieval', *Medieval History Journal* 1, no. 1 (1998): 73–89.
28. Thomas Keirstead, 'Inventing Medieval Japan: The History and Politics of National Identity', *Medieval History Journal* 1, no. 1 (1998): 47–71.
29. Keirstead, 'Inventing Medieval Japan'.
30. Mohamad Tavakoli-Targhi, 'Contested Memories of Pre-Islamic Iran', *Medieval History Journal* 2, no. 2 (1999): 245–275.
31. This rhetoric itself underwent several shifts and turns over the nineteenth century. For instance, the initial idea of restoring South Asia to its glory lost to the invading Muslims in the Middle Ages was replaced at one point of time by a drive to civilize and enlighten an essentially non-modern space. For details, see Thomas R. Metcalf, *The New Cambridge History of India*, vol. 3.4: *Ideologies of the Raj* (Cambridge: Cambridge University Press, 1995).
32. Mukhia, '"Medieval India"', 99–102; Daud Ali, 'The Historiography of the Medieval in South Asia', *Journal of the Royal Asiatic Society* 22, no. 1 (2012): 7–12, see 7–8; Daud Ali, 'The Idea of the Medieval in the Writing of South Asian History: Contexts, Methods and Politics', *Social History* 39, no. 3 (2014): 382–407, see 384–385.
33. Ali, 'Idea of the Medieval', 387–389. For some of the important interventions in this debate, see Harbans Mukhia (ed.), *The Feudalism Debate* (New Delhi: Manohar, 1999).
34. Ali, 'Idea of the Medieval', 394–395.
35. For an analysis of this line of thinking about the past, see Neeladri Bhattacharya, 'Predicaments of Secular Histories', *Public Culture* 20, no. 1 (2008): 57–73.
36. For a similar point for Japanese history, see Keirstead, 'Inventing Medieval Japan', 51. It is to be noted that notwithstanding the various scholarly

reinterpretations of the medieval, it still continues to be the 'penal colony' of public historical imagination. Even now, it remains the place where all negative attributes – like superstition, violence against women, lack of infrastructure, and violence of the caste system – that do not fit into different visions of a modern India are relegated. For a typical example, see Aparajita Banerjee, 'A Medieval India in a Modern Era', *The Hindu*, 13 June 2016, https://www.thehindu.com/opinion/open-page/a-medieval-india-in-a-modern-era/article4302422.ece (accessed on 4 August 2018).

37. Dagenais and Greer, 'Decolonizing the Middle Ages', 438.
38. Dagenais and Greer, 'Decolonizing the Middle Ages', 438.
39. In fact, Catherine Asher and Cynthia Talbot argue that the entire period between the thirteenth and eighteenth centuries – designated traditionally as the South Asian medieval – heralded the 'highly pluralistic human landscape' of modern South Asia. Catherine B. Asher and Cynthia Talbot, *India before Europe* (Cambridge: Cambridge University Press, 2006).
40. Brajadulal Chattopadhyaya, *The Making of Early Medieval India* (New Delhi: Oxford University Press, 2005 [1994]). Also see Ali, 'Historiography of the Medieval', 8–10; Ali, 'Idea of the Medieval', 387–389.
41. Ali, 'Historiography of the Medieval', 10–12; Ali, 'Idea of the Medieval', 397–407.
42. Dorothy Ross, 'American Modernities, Past and Present', *American Historical Review* 116, no. 3 (2011): 702–714, see 702.
43. Jack Goldstone, 'The Problem of the "Early Modern" World', *Journal of the Economic and Social History of the Orient* 41, no. 3 (1998): 249–284, see 250.
44. Goldstone, 'Problem of the "Early Modern" World', 250.
45. Goldstone, 'Problem of the "Early Modern" World', 250–252.
46. This, as Goldstone rightly points out, was a long-drawn process that stretched roughly from 1500 to 1850, which is said to have been characterized by 'proto-industrialization' – a process comprising a slow shift in socio-economic processes between the economy of a relatively static feudal setup and a market- and profit-oriented society. We explore the implications of this formulation for the conceptualization of early modernity in the next section. Goldstone, 'Problem of the "Early Modern" World', 252–253.
47. Sudipta Kaviraj, 'An Outline of a Revisionist Theory of Modernity', *European Journal of Sociology* 46, no. 3 (2005): 497–526, see 508–509.
48. Chatterjee, *Our Modernity*, 19.
49. Dipesh Chakrabarty, 'The Muddle of Modernity', *American Historical Review* 116, no. 3 (2011): 663–675, see 669.
50. Chakrabarty, 'Muddle of Modernity', 669.
51. Wolfgang Reinhard, 'The Idea of Early Modern History', in *Companion to Historiography*, ed. Michael Bentley, 268–279 (London and New York: Routledge, 1997), 271.

52. Björn Wittrock, 'Early Modernities: Varieties and Transitions', *Daedalus* 127, no. 3 (1998): 19–40, see 19.
53. Carol Gluck, 'The End of Elsewhere: Writing Modernity Now', *American Historical Review* 116, no. 3 (2011): 676–687, see 677.
54. Gluck, 'End of Elsewhere', 676–677.
55. Gluck, 'End of Elsewhere', 676–677.
56. Gluck, 'End of Elsewhere', 676–677.
57. Kaviraj, 'An Outline of a Revisionist Theory of Modernity', 525–526.
58. Kaviraj, 'An Outline of a Revisionist Theory of Modernity', 525–526.
59. Gluck, 'End of Elsewhere', see 686.
60. Gluck, 'End of Elsewhere', 686.
61. Gluck, 'End of Elsewhere', 686.
62. Gluck, 'End of Elsewhere', 686.
63. Kaviraj, 'An Outline of a Revisionist Theory of Modernity', 514, 516.
64. Kaviraj, 'An Outline of a Revisionist Theory of Modernity', 514, 516.
65. Sanjay Subrahmanyam, 'Hearing Voices: Vignettes of Early Modernity in South Asia, 1400–1750', *Daedalus* 127, no. 3 (1998): 75–104, see 99–100.
66. Subrahmanyam, 'Hearing Voices', 99–100.
67. Subrahmanyam, 'Hearing Voices', 99–100.
68. Partha Chatterjee and Raziuddin Aquil (eds.), *History in the Vernacular* (Ranikhet: Permanent Black, 2008), 7–8. In the recent years, some scholars have argued against the idea of colonial rule bringing about a profound historical rupture. Instead, they have highlighted the continuities between early modernity and colonial modernity, especially in the intellectual realm. See, for instance, C. A. Bayly, *Recovering Liberties: Indian Thought in the Age of Liberalism and Empire* (Cambridge: Cambridge University Press, 2012); Milinda Banerjee, '"All This Is Indeed Brahman": Rammohun Roy and a "Global" History of the Rights-Bearing Self', *Asian Review of World Histories* 3, no. 1 (2015): 81–112; Caleb Simmons, *Devotional Sovereignty: Kingship and Religion in India* (New York: Oxford University Press, 2020). Some of the contributors of the present volume too emphasize this element of continuity. While certain continuities may indeed have existed, the editors of this volume argue that they could not diminish the fundamentally transforming quality of colonial rule.
69. Kaveh Yazdani offers an alternate perspective to this multi-phase evolution of modernity. Locating the origins of modernity in what is traditionally seen as the High Middle Ages with respect to European history, he argues that versions of modernity emerged in different poly-centric core areas of Afro-Eurasia, as a result of both indigenous historical processes and exchanges across regions. He breaks down the historical development of modernity into several phases – 'early modernity' between the tenth and fifteenth centuries, 'middle modernity'

during the sixteenth through eighteenth centuries, 'saddle period' roughly between 1770 and 1830, and finally 'late modernity' since around 1830. Kaveh Yazdani, *India, Modernity and the Great Divergence: Mysore and Gujarat (17th to 19th C.)* (Leiden: Brill, 2017).

70. Justus Nipperdey, 'The Pitfalls of Terminology: Uncovering the Paradoxical Roots of Early Modern History in American Historiography', *Chronologics: Periodisation in a Global Context*, Hypotheses, 2018, https://chronolog.hypotheses.org/798#_ftnref22 (accessed on 25 June 2021).
71. Terence Cave, 'Locating the Early Modern', *Paragraph* 29, no. 1 (2006): 12–26, see 12.
72. Moshe Sluhovsky, 'Discernment of Difference, the Introspective Subject, and the Birth of Modernity', *Journal of Medieval and Early Modern Studies* 36, no. 1 (2006), 169–199, see 171–173.
73. Koselleck, *Futures Past*, 12–21.
74. Koselleck, *Futures Past*, 21.
75. At the same time, other historians highlight some of the other changes that transpired simultaneously in Europe with Koselleck's 'temporalization of history' and hence can be associated with the idea of early modernity. Wittrock breaks them down into three phases. The first, he argues, entailed the separation of religious and temporal authorities in the twelfth and thirteenth centuries. This established the prospect of the coexistence of a multiplicity of political, social, and cultural domains. This was followed by the rise of absolutist regimes of national kingships, the breakup of the confessional unity of Christendom, an era of bloody religious conflict, and the rise of vernacular cultures. In the third and final phase, Europe saw the emergence of a thriving and dynamic public sphere, new types of political organizations in the form of republican governments, and new modes of collective identities. Wittrock, 'Early Modernities', 22–23, 25–27, 37–38.
76. Sluhovsky, 'Discernment of Difference', 174–178.
77. Sluhovsky, 'Discernment of Difference', 174–178.
78. Sluhovsky, 'Discernment of Difference', 174.
79. Luke Clossey, 'Early Modern World', in *The Berkshire Encyclopedia of World History*, ed. William H. McNeill, Jerry H. Bentley, David Christian, Ralph C. Croizier, J. R. McNeill, Heidi Roupp, and Judith P. Zinsser, 592–598 (Great Barrington, MA: Berkshire Publishing Group, 2005), 593–595.
80. Richards, 'Early Modern India and World History'.
81. Subrahmanyam, 'Connected Histories', 737–739, 746–754.
82. Rosalind O'Hanlon, 'Contested Conjunctures: Brahman Continuities and "Early Modernity" in India', *American Historical Review* 118, no. 3 (2013): 765–787, see 771, 786–787.

83. Velcheru Narayana Rao, David Shulman, and Sanjay Subrahmanyam, *Textures of Time: Writing History in South India 1600–1800* (New York: Other Press, 2003).
84. David Shulman, *More than Real: A History of the Imagination in South India* (Cambridge, MA, and London: Harvard University Press, 2012).
85. Elaine M. Fisher, *Hindu Pluralism: Religion and the Public Sphere in Early Modern South Asia* (Oakland: University of California Press, 2017), 22.
86. Fisher, *Hindu Pluralism*.
87. Jonardon Ganeri, *The Lost Age of Reason: Philosophy in Early Modern India 1450–1700* (Oxford: Oxford University Press, 2011), 6.
88. Ganeri, *Lost Age of Reason*.
89. Shankar Nair, *Translating Wisdom: Hindu–Muslim Intellectual Interactions in Early Modern South Asia* (Oakland: University of California Press, 2020).
90. Nile Green, *Making Space: Sufis and Settlers in Early Modern India* (New Delhi: Oxford University Press, 2012), 226.
91. The Mughals, however, did use cartography extensively in the first half of the seventeenth century in imperial portraiture as a tool of political propaganda. Ebba Koch, 'The Symbolic Possession of the World: European Cartography in Mughal Allegory and History Painting', *Journal of the Economic and Social History of the Orient* 55, nos. 2–3 (2012): 547–580.
92. Irfan Habib, 'Cartography in Mughal India', in *Medieval India: A Miscellany*, ed. Irfan Habib, 122–134 (New York: Asia Publishing House, 1977).
93. Goldstone, 'Problem of the "Early Modern" World', 253–254.
94. Goldstone, 'Problem of the "Early Modern" World', 253–254.
95. Goldstone, 'Problem of the "Early Modern" World', 254–255.
96. Goldstone, 'Problem of the "Early Modern" World', 255–261.
97. Randolph Starn, 'The Early Modern Muddle', *Journal of Early Modern History* 6, no. 3 (2002): 296–307.
98. Starn, 'Early Modern Muddle', 299.
99. Sheldon Pollock (ed.), *Forms of Knowledge in Early Modern Asia: Explorations in the Intellectual History of India and Tibet, 1500–1800* (Durham and London: Duke University Press, 2011), 4.
100. Pollock, *Forms of Knowledge*, 3
101. Pollock, *Forms of Knowledge*, 2–3. Also see Sheldon Pollock, 'India in the Vernacular Millennium: Literary Culture and Polity, 1000–1500', *Daedalus* 127, no. 3 (1998): 41–74.
102. Chakrabarty, 'Muddle of Modernity', 672.
103. Chakrabarty, 'Muddle of Modernity', 672.
104. Chakrabarty, 'Muddle of Modernity', 672.
105. Chakrabarty, 'Muddle of Modernity', 674–675.

106. For the arguments of this paragraph, we are indebted to Tanika Sarkar, who discussed some of these ideas in her Plenary Address in the 'Debating the "Early Modern" in South Asian History' conference held at Ashoka University, Sonipat, Haryana, on 9–10 February 2018.
107. O'Hanlon, 'Contested Conjunctures', 767.
108. Pollock, *Forms of Knowledge*, 4.
109. O'Hanlon, 'Contested Conjunctures', 770.
110. This was pointed out by Sarkar in her Plenary Address at the conference 'Debating the "Early Modern" in South Asia'.
111. In contrast to the increasingly warm welcome that the idea of early modernity has received in the last two decades from historians working on this period, the category has been greeted with reluctance and scepticism from scholars working on the colonial period. The few scholars who use this category mostly do so to refer to the eighteenth century – and in some rare cases the seventeenth century – to talk about the demise of Mughal imperial power, the rise of regional states, and the rise of British colonial commercial-political power. In this sense, early modernity is reduced to the last phase of South Asia's pre-colonial history and the dawn of colonialism. In other words, early modernity is conceptualized as a brief phase of transition from the pre-colonial times to the colonial condition. Kaushik Roy, *War, Culture and Society in Early Modern South Asia, 1740–1849* (London and New York: Routledge, 2011); Philip J. Stern, *The Company-State: Corporate Sovereignty and the Early Modern Foundation of the British Empire in India* (New York: Oxford University Press, 2011); Tirthankar Roy, *An Economic History of Early Modern India* (London and New York: Routledge, 2013).
112. See, for instance, Pollock, *Forms of Knowledge*; Rosalind O'Hanlon and David Washbrook, *Religious Cultures in Early Modern India: New Perspectives* (London and New York: Routledge, 2014); Thomas de Bruijn and Allison Busch (eds.), *Culture and Circulation: Literature in Motion in Early Modern India* (Leiden and Boston: Brill, 2014); Rosalind O'Hanlon, Christopher Minkowski, and Anand Venkatkrishnan (eds.), *Scholar Intellectuals in Early Modern India: Discipline, Sect, Lineage and Community* (London and New York: Routledge, 2017); Tyler Williams, Anshu Malhotra, and John Stratton Hawley (eds.), *Text and Tradition in Early Modern North India* (New Delhi: Oxford University Press, 2018); Raziuddin Aquil and Tilottama Mukherjee (eds.), *An Earthly Paradise: Trade, Politics and Culture in Early Modern Bengal* (London and New York: Routledge, 2020).
113. de Bruijn and Busch, *Culture and Circulation*, 1–20.
114. O'Hanlon and Washbrook, *Religious Cultures in Early Modern India*.
115. Cave, 'Locating the Early Modern', 15.

PART I
RELIGION, IDEOLOGY, IDENTITY

2

Locating the Early Modern in South Asian Sufism

Kashshaf Ghani

What constitutes the 'early modern' for South Asia is a question that has engaged a large number of scholars in recent times. The earliest traces of modernity for South Asia have been argued to have emerged around the sixteenth century as much from the impact of global processes as from developments within the region. The following discussion will explore the nature of this early modernity in the Indian subcontinent with regard to Sufi traditions.

The history of Sufism in this region has been rich and diverse, but most importantly continuous, alongside the rise and fall of political dynasties. This connection between institutionalized Sufi orders and Muslim political authority has deep roots that can be traced to Central Asia and Iran, where state ideology and Sufism have a long history of borrowing from each other.[1] In this tradition, the rise and fall of rulers was intertwined with the idea of sainthood (*wilayat*) in the Persian tradition, where Sufi saints, believed to exercise spiritual sovereignty in God's earthly domain, leased out political authority to rulers over specific territories (*sultanat*). The worldly authority (*walayat*) of a Sufi was demarcated amongst masters of the same or different orders (*tariqa*), and after the death of the master it was conferred on his spiritual successor (*khalifa*). Following such a notion, it is not surprising therefore that the rise and decline of political orders came to be linked with the rise of Sufi orders under living saints or the passing away of influential Sufi masters.[2]

Sufism in South Asia merits a historical analysis not as a monolithic, inward-looking spiritual tradition, but rather as a socio-religious practice deeply embedded in the doctrines of Islamic philosophy while at the same time having strong local connections with the state and society through intellectual and cultural production. While trying to understand what could have constituted *early modernity* for Sufism in this region within such a dynamic history, what can be treated as a point of departure is how Sufism participated in some of the broader trends identified with early modernity. In the period between the sixteenth and eighteenth centuries, early modernity in Sufi activities can be read in terms of three distinct but complementary tendencies. First, there was intense engagement of Sufi orders – regional as well as transregional, old and new, minor and major – with the Mughal state. In an interesting departure from earlier – medieval – times, such new forms of interaction often penetrated both Sufi orders and the imperial household. Members of the royalty became active patrons, and members of Sufi orders were incorporated as courtiers and imperial servants. Second, we see during this period the expansion of Sufi orders and practices, the arrival of new orders, the formation of suborders that led to regional networks, and the emergence of rich cultural production. Finally, the latter part of this period was marked by the rise of reformist traditions that reinterpreted prevailing spiritual discourses, the emergence of new knowledge and practice, and the advent and adoption of European technology, like print. I will explore these three themes in the following three sections.

New Relationships between Sufi Orders and the State

Sufism arrived in South Asia at the close of the twelfth century, around the same time as the Ghurid invasions. As the sultans of Delhi consolidated their authority over the thirteenth and fourteenth centuries, their relationship with the Sufi masters became increasingly complex. While the Suhrawardis showed willingness to accept state patronage and take up public offices, Chishti saints avoided association with temporal authority. Consequently, the relationship between successive Sufi masters and the Delhi sultans can be characterized as ambivalent at best and antagonistic at worst. Even when the Tughlaq sultans extended patronage to the shrine of Baba Fariduddin (d. 1265) in Pakpattan during much of the fourteenth century, they showed distrust and hostility towards his living successors like Nizamuddin Awliya (d. 1325) and Nasiruddin Chiragh-i Dehli (d. 1356).[3] Relationships between the royal authority and Sufi orders improved to some extent in the fifteenth century. However, it was really in the sixteenth century that a paradigmatic shift came about in this respect. This was directly related to the advent of the Mughals in South Asia in 1526 and their building of an empire of subcontinental proportions in this part of the world. In terms of the patronage Mughal emperors extended to Sufis across various mystical orders, the employment that many Sufis enjoyed at the Mughal court and the deep mutual interest of the Mughal elite and the Sufi orders in each other set the sixteenth through the eighteenth centuries in contrast with the antecedent period. This section looks into the nature of this evolving relationship between Mughal power and Sufi authority in course of the sixteenth and seventeenth centuries.

Roots of the close relationship between Sufis and the Mughals can be traced back to the Timurid ancestors of the latter in Central Asia, where during the fifteenth century many Timurid princes were drawn towards the order of Naqshbandi Sufis, particularly their famous master Khwaja Nasiruddin Abdullah Ahrar (d. 1490). Babur was initiated under Ahrar at the time of his birth. He later versified sections of Ahrar's *Risala-i Walidiyya* into Turkish (1528–1529). After taking control of Kabul in 1504, Babur patronized the descendants of Ahrar, even offering one of his daughters in marriage to a Naqshbandi shaikh. Later, Mughal royal women like Bakshi Banu Begum, the sister of Akbar, was married to one of the grandsons of Khwaja Nura, himself the grandson of Ahrar.[4] Having relocated to North India, both Babur and his son Humayun recognized the presence of multiple Sufi orders there and engaged closely with many. This was especially true for popular Sufi orders like the Shattaris and Chishtis, who had strong roots in the region. Babur was familiar with the Timurid practice of shrine visits (*ziyarat*). Immediately upon conquering Delhi, he visited the revered Chishti shrines of Nizamuddin Awliya and Qutbuddin Bakhtiyar Kaki (d. 1235) in Delhi.[5] Later that year, Shaikh Muhammad Ghaus Shattari (d. 1562), a premier saint of the Shattari order, helped Babur capture the fort of Gwalior. These events were the earliest instances of Mughal interaction with Sufi groups other than the Naqshbandis. In the years to come, Humayun aligned himself closely with two Shattari brothers – Shaikh Phul (d. 1562) and Shaikh Muhammad Ghaus. Azfar Moin argues that this relationship helped the emperor create a new form of kingship that drew heavily on astrology and mysticism. All this invited sharp criticism from the larger Timurid kin, who were dismayed at the neglect of the eminent Naqshbandis in favour of local ostensibly pseudo-Sufi orders.[6]

Under Humayun's son Akbar, imperial patronage shifted again – this time towards the Chishti order. In course of the 1560s and 1570s, Akbar made 17 pilgrimages to the shrine of Khwaja Muinuddin Chishti (d. 1236) in Ajmer and displayed great veneration for the living Sufi master Salim Chishti (d. 1572). Mughal accounts attribute the birth of Akbar's son and heir Prince Salim (later Emperor Jahangir) in 1569 to the living grace of Salim Chishti, an event that reinforced the belief of the emperor on Chishti spirituality. Out of reverence, the emperor built a marble mausoleum with lattice screens on the tomb of the saint at Sikri and his new capital city Fatehpur around it. By choosing this living Chishti saint as his object of devotion, the emperor connected himself on the one hand to the saint's predecessor, the renowned Chishti master Baba Fariduddin, and on the other to the nearby shrine of Khwaja Muinuddin Chishti in Ajmer.[7] The attachment was deepened when Akbar built a mosque within the Ajmer shrine in 1571 and embellished the mausoleum in 1579.

In the early seventeenth century, Jahangir introduced spiritual competition for the Chishtis with the revival of the Central Asian Naqshbandis under the charismatic leadership of Khwaja Baqi Billah (d. 1603). In this contested zone of Sufi activities in Mughal North India, the last major transregional Sufi order to emerge was the Qadiri order. Jahangir's son Shah Jahan reverted back to his grandfather's practice of patronizing Chishti Sufis, especially through Muinuddin's shrine at Ajmer. The pendulum swung again with the succession of his son Aurangzeb. Being a strict conformist to *sharia* norms, he forbade imperial women from visiting Sufi shrines for pilgrimage, making structural additions covering tombs, and lime-washing of the sepulchre. However, dissociating himself from shrine practices of his predecessors was easier said than done. In his search for legitimacy after killing his brothers in the race to the throne, Aurangzeb ironically had to take recourse to those very practices of routine visitations and donations to important Sufi shrines in North India as well as in the Deccan. He made customary visits and donations to Ajmer after victory over Dara Shukoh in 1659.[8] In course of his subsequent campaigns in the Deccan, he also paid multiple visits and donations to the shrine of Gesudaraz (d. 1422) in Gulbarga. While Dara's eclectic outlook based on *wujudi* principles[9] invoked the ire of the conservative Naqshbandis like Khwaja Muhammad Masum (d. 1668), the son of Sirhindi (d. 1624), Aurangzeb's image as the orthodox prince and strict upholder of *sharia* norms garnered support from these very Naqshbandis who saw in the Mughal ruler the promise to uphold the interests of Islam.

Deep association between Sufi orders and the emperors also found their way into the employment of Sufis at the imperial court. Alongside the occasional matrimonial alliance, Naqshbandi shaikhs were inducted in the Mughal bureaucracy through appointments in religious offices, thereby creating an 'informal aristocratic Naqshbandi lobby at the Mughal court'.[10] Akbar's administration had individuals linked to famous Chishti saints. Abdul Nabi (d. 1584), the *sadr-i sudur* and the first official in charge of charitable trusts under Akbar, traced his family back to the lineage of Abdul Quddus Gangohi (d. 1537). Abul Fazl's father Shaikh Mubarak traced his family lineage to Sufi Hamiduddin Suwali Nagauri (d. 1274), the spiritual successor of Muinuddin Chishti. The Mughal general and *subadar* of Bengal, Islam Khan Chishti (d. 1613) was the grandchild of Salim Chishti. In a sharp departure from the measured indifference of early Chishti saints for political appointments and largesse, these descendants threw themselves into the royal court, thereby cementing the relation of some Chishti branches with the state through imperial service.[11] This signified a major departure in terms of Sufi–state relationship in comparison with antecedent times.

The devotion that the Mughal elite showed towards Sufis often took the form of the practice of *ziyarat* Akbar's attachment to Chishti Sufism carried a strong performative dimension. Beginning in 1562, this assumed the form of regular *ziyarat* to the shrine of Muinuddin in Ajmer, sometimes during *urs*[12] celebrations, visits to the living Sufi saint Salim Chishti, and occasional visits to the tombs of other Chishti masters like Nizamuddin Awliya, Qutbuddin Bakhtiyar Kaki, Nasiruddin Chiragh-i Dehli, Hamiduddin Nagauri, and Baba Fariduddin.[13] Later Mughal emperors – Jahangir, Shah Jahan, and Aurangzeb, as well as members of the royal household Dara Shukoh and Jahanara – kept up this practice of shrine visits and patronizing construction projects at shrines.

The Qadiri order was single-handedly responsible for attracting members of the Mughal household into a spiritual bond. Mulla Shah (d. 1661), the disciple of the famous Qadiri Sufi Miyan Mir (d. 1635) of seventeenth-century Punjab, was the *murshid* of the Mughal prince Dara Shikoh.[14] Though Dara was deeply drawn towards the five leading Sufi orders in South Asia – Chishti, Suhrawardi, Qadiri, Naqshbandi, and Kubrawi – his primary affiliation however was with the Qadiris. Dara's engagement with Sufism is evident through a series of treatises – both literary and spiritual – he left behind.[15] Dara's sister Jahanara was a devotee of both Chishti and Qadiri Sufis. She had to her credit two Sufi biographies, one titled *Risala-i Sahibiyya* (1641) on her Qadiri Sufi teacher Mulla Shah Badakshi and the other titled *Munis al Arwah* (1639) on Muinuddin Chishti. Regular visits to Ajmer and Kashmir made Jahanara experience the sublime feelings of a *pir-murid* (master–disciple) relationship, through both her immediate Qadiri masters Miyan Mir and Mulla Shah and the hallowed memory of Khwaja Muinuddin. Her attachment to Sufi saints – living and deceased – imparted to her personality a degree of dynamism drawn directly from a sense of deep spiritual devotion that was almost unprecedented in the Mughal *harem*.[16]

As much as Sufi orders flourished by attracting the devotion and patronage of the imperial elite, Mughal sovereignty itself also came to be shaped by Sufi charisma and based on the appropriation of Sufi attributes of authority. The construction of Mughal sacred kingship based on Sufi attributes of spiritual authority became visible from the reign of Humayun, reaching a climax under Akbar. When Humayun succeeded Babur, his reverence for the Shattaris led to their steady elevation at the court. Shaikh Phul and his brother Shaikh Muhammad Ghaus became the spiritual mentors of the emperor. The Shattari brothers were widely known for their knowledge of magic and the sciences of planets. Shaikh Phul is believed to have been endowed with the remarkable ability to gather the spirit powers of planets through miraculous Shattari techniques of invoking the Divine names (*dawat al asma-i husna*). Humayun's interest in occult and astronomical sciences could be the primary reason why he bonded well with the Shattari brothers. Under the influence of the Shattaris, he organized his court rituals on a cosmological basis, reflected in the way he divided his courtly audience through a combination of augury and auspicious planetary positions. On the same principle, the court society was divided into 12 ranks. Lastly, the emperor also connected the powers of planets to his own body by choosing to clothe himself each day depending on planetary positions and colours associated with planets.[17]

While the sudden death of Humayun in 1556 halted the Shattari rise at the Mughal court, the career of Akbar saw the most effective utilization of Sufi authority and charisma for political ends. Akbar's cosmopolitan vision of empire projected through the principle of justice (*adl*) and social harmony among his diverse subject population brought him closer to the Chishtis, who carried a long legacy of cultural adaptation and popularity across a wide cross-section of the South Asian society. Contrary to the politically influential and wealthy Naqshbandis of Central Asia and the Suhrawardis closer home, Chishti spirituality from its inception rested on practices of frugality and asceticism, as well as the avoidance of government service, royal company, grants, and donations. Chishti ideology was deeply influenced by the doctrine of *wahdat al-wujud* (unity of existence),[18] which, when applied to the sociocultural diversity of South Asia, facilitated a dynamic exercise of social dialogue and cultural synthesis. By the time Akbar assumed office, this practice came to be voiced strongly in contemporary Chishti literature: 'The whole world is the manifestation of love (*ishq*), and we see everything as perfect ... there is no precedence of one religion over the other ... you can see His Grace present both in a *kafir* and a Muslim.'[19] In the Chishti outlook, the emperor saw a strong vindication of his own projection of sovereignty. Submission to Chishti authority helped him create a form of Islamic kingship during the 1560s and 1570s. Interestingly, this was followed by the development of Mughal millenarian kingship – one that attained its most hyperbolic phase during the second half of Akbar's rule as well as the reign of Jahangir – by borrowing markers of Sufi charisma and mystical authority.[20]

This brief survey of the intimate involvement of the Mughal emperors and the Sufi orders in South Asia in course of the sixteenth and seventeenth centuries demonstrates the paradigmatic shift that engulfed the relationship between temporal power and mystical authority during this period. My arguments here match those of Azfar Moin, who has recently pointed out that Sufi shrines grew drastically in importance in the post-Mongol world. His work shows that in its patronage of Sufi orders and shrines, the Mughal Empire displayed tendencies comparable to the Safavid and Ottoman Empires, although there were also certain differences between these three major Asiatic Islamicate empires.[21] As a characteristic of early modernity in the realm of Sufism, this radically heightened intermingling of temporal power and Sufi authority was, hence, rooted in the specifics of the developments in South Asia, together with being a part of a shared historical condition.

Expanding Networks, Vernacular Languages, Heightened Engagements

Away from the imperial cities of Agra, Lahore, and Delhi, one important tendency characterized the mystical realm of Sufism in the regional centres in the second half of the sixteenth century.[22] Complementing the changing relations of the Sufis with the state, this new tendency manifested in three ways. First, there was a remarkable geographical expansion of Sufi orders, resulting from the formation of suborders through training and spiritual practice under important masters. Second, cultural productions in regional languages like Hindavi, Dakhni, and Punjabi made increasing appearances during this period. Finally, we find noticeable examples of vigorous engagements with Indic – particularly Brahmanical – as well as foreign devotional and philosophical traditions. These are the historical processes that the present section studies.

The proliferation of Sufi suborders occurred primarily around charismatic personalities who on many occasions combined multiple chains of spiritual training through either their family background or multiple initiations. For instance, in the face of the growing importance of the Naqshbandis at the Mughal imperial court in particular and South Asia in general since the early seventeenth century, two important suborders of the Chishtis grew in strength – the Chishti–Nizami and the Chishti–Sabiri, which traced their origins to Nizamuddin Awliya and Alauddin Ali Sabir (d. 1291), respectively – both notable disciples of Baba Fariduddin. Within these sub-orders, the core Chishti practices of *sama* and *dhikr* came to be supplanted during this period by the primacy of mystical thought (*irfan*), invocation of a sacred lineage (*nasl*), remembering the model behaviour of Prophet Muhammad (*sunnah*), and advocacy of Muslim learning (*ilm*). These suborders spread across regional centres in North India, Gujarat, and the Deccan.

The revival of the Chishti order in North India is credited to Shah Kalimullah Jahanabadi (d. 1729), whose *Kashkul-i Kalimi* (Alms-bowl of Kalimullah) was an important manual for spiritual training, and his successor Nizamuddin Awrangabadi (d. 1730). This spiritual legacy can be traced back to the Chishti master Nasiruddin Chiragh-i Dehli. A disciple of the latter, Kamaluddin Allama (d. 1355) was responsible for establishing the lesser-known Gujarat branch of the Chishti–Nizami order. Kalimullah was initiated into this branch by his master

Shaikh Yahya Madni (d. 1689), the disciple of the reputed Muhammad Chishti (d. 1630) from the Gujarat line. Though he was initially trained under eminent scholars like Shaikh Abu Rida (d. 1690), the famous Naqshbandi saint and uncle of Shah Waliullah (d. 1762), the spiritual brilliance of Kalimullah allowed him to be initiated into the Qadiri, Suhrawardi, Naqshbandi, and Shattari orders as well. Representative of an important development, such non-exclusive approach to spiritual initiation upheld an eclectic tradition which allowed engagements with multiple techniques of spiritual practice rather than isolated experiences. Nizamuddin Awrangabadi from Kakori near Lucknow left behind the treatise *Nizam al-Qulub* (Harmonic Order of Hearts, 1891–1892), which, a century later, inspired the meditative manual *Zia al-Qulub* (Brilliance of Hearts, 1866) by Haji Imdadullah (d. 1899), a master from the Sabiri sub-order of the Chishtis.[23] Preserving the inspiration from their founder-master Alauddin Ali Sabir, the Sabiri Chishtis engaged with meditative (breath control) and bodily techniques based on yoga traditions on a scale unmatched by any branch of the Chishtis.[24]

While Mughal emperors continued to offer regular patronage to important shrines of the Deccan, in and around Khuldabad, it is equally rewarding to explore lesser-known Sufi personalities like Mahmud Khwush Dahan (d. 1617) from Bijapur. Even though these saints do not match up to the charismatic Nizamuddin Awliya and Muhammad Gesudaraz, their writings and practices throw light on unique facets of Sufi activity, like cross-order initiation and training, as seen earlier. Khwush Dahan belonged to a well-known Qadiri family in Bidar but was interestingly trained under a famous Sufi lineage that traced itself back to the renowned Chishti master of Bijapur Shah Miranji Shams ul Ushshaq (d. 1499). He is identified as one of the first Sufis in the Deccan to compose poetry like *Khush Nama* and *Khush Naghz* in Dakhni.[25] Shams ul Ushshaq was succeeded by his son Burhanuddin Janam (d. 1597), the master of Mahmud Khwush Dahan and a prolific author of Sufi treatises in Dakhani like *Irshad Nama* (1582–1583). A treatise by Khwush Dahan titled *Marifat ul Suluk* (The True Knowledge of Wayfaring, 1898) elaborates, in simple form and language, the basic Sufi teachings and practices imparted by him and his master Burhanuddin.[26] This treatise drew from the works of non-Indian masters, like Al-Ghazali (d. 1111) and Ibn al-Arabi (d. 1240), thereby situating Sufism in Mughal India within the larger Islamic world.

The incorporation of women as intended readers and audiences of this kind of literature affirm, first, the widening of the spiritual circuit beyond esoteric teachings and trained disciples and, second, the increasing accessibility of elite Sufi rituals like *dhikr* to the common people in the form of poetical recitation, thereby 'remembering' the attributes and presence of the Divine in one's life. Known as the *Chakkinama* and the *Charkhanama*, some of these poetical compositions from seventeenth- and eighteenth-century Deccan were written by Aminuddin Ala (d. 1675), Shah Hashim Khudawand Hadi (d. 1704–1705), and Shah Kamaluddin (d. 1809–1810). These narratives were meant to be recited and internalized by householder women while grinding grain on the grindstone (*chakki*) and spinning thread on the spinning wheel (*charkha*).[27]

An equally interesting story of the proliferation of Sufi orders unfolded in Bengal, the eastern frontier of South Asia. Since the assertion of Mughal control was still an ongoing and incomplete process here in the seventeenth century, most of the land grants the state made in this region were among the forests of eastern Bengal. In these parts, the Sufis employed the local population to clear forests and expand the agricultural frontier. In the process, local inhabitants were introduced to a Sufi world of Islam in both its Persianized and vernacular forms. In turn, this led to the emergence of a corpus of Sufi literature in Middle Bengali. Examples of such works are Sayyid Murtaza's sixteenth-century text *Yoga Qalandar* and Shaikh Chand's *Talibnama* (1712) – both full of Persian vocabulary and idioms, combined with yogic and *nathapanthi* traditions.[28]

This brings us to another major development during the sixteenth through eighteenth centuries – the increasing importance of vernacular languages as a medium of expression for Sufi spiritual discourse. The earliest traces of such works appear in the form of *doha*s sung in Sufi *sama* assemblies. These were attributed to the Chishti masters Hamiduddin Nagauri and Baba Fariduddin. The trend picked up since the fourteenth century in the form of *masnawi*s in Hindavi. These included Mulla Daud's *Chandayan* (1379) in the fourteenth century. By the sixteenth century, the proliferation of this body of literature started gathering greater momentum. Texts from this period included Mulla Qutban's *Mirigavati* (1503), Malik Muhammad Jayasi's *Padmavat* (1540), and Shaikh Manjhan Shattari Rajgiri's *Madhumalati* (1545). These works fall under the genre of Sufi *premakhyan* (romantic ballads), combining Indic symbols of love and devotion with complex concepts of Sufi spirituality written in simple language. Both Mulla Daud and Mulla Qutban were trained under reputed Chishti Sufi masters Shaikh Zaynuddin and Shaikh Burhan, respectively. The topos of the *virahini* as the longing soul of the woman who suffers from separation and desires for union with her beloved is central to these Sufi romantic tales of Lorik–Chanda, Sohni–Mahiwal, and Sassui–Punhun. In these narratives, the idea of the union leading to the state of unity was largely the impact of the spread of Ibn al-Arabi's *wujudi* doctrines in South Asia.[29] The tales served as cultural artefacts readily accessible by common people, irrespective of their religious affiliation or cultural location.[30] This emergence of Sufi writings in the vernacular in the heartland of South Asia was complemented by similar processes on the margins as well. The case of the Raushaniyya movement in the Pashtun society of modern-day Afghanistan is a good example. The central figure here was Bayazid Ansari (d. 1575), who produced a rich corpus of spiritual literature through the composition of melodies, *diwan*s, *ghazal*s, *qasida*s, *masnawi*s, and *rubai*s in Pashto.[31]

The seventeenth and eighteenth centuries saw further proliferation of Sufi literature in the vernacular. An increasing corpus of texts in Punjabi serves as a case in point. An exploration of this corpus of vernacular Sufi poetry from this region connects us to the spiritual lineage of the masters from the Qadiri order. Their long-standing achievements in the cultural domain of Punjab lay in their prolific contribution to Sufi poetry composed in Punjabi. This literary production was led by some of the most revered Sufi poets like Shah Husayn (d. 1599), Sultan Bahu (d. 1691), Shah Abdul Latif (d. 1752), Bulleh Shah (d. 1752), and Waris Shah (d. 1798).[32] The seventeenth-century quatrains of the Sufi poet Sultan Bahu of Jhang in southern Punjab, for instance, provided a fine exposition of the relationship between man and God. The finest of Sufi *premakhyan*s, with their rich repository of mystical allegory, came from Shah Abdul Latif of Bhit in the Sindh region. His book of poems *Shaha Jo Risalo* (Book of Shah, 1866) contains 30 chapters according to traditional Indian musical modes (*raga*s), many of which he composed himself.[33] Sayyid Abdullah, popularly known as Bulleh Shah, emerged as arguably the greatest Sufi poet in Punjabi.[34] He is also credited with introducing *wujudi* ideas in a reinterpretation of medieval Hindu folktales like Heer–Ranjha.

These vernacular literary expressions were complemented by the cultural translation of mystical ideas from other parts of the world as well as from other devotional paradigms within South Asia. For instance, the sixteenth century saw the production of *Rushd Nama* (1480) by Shaikh Abdul Quddus Gangohi. The shaikh was a staunch proponent of the *wujudi* doctrine of Unity from the Chishti–Sabiri sub-order. It was inspired by the works of the Spanish mystic Ibn al-Arabi, who had a tremendous influence on South Asian Sufis, especially the Chishtis and Qadiris.[35] Gangohi's work reflected the crystallization of an older tradition of bringing together ideas of al-Arabi with those of Hindu *yogi*s and *sannyasi*s. The text carried verses in Hindavi and Persian, identifying *wujudi* beliefs among Sufis with the philosophy and practices of the Shaivite *yogi* Gorakhnath. This signified the heightening of Sufi engagement with Indic religious and philosophical paradigms during this period. It is possible to identify two similar examples of literary works that embody cultural assimilation between Sufi and Brahmanical traditions. In the sixteenth century, Abdul Wahid Bilgrami (d. 1608) wrote *Haqaiq-i Hindi* (Indian Truths, 1566–1567) in the form of a compilation of Hindu devotional songs to the Brahmanical god Vishnu.[36] In this text, he gave Brahmanical hymns Islamic meanings for them to be used in Sufi musical concerts. The other example is Abdul Rahman Chishti's (d. 1683) *Mirat ul Haqaiq* (Mirror of Truths) from the seventeenth century. It carried a Persian rendering of the Sanskrit *Bhagavad Gita*. Here, Krishna's message was depicted in non-contradictory terms to Islamic teachings of the doctrine of *hama ust*.[37]

Emergence of Reformist Traditions

A third major marker of early modernity in South Asian Sufism was the emergence of strong reformist traditions and a new criticality towards devotional practices. These tendencies emerged during the seventeenth century, gained greater momentum during the eighteenth century, and extended into the early nineteenth century. In the intensity and scope of reformist ideologies, these centuries marked a shift from earlier times. Two main tendencies were visible during this period. First, we see the rise of the Mujaddadi tradition among Naqshbandis. The name Mujaddadi was introduced by a highly respected scholar (*alim*) Maulana Abdul Hakim Sialkoti (d. 1657) after Shaikh Ahmad Sirhindi, who was styled as the renewer (*mujaddad*) of Islam in the second millennium (Mujaddad-i Alf-i Thani).[38] Second, there was a shift towards reformist Sufism led by Naqshbandis like Mirza Mazhar Jan-i Janan (d. 1781) and his equally famous disciple Qazi Sanaullah Panipati (d. 1810). This section discusses these and other related historical processes.

The emergence of the reformist tradition was triggered by a sense of 'decline' within South Asian Islam in general and Sufism in particular. Sufi customs and practices labelled as 'innovations' came to constitute the primary target of this reform. Questionable Sufi practices were identified as originating from localized versions of Islam in the regions, influenced by indigenous ritualistic traditions and assimilated through Sufi shrines and spiritual establishments. By the seventeenth century, conservative sections within the Muslim society began raising questions as to whether these mystical traditions constituting a plethora of practices and diverse rituals, which the practitioners claimed was based on traditions of Prophet Muhammad, could at all be connected to the Sunnah of the Prophet. If yes, then what were the practices that can be accepted? If no, then what were those specific innovations (*bidat*) that needed to be reformed in spite of its acceptance within Sufi circles?

During the seventeenth century, Sirhindi came to be recognized in Sufi and scholarly circles as one of the harshest critics of the *wujudi* doctrine.[39] His alternate doctrine of *wahdat al shuhud* originated from a fine distinction in the Sufi idea of union between reality and perception.⁴⁰ Approaching from a Sufi perspective, Sirhindi argued that claims of non-distinction between the Creator and creation were made in a spiritual state where the Sufi saint was in no position to distinguish between reality and falsehood. As a result, the closer he moved towards the realization of Divine beauty, the more he lost control over his rational sense of differentiating between the creation and the Creator. This illusion of unity (*wahdat*), for Sirhindi, remained only in the perception (*shuhud*) of the Sufi, never in actuality (*wujud*). Interestingly, Sirhindi was not a pioneer of the *shuhudi* doctrine,⁴¹ but rather was responsible for imparting it with a doctrinal status and acceptance, vis-à-vis the *wujudi* idea, that it was yet to claim for itself. *Wahdat al shuhud* could never fully replace its *wujudi* antithesis but tried to alter the Sufi experience of Divine reality.⁴²

In effect, the *shuhudi* doctrine could hardly challenge the strong *wujudi* foundations championed by Chishtis and Qadiris. Chishti response in the face of a strong Naqshbandi offensive on *wujudi* doctrines emerged from the pen of Abdul Rahman Chishti in one of his lesser-studied works – *Mirat ul Asrar* (1663), considered a milestone in rearticulating the Chishti spiritual discourse. As a member of the Sabiri branch of Chishtis, Abdul Rahman was a staunch advocate of the *wujudi* doctrine, evident from his copious citations from the *Fusus al Hikam* (1229) and the borrowing of *wujudi* interpretations from the works of Ala-ud daula Simnani (d. 1336).⁴³ Prior to Abdul Rahman, a strong exponent of Ibn al-Arabi's philosophy was the famous Qadiri saint Amanullah Panipati (d. 1550). He worked extensively on the treatises of Ibn al-Arabi to defend his strong position in favour of *wahdat al-wujud*. His depth of knowledge on *wujudi* doctrines led his contemporaries to address him as Ibn al-Arabi-i Thani (the second Ibn Arabi). The famous Shattari saint Muhammad Ghawth of Gwalior (d. 1562) also engaged with the idea of *wahdat al-wujud* in his mystical treatise *Jawahir-i Khamsa* (1525).

The most important eighteenth-century figure in this context was Shah Waliullah, often looked upon as a master of his time (*qaim al-zaman*) and polestar of mystical hierarchy (*qutb*). His Persian work the *Hamaat* (Outpourings, 1735–1736) begins with an outline on the rise and fall of Sufi orders and affiliations, following the basis of the path (*asl-i tariqat*) through which the teachings are continuously 'being renewed along the lines of Renewership (*mujaddidiyya*)'.⁴⁴ Although critical of Sufi practices in general, it is evident that Shah Waliullah could not fully escape the influence of the reputable lineage of Naqshbandi Sufis. He was most critical of the Sufi practices that he came to witness around popular devotion, veneration of tombs, musical concerts and dance, and acts of physical submission to the deceased saint. Therefore, it was less about critiquing the tradition of Sufism in general and more about criticizing its practices whose validity over centuries had become extremely difficult to ascertain. For Waliullah, the only way towards that ascertainment was through the yardstick of the *sharia*. He repeatedly argued that practices that failed to stand the test of Islamic law should be rejected right away.[45] Recognizing the endurance of *wujudi* doctrines, Waliullah's efforts at synthesis and reconciliation (*tatbiq*) between *wujudi* and *shuhudi* ideas are noteworthy.

Another important figure of the eighteenth century was Qazi Sanaullah, a successor of Sirhindi. For him, the primary prerequisite of a true Sufi shaikh was sound academic training in the doctrines of the *sharia* that would lead one towards the intricacies of the *tariqa*. Thus, his works emphasized a harmonious relation between the tenets of the *sharia* and the *tariqa*, as essential for reinstating Sufism as a means of Islamic revival in the eighteenth century. Sanaullah abhorred ideas of superstition and un-Islamic practices, ranging from criticism towards a deep sense of devotion in Sufi beliefs and practices like statements made in a state of intoxication (*sukr*), inner spiritual realities, and actions attesting spiritual stature.

Subsequently, Sufi practices and ethics came to be increasingly read and explained in accordance to the Quran and Hadith as proof texts, while Sufi teachings attained a characteristic of legal treatises, with Sufi masters adopting the approach of legal scholars (*fuqaha*) rather than mystics.[46] Lessons and manuals on spiritual training came to be textualized, marking a noticeable shift from the dominant oral tradition. Manuals of Sufism did exist in writing prior to the eighteenth century, like the *Jawahir-i Khamsa* of Muhammad Ghauth Gwaliyari and Kalimullah Jahanabadi's *Muraqqa-i Kalimi* and *Kashkul-i Kalimi*.[47] However, by the time of the famous Sufi poet Khwaja Mir Dard (d. 1785), written materials and manuals came to substitute the oral *suhbat* (company of the Sufi master).[48] The increasing availability of Sufi teachings and practices in the public domain through print technology was perhaps an attempt at asserting the spiritual legitimacy of these discourses along the models of the Quran and Hadith. The personification of this latter approach was done no better than by Sirhindi, who combined in himself characteristics of a learned *alim* with those of a profound Sufi master (*arif-i tamm al-marifat*).[49]

These reformist tendencies continued well into the early nineteenth century. Shah Ismail 'Shahid' (d. 1831), the grandson of Shah Waliullah and the nephew of Shah Abdul Aziz (d. 1832), together with Sayyid Ahmad (d. 1831) of Rae Bareli, leader of the Mujahidin movement, led the *tajdid* movement in North India by combining the Wahhabi-inspired Tariqah-i Muhammadiya, a Sufi order led by

Sayyid Ahmed.⁵⁰ Sayyid Ahmad was trained in the leading Sufi orders – Chishti, Suhrawardi, Qadiri, and Naqshbandi – by Abdul Aziz, before he went on to integrate these mystical teachings in his own order of the Tariqah-i Muhammadiya, conceived around 1818. The idea of reformism according to this school of thought followed the actions of the Prophet and its proper imbibing throughout all sections of the Muslim community, which called for 'strict conformity to religious law' without compromising on the core Sufi ethics.⁵¹ These reforms were intended at checking heterodox practices repeatedly criticized by Sayyid Ahmad and his followers. These practices included the veneration of Sufi shrines, ritualistic and devotional practices of Shias, and Brahmanical influences at Sufi shrines.⁵²

Conclusion

What emerges from this discussion is that the onset of the sixteenth century marked a paradigmatic shift away from the antecedent period in South Asian Sufism in at least three major ways. The tendencies established around this time stretched well into the eighteenth century and in some cases continued even into the first half of the nineteenth century. In other words, the history of Sufism from the early thirteenth to the early nineteenth centuries cannot be seen as a continuous, uninterrupted, or uniform process; rather, the sixteenth century marked a watershed in this process, in more ways than one. Hence, if the thirteenth to fifteenth centuries are looked upon as the medieval period in the history of South Asian Sufism, then the sixteenth through the early nineteenth centuries deserve a different category in the acknowledgement of the historical difference they exhibited. I argue that this is where the category of early modernity – with its ability to encapsulate both changes that emanated from indigenous processes and those that came about as a result of global changes – becomes useful. It is also clear that the nature of this early modernity encompassed different dimensions of South Asian Sufism, including interactions with the state and society, form and content of cultural expression, as well as theology and doctrine. Let us recapitulate some of these processes as outlined earlier.

First, there was a marked shift in terms of the interactions between Sufi orders and the Islamicate state. With the rise of the Mughal state in the early sixteenth century, new tendencies emerged. By this time, the great Chishti masters were no longer alive; the emergent Mughal state easily lured their descendants into the ambit of imperial patronage and service. Also, with the arrival of the Mughals, Hindustan was once again firmly connected to the larger Persianate world. With the advent of new Sufi orders, spiritual competition for state patronage intensified within South Asia. Relations between the Mughal royalty and major Sufi orders indicate this dynamism, where charismatic masters could access the imperial household and play decisive roles in the formation of empire. Though in the early fifteenth century the Nimatullahi Qadiris of Kerman had started marrying into royal families like the Bahmanis of the Deccan, the Mughals formalized the practice of marrying into Sufi families as an element of statecraft. Alongside this, the tendency of Mughal emperors to elevate their own sovereignty to the heights of sacred kingship and the deep interest of several members of the imperial elite in mystical matters further complicated the relationship of the state with the Sufis. In all these ways, the rise and consolidation of the Mughal Empire in course of the sixteenth and seventeenth centuries heralded a new episode in the relationship between the Islamicate state and Sufi orders.

This was complemented by major developments within the arena of Sufism itself. The sixteenth century saw the expansion of the networks of Sufi orders and sub-orders across South Asia. There was also radical heightening of Sufi engagements with the South Asian population, in terms of the increasing use of vernacular languages as the medium for Sufi literature and ritual. This was accompanied by increasing engagements with literary tropes, spiritual ideas, and cultural symbols of Indic religions and philosophies. Both these processes allowed Sufi influences to spread across large sections of the South Asian population, especially women. Alongside this, there also emerged significant engagements with Sufi ideas from beyond South Asia. This is exemplified by the case of Ibn al-Arabi's discourse on *wahdat al-wujud*, which came to be internalized by South Asian Sufis, especially in the spiritual training and practice of Chishtis and Qadiris, since at least the sixteenth century. Their greatest success lay in adapting that very vision of unity to interact closely with the South Asian cultural world. This could be achieved through a spiritual revival initiated under the dynamic leadership of Sufi masters who operated from a wide network of Sufi centres across South Asia.

In part, this spiritual revival was triggered by the religious significance of the late sixteenth century, when the first Islamic millennium was expected to come to an end in 1591. This event sparked the rise and spread of Islamic millenarianism across Eurasia and provoked complex responses in South Asia. As Mughal emperors projected themselves as saintly messianic figures, the renewers of Islamic faith, and the highest arbiters in religious affairs, Sufi orders like the Naqshbandis grabbed that very moment to mark a historical break in Sufi traditions by calling for a return to the foundational doctrines of Islam. This led to the third development that I have discussed. By the early seventeenth century, there emerged notable reformist voices that were sharply critical of popular Sufi practices, including the philosophical position of *wahdat al-wujud*. While the need to reform technically suggests a return to the roots, this movement, ironically, bridged early modernity and colonial modernity for Sufism by advocating the use of print technology for mass-based dissemination of Sufi texts and treatises.

After the advent of colonial modernity, reformist practices within Sufism continued alongside the rise of the colonial state. The failure of the Revolt of 1857 led Sufi heirs to transform their outlook by reasserting Islamic scriptural and legal traditions, as witnessed in the foundation of the Deoband seminary.[53] Consolidation of British colonialism led to its involvement in matters concerning Sufi shrines and its administration, and, on occasions, gave way to legal interventions into succession disputes. All this transpired while keeping in mind the social position of Sufi shrines and its hereditary successors – many of whom were incorporated as divisional, provincial, and even vice-regal *darbaris* (courtiers).[54] Such a politicized position of the shrine caretaker (*sajjada nashin*) turned out to be crucial with the subsequent introduction of electoral politics in colonial India. The social presence of the shrine and its support to the poor and needy led the colonial administration to even attach the concept of welfare to these institutions, enlisting their support in times of natural calamities.

Notes

1. Blain H. Auer, *Symbols of Authority in Medieval Islam: History, Religion and Muslim Legitimacy in the Delhi Sultanate* (New Delhi: Viva Books Pvt. Ltd., 2012), 25–46; Nile Green, *Sufism: A Global History* (Massachusetts: Wiley-Blackwell, 2012), 125–186.
2. Simon Digby, 'The Sufi Shaykh and the Sultan: Conflict of Claims to Authority', *Iran* 28 (1990): 71–81.
3. Aziz Ahmad, 'The Sufi and the Sultan in Pre-Mughal Muslim India', *Der Islam* 38 (1962): 142–153; Digby, 'Sufi Shaykh and the Sultan'.
4. Stephen Frederic Dale, 'Steppe Humanism: The Autobiographical Writings of Zahir al-Din Muhammad Babur 1483–1530', *International Journal of Middle East Studies* 22, no. 1 (1990): 37–58, in particular see p. 48; Stephen Frederic Dale, *The Garden of the Eight Paradises: Babur and the Culture of Empire in Central Asia, Afghanistan and India 1483–1530* (Leiden: Brill, 2004), 135–186.
5. Simon Digby, 'Early Pilgrimages to the Graves of Muin al-Din and Other Chishti Shaikhs', in *Islamic Society and Culture*, ed. M. Israel and N. K. Wagle, 95–100 (New Delhi: Manohar, 1983).
6. Zahiruddin Muhammad Babur, *The Babur-nama in English (Memoirs of Babur)*, vol. 2, trans. A. S. Beveridge (London, Luzac, 1922), 539–540; Azfar

Moin, *The Millennial Sovereign: Sacred Kingship and Sainthood in Islam* (New York: Columbia University Press, 2012), 97–98.
7. Carl W. Ernst and Bruce B. Lawrence, *Sufi Martyrs of Love: The Chishti Order in South Asia and Beyond* (New York: Palgrave Macmillan, 2003), 98–99.
8. Dara Shukoh was born in Ajmer as the eldest son of emperor Shah Jahan. While his brothers were appointed as administrators in far-off provinces, Dara enjoyed the privilege of staying close to his father in Agra. Aside from administrative responsibilities, Dara had enough time to engage in his interests which spread across the Indo-Islamic cultural, spiritual, and linguistic worlds. He knew Persian and Sanskrit, was interested in the beliefs of multiple faiths, and valued the plurality of Indian culture. Shah Jahan saw Dara as his successor, but Aurangzeb, who had sharpened his military skills in the Deccan, claimed rightful successorship to the throne. With the emperor falling ill, Aurangzeb chose the path of military confrontation to assert his claim on the throne. In this war of succession among the sons of Shah Jahan, it was Aurangzeb who eventually emerged victorious, defeating Dara who was supported by the imperial army.
9. Principles based on the doctrine of *wahdat al-wujud*.
10. Stephen Frederic Dale, 'The Legacy of the Timurids', *Journal of the Royal Asiatic Society of Great Britain and Ireland* 8, no. 1 (1998): 43–58, in particular see p. 49.
11. Abul Fazl Allami, *Akbarnama*, vol. 2, trans. Henry Beveridge (Delhi: Low Price Publications, 2002), 237.
12. Literally, 'wedding'. Popularly understood as the death anniversary of a Sufi saint, celebrating his wedding or spiritual union with God.
13. For Mughal visits to the shrine of Ajmer, see Catherine Asher, 'Pilgrimage to the Shrines in Ajmer', in *Islam in South Asia: In Practice*, ed. Barbara Daly Metcalf, 77–86 (Princeton: Princeton University Press, 2009).
14. Iqbal Sabir, 'Jahangir's Relations with the Contemporary Ulama and Sufis', in *Medieval India 2: Essays in Medieval Indian History and Culture*, ed. Shahabuddin Iraqi, 23–36 (Delhi: Manohar, 2008), 27–29; Muhammad Aslam, 'Jahangir and Hadrat Shaikh Ahmad Sirhindi', *Journal of the Asiatic Society of Pakistan* 10, no. 1 (1965): 135–148; Sajida Sultana Alvi, *Perspectives on Mughal India: Rulers, Historians, 'Ulama' and Sufis* (Karachi: Oxford University Press, 2012), 197–218.
15. Munis Faruqui, 'Dara Shukoh, Vedanta and Imperial Succession in Mughal India', in *Religious Interactions in Mughal India*, ed. Vasudha Dalmia and Munis Faruqui, 30–64 (New Delhi, Oxford University Press, 2014); Supriya Gandhi, 'The Prince and the Muvahhid: Dara Shikoh and Mughal Engagements with the Vedanta', in *Religious Interactions*, ed. Dalmia and Faruqui, 65–101.

16. Afshan Bokhari, 'Between Patron and Piety: Jahan Ara Begam's Sufi Affiliations and Articulations in Seventeenth Century Mughal India', in *Sufism and Society: Arrangements of the Mystical in the Muslim World 1200–1800*, ed. John J. Curry and Erik S. Ohlander, 120–142 (London: Routledge, 2014).
17. Eva Orthmann, 'Ideology and State Building', in *Religious Interactions*, ed. Dalmia and Faruqui, 21–23; Moin, *Millennial Sovereign*, 113–123; N. Elias (ed.), *A History of the Moghuls of Central Asia Being the Tarikh-i-Rashidi of Mirza Haidar Dughlat*, trans. E. Denison Ross (London: Curzon Press, 1972), 398–399; K. A. Nizami, 'Shattari Saints and Their Attitude towards the State', *Medieval India Quarterly* 1, no. 2 (1950): 56–70.
18. The doctrine of the 'unity of being' is identified with Ibn al-Arabi. According to this theory, God and His creation are one, and all creation will eventually return to Him.
19. Muzaffar Alam, 'The Mughals, the Sufi Shaikhs and the Formation of the Akbari Dispensation', *Modern Asian Studies* 43, no. 1 (2009): 135–174.
20. Allami, *Akbarnama*, 237; Moin, *Millennial Sovereign*.
21. Azfar Moin, 'The Politics of Saint Shrines in the Persianate Empires', in *The Persianate World: Rethinking a Shared Sphere*, ed. Abbas Amanat and Assef Ashraf, 105–124 (Leiden: Brill, 2019); Richard M. Eaton, 'The Court and the Dargah in the Seventeenth Century Deccan', *Indian Economic and Social History Review* 10, no. 1 (1973): 50–63.
22. For one such case study on the Sufis of Bansa Sharif in Awadh, see Muzaffar Alam, *The Languages of Political Islam in India c. 1200–1800* (Ranikhet, Permanent Black, 2010), 98–114; Francis Robinson, 'Farangi Mahall and the Sufis of Bansa Sharif', in *A Leaf Turns Yellow: The Sufis of Awadh*, ed. Muzaffar Ali, 98–107 (New Delhi: Bloomsbury India).
23. Ernst and Lawrence, *Sufi Martyrs*, 28–29, 108–109.
24. Carl Ernst, 'Chishti Meditation Practices of the Later Mughal Period', in *The Heritage of Sufism*, vol. 3, ed. Leonard Lewisohn and David Morgan, 344–357 (Oxford: Oneworld Publications); Scott Kugle, 'The Brilliance of Hearts: Hajji Imdadullah Teaches Meditation and Ritual', in *Islam in South Asia*, ed. Metcalf, 212–224.
25. A local dialect of the Deccan that combines Persian, Marathi, Telegu, and Sanskrit.
26. William Chittick, 'Travelling the Sufi Path: A Chishti Handbook from Bijapur', in *The Heritage of Sufism*, vol. 3, ed. Lewisohn and Morgan, 247–265.
27. Richard M. Eaton, 'Sufi Folk Literature and the Expansion of Indian Islam', *History of Religions* 14, no. 2 (1974): 117–127.
28. Richard M. Eaton, *Rise of Islam and the Bengal Frontier 1204–1760* (New Delhi: Oxford University Press, 1997); Ahmad Sharif (ed.), *Banglar Sufi*

Sahitya (Dhaka: Samay Prakashan, Dhaka, 2011). Kashshaf Ghani, 'Practices of Sufism and Islam in Medieval Bengal', in *Sufism in Medieval India*, ed. Raziuddin Aquil (forthcoming).

29. For Indic literary traditions on love and romance in the early Mughal period, see Aditya Behl, *Love's Subtle Magic: An Indian Islamic Literary Tradition 1379–1545* (New York: Oxford University Press, 2012).

30. Madhu Trivedi, 'Images of Women from the Fourteenth to the Sixteenth Century: A Study of Sufi Premakhyans', in *Rethinking a Millennium: Perspectives on Indian History from the Eighth to the Eighteenth Century: Essays for Harbans Mukhia*, ed. Rajat Datta, 198–221 (New Delhi: Aakar Books, 2008).

31. Sergei Andreyev, 'The Rawshaniyya: A Sufi Movement on the Mughal Tribal Periphery', in *The Heritage of Sufism*, vol. 3, ed. Lewisohn and Morgan, 290–318.

32. Christopher Shackle, 'Persian Poetry and Qadiri Sufism in Later Mughal India: Ghanimat Kunjahi and His Mathnawi-yi Nayrang-iishq', in *The Heritage of Sufism*, vol. 3, ed. Lewisohn and Morgan, 435–463; Annemarie Schimmel, *Mystical Dimensions of Islam* (Chapel Hill, NC: University of North Carolina Press, 2011), 344–402; Christopher Shackle, 'Beyond Turk and Hindu: Crossing the Boundaries in Indo-Muslim Romance', in *Beyond Turk and Hindu: Rethinking Religious Identities in Islamicate South Asia*, ed. David Gilmartin and Bruce Lawrence, 55–73 (Florida: University Press of Florida, 2000); Denis Matringe, 'Hir Waris Shah', in *On Becoming an Indian Muslim: French Essays on Aspects of Syncretism*, ed. M. Waseem, 208–237 (New Delhi: Oxford University Press, 2003).

33. Ali Asani, 'Sufi Poetry in the Folk Tradition of Indo-Pakistan', *Religion and Literature* 20, no. 1 (1988): 81–94.

34. Zahiruddin Malik, 'Role of Sufis and Bhaktas in North Western India during the Eighteenth Century', in *Sufism in Punjab: Mystics, Literature and Shrines*, ed. Surinder Singh and Ishwar Dayal Gaur, 158–175 (New Delhi: Aakar Books, 2009).

35. For the impact of *wahdat al-wujud* on Mughal politics and ideology, see Alam, *Languages of Political Islam in India*, 91–98.

36. Muzaffar Alam, 'Assimilation from a Distance: Confrontation and Sufi Accommodation in Awadh Society', in *Tradition, Dissent and Ideology: Essays in Honour of Romila Thapar*, ed. S. Gopal and R. Champakalakshmi, 165–177 (New: Delhi, Oxford University Press, 1996).

37. Muzaffar Alam, 'State Building under the Mughals: Religion, Culture and Politics', *Cahiers d'Asie centrale* 3-4 (1997): 105–128; Alam, *Languages of Political Islam in India*, 88–98; Green, *Sufism: A Global History*, 125–186.

38. On the spread of the Naqshbandi order, see Hamid Algar, 'The Naqshbandi Order: A Preliminary Survey of Its History and Significance', *Studia Islamica*, 44 (1976): 123–152.
39. For a discussion on Sirhindi's works, see Iqbal Sabir, 'Formation of Naqshbandi Mysticism: Studying the Major Writings of Shaikh Ahmad Sirhindi', *Sufism in Punjab: Mystics, Literature and* Shrines, ed. S. Singh and Ishwar D. Gaur, 267–277 (New Delhi: Aakar Books, 2009).
40. The doctrine of *wahdat al-shuhud* (unity of witnessing) argues that according to the principle of *tauhid*, no creation can be united with God. All creations of God may witness His glory but can never achieve Union with Him in principle.
41. Doctrine based on the idea of *wahdat al-shuhud*.
42. Alam, *Languages of Political Islam*, 161–163; On Sirhindi's attempted reconciliation of the two doctrines, see Alberto Ventura, 'A Letter of Shaykh Ahmad Sirhindi in Defense of the Wahdat al-Wujud', *Oriente Moderno* 92, no. 2 (2012): 509–517.
43. Muzaffar Alam, 'The Debate Within: A Sufi Critique of Religious Law, Tasawwuf and Politics in Mughal India', *South Asian History and Culture* 2, no. 2 (2011): 138–159.
44. Marcia K. Hermansen, 'Contemplating Sacred History in Late Mughal Sufism: The Case of Shah Wali Allah of Delhi', in *The Heritage of Sufism*, vol. 3, ed. Lewisohn and Morgan, 319–343.
45. J. M. S. Baljon, 'Shah Waliullah and the Dargah', in *Muslim Shrines in India: Their Character, History and Significance*, ed. C. W. Troll, 189–197 (New Delhi: Oxford University Press, 2004).
46. Alvi, *Perspectives on Mughal India*, 177–193; Arthur R. Buehler, *Sufi Heirs of the Prophet: The Indian Naqshbandiyya and the Rise of the Mediating Sufi Shaykh* (Columbia: University of South Carolina Press, 1998); Marcia K. Hermansen, 'Contemplating Sacred History in Late Mughal Sufism: The Case of Shah Wali Allah of Delhi', in *The Heritage of Sufism*, vol. 3, ed. Lewisohn and Morgan, 319–343.
47. On the genre of meditational treatises from the late Mughal period, see Scott Kugle, 'Sufi Meditation Manuals from the Mughal Era', *Oriente Moderno* 92, no. 2 (2012): 459–489.
48. Annemarie Schimmel, *Pain and Grace: A Study of Two Mystical Writers of Eighteenth-Century Muslim India* (Leiden: Brill, 1976).
49. For a contemporary hagiographical account on Sirhindi by one of his disciples Badruddin, see Carl Ernst, 'The Daily Life of a Saint, Ahmad Sirhindi, by Badr al-Din Sirhindi', in *Islam in South Asia*, ed. Metcalf, 158–165.
50. Harlan O. Pearson, *Islamic Reform and Revival in Nineteenth Century India: The Tariqah-i Muhammadiyah* (New Delhi: Yoda Press, 2008).

51. Marc Gaborieau, 'The Jihad of Sayyid Ahmad Barelwi on the North West Frontier: The Last Echo of the Middle Ages? Or a Prefiguration of Modern South Asia', in *Sufis, Sultans and Feudal Orders*, ed. Mansura Haidar, 23–43 (New Delhi: Manohar, 2004); Marc Gaborieau, 'Criticizing the Sufis: The Debate in Early Nineteenth Century India', in *Islamic Mysticism Contested: Thirteen Centuries of Controversies and Polemics*, ed. F. De Jong and B. Radtke, 452–467 (Leiden: Brill, 1999); Marc Gaborieau, 'A Nineteenth-Century Indian "Wahhabi" Tract against the Cult of Muslim Saints: Al-Balagh al-Mubin', in *Muslim Shrines in India*, ed. Troll, 198–239.
52. N. R. Farooqi, 'Saiyid Ahmad Barelvi, Altaf Husain Hali and the Formation of Muslim Identity in the Nineteenth Century', in *Negotiating Religion: Perspectives from Indian History*, ed. R. P. Bahuguna, R. Dutta, and F. Nasreen, 233–260 (New Delhi: Manohar, 2012).
53. Ernst and Lawrence, *Sufi Martyrs*, 105–127.
54. Muhammad Mubeen, 'Evolution of the Chishti Shrine and the Chishtis in Pakpattan (Pakistan)', in *Devotional Islam in Contemporary South Asia: Shrines, Journeys and Wanderers*, ed. M. Boivin and R. Delage, 119–137 (London: Routledge, 2018); P. M. Currie, *The Shrine and Cult of Muin al-Din of Ajmer* (New Delhi: Oxford University Press, 1989), 164–173.

3

Beginnings of Modernity in South Asia

Natural Philosophy in Persianate Islam

Charles Ramsey

Will believers actually see the Almighty on the Day of Judgement? Could there be multiple worlds? What is the relationship between matter and space, and could there be a void? How does matter evolve and become increasingly differentiated? These inherently modern questions were the subject of heated debate in late-nineteenth-century India, and they continue to draw an array of responses even today. But what if these same questions were seeded around the year 1000 CE, long before they came into bloom in the mid-seventeenth century? One consequence of that would be to make us ponder the temporal boundaries of what defines the modern. In this chapter, I explore the trajectory of a particular intellectual tradition that began prior to and continued through the nineteenth century – a time that is often periodized as the beginning of modernity in this region. In questioning the dative nomenclature of the medieval or Middle Ages of South Asian history, I also question the narrative of an imported and ruptured modernity thrust upon a people without agency.

Much is at stake, for historiography is concerned with more than nomenclature; indeed, it is an adjustment of the lenses through which history is interpreted. Modernity in this part of the world has been defined in terms of colonialism and the reformulation of knowledge in the light of European ideas. It has traditionally been seen to flow from west to east as the product of intellectual enlightenment and technological advancement. But there is a growing sense that India engendered a modernity of its own even before the advent of colonialism. As discussed in this chapter, the circulation of ideas within the Persianate region in general, and between India and Iran in particular, during the few centuries preceding the advent of British colonialism is indicative of a dynamic intellectual environment where powerful and innovative possibilities developed apart from European influence. Defining the period from the sixteenth through the eighteenth centuries as 'early modern', rather than 'late medieval' or the 'Mughal era', affirms such agency of India as a region and pushes historians to examine this period in terms of a complex interplay of local, regional, and global actors.[1]

In the light of space constraints, I will consider mainly the first of the questions I began with – 'will the Almighty be seen?' – and allow this to thread the discussion of this chapter. It is an appropriately religious subject – delicate and complex, and concerns both philosophy and science, that is cosmology, and the nature and substance of all matter.[2] One passage in the Quran, which is often cited in this regard, states that 'Some faces will be radiant on that day, gazing at their Lord' (*Surah al-Qiyamah* 75:22–23). To some, this unequivocally indicates that the Almighty will indeed be seen, but others within the tradition maintain this conclusion – for the formed to see the formless – to be a logical impossibility. It has been a heated debate. Though the question may appear at first glance to be a conundrum of the present age, perhaps inseminated by modern European rationalism and its incredulity of the mythological and pre-scientific patterns of thinking, in actuality it is not new at all.[3] Whether or not the formless could be seen was a question of considerable importance and careful deliberation for seventeenth-century Persianate thinkers in India and Iran.[4] This comes as a surprise to many because of the prevailing nineteenth- and early twentieth-century characterizations of the educational system in the Persianate zone as stagnant and altogether devoid of critical and creative thinking, capable only of the parroting of facts, aphorisms, and legal verdicts.[5] The questions raised, however, and the manner in which many of these seventeenth-century scholars went about constructing arguments and interpreting sacred writings and experiences, are indicative of an approach to knowledge that is inconsistent with such an assessment. Renewed interest in the history of this region has caused a re-evaluation of existing assumptions. The findings indicate that during this period, India and Iran were important centres for the collection and continuance of a great tradition of learning in Central Asia, one which drew resources and energy from all directions – from the Mediterranean, China, and India.[6]

Locating historical benchmarks in South Asian historiography is admittedly a challenge. There was significant destruction and loss of written records caused by invasions and changes of regime. The dismantling and readjusting of social, economic, and educational structures experienced in the violent turmoil of the eighteenth and nineteenth centuries have hindered the historicization of the earlier period.[7] But there are also methodological problems – as Shahzad Bashir has argued – which have prevented a more robust assessment of the intellectual and social developments of this region immediately before the advent of colonialism.[8] As Sheldon Pollock has cautioned, 'we cannot know how colonialism changed South Asia if we do not know what was there to be changed'.[9] To place this in context, it is widely held that there has been no rupture greater in the history of the Islamic tradition than that brought about by the onset of modernity. In the extreme, modernity is portrayed as a European force that was and remains incompatible with the Islamic intellectual traditions.[10] For the Islamist, modernity is a Western malady inflicted upon the 'East'. For the progressive, Islamic tradition is a roadblock for human flourishing. Yet neither camp has produced a nuanced account of what preceded the colonial experience in Persianate India.[11] Bashir concludes:

> If we interpret these actors within the single timeline that has dominated modern academic views of Islam, we turn to moments in the records of earlier Muslims to find clues of understanding the present. This perspective leads to explanatory paradigms centered on notions of linear and unidirectional development, positive or negative evolution, 'medievalism,' and so forth, which have had a nearly universal monopoly on how we understand modern Muslim individuals and movements.[12]

Characterizing the actors and identifying their roles in the unfolding tale of South Asian history is a demanding task that requires revision. However, as Pollock observes, historians are now increasingly imagining an early modernity in the Persianate world as a 'dynamic era of intellectual inquiry'.[13] My aim here is to add texture and nuance to this imagination by exploring the writings of two of the protagonists.

Of the many possible options, one finds the writings of Ahmad al-Faruqi al-Sirhindi (1564–1624) and Sadr al-Din al-Shirazi, also known as Mulla Sadra (1570/1571–1635/1640), to be particularly promising for this purpose. Shaikh Sirhindi and Mulla Sadra, in the Mughal and Safavid empires respectively, contributed to this sense of dynamism by demonstrating the circulation of ideas regionally and the continuity of ideas with intellectual predecessors. Later modernists, from Tabataba'i and Jamal al-Din al-Afghani to Ayatollah Khomeini in Iran, and from Shah Wali Allah and Muhammad Iqbal to Abu'l Ala-Maududi in India, understood themselves to proceed in a channel opened and traversed by these respective forerunners.[14] The progression of these ideas is not associated with Western post-Enlightenment thinking; yet they demonstrate an approach that is more akin to the modern than not. A careful reading of their works underscores what Fazlur Rahman concluded decades ago, namely that the seventeenth and eighteenth centuries represent the 'pinnacle of Persianate philosophy'.[15] Analogously stated, what the British were accomplishing in the mechanical sciences during this time, the Persianates were accomplishing in natural philosophy. As S. Frederick Starr has described in great detail, long before the rise of European Enlightenment and colonial rule – the mainstays of conventional definitions of modernity – thinkers in Central and South Asia were actively debating the measurements of the earth, the shape of the cosmos, the concept of natural evolution, and the contingency of revelation.[16] Far from being otherworldly, these ideas had far-reaching educational, social, and economic consequences. They marked a pathway to modernity that was developing in this region apart from European stimulus. This region of Sanskrit and Persianate confluence experienced an enlightenment of their own during this period, and thinkers like Sadra and Sirhindi progressed in this tradition.

Theirs was a competent and articulate natural philosophy, which must be regarded as advanced in this period by any measure. In rising academic centres like Paris and Pisa, scholastic European philosophers like Thomas Aquinas and Giovanni di Fidanza (St Bonaventure) played a vital role in the proceeding intellectual flourish that emerged in Europe.[17] This was thanks in part, however, to the efforts of thinkers in Central Asia like Ibn Sina (Avicenna, d. 1037) and Al-Biruni (d. *c.* 1050), whose ideas developed in dialogue with their Indian counterparts. The routes connecting these regions enjoyed the protection of tolerant Muslim sultans through the medieval period. In the sixteenth and seventeenth centuries, they were strengthened further by the Mughal emperor Akbar (r. 1556–1605) and his successors. As Jordanon Ganeri argues, they fostered the emergence of a cosmopolitan atmosphere where 'a very definite form of "modernity" developed in Indian Sanskrit philosophy between 1500 and 1700'.[18] This was a period of intellectual flourish in the Indian subcontinent, the substance of which remains to be fully appreciated in academic literature.

The oversight seems to have been caused by the failure to recognize the latent value in works not traditionally regarded as repositories of historical knowledge. There is a considerable body of writings, as Velcheru Narayan Rao observes, that has been seen as something other than history. Significant textual sources have been overlooked because their significance is yet to be deciphered. This is certainly the case for the writings of Sadra and Sirhindi. One reason for this has to do with the contested definitions of modernity itself. Modernity, as William Reddy recounts, has been conceptualized in many quarters by a practical understanding of time and space.[19] The nomenclature of early modern, in this light, signifies the progression towards the view of time and space as basically empty. 'Time ticks away with perfect uniformity,' Reddy explains, 'and space is devoid of gods, goddesses, and other nonhuman agent; and in which history unfolds with no help from providence, destiny, or apocalypse'.[20] But this Western view of temporality as 'empty time and space' conflates scientific discipline with philosophical naturalism. This implies that scientific rigour demands a desacralized cosmos. But as Rao argues, '... there is room for more than one effective temporal frame and pockets or loops of *purāṇic* or mythic valence, of varying intensity, can easily coexist with historical facticity of a highly empirical and analytical type.'[21] Scholars like Rao and Reddy challenge the assumed uniformity within cultures and conversely the incommensurability across different cultures. Their work supports the argument that time and space have been conceptualized in a diversity of ways within primary sources and that these sources are better approached with the assumption of multiple temporalities, rather than a single time frame proceeding from the West.

Modernity has often been equated with scientific temporality and the economic and political application of technology, but as Martin Heidegger notes, the essence of technology is not anything technological. Technological objects are means to an end. The essence of technology, as he explains, is something else entirely and must be understood as a 'way of revealing'.[22] A shift in paradigm, as Bashir argues, allows for multiple temporalities rather than a single timeline. It opens access to and allows the interpretation of genres like Sufi epistles, scriptural commentaries, and poetic treatises, which were previously considered to be lacking in historical value. Paths of knowledge developed over time in many cities and regions that provided a head-start in technological development, which in turn enabled economic progress. Our two authors pondered such a 'revealing'. They sought to comprehend the substance of things seen and unseen in a manner parturient for scientific development, in a way more 'modern' than not. Let us now turn attention towards their context and respective works.

Authors in Context

Born in Safavid Shiraz, Mulla Sadra was educated in the manner typical of the day. He commenced with the foundational subjects known as the transmitted (*naqliyya*) sciences, that is, grammar, and an introduction to the Quran (*tafsir*) and tradition ('*ilm al-hadith*); then, he proceeded to the rational sciences ('*aqliyya*), namely logic, rhetoric, and theology. He studied in Isfahan under prominent masters like Sayyid Baqir Muhammad Astarabadi (known as Mir Damad), Baha' al-Din Muhammad al-'Amili (Shaikh Baha'i), and Mir Findiriski. Sadra's thought reflected, as Ibrahim Kalin summarizes, a synthesis of '*Qur'ān, burhān*, and '*irfān*' – that is, revealed knowledge, peripatetic philosophy, and realized (mystical) knowledge. Each of these masters and their subject matter contributed to his intellectual development. In time, Mulla Sadra became a prolific writer, and his ideas and influence spread across the region.[23] In the main, Sadra presented a robust metaphysical argument for the primacy of existence as the foundational mode of divine self-disclosure. He posited three categories of existence: 'absolute existence' (*mahiyya*), which is not dependent on anything else; 'relative existence', derived from source, which is relative and contingent; and 'self-expanding existence' (*tashkik al-wujud*), which is the gateway between the two.[24]

Tashkik, as we will consider here, imagined an evolutionary approach to the creation process. By synthesizing elements of Ibn 'Arabi's theosophy', as Fazlur Rahman explained, 'Ibn Sina's peripatetic tradition, and al-Suhrawardi's illumination (*ishrāqī*), Sadra's metaphysics constituted the pinnacle of Persianate philosophy'.[25] Otherwise stated, the core ideas of one like Ibn Sina – which were instrumental in simulating European universities in the twelfth century – were also carried forward in the Persianate zone of Central and northern South Asia. In the mid-seventeenth century, Safavid Shi'ism was in the throes of a heated controversy between the Akhbars and the Usulis. As the literalist and legalist attitudes of the former gained strength, dissonant philosophers and Sufis took refuge in other lands.[26] Many of these fled to India, and particularly to the relatively peaceful region of the Punjab. As one of Sirhindi's students, named Abdul Hakim Sialkoti (d. 1656), recounted, it was during this time that Sa'id Sarmad settled in the region and disseminated Sadra's ideas.[27] His migration sheds light upon the spread of ideas through the region, the significance of which becomes clearer through the writings of Ahmad Sirhindi.

Ahmad Sirhindi was born only a few years before Sadra, in the town of Sirhind in Patiala, now in Indian Punjab. Sirhind was the largest fortified town (*qasba*) between Delhi and Lahore. It boasted of splendid gardens and markets and was renowned as a centre for medical care (*yunani tibb*).[28] Having received similar education as Sadra under the guidance of his father and brother, Sirhindi continued his learning under Yaqub Sarfi Kashmiri and Bahlol Badakhshani in Sialkot, where he was also initiated into the prevalent schools of Sufism. Later, while in Delhi around 1593, he came under the guidance of the prominent leader of the highly influential Naqshbandi order in this region, Shaikh Muhammad al-Baqi, whom Sirhindi eventually succeeded upon his death in 1603.[29] The Naqshbandi order, as Annemarie Schimmel examined in detail, was heavily represented in the Persianate world, and the extent of Sirhindi's influence among them cannot be overstated.[30] This explains, for example, why a mystic religious teacher like Sirhindi could be perceived as a challenge to an emperor like Jahangir (r. 1605–1627). Thousands of initiates across the region looked to him as a source of authority and guidance. If not an actual threat to Mughal power, it was most certainly a check. His followers looked at him as the 'reviver of the second millennium (*mujaddid alf thani*)'. This signified that Sirhindi was the divine representative on earth and a corporeal portal to another realm.[31] It had been a thousand years since the passing of Prophet Muhammad, and this marked a profound cosmological progression in the order of creation.³² The time had come for the shift back towards the original point of departure once commenced with the divine command: Be! (*kun fa yakun*).³³ In the same way that a stone launched into the sky must eventually return once reaching its zenith, all that originated at the moment of creation would now retract to the point of origin. Jahangir, as his father Akbar and the Safavid rulers in Iran, sought to cast himself in this millenarian role, but they were held in balance by the power of these Sufis.³⁴

Unlike Sadra, who wrote many books, the primary source for gauging Sirhindi's ideas is epistolary – that is, an extensive collection of letters.³⁵ These letters describe practices, visions, and guidance from a series of spiritual ascensions, the full extent of which was communicated explicitly only to an inner circle of devotees. Such an extravagant claim, combined with the general scepticism towards the mystical Sufi genre, has caused these writings to be regarded by modern academics as more powerful than cogent. Indeed, the corpus has largely been either overlooked or dismissed as fanciful and hagiographical.³⁶ One consequence of this, however, is that the philosophical notions therein are yet to be given significant consideration. For the sake of problematizing the periodization in this context, one emphasizes the theme of multidimensional forces within his works. By this, one means an awareness of the boundaries between the material and the immaterial realms of space and time, and the seventeenth-century attempt to characterize these.

If Sirhindi's letters are read as mere hagiography or spiritual guidance, then a window into this context remains closed and a vital link in this intellectual tradition remains unseen. I am not advocating a new interpretation of Sirhindi's letters, nor will I attempt to go beyond those who have laboured to decipher his account of the 'formless ineffable realm that is beyond space-time'. Rather, I hope to add a degree of historical texture that acknowledges language as a 'living entity, inseparable from the speaker's cultural assumptions'.³⁷ Without demystifying his message, or de-emphasizing the reverence in which he was held, I attempt to approach Sirhindi within his own temporal context.³⁸

Expanding upon the written exchanges between Al-Biruni and Ibn Sina, Paul Hullmeine recounted a time prior to the separation between those working in philosophy, medicine, and mathematics.³⁹ The Sufi hospice (*khanqah*) was not merely a place of other-worldly meditation. Some of these – in ways similar to certain European monasteries – were often centres of learning and discovery. This was particularly the case in the Mughal Empire. The healing tradition, as Seema Alavi argued, 'expanded and was consolidated in tandem with the entrenchment of the Indo-Muslim fabric of the region's society'.⁴⁰ Health was an aristocratic virtue. Medical texts produced and circulated within the *akhlaq* literature codified socially acceptable norms of behaviour and civility within the health regime of the ruling *ashraf*. 'Medicine was a form of healing, central to the building of an imperial political culture,' Alavi concludes.[41] These centres contained libraries and hostels; they were the natural hosts for those travelling in search of knowledge. Mathematics and engineering, with practical benefits in irrigation through the Persian waterwheels (*saqiya* or *rehat*) or in medicine, were brought with the saints and their learned followers to the countless shrines that dotted the pathways across India, Central Asia, and beyond.[42] When read in the light of the rich heritage of the medical sciences, astronomical observations, and advancements in mathematics, a considerably different picture emerges out of this. We can see Sirhindi and Sadra progressing in continuity with this vein of learning, having developed those rigorous mental habits and practices that constituted modernity in the seventeenth century and were indicative of what Heidegger termed the 'essence of technology'.[43]

Sirhindi's spiritual enthronement as the millennial reformer inaugurated a new era of history. As Afzar Moin argued, his status 'pivoted not on a new "doctrine" of interpretation of "law" but on taking the place – bodily and spiritually – of a sacred entity that had existed in the previous era or cycle of time'.[44] Elucidating the hidden symbolism, Sirhindi explained that Prophet Muhammad had two individuations (*ta'ayyun*) – the corporeal and the cosmic, as reflected in the two *mīm*s in his name. From the time of his passing, however, the individuation had gradually shifted from the corporeal to the cosmic, so that the *mīm* was subsumed in the *alif* of divinity (*uluhiyyat*). The auspicious millennium marked the Prophet's transformation into pure spirit, thus creating the need for a restorer (*mujaddid*), one who could navigate the mysteries of the cosmos and discern practical guidance for the faithful. Whereas in the time prior to Muhammad, prophets were sent to provide guidance, in this new era a restorer was sent, and one will continue to arise in each generation until the consummation of time. Unlike those whose gaze was focused on the past, this was a bold and forward-looking attitude. They expected discoveries to be made and fresh guidance to be ascertained. This was also the period of the greatest proliferation of Islamic millenarianism, and one finds it highly significant that it occurred roughly during this same period that we call the early modern.

Sirhindi's exalted status is documented in various regional sources. But in order to appreciate this intellectual environment, the oblique spiritual and intellectual processes associated with millenarianism require disambiguation. One important clue is found in the combined interests in reform or restoration (*tajdid*) – the task of the *mujaddid* – and evolution (*tashkik*), or the graded modulation of all being.[45]

This is a pairing of seminal ideas attributed to Sirhindi and Sadra respectively, but not previously considered together. Sirhindi's concept of the 'unity of [contemplative] witnessing' (*wahdat al-shuhud*) brings forth a complimentary addition to Sadra's discourse. Through the practice of contemplative witnessing, Sirhindi trained others to see with the 'eyes of the heart'. Through the mystical practice of 'imagining of the Shaikh' (*tasawwur-i shaikh*) and of cultivating constant contact (*rabitah*) regardless of physical proximity, the goal of the wayfarer was to abide simultaneously in both realms.[46] This experience seeded the idea that creation is like a thought (*khayal*) manifested by God who is 'true being'.[47] 'Contemplative witnessing' was a spiritual journey into increasingly higher stages towards sublimation (*fana*) into the divine, only then to return to the awareness of personal individuation. Contemplation on this complexity fostered observation into the pattern of nature and the shape of the cosmos.

It is important to recall the metaphysical discourse prevalent among the Sufi philosophers in this context. The underlying unity between spirituality and metaphysics, drawn from Ibn 'Arabi's doctrine of *tawhid* or *wahdat*, was an integral part of this intellectual environment.[48] It provided the semantic framework for the metaphysical quest to understand – and to experience – the paradoxical interrelation of the Creator and the created.[49] This assumed a complex theory of emanation that had direct implications upon how revelation was understood to enter the realm of human understanding. Following in the footsteps of Suhrawardi, leading thinkers in this region – like Sadra's teacher Mir Damad – had categorized the divine 'essence' (*dhat*) to be fundamental and 'existence' as one of the divine 'attributes' (*sifat*). Sadra, however, reversed this order and posited that existence was the source and end of all things. As Sadra explained:

> God's self-praise results in the emergence of the cosmos, and how the cosmos, as the 'stuff' (*jawhar*) of God's self-praise, is nothing other than seamless expression or modes or instantiations of praise. Since being is graded, and multilevel, the more one manifests praise, the more he manifests of being.[50]

Here, we see innovation, progress, and the possibility of disagreement. It is essential to grasp that these seventeenth-century polymaths were not content to simply lift prayers into the air. There was a chartered course, a cartography of the spiritual realm, to guide the wayfarer's quest to observe, experience, and comprehend the inner structure of the world in space and time. Today, we map on screens, but they mapped in the mind, or the tablet of the heart.

Let us put this in perspective. From Aristotle to Ibn Sina, philosophers claimed that change was possible in four categories: quantity, quality, position, and place.

Sadra added a fifth category – substance (*jawhar*) – and this was an idea of great significance. He posited that all *jawhar* – the substance of creation – progressively divides into increasingly complex variants. 'The agent of this essential motion is God,' Sadra wrote, 'and its receptacle, that is, its object, is the human soul with respect to the power of the receptivity of its soul and its passive hylic intellect.'[51] This idea of transubstantiation is a precursor to later theories of evolution, and it was articulated long before Darwin or other natural philosophers in Europe. Sirhindi added that some of this substance is visible to the physical eye, and some is not. All of creation, he explained, is a gradation of existence (*tashkik al-wujud*) expressed in matter and energy, substance seen and unseen. As Sayyid Ahmad Khan – who is often regarded as the 'Father of Islamic Modernism' – explained in the nineteenth century, a person and a tree are of the same *jawhar*, but they are differentiable in degree and refinement.[52] In this light, the composite picture of creation is that of a unified whole, differentiated but coherent, because it is made of one self-unfolding substance that proceeds from an original source.[53] Sayyid Ahmad provided this description as an improvement to European science, but he was in fact drawing back to the work of these Indian and Iranian precursors.

Let us now consider the formation of these ideas in greater detail as this illustrates the continuity and innovation within this line of thinking. In *Afsār* (Part 4), Sadra explored the traditional psychology of Ibn Sina and the spiritual anthropology of Ibn 'Arabi. He underscored the interaction of the soul with the physical and intelligible worlds, and the encounter made possible through sense perception (*takhayyul*) of the objective and 'imaginal world' (*'alam al-khayal*).[54] Ibn Sina's medical examinations, as Fazlur Rahman convincingly argued, had led to an original conclusion, namely that the imagination is a 'physical faculty'.[55] The experience of hypnotic and trance-like states (*waham*) could be so profoundly affective that patients were often unable to differentiate these from actual physical events.[56] But these are activities of the mind rather than departures into another dimension. Sirhindi and Sadra carried forward Ibn Sina's insight, namely that spiritual images are projections of the imagination.

The imaginal world, however, is not an imaginary world. As Henry Corbin explained: 'While an imaginary world is a realm of subjective fantasy that we make up in our heads, an imaginal world is a realm of objective reality that exists between the world of matter and the world of the spirit.'[57] During the period under focus, imagination was regarded as a cognitive function, the bridge between the objective world and the world of spirit. Drawing an example from the life of Moses in the Hebrew Bible, for example, Corbin explained that the 'burning bush' would have been a mere brushwood fire if perceived merely by the sensory functions. Perception, or the contemplative witnessing to the unity of existence (to use Sirhindi's term), is the experience of the imaginal function that bridges the two realms and reveals the theophany. Returning to the initial question of the possibility of seeing the Creator, Sirhindi wrote: 'Coming to this throne, one sees the passing of the innermost of the inner penetrate into the innermost secrets (origin of the origins). Yes! The person who reaches the highest place has the penetrating vision to see the most remotely distant object.'[58] The faculty of imagination, which connects the sensate to the spiritual, acts as an intermediary between the worlds of objective substances and detached intelligible substances.

This cosmology, however, could not have been deduced from mere observation. There was the need for a conceptual guide who could cross the imaginal divide. Rational proofs were constructed through abstraction, but 'contemplative witnessing' (*mushahaba*) was an intuitive way of seeing that unveils what is not perceptible to empirical observation.[59] The difference, as Sadra explained, is 'like someone who knows the definition of sweetness and one who has actually tasted something sweet'.[60] This is a prime example of natural philosophy at work. Recalling Heidegger, this is the essence of technology – 'a way of revealing'.

On Seeing the Creator

Let us return to the issue of seeing the Creator. There are multiple occasions in the Quran that portray anthropomorphic accounts of the divine in general and of seeing Allah in particular. In interpreting *Surah al-Qiyāma* (Q75:23), Sirhindi concluded that the meaning was that the faithful will indeed look upon their Lord, but not in material actuality as experienced presently on the earth. Rather, they will gaze upon an imaginal manifestation of their Lord: 'What one sees cannot be God, but a mere projection of the seer himself.... We cannot see God on the Day of Judgement; for how can He who is above space and time be visible to eyes?'[61] Or as Sadra explained, 'the soul is bodily in its origination and spiritual in its subsistence' (*jismaniyyat al-huduth ruhaniyyat al-baqa'*). For this reason, the transmigration (*tanasukh*) of the present physical body is impossible, as is its corporeal resurrection.[62]

Sadra posited that the system of thought derived from the primacy of existence affects all aspects of cosmology, cosmogony, and eschatology. The 'contemplative witness' – or the wayfarer, to use Buehler's term – journeys through the imaginal gateway to gain understanding of the divine effusion through the cosmos. The perceiving (*shuhud*) of the other realm is both desirable and possible, but this is not to be confused with the actual seeing of Allah, for the divine source of being remains eternally outside of the manifest. To support this view, Sadra cited the

'Commander of the Believers', 'Ali ibn Abi Talib' – the nephew of the Prophet and the fount of the Sufis – who said, 'I have seen nothing but God before it, after it, with it, and in it'. The perception of the Exalted One is accessible to each of God's servants, but this does not indicate the perception of the 'Absolute Existence' because that remains a logical impossibility.[63]

Here again we see the interplay between the religious and the philosophical, as well as the physical and the metaphysical. From a religious vantage, the discussion opens questions about the nature of the afterlife. Will there be a heaven, is there eternal bliss, and what will it be like? Yet in the language of philosophy, the discussion promotes the notion of substantial (*jawhar*) continuity after death. In interpreting passages like *Surah Al-Qissas* (Q28:88), for example, where it is written that 'all things perish except His Face', Sadra emphasized that the passage does not define the nature of the resurrected body. Whereas the present body is finite, the body in the afterlife is perfected and will be significantly different. The gradation of substance that exists in the physical and spiritual realms assumes multiple forms and degrees of intensity, and so the resurrected body will be of a different kind.[64] Contrary to most philosophers before him, Sadra differentiated matter from the principle of individuation. Therefore, individual identity and personhood can exist divorced from physical matter, so bodies in the afterlife are real but immaterial. The corruption of the body at the moment of death does not lead to the disappearance of the human person; rather, the 'person' takes on a different and a higher mode of existence.[65] The discussion, however, is not just metaphysical, for it is concerned with producing a logical argument for 'a higher mode of existence' that interfaces differently with time, space, and energy. The idea is original, and innovative, but the thinker shares a continuance with a long intellectual tradition that endured and flourished in this period.

Conclusion

In this chapter, I have explored the trajectory of a particular intellectual tradition of Islamic natural philosophy that emerged to prominence in the seventeenth century and continued through the nineteenth. I have argued that drawing upon antecedent intellectual traditions, these new interventions by thinkers like Sadra and Sirhindi arose partly in response to the global spread of millenarian ideas at the close of the sixteenth century and with the myriad philosophical challenges that this historical conjuncture produced. The lives and ideas of Sadra and Sirhindi thus offer us windows into the emergence of an indigenous modernity in this context, one that developed independently of any European intervention. At first glance, these appear to proceed down the well-beaten path of medieval Sufi masters, but a close reading of their works shed light upon ways of thinking that were innovative and of ideas that were pushed beyond existing intellectual boundaries and broke new ground. These inhabited a threshold, where new ways of thinking were taking hold. Their respective journeys into this early modernity were moderated by a nuanced set of discreet terms applied to discuss the evolutionary expansion of the universe and its eventual contraction at the end of time. Furthermore, the complimentary nature of their ideas is indicative of a rich and sustained intellectual exchange over generations that began before their time, and that has continued since. There was a conjunction of methods, sources, and vocabulary that testifies to a dynamic environment of enquiry, and this continues to add texture to the picture gradually emerging of a context concomitant with our understanding of early modernity.

In essence, this chapter adds to the argument that modernity has been mischaracterized as a transfer of post-Enlightenment thinking from the West to the East. Such an over-generalization has obscured the existing intellectual traditions which developed in the Persianate world at its own pace and by its own resources. The point is not to deny the importance and power of developments in Europe but rather to call for a recalibration of our understanding of this period in the light of the agency revealed in the civilizational achievements in this region. When South Asians engaged with European technological advancements in the nineteenth century, they did so with a pre-existing intellectual framework that prepared them to perceive and respond to these impulses. There were academic disciplines and preconceived categories that enabled these ideas to be grasped, and even improved upon. There were pathways of knowledge developed over generations and across the many regions of the subcontinent that are indicative of a dynamic intellectual environment where powerful and innovative possibilities arose in harmony with indigenous resources and global influences.

Notes

1. John F. Richards, 'Early Modern India and World History', *Journal of World History* 8, no. 2 (1997): 197–209; David Ludden, 'Imperial Modernity: History and Global Inequity in Rising Asia', *Third World Quarterly* 33, no. 4 (2012): 581–601; Anthony Giddens, *Conversations with Anthony Giddens: Making Sense of Modernity* (Stanford: Stanford University Press, 1998), 94–117; Francis Robinson, 'Islamic Reform and Modernities in South Asia', *Modern Asian Studies* 42, no. 2 (2008): 259–281; R. S. Sharma, *Early Medieval Indian Society: A Study in Feudalisation* (Kolkata: Orient Longman, 2001), 15–18.
2. Seyyed Hossein Nasr, *An Introduction to Islamic Cosmological Doctrines* (Albany: Thames and Hudson, 1993, revised edition), 107–176.

3. Christopher Lane, *The Age of Doubt: Tracing the Roots of Our Religious Uncertainty* (New Haven: Yale University Press, 2011), 14–35.
4. The term 'Persianate' is a cognate of the term 'Islamicate' that signifies the proclivities shared by cultural regions, allowing for the nuanced but important differentiation between an ideal, such as Islam, and its cultural manifestations. For a robust exposition of this term, see Shahab Ahmad, *What Is Islam? The Importance of Being Islamic* (Princeton: Princeton University Press, 2016), 113–120. The term reflects the commonalities of ethos and worldview shared by a wide variety of ethno-linguistic groups.
5. Peter Hardy, *Historians of Medieval India: Studies in Indo-Muslim Historical Writing* (London: Luzac, 1966), 1–19; Wilfred Cantwell Smith, *Modern Islam in India: A Social Analysis* (London: Victor Gollancz, 1946), 44–47; Saiyid Naqi Husain Jafri, 'A Modernist View of Madrasa Education in Late Mughal India', in *Islamic Education, Diversity, and National Identify: Dīnī Madāris in India Post 9/11*, ed. Jan-Peter Hartung and Helmut Reifeld, 39–55 (New Delhi: SAGE Publications, 2006).
6. Mohamad Tavakoli-Targhi, 'Contested Memories of Pre-Islamic Iran', *Medieval History Journal* 2, no. 2 (October 1999): 245–275. To place these developments within a broader context, see S. Frederick Starr, *Lost Enlightenment: Central Asia's Golden Age from the Arab Conquest to Tamerlane* (Princeton: Princeton University Press, 2015), 1–27; Peter Frankopan, *The Silk Roads: A New History of the World* (London: Vintage, 2017), 8–19.
7. Ayesha Jalal, *Self and Sovereignty: Individual and Community in South Asian Islam since 1850* (London: Routledge, 2000), 37–41. Also see Barbara Daly Metcalf, *Islamic Revival in British India: Deoband 1860–1900* (Princeton: Princeton University Press, 1982), 20; Seema Alavi, *Islam and Healing: Loss and Recovery in a Indo-Muslim Medical Tradition 1600–1900* (New Delhi: Permanent Black, 2007), 205–236.
8. Shahzad Bashir, 'On Islamic Time: Rethinking Chronology in the Historiography of Muslim Societies', *History and Theory* 53, no. 4 (2014): 519–544.
9. Sheldon Pollock, 'Introduction', in *Forms of Knowledge in Early Modern Asia: Explorations in the Intellectual History of India and Tibet, 1500–1800*, ed. Sheldon Pollock (Durham: Duke University Press, 2011), 8. This view is gradually being strengthened through the work of regional specialists like Ahmad Dallal, Shahzad Bashir, Shahab Ahmed, and Afzar Moin.
10. Muhammad Qasim Zaman, *The Ulama in Contemporary Islam: Custodians of Change* (Karachi: Oxford University Press, 2004), 7; Wael B. Hallaq, 'On Orientalism, Self-Consciousness, and History', *Islamic Law and Society* 18, no. 3–4 (2011): 387–439.

11. Charles M. Ramsey, 'Orientalist: Friend or Foe?', in *Literary and Non-Literary Response Towards 9/11: South Asia and Beyond*, ed. Nukhbah Langah (New Delhi: Routledge, 2017), 35–48.
12. Bashir, 'On Islamic Time', 543.
13. Pollock, 'Introduction', 10.
14. S. H. Nasr, 'The Quranic Commentaries of Mulla Sadra', in *Consciousness and Reality: Studies in Memory of Toshihiko Izutsui*, ed. Jalal al-Din Ashtiyani, Hideichi Matsubara, Takashi Iwami, and Akiro Matsumoto, 45–58 (Leiden: Brill, 2000).
15. Fazlur Rahman, *The Philosophy of Mullā Ṣadrā* (Albany: State University of New York Press, 1975), 12.
16. Starr, *Lost Enlightenment*, 101–125. Also see Paul Hullmeine, 'Al-Birūnī and Avicenna on the Existence of Void and the Plurality of Worlds', *Oriens* 47, nos. 1–2 (2019): 114–144.
17. George Makdisi, *The Rise of Colleges: Institutions of Learning in Islam and the West* (Edinburgh: University of Edinburgh Press, 1981), 279–281; George Saliba, *Islamic Science and the Making of the European Renaissance* (Cambridge: Massachusetts Institute of Technology Press, 2007), 221–235. Also see F. E. Peters, *Aristotle and the Arabs: The Aristotelian Tradition in Islam* (New York: New York University Press, 1968).
18. Jonardon Ganeri, *The Lost Age of Reason: Philosophy in the Early Modern India, 1450–1700* (Oxford: Oxford University Press, 2011), 244–247.
19. William M. Reddy, 'The Eurasian Origins of Empty Time and Space: Modernity as Temporality Reconsidered', *History and Theory* 55, no. 3 (2016): 325–356.
20. Reddy, 'The Eurasian Origins of Empty Time and Space', 326.
21. Velcheru Narayan Rao, David Shulman, and Sanjay Subramanyam, *Textures of Time: Writing History in South India, 1600–1800* (Delhi: Permanent Black, 2001), 255.
22. Martin Heidegger, *The Question of Technology* (London: Garland, 1977), 12; Albert Borgmann, 'Technology', in *A Companion to Heidegger*, ed. Hubert Dreyfus and Mark Wrathall, 420–428 (Oxford: Blackwell, 2005), 428.
23. Sadra authored some 40 books. Of principal concern here is his work on transcendent philosophy, known as *Asfar* (Journeys). Sadr al-Din Shirazi and Muhammad Ibn Ibrahim, *Al- Ḥikma al-mutaʿāliya fī l-asfār al-ʿaqliyya al-arbaʿa*, ed. Riḍā Luṭfī, Ibrāhīm Amīnī, and Fatḥ Allāh Ummīd (Beirut: Dār Iḥyāʾ al-Turāth al- ʿArabī, 1981), 1:56ff. 427–446.
24. Ibrahim Kalin, *Mulla Sadra* (Oxford: Oxford University Press, 2014), 28, 90; Rahman, *Philosophy*, 12–16. For a highly lucid account, see Zailan Moris, *Revelation, Intellectual Intuition and Reason in the Philosophy of Mulla Sadra: An Analysis of the al-Hikmah al-ʿarshiyyah* (London: Routledge, 2003).

25. Rahman, *Philosophy*, 20.
26. The Safavid dynasty in Iran, founded by Shah Isma'il in 1501, had its origins in Safawiyya, a Sunni Sufi order, but a later policy (*tashayyu'*) succeeded in promoting Shi'ism and condemning competing organizations such as the Sufi orders.
27. Nathan Katz, 'The Identity of a Mystic: The Case of Sa'id Sarmad, a Jewish-Yogi-Sufi Courtier of the Mughals', *Numen* 47, no. 1 (2000): 142–160. Also see Annemarie Schimmel, *Pain and Grace: A Study of Two Mystical Writers of Eighteenth-Century Muslim India* (Leiden: Brill, 1976), 7; Rajmohan Gandhi, *Punjab: A History from Aurangzeb to Mountbatten* (New Delhi: Aleph Books, 2013), 60–62.
28. Mansura Haidar, 'Medical Works of the Medieval Period from India and Central Asia', *Diogenes* 55, no. 2 (2008): 27–43. During the reign of Akbar, Sirhind spread for some 3 *kos*, or approximately 10 kilometers. The city was ransacked repeatedly in the eighteenth century and never regained its former stature.
29. For a highly cogent description, see Arthur F. Buehler, *Sufi Heirs of the Prophet: The India Naqshbandiyya and the Rise of the Mediating Sufi Shaykh* (Columbia: University of South Carolina Press, 1998). There is an erroneous tendency in some quarters to emphasize Sirhindi as an opponent to mystical exaggeration, and a champion for the sober reification of *shari'ah*, but this does not adequately account for his stellar rise in station among the Sufi elite.
30. Though Sadra apparently was not initiated in a Sufi order, contact and understanding of the mystical are implicit in his work. Annemarie Schimmel, *Mystical Dimensions of Islam*, 2nd edition (Chapel Hill: University of North Carolina Press, 2011), 263–267; Jamal Malik, *Islam in South Asia: A Short History* (Leiden: Brill, 2008), 170–171; Kalin, *Mulla Sadra*, 35, 62–63, 161.
31. Schimmel, *Mystical Dimensions of Islam*, 267–269; Sajida S. Alvi, 'Mujaddidi Sufi Order's Ascendancy in Central Asia through the Eyes of Its Masters and Disciples (1010s–1200s/1600s–1800s)', in *Reason and Inspiration in Islam: Theology, Philosophy, and Mysticism in Muslim Thought: Essays in Honour of Herman Landolt*, ed. Todd Lawson, 407–418 (London: I.B. Tauris, 2005). For other significant perspectives in English, see Yohanan Friedmann, *Shaykh Ahmad Sirhindi: An Outline of His Thought and a Study of His Image in the Eyes of Posterity* (Montreal: McGill Queen's University Press, 1971); Muhammad Abdul Haq Ansari, *Sufism and Shari'ah: A Study of Shaykh Ahmad Sirhindi's Effort to Reform Sufism* (Leicester: Islamic Foundation, 1986); J. G. J. ter Haar, *Follower and Heir of the Prophet: Shaykh Ahmad Sirhindi (1564–1624)* (Leiden: Het Oosters Instituut, 1992).
32. The stalwart master of Delhi, Shah Wali Allah, for example, shortlisted Sirhindi as one of the 'most faithful servants of God ever'. See J. M. S. Baljon, *Religion and Thought of Shāh Walī Allāh* (Leiden: Brill, 1986), 200.

33. Mohammed Rustom, *The Triumph of Mercy: Philosophy and Scripture in Mulla Sadra* (Albany: State University of New York Press, 2012), 119.
34. Sanjay Subrahmanyam, 'The Eurasian Context of the Early Modern History of Mainland South East Asia, 1400–1800', *Modern Asian Studies* 31, no. 3 (1997): 735–762.
35. The collected letters (*maktubat*) are available in Persian and Urdu, and a good number of these have been carefully rendered into English by Arthur F. Buehler, *Revealed Grace: The Juristic Sufism of Ahmad Sirhindi (1564–1624)* (Louisville: Fons Vitae, 2012). The edition I consulted in Urdu is Aḥmad Sirhindi, *Maktubat-i Imam-i Rabbani*, ed. Nur Aḥmad, 3 vols. (Karachi: Educational Press, 1973).
36. Shahzad Bashir, *Sufi Bodies: Religion and Society in Medieval Islam* (New York: Columbia University Press, 2012), 8. Bashir demonstrates the value of epistolary and hagiographic writings from this period as sources of knowledge and draws attention to the academic tendency to overlook their importance.
37. Buehler, *Sufi Heirs*, xvii
38. Bashir, *Sufi Bodies*, 544.
39. Hullmeine, 'Al-Birūnī and Avicenna', 115. Boris A. Rosenfeld and Ekmeleddin Ihsanuğlu, *Mathematicians, Astronomers, and Other Scholars of Islamic Civilisation and Their Works (7th–19th c.)* (Istanbul: Research Center for Islamic History, Art, and Culture, 2003), 126.
40. Alavi, *Islam and Healing*, 4.
41. Alavi, *Islam and Healing*, 4.
42. J. S. Mishra, 'New Light on Albiruni's Stay and Travel in India', *Central Asiatic Journal* 15, no. 4 (1972): 302–312; Mario Kozah, *The Birth of Indology as an Islamic Science: Al-Biruni's Treatise on Yoga Psychology* (Leiden: Brill, 2016), 8–34. Michael H. Fisher, *Migration: A Human History* (Oxford: Oxford University Press, 2013), 33. Nile Green, *Indian Sufism Since the Seventeenth Century: Saints, Books, and Empires in the Muslim Deccan* (New York: Routledge, 2006), 90.
43. Reddy, 'The Eurasian Origins of Empty Time and Space', 326.
44. A. Azfar Moin, *The Millennial Sovereign: Sacred Kingship and Sainthood in Islam* (New York: Columbia University Press, 2014), 1–16.
45. Sajjad Rizvi, *Mullā Sadrā and Metaphysics: Modulation of Being* (London: Routledge, 2009), 64–72.
46. Muhammad Hisham Kabbani, *Classical Islam and the Naqshbandi Sufi Tradition* (Fenton: Islamic Supreme Council of North America, 2004), 285, 569. Also see Mauro Valdinocci, 'A Model of Sufi Training in the 21st Century: A Case Study of the Qadriyya in Hyderabad', in *South Asian Sufis: Devotion,*

Deviation, and Destiny, ed. Clinton Bennett and Charles M. Ramsey, 31–43 (London: Continuum, 2012); Buehler, *Sufi Heirs*, 201–203.

47. Yohanan Friedmann, 'Religious and Political Ideas of Shaikh Ahmad Sirhindi', *Rivista degli Studi Orientali* 36, no. 1 (1961): 259–270; Buehler, *Sufi Heirs*, 269. The influence of Sirhindi and Sadra in the development of Shah Wali Allah's thought has been well-documented. In broad terms, Wali Allah attempted to synthesize Sufi-philosophical cosmologies into a descriptive system. For greater detail, see Rahman, *Philosophy*, 90–91; Kalin, *Mulla Sadra*, 22.
48. S. H. Nasr, 'Mulla Sadra and the Doctrine of the Unity of Being', *Philosophical Forum* 4, no. 1 (1972): 153–161.
49. William C. Chittick, 'A History of the Term "Waḥdat al-wujūd"', in *Search of the Lost Heart: Explorations in Islamic Thought*, ed. Mohammed Rustom (Albany: State University of New York Press, 2012), 71–78. The central question was whether 'everything is from Him [God]' (*hama az ust*) or 'everything is Him' (*hama ust*).
50. Mohammed Rustom, *The Triumph of Mercy: Philosophy and Scripture in Mulla Sadra* (Albany: State University of New York Press, 2012), 119.
51. Rustom, *The Triumph of Mercy*, 144. Translation of Sadra, *Tafsīr* 1:112–113.
52. Sayyid Ahmad Khan, *Tabyīn al-kalām*, vol. 2 (Aligarh: Sir Sayyid Academy, 2004), 55. For a highly lucid account of Sadra's ideas of substantial motion, see Zailan Moris, *Revelation, Intellectual Intuition and Reason in the Philosophy of Mulla Sadra: An Analysis of the al-Hikmah al-ʿarshiyyah* (London: Routledge, 2003).
53. The most direct translation of the term *paidā* is 'birthed', but it can also be rendered as 'generated', 'begot', or 'came forth from'. This is the term used in the earliest Urdu translations, and it is linguistically consistent with the pre-existing Persian version translated by Wali Allah, Shah ʿAbd al-Aziz, and Shah Rafiʿ al-Din. In the Arabic Quran, God made (*khalq*) rather than 'begot' the heavens and the earth.
54. Kalin, *Mulla Sadra*, 30.
55. Lenn E. Goodman, *Avicenna* (Ithaca: Cornell University Press, 2006), 176.
56. Fazlur Rahman, *Avicenna's Psychology* (London: Oxford University Press, 1949), 98–99. For another cogent examination, see Jon McGinnis, *Avicenna* (New York: Oxford University Press, 2010), 89–116.
57. Henry Corbin, *Creative Imagination in the Sufism of Ibn ʿArabi*, trans. Ralph Manheim (Princeton: Princeton University Press, 1969), 80.
58. Buehler, *Sufi Heirs*, 257.
59. Kalin, *Mulla Sadra*, 62; Sayeh Meisami, *Mulla Sadra* (Oxford: Oneworld, 2013), 43–52.

60. Kalin, *Mulla Sadra*, 35.
61. Sayyid Ahmad Khan, *Tafsir al-Qur'ān*, vol. 3 (Aligarh: Institute Press, 1883), 204–208.
62. Kalin, *Mulla Sadra*, 30.
63. Henry Corbin, 'Le Thème de la résurrection chez Mollâ Sadra Shirazi (1050/1640) commentateur de Suhrawardi (586/1191)', in *Studies in Mysticism and Religion Presented to Gershom G. Scholem*, ed. E. E. Urbach and R. J. Zwi Werblowski, 71–115 (Jerusalem: Magnes Press, 1967).
64. Kalin, *Mulla Sadra*, 158, citing *Afsār* iv. 2.176. For greater detail, see Sajjad H. Rizvi, *Mulla Sadra Shirazi: His Life, Works and the Sources for Safavid Philosophy* (Oxford: Oxford University Press, 2007), 311; Christian Jambet, *The Act of Being: The Philosophy of Revelation in Mullā Sadrā*, trans. Jeff Fort (New York: Zone, 2006), 394–396.
65. Kalin, *Mulla Sadra*, 160. Sadra concluded his presentation with a quotation from Jesus: 'One who is not born twice will never reach the heavens of the afterlife' (*cf.* Gospel of St. John 3:3).

4

Contestations and Negotiations
Early Modern Individualism in Jain Heterodoxy, *c*. 1470–*c*. 1770

Shalin Jain

While debating the 'early modern' in South Asian history, it is pertinent to acknowledge that the concept of 'medieval' is rooted in Orientalist discourse. Borrowed from Europe, the tripartite periodization has continued to loom large over the writing of South Asian history. In this chapter, however, I discuss the nature of early modernity in South Asia between the fifteenth and the seventeenth centuries in terms of some specific historical tendencies that characterized the history of Jainism. In terms of religious practices, Jainism witnessed the rise of individualistic consciousness and a new criticality during the period. In this context, I trace the formation of the individual as a category of analysis through the case study of two individuals from the Jain community. I further argue that the spirit of individualism, dialogue, debate, and dissent that characterized early modernity in Jainism in South Asia was derailed with the advent of colonial modernity.

Individualism and Early Modernity

There is a persisting uncertainty regarding the sites of differences and similarities with regard to medievalism and modernity across spaces; should one look into the material content of mundane life in order to locate patterns of common experiences, or in the world of ideas? European notions of modernity and their transplantation in the Asian context have ended up making tradition and modernity two opposite poles. However, both of these require to be seen in terms of interactions, more as overlapping circles than disconnected ones. As Franz-Josef Arlinghaus has argued, '... with respect to self-esteem, self-consciousness and (if at all) "autonomy" there are more similarities than differences between medieval and modern ways of being "individual"'.[1] Engagement with the concept of the individual as a site that generates cultural narratives offers a good point of entry for constructing connected histories of ideas, knowledge, and cultural production. In the case of Europe, the window to modernity was largely opened by individuals since the time of the Renaissance. This is what emerges from the works of scholars like Carlo

Ginzburg, Emmanuel Le Roy Ladurie, and Natalie Zemon Davis. Their 'new histories' reveal this by focusing on individual behaviour, choices, and experiences of characters like Menocchio and Martin Guerre.[2] The individual has been one of the key categories through which the advent of modernity has been explained in recent times. However, this exercise requires locating spaces of modernity, memory, interaction, and production across boundaries of space and time, as well as across periods of dynamic, often divergent, political and social developments. This creates the historiographical problem of situating both the individual and modernity within the existing overlapping, yet complex, relationship between medieval and early modern. Spaces for individual assertion, dissent, and diversity of opinions as well as levels of acceptance in such societies should be understood as parameters of their indigenous modernity.

In order to develop the premise of individualism, it becomes imperative to contextualize the issue within the larger debate. Scholarship on individualism and its functionality in South Asia has focused overwhelmingly on monotheistic contexts and the categories of community leadership – monarchs, nobles, religious preachers, and trendsetters.[3] The roles of common people and processes active on the margins of history but negotiating the formation of an individual engaged in heterodox projects and non-monotheistic religious traditions have largely been ignored. This approach has complemented the persisting hegemony of the category of the medieval in South Asian historiography, where until recently the traditional structural model did not allow scope for histories of dissent or the individual beyond the project of empires. Here, the dominant trend has been to project the common individual as an obedient, orthodox subject on the basis of official memoirs or court chronicles. Taken at face value, these textual narratives can produce the image of a society dominated entirely by the community with no space for manoeuvre by ordinary individuals. In this framework, dissent or innovations are mostly appropriated within the normative discourse, eclipsing the scope for differences, doubts, and arguments. In opposition to this, the present chapter is driven by an urge to re-define existing identities beyond normative contexts through a focus on unconventional individual attempts to embrace, surpass, and resist such definitions. In the history of South Asian Jainism, there have been instances of alternate, multiple, and vernacular modernities. They problematize the idea of European exclusivity in terms of the emergence of modernity. There are cases in South Asia too where individual identity was constructed and redefined constantly by dissenting personalities who simultaneously contested as well as negotiated asymmetrical power relations. This chapter locates diverse sites of everyday interactions, appropriations, and interpretations that made diverse political statements and created spaces of subjectivity. I will focus on two eminent Jain individuals. The first is Lonka Shah, a fifteenth-century lay preacher of the Sthanakvasi Jain tradition from the Kathiawad region of Gujarat. The second is Banarsidas, an early seventeenth-century Shwetambar Jain from the Middle Gangetic Basin. Their lives reveal the nuances, complexities, and conflicts involved in the shaping of the rise of individualism as a marker of early modernity in South Asia.

Our existing understanding regarding the parameters of religiosity of this period needs to be nuanced in view of the textual expectations about what an individual as well as his or her conduct ought to have been. This is because conflicts arising out of individual actions became increasingly popular in heterogeneous ways during these centuries, defying both conservative and communitarian authorities. Therefore, merely reconstructing a social history through the information contained in the texts is not sufficient. The material aspect of the texts – the conditions and processes through which these texts were produced, circulated, exchanged, read, shared, and performed – also becomes vital. Another significant aspect is the issue of agency in relation with the intellectual and religious networks of Jain merchants. Here, reconciliation between worldly occupation and spiritual salvation seems to have been a problem for the merchants. One also has to address the issue of tensions between individual aspirations and collective needs in the kin and business networks as well as those of religious attitudes and institutions. The principal objective for me is to trace the nature of early modernity by analysing the relationship between the individual and the collective.

I plan to locate diverse sites of interaction and negotiation in the South Asian context rather than contrasting with the European 'others' and their religion. The fifteenth through the seventeenth centuries witnessed both the revival and the rise of intense disputations and critical engagements within the religious landscape of South Asia. Several intellectuals, regional state officials, and even lay individuals grew critical of all formal religious hierarchies. Reworking, reactivating, and revitalizing of tradition were practised generously within the Jain community. At times, such attempts were reflections of being a collective movement of a section of society to go beyond the dependence on the clergy. In many such crucial attempts, certain individuals were at the apex, acting as the central agency through which such heterodoxies found momentum. Since the fifteenth century, there were certain individual projects within South Asian Jainism which demonstrated attempts to mobilize religion into building unorthodox or individual campaigns, mostly in opposition to organized religion. Sometimes, such attempts also emerged in negotiation with organized religion or enjoyed the support of the latter. The concept of the individual was not merely imposed from the above but grew within the communities themselves. By the seventeenth century, a new intellectual tendency increasingly facilitated the processes of individual-building at the expense of the community. The following sections will discuss some of these processes.

Prelude to Early Modern Individualism: Lonka Shah

Let us start with our analysis of the two Jain individuals who were active in different times and spaces, but who shared a common agenda of dissent and heterodoxy. The first, Lonka Shah, was a lay scribe-turned-preacher while the other, Banarasidas, remained a merchant householder throughout his life. Lonka Shah, who lived mostly in Ahmedabad in Gujarat in the fifteenth century, moved beyond the normative discourse of the existing Jain theology by rationalizing his opposition to idol worship. In his critical ways, Lonka could neither favour the dominant structure of the community and religion nor leave any personal writings; this led to his memory being repressed. The scant information available about him was either censored or reinterpreted by the organized religion and by modern stakeholders. In spite of his immense contribution to Jain sectarian and canonical tradition, our knowledge about him is somewhat obscured because of these mediators. By the time one reaches the case of Banarsidas and his friends in the seventeenth century, heterodoxy did not remain an isolated case; rather, it continued the traditions of Jain scepticism and dissent of the preceding centuries. However, Banarsidas, who remained mobile between Agra, Jaunpur, and beyond, was vocal enough to write arguably the first autobiography in the Indian tradition with distinctly modern sensibilities.[4] He used the colloquial language of the metropolitan zone of Mughal North India. Notwithstanding his provocative rational thoughts and actions, he did not challenge the Jain tradition or canonical literature like Lonka Shah. Owing to the duality of his thoughts and actions, he enjoys a respectable individual space within the Jain tradition initially as a cosmopolitan and later as an orthodox Jain.

The historical biography of Lonka Shah remains uncertain for the lack of reliable sources. There are very few references based on the textual tradition of Lonka *gaccha* – a puritanical, reformist Jain movement which is opposed to image worship and whose origin is credited to Lonka Shah.[5] Most of the texts of the Lonka *gaccha* tradition are poems or songs of a hagiographic or biographical nature. The contemporary Lonka *gaccha* tradition itself has lost all written sources and retains no cultural memory anymore on the doctrinal views of Lonka or the earlier Lonka *gaccha* teachers (*acharyas*). Hence, the notions about the life, teachings, and sect of Lonka Shah are more of a recent construct, coming out of conflicting sectarian discussions and debates between Sthanakavasi and *murtipujak* traditions in the late nineteenth and early twentieth centuries. For the first group, Lonka Shah has been a great reformer embodying the true ethos of Jainism, while the second tradition sees him as an aberration and portrays him as a villain. Our analysis about him is largely based on the research conducted by Peter Flugel, who has utilized sources available from both the sides to situate Lonka Shah in his historical milieu and Jain philosophical traditions.[6] Flugel has given a well-researched argument on how no consensus exists on the nature of Lonka's influence on the formation of an iconic mendicant tradition, which emerged in the aftermath of his protest.[7]

Lonka Shah was either a Porwad or Shrimali– that is, one of the three most important castes among the Shwetambar Jains. There is no clear evidence about where he spent his early days; in all probability, he grew up in Limbdi in the Kathiawad region of Gujarat. Later on, he settled in Ahmadabad. Here, he emerged as a learned layman with powerful connections with the Muslim authorities in Ahmadabad. According to one Orientalist view about Jainism,

> ... one effect of the Mohammedan conquest [...] was to drive many of the Jaina into closer union with their fellow idol-worshippers in the face of iconoclasts. Another effect was to drive others away from idolatry altogether. No oriental could hear a fellow oriental's passionate outcry against idolatry without doubts as to the righteousness of the practice entering his mind. Naturally enough it is in Ahmadabad, the city of Gujarat that was most under Mohammedan influence, that we can first trace the stirring of these doubts.[8]

In this interpretation, the rationalization of ideas of Lonka Shah has been attributed to the influence of Islam, denying the man any agency of his own. This is an early-twentieth-century Orientalist generalization, one which did not understand the nuances of indigenous tradition of non-idolism and categorized both the milieu and the individual as medieval, thereby denying an individual the scope of the agency or articulation of selfhood in modern terms.

Due to his profession of a scribe (*lekhak*) and expertise in calligraphy, Lonka Shah could gain access to the sacred texts for the purpose of copying them. For instance, when a Jain layman gave him a Jain text titled *Dashavaikalika Sutra* for copying, he took it home and started reading it. Much impressed, he got two copies made with the help of his widowed daughter and retained one copy for himself for further study. Thereafter, he became a keen student of the Jain scriptures. Though one does not get any contemporary works by Lonka Shah or his followers, all the

Jain legends accept his profession as a scribe. This indicates his ability to read and internalize important texts. He thus cannot be rejected as an ignorant manuscript copyist. It was his readings of these texts of the Jain tradition that was the origin of the various ideas of Lonka. His study of *Acharanga Sutra* and *Dashavaikalika Sutra*, for instance, discovered that the discipline and morality required by these texts were rapidly diminishing due to the laxity and undisciplined behaviour of Jain monks. Great slackness had also crept into the contemporary mendicants, as they had come to possess not only books and clothes but also material wealth. At times, there were also quarrels among them, attracting public criticism for unethical conduct.[9]

Though the immediate milieu of Lonka Shah was marked by Islamic influence, one cannot forget that image-worship hardly found any reference in the Jain scriptures. In late-fifteenth-century Gujarat, the destruction of some temples by the officials of the regional sultanate has been attributed to the provocations of Lonka Shah.[10] However, the Islamic stand against idol worship would have actually made his job easier. He took advantage of these circumstances in propagating his doctrines. He declared his disbelief in several essential Jain rites like as *paushadha*, *pratikramana*, *pratyakhyana*, and even charity. Though the worship of images was very popular among the Jains of his time, he argued that the practice went against scriptural prescriptions. He then started preaching what according to him was the authentic Jain religion, which did not ordain image worship. He argued that the institution of the temple, with its concentrated wealth, power, and burden of rituals, was the main source of corruption; it stood in opposition to the moral path shown in the ancient scriptures. According to him, the erection of the idols in temples involved digging, quarrying, and other construction activities; all of this was harmful to minute life-forms. In this way, Lonka Shah provided a moral cover to his campaign against temple construction. By challenging temple worship, he wanted to force the Jain laity to opt for a more moral and mobile life. In addition to this, he pointed out that the practices of the temple administrator monks did not have any basis in the ancient texts. All these arguments infuriated the monks, especially since Lonka was only a layman; according to the monks, he had no right to preach.[11]

The campaign of Lonka Shah became popular once a Jain *sangha* (religious group) arrived in Ahmedabad and met him. The leader of the group was Sambhuji. His granddaughter Mohabai was a child widow. Both Sambhuji and this girl were greatly attracted by the teachings of Lonka. Other lay members of this group also joined the assembly of Lonka's preaching. This enraged the monks accompanying the *sangha*, and they left in a huff. However, about 45 lay members of the *sangha* stayed on in Ahmedabad and became the disciples of Lonka by formally accepting *diksha* (initiation) from him on Jaishtha Sukla, 1474. Lonka did not become a monk himself but remained a lay preacher throughout his life. Many of his disciples became *muni*s (monks). Among them, *muni* Sarvaj, *muni* Bhanaji, *muni* Munaji, and *muni* Jagmalji subsequently became well-known preachers. Lonka himself, though a layman, was called *muni* Dayadharma by his followers, and the sect he founded came to be popularly known as Daya *gaccha*. Lonka was followed by his disciple Rupa Rishi, whom he had ordained in Surat. The next head of this group was Jiva Rishi; however, by his time sub-groups began to emerge within the order. One *muni* Bija started another sect called Bijamata in 1513. It seems that another dominant Jain sect Tapa *gaccha* tried to take on such challenges during this period by making strict rules for Jain monks and enforcing them rigorously. This process was initiated by Anand Vimal Suri (1490–1540), who practised severe penance for 14 years to create a positive impression of Jainism on the masses. According to the Jain tradition, he was successful in regaining the influence of Jainism. Both the Lonka *gaccha* tradition, which was founded in the 1470s by one of Lonka's followers named Bhanaand, and the Sthanakavasi tradition, which was established in the early seventeenth century by different groups of dissenting *sadhu*s (ascetics) of the Lonka *gaccha*, objected to the re-emergence of idol worship within the Jain tradition. Reform movements of the later period, like Bijamata, Sthanakavasi, and Terapantha, borrowed heavily from the Lonka *gaccha* tradition. These individual efforts and reasons made a case for dissent within the faith and thus gradually created alternate spaces in parallel to the mainstream. By invoking puritanical ideas of original Jainism while refashioning them to suit the fifteenth century, what the dissenting voice of Lonka Shah in effect launched was an important revivalist tendency within Jainism.

The Quest for Individual Agency: Banarasidas

My second case study concerns the seventeenth-century Jain merchant named Banarsidas, whose career spread from Agra to Jaunpur and redefined the relationship between individual, text, and society. The persona of Banarsidas reflects a contrast between orthodox religiosity and individual rationality, which could not be reconciled given the two forms of life he lived. In the public domain, he was a reformer and a translator. However, as his autobiography *Ardhakathanak* shows, his private actions spoke of contestations and concealments. In the public sphere, he wrote and translated Jain philosophical texts like *Samaysar Natak, Gommatsaar, Dhyanbattisi, Adhyatam ke Geet*, a hymn titled *Shivmandir*, and many other texts concerning Jain philosophy.

However, writing his autobiography, *Ardhakathanak,* two years before his demise, he acknowledged and repented what he perceived as his misdeeds, unbecoming of a Jain. This shows a constant clash between prescribed public life and its critique in the personal life by means of deviating from convention. Across these two conflicting spheres of life, reconciliation was very much there. Banarasidas and his literary circle re-explored and redefined the religious texts which communally carried a normative meaning, as if they were stagnant in the time of their writing. In writing a philosophical treatise titled *Samaysaar,* Banarsidas filtered down a tradition according to his own worldview.[12] The literary knowledge of Banarsidas evolved through his engagements with different types of texts. During his bad days in Agra, he passed his time singing Shaikh Qutban Suhravardi's *Mirigavati* and Mir Sayyid Manjhan Shattari Rajgiri's *Madhumalati* – two mystical Sufi poems composed in Hindi verse. For him, these were ballads of love. For us, however, these present cases of early sixteenth-century textual traditions re-cast for seventeenth-century audiences through the oratory skills of an educated intellectual. Thus, the moment of oratory was the moment of recreation as well, as the orator had the agency of interpolation and exposition in his relation to the original text. John E. Cort talks about vernacular culture and the practice of translation in seventeenth-century North India. However, such translation was not a form of mere transmission. In a predominantly illiterate society, the moment of translation also becomes that of creation. *Ardhakathanak* is full of instances of oratory.[13] On several occasions, Banarsidas and his intellectual circle assembled to recite various popular literary texts. I argue that such moments empowered individuals with the agency to navigate a text and its audiences across time. One should remember that *Ramcharitmanas* first became more popular through the performative acts of Ramlila and then the reading of the text.[14]

Here, individualism also becomes a signifier of choices. Contrary to the circumscribed image of medieval Indian merchants, Banarsidas exercised his individual choices whenever he could afford to do so. In this context, sexuality, pleasure, and knowledge can be taken as the attributes of individual creativity. The youthful pangs of Banarsidas were not taken positively by his community, but he did not face any punishment beyond a mild reprimand.[15] If the scope for expressing individual opinions is taken to be an indication of the nature of the times, this instance is revealing. In Italy, Mennocchio of the Inquisition records challenged the virginity of Mother Mary. In South Asia, Banarsidas of *Ardhakathanak* pondered over the existence of Lord Shiva.[16] However, as a societal response, the first was burned at the stake, while the second lived a full life. When Banarsidas started deviating from the normative course of life prescribed by the community leaders, Jain elders reprimanded him and advised him to mend his ways.[17] However, Banarsidas refused to adhere to such suggestions and kept pursuing his passions.[18] His community allowed him that space. Given the circumstances of a parochial communitarian world of the times, individualism requires to be acknowledged as a two-way function. Not only did Banarsidas show the will to make and adhere to his own choices, but his community too seems to have been tolerant enough to let him have his ways, albeit with strong reservations. He was not subjected to either excommunication or censorship, even as he continued with his adventures with eroticism.[19]

The aforementioned deviations from the usual communitarian discipline took place in spite of the fact that Banarsidas was well-trained in Jain religious philosophy, rituals, and ceremonies. He knew the 14 precepts or *niyama*s and *ashthanika*s, that is, the eight days of Jain religious ceremony. He was also familiar with the 12 *vrata*s (rituals) prescribed for the Jain householders. In all these ways, he was a typical member of his community. Yet his rebellious attitude becomes evident from his experiments with diverse religious practices and beliefs. For example, he let two Hindu monks guide him on two different occasions on following Hindu practices with the assurance of good luck. He also studied a ninth-century Digambar text, *Gommatsaar*, of Nemichandra, a Digambar monk, during the times of difficult Shwetambar–Digambar sectarian relationship. Here, one needs to appreciate the fuzziness of religious and sectarian identities too. Identity segregation in the seventeenth century was not as important in the case of Jains as it has been made out to be in the last two centuries. Thus, himself a Khartar *gaccha* Shwetambar Jain, Kharagsen, the father of Banarsidas, went on a pilgrimage along with a Digambar Jain, Rai Dhanna. When Hiranand, a Shwetambar Jain Oswal, organized a *sanghayatra* for Sammet Shikhar a few years later, Kharagsen yet again did not hesitate to accompany him. These two examples indicate that pilgrimage was often thought more as a social event than only a strictly religious one. Contrary to the rhetoric of divine legitimation that characterizes contemporary court chronicles, the author of *Ardhakathanak* humanizes human vanity. In fact, the text is a part of a new genre in Hindi literature, one where many texts were humanizing and personalizing narratives through a focus on relationships between humans or between humans and nature. It was beyond the categories of divine–human, patron–client, state–subject, or exploiter–victim relationships that formed the basis of a vast range of medieval texts.[20] This strong human element is visible throughout the text of *Ardhakathanak*, in narrating how Banarsidas was being repeatedly reprimanded by the elders of the community for his ostensible waywardness and how despite his repeated misdeeds and misconduct, he was always accommodated and embraced.[21]

The recoverable expression of such individual emotions is a relatively recent phenomenon in human history. Usually, emotions – feelings and their expressions – are seen to be shaped by culture and learnt or acquired in social contexts. What somebody can and may feel and express in a given situation depends substantially on social norms and rules. Though the expression of emotions has not been rare in South Asian literary traditions, it has largely comprised the expression of eroticism. However, emotions also function as the individual agency contributing to larger social groups, communities, and movements. This dimension of emotions is embedded in the text of *Ardhakathanak*, where it manifests through the interplay of thoughts and feelings of the author. However, Banarsidas also introduced a sense of platonic emotions, visible in his friendships or in his lamenting for his deceased children. This serves to humanize his thought process, something that rarely found literary expression in the medieval context. Banarsidas and his friends followed virtually a secret anarchist way of life that revolted against the established norms of Jainism. In many cases, the proclamation of Banarsidas' individualism took the form of nudity and erotic acts within the circle of his close friends.[22] For him, these acts were a means to subvert public norms in his private domain.[23] Alongside this, emotions of friendship also occupy an important place in the narrative. For instance, Banarsidas writes how one Narottam befriended him in spite of the discouragement of his own father. The text also reveals how Narottam's subsequent death left Banarsidas devastated and how he wept for days.[24]

The text is an instance of a cosmopolitan, interactive, and popular literary production that emerged in South Asia around this time. The range of literature discussed by Banarsidas was predominately Jain, but his cosmopolitan vocabulary revealed the larger context of which he was a part. Here was an individual acting under various influences and responding to them through his own agency. That is why Banarsidas could freely accommodate Persian words like *mulk*, *shariyati*, *dervish*, *fakir*, and *ashiqi* within his narrative and also write about injuring himself on hearing about the demise of the Mughal emperor Akbar. This speaks of intimate yet complex connections between the imperial and popular realms. The text also mentions other details that are relevant in this context. One incident concerns Shantidas Jauhari of Ahmedabad not sending the best jewels to the Mughal court owing to his ambivalence towards the last years of the reign of Shah Jahan, leading to the protest of imperial authorities against his ways of functioning in the form of blackmail.[25] In another instance, Banarsidas, in spite of having all the sense of loyalty towards the invisible, distant monarch, loathed the dominance of Mughal officials at the local level.²⁶ Through these anecdotes, the text provides an important window into these complex and constant social interactions.

This was the nature of the social milieu in which Banarsidas cultivated a value system conducive for the dominant structures of faith, community, and state. However, there are too many instances within the text that foreground the spirit of individualism vis-à-vis the structures of collectivism. In this context, the individual's defeat against the structures of dominance becomes explicit only towards the end of the text. Much of the narrative projects Banarsidas as an individual struggling all through his career, betraying and challenging his Jain identity. But the endless failures force him in the end to surrender his individualism in favour of structures of religiosity as an act of repentance. He becomes a devout Jain, lamenting his follies.²⁷ In fact, it is here that the fluidity that exists between individual and community unfolds fully. But for the act of repentance, the author of *Ardhakathanak* could have eulogized his life as a Jain reformer celebrating his literary and communitarian successes rather than his mercantile failures, familial ups and downs, and emotional bondings and breakdowns. The very act of innocence at the fag end of his career becomes the act of repentance, forcing the author to divulge the dark episodes of an individual self.²⁸ However, in the quest for locating the modern within the so-called medieval context, one cannot and should not polarize the two. The content of the change requires to be assessed in terms of the process rather than in terms of a final outcome. Thus, issues like the status of women or child mortality – as gleaned from *Ardhakathanak* – have to be discussed with an understanding that individuals were ultimately a part of the context and culture of a medieval society. Ideas and practices did not necessarily permeate each other all the time. Instead, there were fault lines that essentially merge medieval trends and modern tendencies into the grey zone of early modernity.

Situating the Early Modern in the Jain Tradition

Moving beyond the material aspects of early modernity as discussed in the beginning of this chapter, I take humanistic rationality of individual agency as one of its major attributes in South Asia. Here, the heterodoxies of Lonka Shah and Banarsidas served as a prelude to future debates and struggles for individualistic expressions. These figures act as the markers of historical continuities across the medieval and colonial modern sensibilities. The emergence of the individual in the process, in turn, helped the fostering of other fundamental qualities of the future, like criticism and interpretation. The ability to question existing norms had not yet become a vertical act in terms of social hierarchies; subordinates had not yet started questioning their superiors in explicit terms. The tendency to question whatever was found to be illogical was more horizontal. The changing material concerns created a new environment for questioning moral premises and religious orthodoxy. However, these instances of heterodoxy were not necessarily in continuation with preceding and future traditions of Jain scepticism and dissent – neither did they constitute mainstream religious knowledge; clouds of orthodoxy continued to remain the dominant social force.

The extent of religiosity in the public life of the early modern times could be a matter of debate, but cultural practices, literary heritage, and collective memories cannot be totally detached from the contemporary milieu of prevalent religious beliefs and practices. Certainly, one cannot imagine early modernity in South Asia as an age of pure reason and unprejudiced science, but this was also the case elsewhere. However, challenging the existing universally applicable method of determining the truth content of any claim and assessing the pre-determined morality of an act could be seen as indications of a new rationality and reasoned debate. Here the dissenting views of Banarsidas, a merchant from the Gangetic Plains, and the alternate visions of Lonka Shah, a householder of Shwetambar Tapa *gaccha* from Gujarat, become important. Their disagreements signified reasoned thinking minds. In their tendency of engaging with disagreements with others through debates and writing, we find the first signage of the gradual emergence of a public sphere.[29] Here, one can see a particular type of humanism, which led these intellectuals to stay open to the evolving moral situation and not give in to the ideological rigidity of the prevalent orthodoxies. In course of their education, Lonka Shah and Banarsidas moved from being indifferent to being contemptuous towards the prevalent religious practices of their times. For them, the rationalization of thought was a process characterized by repeatedly challenging existing religious beliefs and orthodoxies. This made their views quite unique and essentially different from the rationality of earlier times. Rationality was now becoming increasingly autonomous of the realm of orthodox scholarship. Challenges to and negations of existing belief systems, even though often in subtle terms, were becoming increasingly rampant. New networks of knowledge were emerging through a complex interplay between ideas, personalities, and events. This was the essence of the early modern condition within South Asian Jainism.

However, the world of Banarsidas was lost by the early eighteenth century. In fact, the urge to discover a homogeneous monotheism as well as to create a minority selfhood started juxtaposing itself against the dominant narrative of the majoritarian 'others'. The hardening of the communal boundaries and the growth of fixed social and religious categories of caste and religion started proliferating from this time onwards. The colonial knowledge system had already identified

Christianity as a superior, Western, non-Indian religion and counterposed it against Indic religions. This compartmentalization delegitimized a whole range of pre-colonial knowledge forms. By the late nineteenth century, possibilities of continuation of the cosmopolitanism that had marked the early modern condition in South Asia were further negated by the rise of revivalist rediscoveries of the Indic religions. In a way, the experience of colonialism in its process of building binaries based on religious and sectarian identities scuttled the intellectual potential of South Asia's own early modernity. Peter Flugel has already referred to this scenario in the context of Jainology.[30] These revivalist and puritanical tendencies took the whole religious system towards a metaphysical direction, forgetting their practical implications and treating religion as something frozen in time. This approach of Indic puritanism was very much commensurable with the notions of Christianity and Western philosophy but incommensurable with the pre-colonial past and especially with the environment of scepticism and debate that was the hallmark of South Asian early modernity. Thus, religion became a category of equivalence by all means. Under the hegemony of colonial modernity, the public life of religion had to be refashioned to be necessarily distinct from the 'secular' world of the West. In the process, the various local concepts of religion were subsumed within a universal idea of religion.

One needs to appreciate the fact that an act of retrieval and translation of the texts also meant their transposition. The quest of self and the other required valid explanations for both followers and critics. This led to a great deal of tension between polemics and accord. In the colonial milieu, the chief concern of religious communities was to persuade their audiences (both the supporters and the opponents) of their superiority vis-à-vis the inferiority of the others. Evolving an appropriate universal vocabulary and literary practices to achieve this became a major concern. Whatever did not suit the agenda of a linear progress of a religion had to be either eliminated or suppressed. These urges of comparisons and equivalences led to deep transformations in the conceptualization and expression of the social and cultural project of religions. Here, Jainism was successful in positioning its relationship with Christianity, Hinduism, and Islam. However, exactly like Hinduism and Islam, Jainism too gradually drifted away from the open world of indigenous beliefs and practices that marked the few centuries preceding the advent of colonialism.[31] For instance, the moment Jainism clashed with the Arya Samaj movement in colonial Punjab, the deployment of rhetorical modes became crucial for each community to counter the competing claims of the other.[32] Thus, the historical conditions and requirements of the nineteenth and twentieth centuries led to the disinheritance of many tendencies of diversity and dialogue in the face of religious competition and the quest of developing a refashioned religion.

The parameters of religiosity, in terms of the expectations about individual and collective conduct, remained contested throughout the period under focus. Conflicts arising out of individual actions became increasingly popular in heterogeneous ways, defying both state and religious authorities. Two distinct tendencies co-existed – an urge to define religion in normative contexts and individual attempts to embrace, surpass, and resist such definitions. The interactions between individual, religion, and politics against the backdrop of anti-orthodox campaigns as well as the tensions between religion, individuals, and the processes of de-legitimization or re-legitimization were important elements in the process. If the centuries earmarked as early modern were a time of disagreements, debates, and departures on the part of Lonka Shah and Banarsidas, they were also one of continued dominance of the religious orthodoxy over the popular psyche owing to the deeply rooted theological structures. It is for this reason that the example of these two figures does not serve as a clean break from the medieval past; rather, the overlap between the two contradictory tendencies comprises the ambivalence and overlaps that early modernity represented in the field of Jainism in South Asia.

Thus, the early modern condition in South Asia needs to be conceptualized not only in terms of changes in the material world but also in terms of those churning in the intellectual realm that led to the emergence of didactic worldviews. Early modern cosmopolitanism was characterized by tendencies that were complex, multi-layered, at times contradictory, and, most of all, human. The multi-layered complexities of the lived experiences of people like Lonka Shah and Banarsidas provide us windows into this cosmopolitanism. In many cases, religious and sectarian identities were questioned, sometimes they were erased, and in some cases they were replaced by a cosmopolitan identity. However, these tendencies were derailed by the rise of colonial modernity. Far from being further blurred, the boundaries of religious identity started hardening at the cost of the ideas of cosmopolitanism. In fact, the quest for a homogeneous monotheism got mixed into the colonial imperative of creating a comfortable echo chamber for the notions of European superiority. Thus, the early modern tendency of theological orthodoxies gradually getting diluted under the influence of debates, dialogue, and cosmopolitanism suffered a major setback and went in the reverse instead. The role of the intellectual as a public man within the wider mundane world was lost again, and religiosity reasserted itself as the central marker of individual identity.

The project of modernity as a universal promise remained unfulfilled due to its inbuilt limitations. At the same time, one needs to problematize the category of medieval as well. The medieval in South Asia, much like the modern, was neither uniform nor homogeneous. Both categories were porous, overlapping, extending, and intervening into each other. The very overlapping of scepticism, heterodoxy, and dissent across periods of history shows continuity beyond different historical periods. It is at the grey zone between the two that the early modern needs to be located.

Notes

1. Franz-Josef Arlinghaus, 'In and Out, Then and Now: The Conscious Self and Its Relation to Society in Pre- modern and Modern Times', *Medieval History Journal* 18, no. 2 (2015): 1–26.
2. Carlo Ginzburg, *The Cheese and the Worms: The World of a Sixteenth Century Miller* (New Jersey: John Hopkins University Press, 1992); Emmanuel Le Roy Ladurie, *Montaillou: Cathars and Catholics in a French Village, 1294–1324* (New York: Penguin Books, 1978); Natalie Zemon Davis, *The Return of Martin Guerre* (Cambridge: Harvard University Press, 1983).
3. Iqtidar Alam Khan, *Akbar and His Age* (New Delhi: Northern Book Centre, 1999); Shireen Moosvi, *Episodes in the Life of Akbar: Contemporary Records and Reminiscences* (New Delhi: National Book Trust, 1994); Corinne Lefevre, 'The Majālis-i Jahāngīrī (1608–11): Dialogue and Asiatic Otherness at the Mughal Court', *Journal of the Economic and Social History of the Orient* 55, nos. 2–3 (2012): 255–286; Corinne Lefevre, 'Recovering a Missing Voice from Mughal India: The Imperial Discourse of Jahāngīr (r. 1605–1627) in His Memoirs', *Journal of the Economic and Social History of the Orient* 50, no. 4 (2007): 452–489; Charlotte Vaudville, *A Weaver Named Kabir: Selected Verses, with a Detailed Biographical and Historical Introduction* (New Delhi: Oxford University Press, 1997); John Stratton Hawley, *Three Bhakti Voices: Mirabai, Surdas, and Kabir in Their Time and Ours* (New Delhi: Oxford University Press, 2005).
4. Literary critics see the genre of autobiography as a retrospective prose narrative produced by a real person concerning his own existence, focusing on his individual life, in particular on the development of his personality; accordingly, the author, the narrator, and the protagonist must share a common identity. Linda R. Anderson, *Autobiography: New Critical Idiom* (New York: Routledge, 2001), 2–3.
5. Muni Kantisagar, 'Sri Lonkashah ki Parampara aur Uska Agyaat Sahitya', in *Muni Shri Hazarimal Smriti Granth*, ed. Sobhachandra Bharill, 214–253

(Byavar: Muni Shri Hazarimal Smriti Granth Prakashan Samiti, 1965); Alamshah Khan, 'Lonka Gaccha ki Sahitya Sewa', in *Muni Shri Hazarimal Smriti Granth*, ed. Bharill, 203–213.

6. Peter Flugel, 'The Unknown Lonka Tradition and the Cultural Unconscious', in *Jaina Studies*, ed. Colette Caillat and Nalini Balbir, 181–271 (New Delhi: Motilal Banarsidass Publishers, 2008).

7. Flugel, 'Unknown Lonka Tradition'.

8. Sinclair Margaret Stevenson, *The Heart of Jainism* (London: Oxford University Press, 1915).

9. Malvania Dalsukh, 'Lonkashah aur Unki Vichar Dhara', in *Gurudev Shri Ratna Muni Smriti Granth*, ed. Vijay Muni Shastri and Harishankar Sharma, 365–438 (Agra: Gurudev Smriti Granth Prakashak Samiti, 1964).

10. Mohanlal Dali Chand Desai, *Jain Sahitya No Sankshipt Itihaas* (Bombay: Omkar Suri Gyan Mandir, 1933), 495–496.

11. Muni Gyansundar, *Shreeman Lonkashah* (Falaudi: Shree Ratna Prabhakar Gyan Pushpamala, No. 167, 1936), 110–117, 177–183, 326–336; C. B. Sheth, *Jainism in Gujrat, A.D. 1100 to 1600* (Bombay: Vijayadevsur Sangh Publication, 1953), 233–234.

12. Banarsidas, *Natak Samaysaar* (1636), commentary by Buddhilal Shravak (Bombay: Jain Garnthratnakar, 1929).

13. John E. Cort, 'Making It Vernacular in Agra: The Practice of Translation by Seventeenth-Century Jains', in *Tellings and Texts: Music, Literature and Performance in North India*, ed. Francesca Orsini and Katherine Butler Schofield, 61–105 (Cambridge: Open Book Publishers, 2015).

14. Philip Lutgendorf, 'Ram's Story in Shiva's City: Public Arenas and Private Patronage', in *Culture and Power in Banaras: Community, Performance, and Environment, 1800–1980*, ed. Sandria B. Freitag, 34–61 (Berkeley: University of California Press, 1989).

15. Banarsidas, *Ardhakathanak* (1641), translated and annotated by Mukund Lath as *Ardhakathanak: Half a Tale* (Jaipur: Rajasthan Prakrit Bharati Sansthan, 1981), verse 170, 237.

16. Banarsidas, *Ardhakathanak*, trans. Lath, verse 263, 244.

17. Banarsidas, *Ardhakathanak*, trans. Lath, verse 200, 239.

18. Banarsidas, *Ardhakathanak*, trans. Lath, verse 201, 239.

19. Banarsidas, *Ardhakathanak*, trans. Lath, verse 202, 239.

20. The famous Jain biography of Shwetambar saint Hiravijay Suri, *Hirsaubhgya Kavya*, is a divine–human text; Gujarati text *Sri Rajsagar Suri Niravan Raas* too takes human relations to divine will. Surdas and Tulsidas humanized God but only to set a normative trend. Banarsidas and Lonka Shah humanized experiences of the society within temporality without looking for an external

agency. Humans thus became autonomous in their endeavours. See Devavimal Gani, *Hirasaubhagya Kavya*, ed. Pandit Shiv Dutt and K. P. Parab, *Kavya Mala* (Bombay: Tukaram Javaji, 1900), 67; Tilaksagar, *Sri Rajsagar Suri Nirvana Raas*, Gujarati, 1723 VS, MS. Accession No. 13771 (Koba: Sri Kailash Suri Gyan Mandir, Mahavir Jain Aradhana Kendra).

21. Banarasidas, *Ardhakathanak*, trans. Lath, verses 199–201, 239.
22. Banarasidas, *Ardhakathanak*, trans. Lath, verses 603, 270.
23. Banarasidas, *Ardhakathanak*, trans. Lath, verses 601–605, 269–270.
24. Banarasidas, *Ardhakathanak*, trans. Lath, verses 477–485, 259–260; verses 490–496, 261.
25. M. S. Commissariat, 'Imperial Mughal "Farmans" in Gujarat', *Journal of the University of Bombay* 9, no. 1 (1940): 1–56.
26. Banarasidas, *Ardhakathanak*, trans. Lath, verses 462–464, 258.
27. Banarasidas, *Ardhakathanak*, trans. Lath, verses 649, 652–654, 273–274.
28. Banarasidas, *Ardhakathanak*, trans. Lath, verses 652–654, 274.
29. Farhat Hasan, 'Forms of Civility and Publicness in Pre-British India', in *Civil Society, Public Sphere and Citizenship: Dialogue and Perceptions*, ed. Rajeev Bhargava and Helmut Reifeld, 84–105 (New Delhi: SAGE Publications, 2005).
30. Peter Flugel, 'The Invention of Jainism: A Short History of Jaina Studies', *Journal of Jaina Studies* 1, no. 1 (2005): 1–19.
31. Such deviations within Jainism take us to the question raised by Talal Asad in another context, that is, what actually constitutes the anthropology of Islam, the universal 'discursive tradition' preserved and transmitted by learned men, or more malleable and differentiated meanings created by local or popular tradition. See Talal Asad, *Genealogies of Religion: Discipline and Reasons of Power in Christianity and Islam* (Baltimore: John Hopkins University Press, 1993).
32. John E. Cort, 'Jain Identity and the Public Sphere in Nineteenth-Century India', in *Religious Interactions in Modern India*, ed. Martin Fuchs and Vasudha Dalmia, 99–137 (New Delhi: Oxford University Press, 2019).

PART II
ECONOMY, ENVIRONMENT, SOCIETY

5

Early Modernity and South Asian Economic History

Problematic, Periodization, Processes, and Possibilities

Rajat Datta

For South Asian history, the period between the mid-sixteenth century and the 1830s conventionally gets clubbed into the ambiguous and historiographically challenged rubric of 'medieval' history. This owes mainly to the enduring obsession of most historians writing from within the subcontinent with treating the term 'medieval' as equivalent to an Indo-Persian political system that stretched from the thirteenth century to the eighteenth. The thought of breaking it up into discrete components and tagging these to a different schema of periodization generates an anxiety which almost borders on hysteria. Since Meena Bhargava and Pratyay Nath, the editors of this volume, have extensively critiqued the notion of the medieval, this chapter will not get into the issue, except to say that the standard literature on this is overwhelmingly fiscal, with static parameters. This has resulted in an idiosyncratic analytical trap. While severe social inequalities and sharp conflicts in society are recognized, they are posited within a surprising degree of changelessness in the larger context. The critical variable influencing change or otherwise is assigned to cycles of state formation – one in the thirteenth and fourteenth centuries, and the second in the sixteenth and seventeenth centuries. Both the cycles are determined by the ability or inability of the state to refine its tax-assignment systems. While this fiscal drive tended to maximize appropriation and hence fall regressively on the poorest in the countryside, it did so while subverting 'superior cultivation' as well as simultaneously increasing the distance between the rural rich and poor.[1] Stasis is implicit in this model because it ascribes one single cause to explain the same sort of change over six centuries. This remains by far the most structurally coherent overview of what I call the seamlessness of the medieval in Indian history. The more things changed, the more they remained the same in this framework, because the nature of the state is assumed to have remained the same through more than half a millennium. However, historians of this disposition use terms like 'Mughal India', 'late medieval India', or 'late pre-colonial India' as a nod to some unexplained difference after the sixteenth century;

nevertheless, they land up projecting South Asia as unique, exotic, and somehow detached from global history.

We need a different characterization, namely the 'early modern', as a way of breaking out of this idea of seamlessness. Perhaps convinced that the term 'early modern' is driven by overtly Eurocentric considerations, this category has usually not been a part of the works of Indian historians while thinking of the periodization of South Asian history.[2] This chapter reflects on the appropriateness of this category in analysing the political economy of India roughly between the sixteenth and early nineteenth centuries. It contends that this period saw several features which retained their coherence over the long term, and which essentially differed from the previous three centuries even though they were derived from them. At a general level, modernity need not necessarily always be about birthing the new; it can also be about *how old things*, even cultural practices, *are done differently* to suit new circumstances, as well as introducing new practices to suit the old. The introduction of tobacco, chilies, or European languages in sixteenth-century India and their dissemination into the cultural practices of diet, consumption, and communication come to mind as examples of such newness and continuities. This chapter explores *four P*s: *problematic, periodization, processes*, and *possibilities*. The major explanation I offer to highlight the differences of these centuries for South Asia focuses on some critical economic changes which characterized them.

Problematic

In spite of the traditional historiographical conservatism, the notion of early modernity as a period in Indian history has begun to touch the shores of India's historiographical insularity. This term has emerged as a counterpoint to the static and moribund notions of a medieval that stretches though a millennium before the eighteenth century. In an earlier attempt, John Richards explicitly rejected the term 'early modern' as Eurocentric and argued instead that it was merely 'an attempt to capture the reality of rapid, massive change in the way humans organized themselves and interacted with other human beings and with the natural world'. It was in this sense that he applied the category in the South Asian context.[3] Sanjay Subrahmanyam looked at geographical explorations redrawing and re-imagining the world by opening up new frontiers. At the socio-economic levels, he emphasized the heightened struggles between the sedentary and pastoral modes of economic activity. At the level of polities, he drew our attention to the development and use of the ideology of universal sovereignty by many monarchs and the wide spread of millenarian beliefs across societies.[4] Richard Barnett saw early modernist historians as revisionists who were responding to the growing evidence of continuity of local and regional economic growth, ecological pragmatism, and political realism of entrepreneurial activity indigenous to India. For him, the new historiographical impetus freed itself from Eurocentric, Mughal-centric, and essentialist viewpoints in terms of periodization.[5]

These interventions caution us against the two related pitfalls – Eurocentrism (or, European exceptionalism as an immanent given) and teleology.[6] Instead, the emphasis is on systems which ought to be more scrupulously seen as interconnected 'multiple modernities'.[7] In its west European context, 'early modern' refers to a complex of traits to include coherent national units, increased rationality, growing literacy, urbanization, denser market relations, as well as the rise of ideas about individualism, self-interest, and privacy. Many of these now appear overdrawn, over-emphasized, and anachronistic. On the question of the coherence of the early modern state in Europe, for instance, the evidence is riddled with ambiguities. Conflicts between the state and powerful landed gentries enjoying power though intricate webs of familial connections were endemic; and the state could only function through a web of patronage and clientage which stretched from the royal courts to the local communities.[8] As Daniel Nexon argues, sixteenth-century Europe was made up of 'segments of dynastic agglomerations' which were incorporated by dynastic rulers 'via conquest, or dynastic unions' but who could only hold them 'through distinctive contracts that either pre-existed their incorporation or were negotiated as conditions for compliance with resource and military demands'.[9] Another overview of early modern Europe reveals that

> ... existing political structures put more limits on the level of actual control even the most 'absolute' monarch could impose.... Civil law, which regulated the private relations between individuals in such matters as inheritance and the exchange of property, was based on custom, as well as written codes, and thus was nearly impossible for monarchs to change.[10]

Was European agriculture more advanced or more efficiently organized during this period? The answer is largely in the negative. As I have argued elsewhere, at least the yield ratios in Europe do not overwhelmingly suggest that. They ranged from a measly 4:1 in seventeenth-century Poland, 5:1 in Germany, and about 10:1 in eighteenth-century Netherlands and England. Agricultural surpluses were often uncertain, and in most of the continent, except in the more urbanized areas like the Low Countries and parts of England, they depended on the vagaries of the harvest and the plethora of feudal dues, rents, and tithes. The effect of the urban pull (except in close proximities of major towns in England and in the Low Countries) on this remains uncertain, as the urban population in the more advanced areas of northern Europe was about 8 per cent, which marked an increase by 4 per cent in the 150 years between 1600 and 1750.[11]

For Lieberman, the period between the ninth and early nineteenth centuries across Eurasia was of 'lurching' changes, broadly

> ... driven by a synergistic mix of material expansion, wider cultural circulation, interstate warfare, and the deliberate and unintended effects of state actions. All served to enhance the attractive and coercive potential of privileged cores, to reduce the autonomy of local centers, to pacify rural society, and to spin webs of economic and cultural inter-dependence. Most basically, material expansion ... agrarian and commercial growth as well as the post-1500 diffusion of firearms, magnified the physical superiority of emergent political cores.[12]

Did South Asia not witness similar (but not mimetic) changes? Whatever the variations, one aspect is now clear – there were no exclusive cultural preconditions enjoyed by Europe which were not available to other regions across the Eurasian landmass. As Jack Goody has persuasively argued, many of the so-called European-specific cultural traits of modernity (rationality and an embedded individuality, for instance) existed elsewhere in equal measure before the 'triumph' of capitalism in Europe. Also, much of the rationality of European economic behaviour, including the so-called propensity of technological maximization, was derived from the cumulative *longue duree* of global economic intersections since the first millennium CE, if not earlier.[13] If European modernity was derivative, then the question is what sort of anterior modernity (or modernities) did western Europe manage to latch onto and then redirect that to suit its own ends? Answers to this question will emerge from the ways in which we assess the period between the fourteenth and the eighteenth centuries, but with a sixteenth to eighteenth century global core.

In Jack Goldstone's schematic framework for this period, the great arc from Japan to Ottoman Turkey via India and Southeast Asia displayed various combinations of features which also prevailed in contemporary Europe – agro-commercial expansion, urbanization, global trade networks, dynamic mercantile classes, and increasingly bureaucratized political regimes.[14] Such views are in concordance with some recent revisions in global economic history that have reassessed the economic transition between the sixteenth and eighteenth centuries from the perspective of non-European – particularly Asian – societies, notwithstanding the likes of David Landes and Eric Jones, who would push in the direction of European exceptionalism. The current historiographical reassessments 'provincialize' Europe by positing a relatively backward Europe compared to the Asian giants, particularly China. The revisionists include a formidable list of economic and social historians.[15] The revisions range from the scaling down of average growth rates in 'modernizing' Europe before 1870 – even then at only around 2 per cent per annum – to a lifting of the ceilings of the neo-Malthusian cycles that had stood as the main motor of pre-industrial economic development.[16] For Kenneth Pomeranz, no matter how far back we may push the origins of capitalism in general, industrial capitalism, in which the large-scale use of inanimate energy allowed an escape from the common constraints of the pre-industrial world, only emerged in the 1800s to set the context of the 'great divergence'. Anything prior to that was coeval or even in favour of Asia than Europe.[17]

How have these views changed the perspective about South Asia? From the standpoint of Asian historiography, the answer to this question is that while there is a growing body of literature in this direction, there is still a long way to go before one can speak of a genuine comparative economic history from an Asian perspective. However, from a civilizational perspective, K. N. Chaudhuri has traced four points of unity within Asia before 1750: first, unity in the 'ground floor' of material life; second, the unity of a commonly shared space by four separate civilizational identities – Islamic, Indic, South East Asian, and Chinese; third, certain unifying principles of economic production strongly oriented towards agriculture and agro-commercial production, which tended to maximize the production of cereals; and fourth, 'the interaction between the long-term and the random, between events and tendencies'.[18]

However, most historians studying Asian regions agree upon certain common trajectories in Asian economies, particularly shared experiences of precocious economic growth, followed by colonial subordination in the nineteenth century. Looking at the comparative history of commercial developments in China and Japan in the seventeenth century, William Atwell states that the 'boundaries between national and international history in early modern East Asia were far from clear cut'.[19] Sanjay Subrahmanyam sees a similar process of convergence – albeit with an appropriate time lag – between South Asia, West Asia, and Southeast Asia, in economic expansion, commercialization, fiscal intermediation, and relations between state and society.[20]

Several processes which can be highlighted for this period in South Asian history are comparative and convergent at regional and global levels. While the medieval was characterized by relative localism, early modernity comprised rapid circulation of people, commodities, technologies, and ideas. Economic expansion, new maritime connections, the availability of New World gold and silver, and the rise of a truly connected world economy to which exports from South Asia contributed hugely, were some of the shared developments. The rapid growth in population everywhere, the clearing of forests, intensification of land use and expansion of cultivation, and the diffusion of several new technologies, including introduction of crops from the New World, especially chillies and tobacco, were further forms of such connections.

Therefore, to me the notion of early modernity invokes two related issues – commensurability and convergence on a global scale. Instead of a linear narrative, early modernity invokes an idea of convergent and multipolar modernities. Britain's emergence does provide a universalizing history of European modernity, as Holland, which had witnessed precocious growth in the seventeenth and eighteenth centuries, began slipping in the nineteenth, and the Iberian Peninsula had already exited from this race. Divergences began to arise since the nineteenth century, but this is an aspect not dealt with in this chapter.

Periodization

So, what do all these issues indicate about periodization? First, the term 'early modern' is not used as a definitive 'stage' of development; once it is rid of its European exceptionalism, it becomes uncoupled from any *a priori* (also teleological) history of capitalism (in a Marxian sense), which had characterized a periodization of history oriented towards a model of modern world economy. Second, the category of early modern invokes a sense of global interconnections and thus opens the possibility of a universal periodization prior to the nineteenth century, one which bypasses the ancient–medieval–modern triptych of the European Enlightenment. At the material level, the notion of early modernity invokes coevalness over a long period of about three centuries. It forces us to rethink modernity not as an inevitable western phenomenon (with Japan as an exception, thrown in for good measure) but something which had a more contested emergence, was regionally heterogeneous, and was a product of conjunctural processes, rather than some innately structural superiority.

In order to better understand this issue of periodization, and why the centuries between the sixteenth and the early nineteenth deserve a new nomenclature, one has to keep in mind some fundamental macro-level developments which occurred in various regions of South Asia during this time. Matching the global tendency of the growth of large, stable states that attained size, efficiency, and territorial reach not seen since antiquity, South Asia witnessed the rise of the Mughal Empire. It established its suzerainty over nearly the entire subcontinent for the first time since the Mauryas. In terms of scale and wealth, the empire compared favourably with the contemporary Ottoman and Safavid empires and with any state in Europe. Confronted with the greatly increased costs of firearms, states turned their attention to improving their land-tax assessment and collection. Administrative stability necessitated greater efficiency, increased availability of credit, and systematic record-keeping. Mercantile groups in possession of capital, as well as those who had skills like calligraphy, writing, and accounting, rose in social importance in this environment. Competing regional states as well as European trading companies required their skills, enabling the rapid ascent of revenue farmers, bankers, merchants, and scribes. In this setting, the period witnessed the emergence of new social groups in South Asian society, especially of scribal and commercial communities.

Cultural pluralism was a hallmark of these centuries, and this added further diversity to indigenous societies that were already heterogeneous. The hallmark of the early modern state was its pluralism, a product of its need to strike a balance between the needs of denominational and popular variants of Islam, a majority Hindu community deeply rooted in its Sanskritic traditions, the syncretic religious and cultural traditions of diverse ethnic communities, and diasporic communities of Christians, Jews, and Parsis, whose voices and aspirations were heard and met by emperors with an amazing degree of equanimity. Through a continuous process of fusion and synthesis, Indic and Islamicate traditions came together to produce a cosmopolitan world in both imperial and regional settings. The declining influence of any one religion on the imperial governments and the reflection of this incorporative polity on art, architecture, music, and other cultural productions characterized the period in the South Asian context.[21] Also evident was the simultaneous growth of Persian as the new cosmopolitan language alongside vernacular literary and aesthetic forms that regional elites cultivated as they sought to develop local idioms for the expression of their authority.[22] The spread of mystic and devotional movements was linked to these developments. In this context, the trajectory of developments in South Asia seems at variance from its European counterparts where the processes of homogenization rather than diversification and pluralism appear more pronounced.

Overall, there can be no doubt that things were different in India after the sixteenth century. Some of these differences were an aggregative expansion in production, growth of fiscal-military state apparatuses, the diversification of mercantile activities, growing sophistication of peasant and artisan production systems, massive percolation of a cash nexus, and the emergence of a cultural world characterized by pluralist ecumenism. The sixteenth century ended the 'medieval' and ushered India into a global world of early modernity, a process which continued till the end of the eighteenth century – some would argue even up to the 1830s – before it was finally turned around and incorporated into colonial modernity.

These broad features could develop because of the changing components of the region's political economy in this period. The constituents of this were private property in land, along with a vibrant market in land and in rights over land, and a shift from the informal to the contractual in matters of economic and fiscal transactions. A favourable land–labour ratio made it possible to concentrate agricultural production in lands of high intrinsic fertility and, in turn, to get higher yields per acre than in the nineteenth century. The agricultural systems were complex, with most lands producing two harvests (*do fasla*) and some producing three (*sih fasla*) or more crops per year. This was accompanied by a major increase in the variety of agricultural products, and in the quantum of the agrarian surplus, owing to the introduction and quick dissemination of a whole range of food and cash crops from the New World after the sixteenth century. Several primary and intermediate cities, interwoven by network of supply lines, flourished, and a substantially large percentage of almost 15 per cent of the population lived in such places. The countryside saw commercialized production and manufacturing. Most of the producers produced at least part of the time for a market, while some – probably along the coast and closer to primate cities – produced primarily for it. The economy also received a massive injection of silver bullion from the New World, leading to a phenomenal expansion of money circulation and monetization. This occurred alongside pervasive cash-based exchanges based on a trimetallic monetary system (gold, silver, and copper currencies) and backed up by elaborate (subcontinental) networks of sophisticated financial institutions. Key roles under these circumstances were played by specialized communities of merchants, each of whom were engaged in a distinctive branch of trading or double-ended money ventures with local economies as well as with the European trading companies. All this functioned in conjunction with a political system in which the elite consumed their incomes in urban areas or hypothecated in advance to a class of specialized rural bankers and moneylenders who often farmed such revenue assignments.

Processes

There are three aspects of the economy which I want to specifically discuss, as these have a direct bearing on the economic framework I intend to construct for this period. These are issues of monetization, rural production systems, and prevalence of a rural demand for non-agricultural goods.

The issue of monetization is quickly resolved as there is an enormous literature testifying to its uniqueness and magnitude. The sixteenth century was a period when the world simultaneously started using more money. This expansion was not European in origin, though Europe contributed enormously to it.[23] Practically all states from Japan in the east to England in the west were engaged in major fiscal reforms or were facing some sort of financial strain trying to match mounting expenses with stationery incomes around this time.[24] The reasons for the global demand for silver were perhaps more Asian than European. Europe, particularly the Iberian Peninsula, became crucial in adding massive quantities of silver and gold to the global fund of precious metal during the seventeenth and eighteenth centuries. Nor can it be said that Europe was using more money than the Eurasian economies in the sixteenth and seventeenth centuries. Out of the silver that Europe extracted from the New World every year, at least 40 per cent found its way to Asia, particularly to China and India.[25] In any case, the relationship between the regions at the vanguard of the discoveries in New World silver and the productive or money-using capacities of European economies was never a direct one. Spain hardly invested the treasure it acquired in the development of its economy, losing sometimes as much as 40 per cent of its American wealth directly to the Philippines.[26] On the other hand, regions, like England and Holland, which became the epicentres of Europe's economic expansion, hardly engaged in the colonial extraction of bullion. France, for instance, was scarcely affected by the excitement of New World silver – gold was never used. Even silver coinage was sometimes too strong a currency; billon currency circulated sluggishly.[27]

There is no doubt about India's importance in this global redistribution of bullion. The region that compares with this is China, which by all accounts received the lion's share from predominantly two sources – the New World and Japan.[28] India, on the other hand, received silver in a multilateral system of exchange from a whole range of sources in which there was a very important Asian component. In fact, the amount of bullion which arrived in India from Asian countries during the sixteenth through seventeenth centuries is said to have been excess of what was being sent from Europe, a pattern which changed late in the eighteenth century. Contrary to Immanuel Wallerstein's belief, the imported bullion, particularly the silver, was not hoarded (though, some of it, particularly gold, may have been hoarded).[29] Most of the bullion was immediately converted into money because precious metals were a medium of exchange for commodities received. Their circulation was vital in ensuring continuity in the investment and procurement of exportable commodities, including food grains. Thus, each additional unit of bullion brought into the economy resulted in an increment in India's overseas trade and was immediately converted into money to enable merchants to raise the necessary purchasing power.

There was a significant impact of silver inflows on India's economy. First, this enabled the fiscal refinements of the Mughal state. As the Mughal imperial frontiers advanced, so did the boundaries of India's silver-guzzling systems. It was additionally transforming the fiscal bases of the Mughal state, making it possible for them to extract and redistribute enormous amounts in silver currency.[30] Revenue, commercial deals, even workers' wages, came to be recorded and transacted in silver rupees.[31] Secondly, there was a phenomenal expansion in minting activity. Between 1576 and 1705, Mughal mints each year coined over 150 tonnes of silver in order to maintain an exceptional metallic purity of the currency.[32] Thirdly, there was a major expansion in the activities of bankers and money dealers throughout the length and breadth of the subcontinent, as is testified by the following description of a French traveller, Jean Baptiste Tavernier. In the early seventeenth century, he noticed that 'a village must be very small indeed if it has not a money-changer, called *shroff*, who acts as a banker to make remittances of money and issue letters of exchange (*hundi*)'.[33] In the same period, European currencies suffered periodic bouts of debasement, leading to severe short-term increases in the price of goods. Even China could not escape this fate in the seventeenth century. Yet the silver currency of Mughal India was never debased between 1556 and 1707, not even during the massive monetary crisis which convulsed much of Eurasia in the mid-seventeenth century.[34]

On the question of rural production systems, I draw upon some of my findings from Bengal. Though towns like Qasimbazar (in present-day West Bengal) or Dhaka (the capital of present-day Bangladesh) continued to function as centres of high production, there was a dispersion of production centres all over the countryside. The production of cotton textiles spread out of its primary zones around Nadia in the west and Dhaka in the east to Lakshmipur and Chittagong on the eastern fringes, to Bishnupur in the west, and to Medinipur on the southwestern edges of the province. Silk manufacture spread out of the core area – the Murshidabad–Qasimbazar axis – to cover large areas of Rajshahi in the north and Bishnupur in the west.[35] The expansion of overseas trade also introduced a greater diversification of production. The production of new commodities like indigo and opium expanded rapidly. Between 1740 and 1828, production centres of indigo mushroomed all over central and north-western Bengal, whereas opium cultivation took roots in the northern and north-western margins of the province. This meant that non-agricultural production tended to gravitate substantially to the rural areas. Contemporary evidence indicates that depending on the commercial importance of a locality, between 27 per cent and 15 per cent of the people living in Bengal's villages were artisans. Rangpur had a concentration of 207 artisans per square mile of territory at the turn of the eighteenth century.[36] There was thus a new consolidation of the rural economy and its intensive commercialization.

Rural developments were matched by developments at the intermediate – 'rurban' – levels. Much over northern and eastern India, a salient feature of the early modern reconfiguration seems to have occurred in the changing nature of these rurban settlements that were called *qasba*. Between the thirteenth and eighteenth centuries, these transited from being outlier garrison towns to becoming commercial centres and often commercial-cum-administrative centres of local gentries and traders.[37] In Bengal, the spatial equivalent of the north Indian *qasba* was the *muffassal*.[38] This kind of development was not limited to South Asia. As Suraiya Faroqhi shows, in the Ottoman Empire too, small towns emerged as marketing centres for taxes collected in grain. They also grew along transit routes and caravanserais. In an empire whose revenues came mainly from agriculture, markets were an essential means of transforming produce into money. In the words of Faroqhi, 'while not all markets turned into towns, many of them did so'.[39]

On the question of rural demand for non-agricultural (that is, commercial and industrial) goods, the expansion of production centres in the countryside resulted in movements in that direction. Evidence from Bengal indicates that peasants could procure 'industrial' goods like 'threads, coarse weaving cloths, mats made of split bamboos, brass and cassie (tutenag) plates, kodallies (spades), ploughs, plough shares and ruts for winding threads' from merchants who brought these to the villages, often on boats during the seasonal inundations of its rivers.[40] The requirement of so-called industrial goods in the countryside would also be a function of demand, not merely from the artisanal sectors, but from a whole range of consumers. Detailed lists available show that landed proprietors maintained large households and officials. In addition, there were occupational groups like the *putwa*s (silk-worm breeders), *tanti*s (weavers), *chotoor*s, (carpenters), *chassar*s (silk winders), *moochi*s (cobbler), *kasari*s (brass-makers), *sonar*s (goldsmiths), *shroff*s (moneychangers), *bania*s (traders), and the literate-cum-ritual gentry, like the brahman and the *maulvi* (learned Muslim teacher or doctor of Islamic law).[41]

Such evidence of rural occupational groups living in close proximity should not lead to any erroneous notion of these villages as 'little republics' or relatively self-sufficient entities. The relationships between occupational groups in villages were mediated by a variety of non-monetized and monetized modes of remuneration. The evidence of the existence of *shroff*s at the village level serves to highlight the commercial dynamics embedded in the rural economy.[42] Likewise, while local consumption requirements in villages were often met from local resources, a range of external goods had to be brought in linking merchants operating from the nodal *qasba* through an interconnected network of intermediaries to the village market (*haat*) level.⁴³ The important aspect of this period is the evidence that such networks were solidifying across regions, except perhaps in the most inaccessible parts. Even here, trade existed as can be seen from the following testimony of Abul Fazl regarding the trade between the mountains and plains in the province of Awadh *c.* 1580:

> From the northern mountains quantities of goods are carried on the backs of men, of stout ponies and of goats, such as gold, copper, lead, musk, tails of the *kutas* cow [the yak], honey, *chuk* (an acid composed of orange juice and lemon boiled together), pomegranate seed, ginger, long pepper, majith [producing a red dye] root, borax, zedoary, wax, woollen stuffs, wooden ware, hawks, falcons, black falcons, mertins, and other articles. In exchange they carry back white and coloured cloths, amber, salt, asafoetida, ornaments, glass and earthen ware.⁴⁴

Possibilities

The picture of the Indian economy squares well with the broad economic contours of the most advanced areas of Europe and Eurasia in the period under focus. The features outlined by Jan de Vries and Van der Voude for the early modern Dutch economy – the most advanced among contemporary European economies around this time – can be applied with some modifications to India in this period.⁴⁵ Markets, for both commodities and the factors of production (land, labour, capital), were reasonably free and pervasive. Agricultural productivity was adequate to support a complex social and occupational structure that made possible a far-reaching division of labour. The state, despite its extractive profile, was paternalistic, attentive to property rights, anxious about – but not opposed to – movements of people, and not indifferent to the material conditions of life of most inhabitants. Finally, there existed a level of technology and organization capable of sustained development and of supporting a material culture of sufficient variety to sustain market-oriented consumer behaviour.

The question is, in a processual sense, what do I make of all this growth? Is there a globally compatible economic framework for these centuries, which, even if derivative, can be applied to explain South Asian economic history in a comparative and convergent fashion? Some derivativeness is unavoidable. As Shmuel Eisenstadt and Wolfgang Schluchter remark, 'we cannot avoid western concepts, but we can make them flexible, so to speak, through differentiation and contextualization. Such an attempt entails developing diverse perspectives in order to analyse these civilizations and encourage an intercultural dialogue between them'.[46] With this caveat in place, I suggest some possibilities and tentative combinations.

First, the patterns exhibited by the early modern Indian economy can be studied with reference to two global growth models – one of the 'extensive' kind, and the other of the 'Smithian' kind. In the extensive growth framework, productivity and output grow quantitatively as functions of either demographic or territorial expansion, or both. These are not accompanied by commensurate, or very slow, changes in inputs like capital or new technologies, thus leaving land and labour as the two factors to influence growth.[47] The other model is of the 'Smithian' kind, where growth is driven by increased specialization caused by the geographical expansion of markets. As markets expand, each site can specialize more in the production of one good and purchase other goods from specialized producers at another site. 'Smithian' growth also occurs when returns from specialized economic activities produce higher productivity and, hence, higher per capita incomes per capita as well as total growth. These can come from specialization across different societies that accompany increased long-distance trade, from regional, or urban or rural, specialization accompanying increased domestic trade and urbanization, or from increased occupational specialization accompanying expanding population density and local circulation of goods and services.[48]

Problem arises if we expect 'Smithian' growth to be reproduced on a national scale in a land so large and as diverse as India. All these processes, in some form or the other, can be documented in India at the level of regional economies by incontrovertible evidence of the steady and incremental supply of precious metals through a massive increase in the export trade from various regions, the accretion and densification of market places, the accelerating pace of occupational specialization among artisans, and the intensification of inter-regional diversification among markets (like raw cotton being sourced from the Deccan for Bengal's cotton manufactories).

The situation was not substantially different even in the most advanced economies of north-western Europe in this period. The market-driven growth of 'core areas' in western Europe during the preceding centuries was real enough and was undoubtedly one crucial precursor of industrialization, but it was probably 'no more conducive to industrial transformation than the very similar processes of commercialization and "proto-industrial" growth occurring in various core areas in Asia'. The patterns of scientific and technical development that were taking shape in early modern Europe 'did not by themselves guarantee that Western Europe would wind up on a fundamentally different economic path from, for instance, East Asia'.[49] One can thus justifiably claim that the economic frame of reference for early modern India would be the combined existence of 'extensive' with 'Smithian' growth with some sectoral propensities (in textiles, for instance) to move from the former to the latter.

However, both situations have some ingrained limitations. In a situation characterized by extensive growth, population and total output grow in tandem, so that per capita incomes become stationary or may even decline in an inflationary situation. In India, low wages, very small technological changes, and low subsistence thresholds would suggest such possibilities. Yet, as Tirthankar Roy suggests, despite the income differentials between the two, the average peasant in the province of Bengal was in no way poorer than their European counterparts in terms of income. On the point of caloric adequacy, the Bengali peasant was as well-placed as their counterparts in Europe and the Yangtze Delta in the mid-eighteenth century.[50] In another study, Prasannan Parthasarathi has argued that household incomes of agricultural workers in southern India could be four times higher than subsistence requirements and that weavers' wages were comparable with – if not higher than – that being earned by European weavers.[51] On the other hand, in the 'Smithian' model, there is no automatic technological improvement to a new threshold; gains can therefore remain modest, to be quickly counterbalanced by population growth, and may cease when specialization, trade, or density in a given society reaches a plateau.[52] The point is that such bottlenecks were not exclusive to Asian societies alone. Economic disparities and growth-demography scissors operated in Europe too.[53]

Conclusion

By all accounts, South Asia recorded very impressive and uninterrupted economic growth over two centuries. It certainly appears superior in many respects to what Europe was undergoing in the same period. It paralleled China, which in the same period witnessed rapid agricultural specialization and commercialization, steady expansion in the handicraft sector, a significant increase in the volume of interregional trade, and monetization on an apparently massive scale.[54] Japan, the so-called Asian 'exception', exhibited the same features of economic growth – commercialized agriculture and expanding handicraft production, accompanied by burgeoning urban and monetary growth.[55] The question is: were Europe, and tangentially Japan, surging ahead than South Asia? This seems quite unlikely, as it is clear that in Japan's case, as in the case of contemporary Europe as well as South Asia, these tendencies were achieved in farming and manufacturing primarily by the use of human labour, and all had developed, within the confines of their own conditions, rational and sensible ways to manage resources.[56]

Early modern Europe did not comprise economies undergoing revolutionary transformations. There is little to suggest that western Europe's economy had decisive advantages earlier then, either in its capital stock or economic institutions, that made industrialization highly probable there and unlikely elsewhere.[57] Instead of a 'dramatic' break, early modernity in the field of economy in Europe showed an 'organic continuity with the later middle ages', except in two areas: first, an absolute and relative increase in the use of money and, second, population growth in conjunction with a higher degree of urbanization.[58] This was also the case in South Asia. Recent revisions in European economic history show a very moderate economic growth, even in the most economically advanced places. What is indicated instead is a gradual demographic upswing, a slow advance in the living conditions of people, and a better fund of consumption goods, especially from the New World and from the tropics.[59] The early modern period in Europe was a transitional age when the structures of the 'medieval' were still alive, though changes were slowly occurring that eventually led to others, but there was no inevitability about them. They were also slow as they staggered over five centuries or so. The greater part of the European economy retained its feudal and agrarian character for a long time. Manorial estates still provided the framework for working the arable, but within this traditional framework, some elementary forms of a market economy started operating through the growth of small market towns, monetization, and the attenuation of serfdom.

These slow changes over many centuries elicit a few cautionaries. First, we must use the term 'modern' with great care, and certainly not as a definitive stage of development, and also void it of its European exceptionalism. We also have to rid ourselves of any fascination with the British economic experience of the nineteenth century as a teleology. This means we must also use the term 'early modern' by uncoupling it from the history of a textbook kind of western capitalism. As Goldstone remarks, there is no universal 'pre-modernity'; rather, a 'wide range of societies with distinctive cultures and structures went through their own historical development over centuries before and after Western contact'.[60] An *a priori* understanding of modernity as *capitalist* modernity is no longer a model one needs to explain *pre-capitalist* (in a broad sense) forms of capitalism, or, to put it another way, forms of proto-capitalisms that emerged across Eurasia and South Asia in almost the same time in history.

From a comparative Asian perspective, it is thus possible to argue that modernities could assume different forms and could very well be non-capitalist in economic orientation; alternatively, they could be capitalist modernities but conceivably of *different types* of *capitalism*. European exceptionalism before the nineteenth century cannot be pushed beyond a point. The market-driven growth of core areas in western Europe during the preceding centuries, though visible in some respects, was probably no more conducive to industrial transformation than the very similar processes of commercialization and 'proto-industrial' growth occurring in various core areas in Asia.[61]

Second, the pitfall in comparative economic history is the assumption of national-level economic indicators to justify this search for a singular capitalist modernity, or its absence.[62] The first level of difference is that early modern empires, especially in the Asian part of Eurasia, were very significant in terms of the diversity of political, institutional, and cultural processes that they embodied. A look at South Asia will substantiate this. Ecological diversities facilitated distinct agrarian regimes, from wet rice agriculture in the high rainfall zones, to intermediate wheat zones, to millet zones in dry and semi-arid areas. Economic activities therefore ranged from high-density sedentarized agriculture and agropastoralism, to high nomadism, depending on the environmental conditions in which people found themselves.[63] Outside the agrarian sectors, the Mughals were repositories of multifarious social and cultural participants in the state, in commercial transactions, and in productive labour. Additionally, unlike contemporary European states, the early modern South Asian and Ottoman ones were redistributive of the imperial fiscal resources.[64] In India, there was also a massive expansion in oceanic trade far beyond what occurred, for instance, under the contemporary Ottoman Empire.[65] These enabled a deep monetization of the economy in South Asia, more extensive than in the Ottoman Empire,[66] through the circulation of cash. They also helped powerful and rich agro-commercial gentries to consolidate themselves in the regions. The regions were in turn deeply embedded in commercial networks of ascending scales and magnitude. Looking at these kinds of growth trajectories of India's economy in the seventeenth and eighteenth centuries in a global perspective holds the key for understanding the larger experience of early modernity here.

Third, the term 'early modern' brings in global interconnections. One is now able to see Indian history in a global economic context, the absence of which has been a singular failure of most of Indian historiography which is characterized in a large measure with an almost self-imposed insularity for much of the past till the advent of British colonialism. With the British conquest of Bengal in 1757, Indian historiography becomes frenetically engaged with a saga of India's incorporation in a world process as a subordinated entity. This traditional insularity needs to be broken by the insertion of the early modern into Indian historiography which, I submit, enables Indian history to become part of a wider global history *before* colonialism. The notion of early modernity also forces us to rethink the binary separations between medieval and modernity. At a conceptual level, it allows a reconceptualization of modernity as a phenomenon which had a more troubled emergence, was slower in its trajectory than is usually imagined, was geographically disparate even in its core areas, was a product of more convergent changes, and was not an immanent phenomenon somehow culturally embedded in the western ethos.

Notes

1. *The Cambridge Economic History of India,* vol. 1: *c. 1200–c. 1750*, ed. Irfan Habib and Tapan Raychaudhuri (Delhi: Orient Longman, 1982).
2. Here I refer to those who write on Indian history and generally reside in the country.
3. John F. Richards, 'Early Modern India and World History', *Journal of World History* 8, no. 2 (1997): 197–209.
4. Sanjay Subrahmanyam, 'Connected Histories: Notes towards a Reconfiguration of Early Modern Eurasia', *Modern Asian Studies* 31, no. 2 (1997): 735–762.
5. Richard Barnett (ed.), *Rethinking Early Modern India* (New Delhi: Manohar, 2002).
6. Victor Lieberman, 'What Strange Parallels Sought to Accomplish', *Journal of Asian Studies* 70, no. 4 (2011): 931–938.
7. S. N. Eisenstadt, 'Multiple Modernities', *Daedalus* 129, no. 1 (2000): 1–30.
8. Julia Adams, *The Familial State: Ruling Families and Merchant Capitalism in Early Modern Europe* (Ithaca: Cornell University Press, 2005); Peter Musgrave, *The Early Modern European Economy* (London: Macmillan Press, 1999), 95.
9. Daniel H. Nexon, *The Struggle for Power in Early Modern Europe: Religious Conflicts, Dynastic Empires and International Change* (Princeton: Princeton University Press, 2009), 83.
10. Mary Weisner-Hanks, *Early Modern Europe, 1450–1789* (Cambridge: Cambridge University Press, 2006), 288–289.
11. Rajat Datta, 'Before the Great Divergence: The Early Modern South Asian Agrarian Economy in a Global Perspective', in *China, India and Alternative Asian Modernities*, ed. Sanjay Kumar, Satya P. Mohanty, Archana Kumar, and Raj Kumar, 185–202 (London and New York: Routledge, 2019).
12. Lieberman, 'What Strange Parallels Sought to Accomplish', 932.
13. Jack Goody, *The East in the West* (Cambridge: Cambridge University Press, 1996).
14. Jack Goldstone, 'Efflorescences and Economic Growth in World History: Rethinking the West and the Industrial Revolution', *Journal of World History* 13, no. 2 (2002): 323–389.

15. See, for instance, Kenneth Pomeranz, *Before the Great Divergence: China, Europe and the Making of the Modern World Economy* (Princeton: Princeton University Press, 2000); Andre Gunder Frank, *ReOrient: Global Economy in the Asian Age* (Berkeley: University of California Press, 1998); R. Bin Wong, 'The Search for European Differences and Domination in the Early Modern World: A View from Asia', *American Historical Review* 107, no. 2 (2002): 447–469; Sevket Pamuk, 'Institutional Change and the Longevity of the Ottoman Empire, 1500–1800', *Journal of Interdisciplinary History* 35, no. 2 (2004): 225–247; Jack Goody, *The Eurasian Miracle* (Cambridge: Polity Press, 2000); Jack Goldstone, *Revolution and Rebellion in the Early Modern World* (Berkeley: University of California Press, 1991).
16. Randolph Starn, 'The Early Modernity Muddle', *Journal of Early Modern History* 6, no. 3 (2002): 296–307, see 306
17. Pomeranz, *Great Divergence*, 1–19.
18. K. N. Chaudhuri, 'The Unity and Disunity of Indian Ocean History from the Rise of Islam to 1750: Outline of a Theory and Historical Discourse', *Journal of World History* 4, no. 1 (1993): 1–21, see 8.
19. William S. Atwell, 'Some Observations on the "Seventeenth Century Crisis" in China and Japan', *Journal of Asian Studies* 55, no. 2 (1986): 223–244, see 237.
20. Sanjay Subrahmanyam, 'State Formation and Transformation in Early Modern India and South-East Asia', *Itinerario* 12, no. 1 (1988): 91–109.
21. For a comprehensive perspective of such plurality, see Harbans Mukhia, *The Mughals of India* (New Delhi: Blackwell Publishing, 2004).
22. Compare the following texts: Muzaffar Alam, *Language of Political Islam India, 1200–1800* (New Delhi: Permanent Black, 2005); Allison Busch, *Poetry of Kings: The Classical Hindi Literature of Mughal India* (New York: Oxford University Press, 2011).
23. John F. Richards (ed.), *Precious Metals in the Later Medieval and Early Modern Worlds* (Durham: Carolina Academic Press, 1983) was one of the earliest collections of seminal essays to explore the connection between global precious metals movements and money use.
24. Niels Steensgaard, 'Commodities, Bullion and Services in Intercontinental Transactions Before 1750', in *The European Discovery of the World and Its Economic Effects on Pre-industrial Society, 1500–1800: Papers of the Tenth International Economic History Congress*, ed. Hans Pohl, 9–23 (Stuttgart: F. Steiner, 1990), 19.
25. Ward Barrett, 'World Bullion Flows, 1450–1800', in *The Rise of Merchant Empires: Long-Distance Trade in the Early Modern World, 1350–1750*, ed. James D. Tracy, 224–254 (Cambridge: Cambridge University Press, 1990); Renate Pieper, 'The Volume of African and American Exports of Precious

Metals and Its Effects in Europe, 1500–1800', in *European Discovery of the World*, ed. Pohl, 113.

26. John J. TePaske, 'New World Silver, Castile and the Philippines, 1500–1800', in *Precious Metals*, ed. Richards, 425–446, see 434, 442–45.

27. Jean Meuvret, 'Monetary Circulation and the Use of Coinage in Sixteenth- and Seventeenth-Century France', in *Essays in European Economic History, 1500–1800*, ed. Peter Earle, 89–99 (Oxford: Clarendon Press, 1974).

28. One billion ounces of silver bullion apparently coursed through the Chinese economy every year, which allowed a massive improvement in the state's fiscal health. Kenneth G. Deng, 'A Critical Survey of Recent Research in Chinese Economic History', *Economic History Review* 53, no. 1 (2000): 1–28; Albert Feuerwerker, 'State and Economy in Late Imperial China', *Theory and Society* 13, no. 3 (1984): 297–326.

29. Immanuel Wallerstein, *The Modern World-System: Capitalist Agriculture and the Origins of the European-World Economy in the Sixteenth Century* (New York: Academic Press, 1974), 41.

30. John F. Richards, 'Mughal State Finance and the Premodern World Economy', *Comparative Studies in Society and History* 23, no. 2 (1980): 285–308; Frank Perlin, 'Money-use in Late Pre-colonial India and the International Trade in Currency Media', in *The Imperial Monetary System of Mughal India*, ed. J.F. Richards, 232–373 (Delhi: Oxford University Press, 1987).

31. Irfan Habib, 'A System of Trimetallism in the Age of "Price Revolution": Effects of the Silver Influx on the Mughal Monetary System', in *The Imperial Monetary System of Mughal India*, ed. John F. Richards, 137–170 (New Delhi: Oxford University Press, 1987), 153–155.

32. By comparison, French mints between 1631 and 1680 processed only 75 tonnes of silver per year. Shireen Moosvi, 'The Silver Influx, Money Supply, Prices and Revenue-Extraction in Mughal India', *Journal of the Economic and Social History of the Orient* 30, no. 1 (1987): 47–94, see 58.

33. Jean-Baptiste Tavernier, *Travels in India, 1676*, trans. V. Ball, ed. William Crooke, Indian edition (Delhi: DK Fine Art Press, 2007), 24.

34. Goldstone, *Revolution and Rebellion*. Also see Neils Steensnsgaard, 'The Seventeenth Century Crisis and the Unity of Eurasian History', *Modern Asian Studies* 24, no. 4 (1990): 683–697; Habib, 'A System of Trimetallism in the Age of "Price Revolution"'.

35. Based on Irfan Habib, *An Atlas of the Mughal Empire: Political and Economic Maps with Detailed Notes, Bibliography and Index* (Delhi: Oxford University Press, 1982), 46.

36. Rajat Datta, *Society, Economy and the Market: Commercialization in Rural Bengal, c. 1760–1800* (New Delhi: Manohar, 2000), 189–191.

37. Rajat Datta, 'The Rural–Urban Continuum and the Making of a Proto-Industrial Economy in Early Modern India: A View from the East', in *Cities in Medieval India*, ed. Yogesh Sharma and Pius Malekandathil (New Delhi: Primus, 2014).
38. The position of the *muffassal* was explained by the 1777 report of the Amini Commission in the following words: 'the head court of a zamindar is *sadar* with respect to the villages or *tarafs*, or subordinate parts of which it is composed, and is mofussil [*muffassal*] with respect to the *cutcherry* at Murshidabad or Calcutta'. The Amini Commission Report vide R. B. Ramsbotham, *Studies in the Land Revenue History of Bengal, 1769–1787* (Calcutta: Humphrey Milford, 1927), 109–111.
39. Suraiya Faroqhi, *The Ottoman and Mughal Empires: Social History in the Early Modern World* (London: IB Taurus, 2019), 164.
40. Oriental and India Office Collections, India Office Records, Proceedings of the Board of Revenue, Miscellaneous, Sayar, P/89/41, 15 April 1794.
41. Datta, *Society, Economy and the Market*, 189–190.
42. Datta, 'The Rural–Urban Continuum', 94–95.
43. B. R. Grover, 'An Integrated Pattern of Commercial Life in the Rural Society of North India during the Seventeenth and Eighteenth Centuries', *Proceedings of the Indian Historical Records Commission* 37 (1966): 121–153; Datta, 'The Rural–Urban Continuum'.
44. Abul Fazl, *The Āīn-i Akbarī*, vol. 2, trans. H. S. Jarrett (New Delhi: Low Price Publications, 2001), 183.
45. Derived and modified from Jan de Vries and Peter van der Woud, *The First Modern Economy: Success, Failure, and Perseverance of the Dutch Economy, 1500–1815* (Cambridge: Cambridge University Press, 1997), 721.
46. Shmuel N. Eisenstadt and Wolfgang Schluchter, 'Paths to Early Modernities: A Comparative View', *Daedalus* 127, no. 3 (1998): 1–18, see 15.
47. Derived from E. J. Jones, *Growth Recurring: Economic Change in World History* (Oxford: Oxford University Press, 1988).
48. Morgan Kelly, 'The Dynamics of Smithian Growth', *The Quarterly Journal of Economics* 112, no. 3 (1997): 939–964. For a discussion of Smithian growth in eighteenth-century England's textile production, see Prasannan Parthasarathi, *Why Europe Grew Rich and Asia Did Not: Global Economic Divergence, 1600–1850* (Cambridge: Cambridge University Press, 2011), 109–113.
49. Kenneth Pomeranz, 'Beyond the East–West Binary: Resituating Development Paths in the Eighteenth-Century World', *Journal of Asian Studies* 61, no. 2 (2002): 539–590.
50. Tirthankar Roy, 'Economic Conditions in Early Modern Bengal: A Contribution to the Divergence Debate', *Journal of Economic History* 70, no. 1 (2010): 179–194.

51. Parthasarathi, *Why Europe Grew Rich*, 42–45.
52. Kelly, 'The Dynamics of Smithian Growth'.
53. See, for instance, Carlo M. Cipolla, 'The Decline of Italy: The Case of a Fully Matured Economy', *Economic History Review* 5, no. 2 (1952): 178–187; John H. Eliot, 'The Decline of Spain', *Past and Present* 20, no. 1 (1961): 52–75; Henry Kamen, 'Decline of Spain. A Historical Myth?' *Past and Present* 81, no. 1 (1978): 24–50; Michael R. Weisser, 'The Agrarian Depression in Seventeenth Century Spain', *Journal of Economic History* 42, no. 1 (1982): 149–154.
54. Lee, 'East Asia in the Age of Global Integration', 18–19.
55. Chie Nakane and Shinzaburo Oishi, *Tokugawa Japan: The Social and Economic Antecedents of Modern Japan* (Tokyo: Tokyo University Press, 1990); Conrad Totman, *A History of Japan* (Oxford: Basil Blackwell, 2000), 231–236.
56. Thomas C. Smith, 'Farm Family By-employments in Pre-Industrial Japan', *Journal of Economic History* 29, no. 4 (1969): 687–715.
57. Pomeranz, *Great Divergence*; Goldstone, 'Efflorescences and Economic Growth in World History'.
58. Harry A. Miskimin, 'Agenda for Early Modern Economic History', *Journal of Economic History* 31, no. 1 (1971): 172–183.
59. Musgrave, *Early Modern European Economy*.
60. Jack Goldstone, 'The Problem of the "Early Modern" World', *Journal of the Economic and Social History of the Orient* 41, no. 3 (1998): 249–284, see 251.
61. Pomeranz, *Great Divergence*.
62. Pomeranz, 'Beyond the East–West Binary'.
63. David Ludden, *An Agrarian History of South Asia* (Cambridge: Cambridge University Press, 1999). Also see Ramya Sreenivasan, 'A South Asianist's Response to Lieberman's Strange Parallels', *Journal of Asian Studies* 70, no. 4 (2011): 983–993.
64. Huri Islamoglu, 'Modernities Compared: State Transformations and Constitutions of Property in the Qing and Ottoman Empires', *Journal of Early Modern History* 5, no. 4 (2001): 353–386; Dina Rizk Khoury, 'Administrative Practice between Religious and State Law on the Eastern Frontiers of the Ottoman Empire', *Shared Histories of Modernity: China, India and the Ottoman Empire*, ed. Huri Islamoglu and Peter C. Perdue, 46–74 (New Delhi: Routledge, 2009).
65. Faroqhi, *The Ottoman and Mughal Empires*, 263.
66. Faroqhi, *The Ottoman and Mughal Empires*, 100, 237.

6

Markers of the Early Modern

Ecology, State, and Society in Rajasthan

Mayank Kumar

Defining any historical era is a difficult task, mainly because historical processes are never linear; they crisscross, overlap, and exhibit contradictory tendencies. To further compound the problem, in addition to addressing the issue of periodization, we are dealing with the category of modernity in this volume. Both these notions – periodization and modernity – have extremely chequered histories. For South Asia, these terms carry considerable historical baggage and are prone to misappropriation.[1] One of the important components of the baggage, as pointed out in the introduction to this volume, is the tendency to evaluate Indian history with a Eurocentric approach. Following the conventional division of European history into the classical ancient, the dark medieval, and the rational modern, the Indian past too was categorized into the Hindu or ancient, Mohammedan or medieval, and British or modern periods. This categorization of Indian history along religious lines at the hands of British colonial administrator-historians restricted the evaluation of India's past in terms of other variables for a long time.[2] Departures towards the modern and the concomitant rupture from past has never been a straight path for any society. It is in response to these concerns that the category of early modernity has emerged in historical thinking in recent decades. However, expecting the beginning of the early modern condition in all the societies at the same time and in the same measure may also lead us into problematic territory. Every society went through different processes to the extent that even the most prominent features of early modernity manifested at different point of time in different places.[3] For much of the Indian subcontinent, the early modern condition in the field of political economy comprised the rise of the centralizing administrative machinery of the Mughal Empire during the sixteenth and seventeenth centuries. For Rajasthan, however, the arrival of early modernity was signified by transition from tribal kin-based political formations to centralized state apparatus in course of the seventeenth century.[4]

It should also be noted that conventional historiography on India between the sixteenth and eighteenth centuries has not accorded due importance to environmental factors.⁵ A plausible reason could be the kind of sources that historians have traditionally relied upon – Persian court chronicles and vernacular literary texts, which did not furnish a lot of information about environmental conditions. Even when administrative documents like village-level documents from the latter part of the seventeenth century became available at the Rajasthan State Archives, Bikaner, the focus of historical investigation remained largely on agrarian history. A close examination of these records, however, offers insights not only into the functioning of the state apparatus⁶ but also into the ways society negotiated nature and appropriated different types of natural resources.⁷ They also bear testimony to how people wrestled with environmental factors like adverse climatic conditions.

This chapter highlights the various markers of the early modern condition in South Asia by studying various polities in Rajasthan from the seventeenth and the eighteenth centuries. Broadly speaking, these markers comprised constant efforts of the state machinery to establish a centralized mechanism through which it could ensure the greatest possible appropriation of natural resources and social surplus.⁸ On the one hand, these efforts took the form of the construction of 'mega structures' to augment the irrigation potential of the region.⁹ On the other hand, the state showed increasing keenness on regulating the domestic and social lives of the subject population.¹⁰ The chapter begins with a broad survey of the region in question and the kinds of sources available for studying it. This is followed by three sections which examine different markers of the early modern. The first among these examines the nature and significance of intensive documentation of geographies and mapping of the resources – natural as well as human – that the state was interested in. The second section analyses the increasing expansion of state enterprise, especially the way it channelized natural drainage to support the expansion of agrarian environment. In time, this helped the agrarian sector emerge as the primary source of revenue, although pastoral activities remained important means of livelihood. The final thematic section studies various instances of intrusion of the state in the domestic affairs through juridical and social means.

Region and Sources

In terms of ecological conditions, Rajasthan cannot be termed as a homogeneous unit. The Aravalli Hills render north-western Rajasthan arid, whereas south-eastern Rajasthan remains semi-arid. In the absence of snow-fed rivers, most of the agrarian production has been dependent on the monsoon. Any delay or disruption in the monsoons resulted in drought and even famine during the period under focus, which could play havoc with the economy. The population density in the arid region of Rajasthan was meagre; pastoral activity, which dominated the socio-economic landscape, supplemented agricultural economy here. The practice of intermixing of crops was quite prevalent across the whole region.

However, the strategic location of Rajasthan between the ports on the western coast of the Indian subcontinent and the fertile plains of North India provided the region with a prominent position in trade networks. Despite the expansion of trans-oceanic trade after the coming of European trading companies in the Indian Ocean, the centrality of Rajasthan in the overland trade routes to Sind and Multan as well as West Asia did not diminish.[11] The landscape of the region was an additional factor in the flourish of this trade network. The general aridity, limited rains, and the absence of perennial rivers induced the movement of traders across Rajasthan round the year. Ecological factors thus facilitated the integration of the economy of the region with global commercial networks.

There is a wide range of official documents available for this period in the Rajasthan State Archives, Bikaner. These include local-level documents like *arzdasht*s (local petitions), revenue reports, *arhsatta*s (ledgers of receipts and expenditure), imperial directives issued by the *pargana* officials, and administrative manuals. The fact that these documents were written in the vernacular testify to the fact that the local vernacular had become the administrative language by the seventeenth century. These sources reveal the nature of official responses to various instances of natural distress. By implication, they also provide us glimpses into contemporary sociopolitical responses and concerns. The information from these documents supplements the information offered by literary and epigraphic sources of this period. The importance of these documents is not confined to the fact that they provide vital information to identify the various markers of the early modern condition; rather, the sheer fact that these documents were generated is in itself a definitive marker of this condition for this region.

Documenting Geography: Going beyond the Normative

One of the markers of the advent of early modernity in this region comprised state-driven initiatives towards extensive documentation of the landscape. Though landscapes were also described and documented earlier, one witnesses a major change in South Asia from the sixteenth century onward. Unlike earlier descriptions which usually followed normative-canonical narrative, depictions by authors like Abul Fazl for the Mughal Empire and Diwan Munhot Nainsi for the Marwar *pargana* now focused on a more realistic sketch of the landscape, often giving due considerations to those elements that were of strategic interest from the point of view of the state.

This point becomes clear in view of some instances drawn from seventeenth-century Rajasthan. Nainsi, the Revenue Minister of Marwar in the second half of seventeenth century, visualized Marwar as a political unit and described it accordingly. While compiling an administrative manual for the Marwar region, he described the landscape of Bikampur in great details. He listed, for instance, various ponds, their distance from Bikampur, and duration of availability of water in each waterbody.[12] His documentation indicates that the state did not neglect the non-agrarian areas of its realm; rather, it recorded its strategic significance carefully as a part of the intensive mapping of the landscape. In his documentation of the region, Nainsi mentioned various markers of landscape, especially rivers and mountains. While describing the river Banas, he recorded that it originates from a mountain named Jargara, which is 29 *kos* from Udaipur, and merges with the river Chambal in the Harauti region. Furthermore, Nainsi traced the course of the river with respect to major physical landmarks and villages. He also mentioned the nearby hills in order to locate the river in its larger geographical context. In documenting the pattern of village settlements in the region of Mewar, Nainsi showed a similar eye for detail by dividing them into three categories: those situated on hills, those located on a plateau, and the rest.[13] This concern for documenting the realms meticulously also manifested itself in other mediums. Neelima Vashishatha, for instance, makes an important observation that the painted depictions of landscape also became increasingly realistic during this period.[14]

Nainsi's documentation of landscape also reveals a larger understanding of society. For instance, he recorded that it was once suggested that land could be divided between Hardas and Sekhas on the basis of the grass it supported. Sekhas would take control of land which produced *karar* (*Dichanthium annulatum*), while the Hardas would get that which grew *bhurat* (*Cenchurus biflorus*).[15] This indicates that the nature of vegetation had emerged as a means of identifying different ecological zones by this time. Even the kind of grass grown in a particular region could become the basis of identification of land to be divided for political purposes.

Similarly, Nainsi documented that when Rao Jodha, a ruler of Marwar, defeated Rana Kumbha, a ruler of Mewar, it was decided that the land which sustained trees of *babool* (*Acacia nilotica*) would be bestowed to Marwar, whereas the land which grew *amla* (*Phyllanthus emblica*, or Indian gooseberry) would go to Mewar.[16] This not only bears out lose interactions between environment and sociopolitical life, but Nainsi's documentation of this also indicates an increasing awareness of this phenomenon at the state level. In sum, this increasing tendency of the state to chart out the realms and map its resources was something new for

Rajasthan in the seventeenth century. It revealed an increasing concern of the state to monitor and control the countryside for the sake of governance, something that needs to be recognized as a prominent marker of early modernity in this part of the world. I will return to this issue in the subsequent sections.

State Stretching Its Arms

This kind of extensive documentation of landscape helped states enumerate the potential resources they could harness. Water was the most limiting factor for agricultural production in Rajasthan. The supply of water by natural precipitation was meagre and sporadic. The long-term as well as the short-term variations in the climate and rainfall would often ruin the crops and dry up the fodder, making the living conditions difficult for the people. Recurrent droughts and famines could also result in bouts of peasant migration. All this necessitated political authorities to be accommodative in their attitude towards revenue realization and to extend necessary relief to safeguard their long-term interests. This suggests that the state of this period was making earnest efforts to directly communicate with the peasantry and involve itself in improving their conditions. If not by choice, then definitely under the compulsions of natural exigencies, the ruling elites were forced to secure the well-being of the peasantry, who provided the much-needed manpower for cultivation.[17] Similarly, by curbing the powers and privileges of intermediaries, polities of Rajasthan in the seventeenth and eighteenth centuries started becoming increasingly accommodative of the concerns of various sections of society who were engaged with economic activities.

Massive Investment for Greater Gains

Given the absence of perennial rivers and the erratic nature of rainfall, the state tapped into the only viable alternate option for making water resources available for the people – artificial methods of irrigation.[18] Since the sixteenth century, there were increasing efforts in Rajasthan to make optimal use of geographic features. For instance, given that the region received monsoon rains only for a couple of months, the state started making heavy investments in channelizing seasonal rivers to create big reservoirs of water. Such efforts had also been undertaken earlier both in Rajasthan in particular and in the Indian subcontinent in general. But what was different in the enterprises undertaken in the projects in the sixteenth through eighteenth centuries was the massive scale of investments and direct interventions by the highest decision-making authorities.[19] The tradition of building waterbodies can be seen in various parts of Rajasthan as well.[20] Apart from tanks located in the natural depressions, large waterbodies were constructed with the help of state intervention. The only precondition for this was a specific kind of topography – a hilly terrain leading to formation of narrow gorges. The gorges between two hills on either side offered an ideal location for the construction of an earthen dam, ultimately leading to the creation of a large waterbody, like a lake. A few prominent waterbodies that emerged since the sixteenth century include the Udaisagar built in 1564,[21] the Raj Summand constructed in Mewar between 1662 and 1675,[22] and the Manasagar excavated near Amber in the early eighteenth century.[23] Let us look closely at some of these. An embankment of Pichhola Lake, allegedly constructed by a Banjara at the end of the fourteenth century, was raised by Rana Udai Singh in 1560. The lake is about 2.5 miles long by 1.25 miles broad. It has an area of over one square mile and a capacity of holding 418 million cubic feet of water. In the middle of it stand the two island palaces – the Jagmandir and the Jagniwas. The former was built by Rana Jagat Singh I (r. 1628–1652) and the latter by Jagat Singh II (r. 1734–1751).[24] Another lake, Udaisagar, lies 8 miles east of Udaipur. It is 2.5 miles long by 1.5 miles broad; its area is about 2 square miles, and it drains 185 square miles of the land. The water is held up by a lofty dam of massive stone blocks, thrown across a narrow outlet between two hills, a little to the south of Debari at the eastern entrance to the Girwa or Udaipur valley. The embankment, built by Rana Udai Singh between 1559 and 1565, has an average width of 180 feet.[25]

Maharana Raj Singh (r. 1662–1680), a Sisodia Rajput ruler of the kingdom of Mewar, is credited with the construction of the Raj Summand by a eulogy posted on the embankment.[26] The Raj Summand is situated approximately 60 kilometres north by northeast of Udaipur. It is 3 miles long by 1.5 miles broad. Its catchment area is spread across 195 square miles and has an area that roughly covers three square miles. Its construction served to alleviate the sufferings of a starving population, even though the irrigation potential of this lake was restricted owing to the absence of any provisions for canals.[27] The tradition of development of big reservoirs by constructing a dam across a river or rivulet continued in Mewar in subsequent years. Later lakes are exemplified by the Jai Sammand, also known as Dheber Lake. It lies about thirty miles south-east of Udaipur and 969 feet above sea level. It receives the drainage of around 690 square miles and has an expanse of approximately twenty-one square miles. The earthen dam is 1252 feet long and 116 feet in height; its breadth at the base is seventy feet and at the top sixteen feet.[28]

There is evidence of the construction of dams for the Amber region as well. There exist a number of dams, with roughly similar designs and dating back to the eighteenth century or earlier. One of these is the Mansagar dam. It is located more than 1 mile to the northeast from the city of Jaipur. The tract that was eventually occupied by the lake was a marshy land earlier. It also formed the bed of a rivulet which, passing through a narrow gorge in the hills, used to flow towards the northeast. This rivulet called Darbhavati was dammed in 1735. In absence of any evidence pointing to the contrary, one might conjecture that the specialized knowledge related to the problem of dam-building, reflected in the basic design of the Mansagar dam, was an indigenous tradition.[29]

Nomenclatures as well as inscriptions on these massive structures reveal a lot about what can be called a marker of early modernity. The rulers who constructed the structures made lofty claims in these texts and declared absolute sovereign rights over territories across their realms. Due to the construction of large waterbodies, the possibilities of irrigation in the region increased greatly; the rulers took the entire credit for the resultant growth in agrarian production. Moreover, huge investments in the construction activities were also seen as an evidence of the superior capabilities of the ruling dynasty. As opposed to numerous land grants issued in the vernacular, the sites of these structures carried assertive eulogies of the rulers in Sanskrit. This shows a tendency of cultural appropriation of models of monarchical absolutism – a process that gradually became dominant across the various principalities of the region during this period.[30]

Agrarian Expansion and Administrative Interventions

Deeper and closer association of the landed nobility with the resources of the land was always a cause of concern for ruling dynasties. However, several changes emerged in the relationship between ruling dynasties and rural intermediaries in course of the sixteenth and seventeen centuries with greater integration of the various principalities of Rajasthan with the Mughal imperial agrarian-fiscal-military apparatus. This led to a greater centralization of the administrative machinery in the region, which represented a new historical phenomenon.[31] Without the ruling dispensation having a somewhat accurate account of the landscape as well as its natural and social resources, it was almost impossible for the state to exercise effective control over the landed nobility in earlier times. However, with the increasing generation of records of the resources and increasing independence from the intermediaries, there was a considerable centralization of power and authority even for the far-flung areas of the kingdom during this period.

*Arzdasht*s, or petitions written by the *amil*s, *faujdar*s, or other officials of the *pargana* to the ruler at Amber, provide us a peek into the communications that transpired between village-level officials and the office of the kings. These officials regularly reported to the ruling authorities about various revenue-related and administrative details of the areas under their control. *Arzdasht*s documented concerns of local officials and communities along with the responses and remedies. Since agriculture was the mainstay of the economy, the ruling dispensation was always eager to keep themselves updated about the status of agrarian production. For example, Amar Chand and Sahib Ram, *vakil*s of the Amber court, recorded that due to meagre but delayed rains till the month of Bhadava, only *moth* could be sown this year.[32] Similarly, Vakil Ajitdas and Man Ram informed the state that due to drought, not even *moth* could be sown this year.[33] Information regarding agrarian production helped central authorities reduce possibilities of corruption by the intermediaries. These documents also suggest that officials appointed by central authorities were given the task not only to extend the area under cultivation but also to ensure proper cultivation even in the eventualities of delayed rains. The fact that directives like these came directly from the royal court is a clear indication that the power of intermediaries was being reduced and centralization of power was on the ascent.

In the agrarian economy, the *bohra*s (moneylenders) constituted an important group of intermediaries. Generally, the *bohra*s were eager to extend loans to the peasantry. But when agriculture would be threatened by natural exigencies, they would refrain from providing loans. At times this would provoke intervention from the political authorities to ascertain that credit was made available. For instance, reports of widespread refusal by the moneylenders to provide loans in every *pargana* in 1731 led the *diwan* (financial offer) to issue instructions. They compelled the *bohra*s to advance half the grain that they had recovered in the previous *rabi* harvest as seed-loan to the peasants so that the *rabi* cultivation in the current year could commence.[34]

Moreover, the rulers in Rajasthan imposed several restrictions on the functioning of the *bohra*s on various occasions to redress the hardships faced by the peasantry owing to reduction in agricultural production. The general principle in regard to all loans – *tagai* as well as loans advanced by the *bohra*s – was that the debt incurred in the current harvest period had to be recovered immediately after the harvest or within the same fiscal year. Arrears on the older loans could only be demanded if the output of the current harvest was considered adequate. The state's attempt to discourage the recovery of old loans by the *bohra*s suggests that such loans were generally unrecoverable and therefore written off.[35] It was perhaps also driven by the awareness that excessive exploitation of peasantry would compel them to migrate and thereby erode the possibilities of revenue generation.

Such detailed documentation of agrarian relations was done with a purpose and this was reflected in day-to-day administration. Apart from the obvious use in land-revenue administration, we find society in general and the state in particular making use of the documented information. As discussed previously, the construction projects of the various artificial waterbodies were derived from this kind of information. The state was aware of the locational specificities of the land and the assessed land revenue that varied according to the nature of irrigation deployed by the peasants.[36] The differences in land-revenue rates also reflect this phenomenon. This further testifies to the fact that the state was making increasing use of documentation available at hand. Determination of land revenue according to the means of irrigation also testifies to the extent of intervention made by the ruling sections of the society during this period.

Documentation of ecological as well as sociopolitical conditions provided ample opportunities for the state to promote its agenda. While negotiating disputes over the use of water for irrigation purposes in the semi-arid climate, the political classes had the platform to promote their own interests. Rulers not only arbitrated on the issue of ownership of the means of irrigation but also issued directives on the amount of water to be distributed.[37] It is not surprising that most of the disputes over water uses were about illegal excavation of the canals and draining of the water by the peasantry for irrigation.[38] There is even evidence of the excavation of dams to secure water for irrigation. The state meted out appropriate punishments in such cases; the money collected as fine would be deposited in the exchequer.[39] At times, the state had to arbitrate between claimants over the use of irrigational devices.[40] It is interesting to also note that the political authorities would often expand the agricultural domain by digging new wells in the villages.[41]

Thus, what emerges is that one of the characteristics of the political economy of Rajasthan in the seventeenth and eighteenth centuries – that set it apart from the earlier times – was the expansion of the agricultural realm at the behest of state power as well as the state acquainting itself with and using various facets of the natural environment to further its agenda of politico-administrative centralization.

Taxation on Social Uses of Natural Resources

Unlike settled agricultural zones, pastoral communities were semi-nomadic and had well-developed 'networks of circulation of mobile wealth'.[42] Very crucial for the polities of frontier regions, this wealth, however, was difficult for states to tax. Nevertheless, with the advent of increasingly comprehensive documentation of their natural and human landscape, such taxation also gradually became possible.

Livestock-rearing communities were taxed on the basis of the number of families in the community or in terms of the number of kitchens they maintained. The tax of this latter kind was known as *dhuan bhachh* (smoke from the chimney of the kitchens). It was a poll tax and was realized from each household at the rate of one rupee. It was a major component of the *rokad-rakam* (non-agricultural taxes collected in cash) and contributed around 40 to 50 per cent of the total income of states. Similarly, another tax by the name of *talibab* was levied on non-agricultural communities at the rate of 4 rupees per family.[43] The rulers of Bikaner imposed an extra cess of eight *anna*s per camel load of goods brought to the kingdom by itinerant merchants for sale.

Recognizing the value of animal husbandry to the economy of the kingdoms, the rulers often intervened to regulate the usage of grass and fodder. It was mandatory, for instance, for the cultivators to share one-fourth of the grass produced by them with the state.[44] Moreover, there is considerable evidence of administrative regulation of grazing grounds. To augment its resources, the state charged *singothi* – a tax of one paisa per head of cattle.[45] Since the rearing of livestock was a prominent occupation in the western part of Rajasthan, the cultivator had to give a share of the grass produced in his field to the state. In Marwar, the rate was one bullock-cartload of grass per plough of land. Furthermore, there was tax on the sale of grass in the region, 'charged at Rs. 2.50 on the first Rs. 100 worth of fodder, and Rs. 1.50 upon every successive Rs. 100 worth'.[46] Extensive documentation of natural resources, combined with an efficient administrative mechanism, helped states to collect penalties on different kinds of illegal usage of natural resources. For instance, the felling of green trees or defacing the village pond through use of dyes was subject to penalty.[47] Similarly, killing of buffaloes and unauthorized cutting of grass were also punishable offences.[48] Even the cutting of grass grown on hills and forests was considered an offence.[49] Pastures increasingly came under state control since they provided food for cattle, which were important in both agriculture and transportation, and horses, which had an important role in warfare.[50]

Thus, be it through the construction of large public waterworks, bypassing rural intermediaries while dealing with peasant communities, or imposing control over natural resources, states in Rajasthan during the period under focus increasingly exhibited a definite tendency of centralization as well as rapid expansion in their mechanisms of control and governance. This set them apart from the historical processes of earlier times, creating a sense of a historical break. The next section shows how this heightening state-intervention also made its way into the domestic world of the subjects.

Regulating the Domestic: Judicial Processes and Social Norms

Highlighting the significant role of the king as dispenser of justice, Corinne Lefevre cites the memoirs of Jahangir, who wrote:

> After my accession, the first command issued by me was to have a chain of justice (*zinjir-i- 'adl*) hung so that if those charged with administering the courts were slack or negligent in rendering justice to the downtrodden, those who had suffered injustice could have recourse to the chain and pull it so that the sound would cause awareness.[51]

Lefevre argues that in doing so, Jahangir was publicly adhering to established normative models of kingship embodied by kings David and Anushirwan. The remainder of the memoirs is peppered with passages in which the Mughal monarch administers justice not only to his human subjects but also to the animals of his empire. He is also keen on underlining his impartiality in the dispensation of justice.

During the period under focus, we find a similar concern of Rajput monarchs about the dispensation of justice as a vital part of their kingship in the various principalities of Rajasthan. By asserting their personal prerogative to deliver justice, kings of these principalities discreetly undermined the social prestige of various intermediaries. A careful evaluation of *arhsatta*s indicates that in course of the seventeenth and eighteenth centuries, Rajasthan saw a steady rise of monarchical authority at the expense of the traditional power of intermediaries. As mentioned earlier, one of the sixty-eight categories of information was known as *hasil farohi*, which means the collection of money, deposited as fine at the court at *pargana* level. The documents of this category also provide information on the various crimes committed in the region and the punishment awarded. In turn, they offer us a peek into the workings of the legal world of the region. Dilbagh Singh argues that a closer examination of judgments recorded in these documents

> ... give a nuanced picture of the state – here it appears to be overarching in its authority and not hesitant to put its administrative apparatus to full use in regulating affairs of the state and society down to the level of village, its distinct social groups, the family, and even its individual members.[52]

The authority exercised by the state not only pertained to the management of its agrarian resources but also extended to flora and fauna as well as the private affairs of the household. Perhaps it was under the influence of their close associations with the Mughal emperors – for whom justice served as one of the defining characteristics of kingship – that asserting their right to deliver justice emerged as a means for the kings of Rajasthan to consolidate their claims towards sovereign authority over their realms.

This point is further illustrated by the references to legal interventions by the states in the domains of social norms and marital disputes. Observance of social norms is one of the prerequisites for reinforcing the authority of ruling dispensations. For the kings under consideration, the right to deliver justice emerged as a tool for reiterating and reinforcing social norms. States regularly extended their arms to regulate the social order, thereby conveying the message that social status and hierarchy were to be protected, with the position of the king elevated above all the subjects of the empire. States increasingly came to expect strict adherence to social norms, be it in domestic affairs or at the highest official level. Challenging the authority and appropriateness of decisions of the elders or arguments with them was seen as violations of the conventional code of conduct regulating the social fabric. It is important to note that the onus of adhering to the code of conduct was also applicable to the elders of the family. Even elders would be castigated for unbecoming behaviour towards the young.[53] In social disputes, states would usually direct caste *panchayat*s to resolve issues in accordance with established traditions and conventions of the community, known as *wajabi*.[54] Through these processes, states increasingly emerged as protectors and enforcers of social norms during this period.

Alongside this, states started regularly intervening in the domestic affairs of families. In a way, this opened a possibility for women to get redressal in cases of sexual abuse, even within the patriarchal social formation of the times. Given the nature of documentation available, it is not easy to chart out the routes of communication through which the matters of the family reached the apex level. Yet it is certain that the individuality of women came to be well-established as far as judicial proceedings were concerned. *Hasil farohi* documents are full of references for *chamchori* (the theft of the body) in the sense of any form of sexual misconduct, including adultery and rape. There are instances where another term *joravari* was prefixed to *chamchori*, implying the use of force – possibly referring to rape or attempt to rape. We find increasing documentation of states adopting a strong posture against such crimes in a bid to control the sexual morality of society. Punishments were meted out even when such crimes were collective ones. For example, when in 1749 an allegation was made against the residents of a village named Ramparsadi for engaging in *chamchori*, the state fined the residents a collective sum of 101 rupees.[55]

We also get glimpses through a very informative document known as *Sanad Parwana Bahi* of the Marwar region. This text has plenty of evidences where the complainant was a woman. In fact, many women filed cases in their individual capacity with the state. Kailash Rani points out that there are evidences where women petitioned the state – and also received approval – for remarriage.[56] This indicates that even when a woman was in the 'custody of someone', known locally as *roti sata*, she enjoyed the individuality of approaching the state apparatus to seek justice for her grievances.[57] The state also seems to have created by this time a robust legal sphere where women enjoyed a great deal of rights in the eyes of royal and legal authority.

All this indicates the emergence of new forms of legality, where the various states of Rajasthan increasingly established themselves as the ultimate authority for settling legal disputes during the period under focus. Their own anxieties reflected by their repeated interventions in upholding social norms and order at the local level were reciprocated by the state's legal sphere gaining acceptance of the subjects as the paramount forum for the redressal of legal grievances.

Conclusion

What emerges from this discussion is a picture of complex interactions between state, society, and environment. We have seen that during the period from sixteenth through eighteenth centuries, the various Rajput polities of Rajasthan showed a remarkable inclination to devise penetrative and centralizing administrative mechanisms. This was a time when these states emerged out of their tribal kin-based status and increasingly transformed into robust monarchical entities in close association with the Mughal Empire. This chapter has highlighted three main processes that signified the early modern condition that comprised the historical context for this. The first of these comprised the rising inclination of states to document their realms and resources for concerns relating to governance. Next, the information thus generated helped states intervene directly at the local level, increasingly bypassing rural intermediaries. These interventions took the form of the expansion of agriculture, welfare measures like the construction of water bodies, and proliferation of state regulations like those imposed on the use of grazing grounds. Thirdly, there was a gradual rise of monarchical authority and rapid expansion of new forms of legality for upholding social norms and controlling social morality. In the process, the state steadily emerged as a legitimate forum for redressing legal matters for local society. Collectively, these historical processes comprised a new condition – early modernity, one that brought about a major shift from the historical landscape of antecedent times.

Notes

1. Partha Chaterjee, *Nation and Its Fragments: Colonial and Postcolonial Histories* (Princeton: Princeton University Press, 1993); Romila Thapar, 'Decolonizing the Past: Historical Writings in the Time of Sachin and Beyond', *Economic and Political Weekly* 40, no. 14 (2005): 1442–1448.
2. Equally important has been the newly founded nation's tryst, initially with religious divide and subsequently with caste-based vote-bank politics. See Gyanendra Pandey and Yunus Samad, *Fault Lines of Nationhood* (New Delhi: Roli Books, 2007); Bipan Chandra, *Communalism in Modern India* (New Delhi: Vikas, 1984).
3. S. C. Misra, *The Rise of Muslim Power in Gujarat: A History of Gujarat from 1298 to 1442* (New Delhi: Munshiram Manoharlal Publishers, 1982), 34–44; Kathleen Morrison, *Fields of Victory: Vijayanagara and the Course of Intensification* (New Delhi: Munshiram Manoharlal Publishers, 2000).
4. G. D. Sharma, *Rajput Polity: A Study of Politics and Administration of the State of Marwar, 1638–1749* (New Delhi: Manohar Publications, 1977); G. S. L. Devra, *Rajasthan ki Prashashnik Vyavastha* (Bikaner: Dharti Prakashan, 1981).
5. Mayank Kumar, *Monsoon Ecologies: Irrigation, Agriculture and Settlement Patterns in Rajasthan during the Pre-Colonial Period* (New Delhi: Manohar, 2013), 13–39; Meena Bhargava (ed.), *Frontiers of Environment: Issues in Medieval and Early Modern India* (Hyderabad: Orient Blackswan, 2017), 2–6.
6. Suraj Bhan Bhardwaj, *Contestations and Accommodations: Mewat and Meos in Mughal India* (New Delhi: Oxford University Press, 2016).
7. Tanuja Kothiyal, *Nomadic Narratives: A History of Mobility and Identity in the Great Indian Desert* (New Delhi: Cambridge University Press, 2016).
8. Sumit Guha, 'Claims on the Commons: Political Power and Natural Resources in Pre-colonial India', *The Indian Economic and Social History Review* 39, no. 2–3 (2002): 181–196; Mayank Kumar, 'Vagaries of Monsoon, Resilience of Society: Revisiting Nature of Socio-Political Structures during Early-Modern Rajasthan', *Studies in History* 32, no. 2 (2016): 209–230.
9. Rajiv Sharma and S. A Nadeem Rezavi, 'Aspects of Hydraulic Engineering in Medieval Rajasthan: A Case Study of Water System in Jaigarh Fort', in *Art and Culture*, ed. Ahsan Jan Qaisar and Som Prakash Verma, 129–133 (Jaipur: Publications Scheme, 1993); I. A. Khan and Ravindra Kumar, 'The Mansagar Dam of Amber', in *Ancient and Medieval Technologies in India*, ed. Anirudha Ray and S. K. Bagchi, 25–40 (New Delhi: Sundeep Prakashan, 1986).
10. Dilbagh Singh, 'Regulating the Domestic: Notes on the Pre-colonial State and the Family', *Studies in History* 19, no.1 (2003): 69–86, see especially 85.

11. Kothiyal, *Nomadic Narratives*, 133–150.
12. Munhot Nainsi, *Munhot Nainsi ri Khyat*, ed. Badri Prasad Sakariya, vol. 2, *1657–66* (Jodhpur: Rajasthan Oriental Research Institute, 1962), 134–139.
13. Munhot Nainsi, *Munhot Nainsi ri Khyat*, ed. Badri Prasad Sakariya, vol. 1, *1657–66* (Jodhpur: Rajasthan Oriental Research Institute, 1960), 37–42.
14. Neelima Vashishatha, 'Unnisvi Shatabdi mein Marwar ki Chitrankan Parampara mein Naveen Prayog', Prof. R. P. Vyas Memorial Lecture, Session 34, Rajasthan History Congress, 2019, 1–24.
15. Nainsi, *Munhta Nainsi ri Khyat*, vol. 1, 890.
16. Munhot Nainsi, *Marwar-ra-Pargana-ri-Vigat*, ed. Narain Singh Bhati, vol. 1, *1657–66* (Jodhpur: Rajasthan Oriental Research Institute, 1968), 36.
17. James C. Scott, *Seeing Like a State: How Certain Schemes to Improve the Human Condition Have Failed* (New Haven: Yale University Press, 1998), 185. Also see Sumit Guha, *Health and Population in South Asia from the Earliest Times to the Present* (Ranikhet: Permanent Black, 2001).
18. Dilbagh Singh, *The State, Landlords and Peasants* (New Delhi: Manohar, 1992), 18; Also see B. L. Bhadani, *Peasants, Artisans and Entrepreneurs: Economy of Marwar in the 17th Century* (Jaipur: Rawat Publication, 1999).
19. Yogesh Sharma, 'The Circuit of Life: Water and Water Reservoirs in Pre-modern India', *Studies in History* 25, no. 1 (2009): 69–108; David Mosse, *The Rule of Water: Statecraft, Ecology and Collective Action in South India* (New Delhi: Oxford University Press, 2003); Anil Agarwal and Sunita Narain (eds.), *Dying Wisdom: Rise, Fall and Potential of India's Traditional Water Harvesting Systems* (New Delhi: Centre for Science and Environment, 1997); Mayank Kumar, 'Adaptations to Climatic Variability: Irrigation and Settlements Patterns in Early Medieval Rajasthan', *Medieval History Journal* 17, no.1 (2014): 57–86.
20. Anupam Misra, *Rajasthan ki Rajat Booden* (New Delhi: Gandhi Shanti Pratishthan, 1995).
21. Nainsi, *Munhot Khyat*, vol. 1, 30.
22. Shyamal Das, *Vir Vinod*, ed. Badri Prasad Sakariya, vol. 2 (Jodhpur: Rajasthan Oriental Research Institute, 1960 [1884]), 578–634, 2204.
23. Khan and Kumar, 'The Mansagar Dam of Amber'.
24. K. D. Eriskine, *Rajputana Gazetteers*, vol. 2A, *The Mewar Residency* (Ajmer: Scottish Mission Industries Co. Ltd., 1908), 109.
25. Eriskine, *Rajputana Gazetteers: Volume 2-A*, 9.
26. Neelima Vashishatha, 'A Note on the Sculptures of the Raj Samudra Lake in Rajasthan', in *Art and Culture*, ed. Qaisar and Verma, 111.
27. Eriskine, *Rajputana Gazetteers: Volume 2-A*, 9.
28. Eriskine, *Rajputana Gazetteers: Volume 2-A*, 8–9.
29. Khan and Kumar, 'The Mansagar Dam of Amber'.

30. Norbert Peobody, *Hindu Kingship and Polity in Pre-colonial India* (Cambridge: Cambridge University Press, 2003); R. P. Bahuguna, 'Religious Festivals as Political Rituals: Kingship and Legitimation in Late Pre-colonial Rajasthan', in *Revisiting the History of Rajasthan: Essays for Prof. Dilbagh Singh*, ed. Suraj Bhan Bhardwaj, R. P Bahuguna, and Mayank Kumar, 84–92 (New Delhi: Primus, 2017).
31. Mayank Kumar, 'Situating the Environment: Settlement, Irrigation and Agriculture in Pre-Colonial Rajasthan', *Studies in History* 24, no. 2 (2008): 211–233.
32. *Arzdasht, Bhadva Vadi* 7, 1774 vs./AD 1717 & *Arzdasht Sawan Sudi* 9, 1752 vs./AD 1695 Historical Section, Jaipur Records, Rajasthan State Archives, Bikaner (henceforth, HS, JR, RSAB.) Traditionally, Bhadva is the third month of rainy season and usually the last one also.
33. *Arzdasht, Falgun Sudi* 11, 1751 vs./AD 1694 HS, JR, RSAB.
34. Madhvi Bajekal, 'Agricultural Production in Six Selected "Qasbas" of Eastern Rajasthan (c.1700–1780)', Unpublished PhD Thesis (London: University of London, 1990), 85.
35. Bajekal, 'Agricultural Production', 85.
36. Bhadani, *Peasants, Artisans and Entrepreneurs*, 34–80.
37. *Sanad Parwana Bahi, Sawan Sudi* 2, 1765 vs./AD 1708, Jodhpur Records, RSAB.
38. *Sanad Parwana Bahi, Jeth Sudi* 9, 1825 vs./AD 1768, Jodhpur Records, RSAB.
39. *Arhsatta*, Village Raitoli, Pargana Dausa, 1825 vs./AD 1768; Village Dhamorki, Pargana Chatsu, 1775 vs./AD 1718; Qasba Baswa, Pargana Bhartri, 1774 vs./AD 1717, HS, JR, RSAB.
40. *Sanad Parwana Bahi, Kartik Vadi* 11, 1768 vs./AD 1711, Jodhpur Records, RSAB.
41. *Sanad Parwana Bahi, Kartik Vadi* 11, 1768 vs./AD 1711, Jodhpur Records, RSAB.
42. Kothiyal, *Nomadic Narratives*, 41–50.
43. P. W. Powlett, *Gazetteer of Bikaner* (Calcutta: Office of the Superintendent of Press, 1874), 162.
44. *Kagad Bahi* 1827, vs./AD 1770, Bikaner Records, Rajasthan State Archives, Bikaner. The state required large amount of grass for the cavalry and the elephants.
45. Bhadani, *Peasants, Artisans and Entrepreneurs*, 86; Nainsi, *Vigat*, vol. 1, 158–160.
46. Bhadani, *Peasants, Artisans and Entrepreneurs*, 223.
47. *Arhsatta, Qasba* Malpura, *Pargana* Malpura, 1791 vs./AD 1734, HS, JR, RSAB.

48. *Arhsatta*, Village Kiratpura, *Pargana* Bahatri, 1774 vs./AD 1717; *Arhsatta*, *Pargana* Bahatri, 1786 vs./AD 1729; *Pargana* Malrana, 1772 vs./AD 1715, HS, JR, RSAB.
49. *Arhsatta*, *Pargana* Bahatri, 1786 vs./AD 1729; *Pargana* Malrana, 1772 vs./AD 1715, HS, JR, RSAB.
50. *Sanad Parwana Bahi, Jeth Sudi* 9, 1825 vs./AD 1768, Jodhpur Records. RSAB; Also see Abhimanyu Singh Arha, 'Hoofprint of Empire: An Environmental History of Fodder in Mughal India (1650–1850)', *Studies in History* 32, no. 2 (2016): 186–208; Norman Ziegler, 'Some Notes on Rajput Loyalties during the Mughal Period', in *Kingship and Authority in South Asia*, ed. John F. Richards, 215–251 (Madison: University of Wisconsin-Madison, 1978); Dirk H. A. Kolff, *Naukar, Rajput and Sepoy: The Ethnohistory of the Military Labour Market in Hindustan, 1450–1850* (Cambridge: Cambridge University Press, 1990); Guha, 'Claims on the Commons', 181–196.
51. Corinne Lefevre, 'Recovering a Missing Voice from Mughal India: The Imperial Discourse of Jahangir (r.1605–1627) in His Memoirs', *Journal of the Economic and Social History of the Orient* 50, no. 4 (2007): 452–489, 470.
52. Singh, 'Regulating the Domestic', 85.
53. Singh, 'Regulating the Domestic', 72.
54. Nandita Prasad Sahai, *Politics of Patronage and Protest: The State, Society and Artisans in Early Modern Rajasthan* (New Delhi: Oxford University Press, 2006).
55. Singh, 'Regulating the Domestic', 76.
56. Kailash Rani, 'Claims and Counterclaims: Widow Remarriage in Eighteenth Century Marwar', in *Revisiting the History of Rajasthan*, ed. Bhardwaj, Bahuguna and Kumar, 294–307.
57. Kailash Rani, 'Roti Satta ka Samajshastra: Marwar ke Samaj me Stri Dasta ka Ek Roop', *Pratimaan: Samay, Samaj avam Sanskriti*, vol. 15 (January–June 2020), 352–368.

7

Through the Prism of Environmental History

Defining the Early Modern in South Asia

Meena Bhargava

As the world moved into the twenty-first century, 'modernity' was 'out there for everyone to see and no questions asked', observed Christopher A. Bayly.[1] To begin with, there was a fair amount of consensus with Bayly's definition of modernity and its origins. But with the deepening of historical research and scholarship, that consensus has become a thing of the past. Modernity has increasingly come to be constructed in several different ways, with none attributing to it the characteristics of an objective reality or speaking of it in the 'singular', thus leading to 'subjective modernities'.[2] With the querying of 'singular modernity' and that 'one-size-fits-all conception of development' evolved the notion of early modernity in different parts of the world, pointing towards different regions pursuing alternate paths into the modern world and experiencing modernity in different ways. In the context of South Asia, a few scholars observed that India along with China led the world economy – whether in crafts, agriculture, trade and commerce – until about the middle of the eighteenth century. Not just that, India in the seventeenth century could boast of traders like Abdul Ghafoor and Virji Vora, who by themselves wielded more capital than all the East India Companies of Europe put together. In addition, reason, philosophy, and intellectualism were deeply rooted in the centuries – mid-sixteenth to the eighteenth centuries.[3] As indicated in the introduction to this volume, this is roughly the period that has been carved out of the traditional category of the medieval period of South Asian history and has come to be identified in recent historiography as the time of early modernity.

In this chapter, I explore the nature of the early modern condition in South Asia in the domain of human–environment relationships.[4] I argue that the period between the sixteenth to the eighteenth centuries in South Asia, like in every other part of the world, witnessed processes by which human beings vigorously intervened in the natural environment with heightened pace and magnitude of change.[5] Early modernity in South Asia also witnessed growing population, rapidly moving anthropogenic change, and heightening effects of collective human action on the ecosystems. Like in the global context, when the total number of human beings nearly doubled from 400–500 million in 1500 to 850–950 million in 1800, there were patterns of growing population in South Asia too, especially during the period between 1601 and 1801. Even as the society relied on human, animal, wind, and water power, South Asia witnessed rapid changes in the natural world; there was intensified human land-use, and with technological shifts, humans brought material changes and manipulated the material world. I discuss these transformations in detail in the two sections of this chapter, outlining the meanings of early modernity in the field of human–environment relationships in South Asia and concluding with the shifts that appeared with the rise of colonial modernity in the nineteenth century.

Human Intervention and Land-Use Patterns

In this section, I analyse human interventions, the modification of natural environment, and the rapid changes in land use that early modernity in South Asia brought about. Environmental processes in South Asia during this period facilitate the understanding of demography, settlement patterns, and ecological change. Climatic and biotic factors – drought, flood, famine, and epidemics – might have put some constraints on the growth of population in the region, but for the period of 1601–1801, we notice a compound annual rate of population growth of about 0.2 per cent. On the basis of *pargana*-wise[6] statistical data provided in Abul Fazl's late-sixteenth-century text *Ain-i Akbari* on cultivable area, crop yields, land revenue, prices, wages, retainers of *zamindar*s, W. H. Moreland estimated the population of India in *c.* 1601 at 100 million. Kingsley Davis revised this to 125 million by taking into account areas that Moreland had not considered. On the basis of further investigations on area statistics, productivity, and taxation data, Shireen Moosvi estimated the population of India in *c.* 1601 to be around 145 million, which went up to 207 million by 1801. There is no reliable data to construct population statistics prior to 1601, but if it is accepted that the population increased at the rate of 0.2 per cent in the period 1601–1801, then the population in *c.*1101 should have been around 72.5 million.[7]

With rising human numbers and increasing pressure on the land, human settlement and sedentary cultivation expanded; in turn, this led to ecological change. Emphasizing the importance of ecology to understand demography and settlement patterns, and to compute the extent of cultivated land around *c.* 1600, Moosvi argues that it is the limits of the agricultural zone which constitute the main frontier between the territories of nature and of man.[8] Agriculture was the single most important means by which humans changed the land and its ecosystems. As land use intensified, the forests retreated. It is difficult to establish the extent of forests in the period prior to the sixteenth century. But some assessment can be ventured on the basis of the proximity of forests to the capital city of Delhi. In the thirteenth century, forests stretched along the Aravalli hills up to south-west Delhi, making it difficult for the sultans of Delhi to control this region. The middle Doab region in modern western Uttar Pradesh, with its extensive stretches of forests, connected with sub-montane forests by ravines and jungle running along the rivers Yamuna and Ganga in the thirteenth century. This too obstructed political control. Travellers traversing the region between Badaun and Delhi often encountered tigers in this forest. In the latter half of the fourteenth century, the territory north of Badaun, that is, modern Rohilkhand (then known as Katehr), was so densely forested that herds of wild buffalo and Indian bison (*gaur*) roamed freely and were known to have been hunted by Sultan Firuz Shah Tughluq. None of these patterns were visible any longer in the sixteenth century and the Doab region was almost completely under cultivation by *c.* 1600.[9] Commenting on the seventeenth century, Pelsaert mentioned complete lack of trees in the region – a sign of clearance of forests and the emergence of agrarian settlements.[10] Further, evidences from the seventeenth and the eighteenth centuries regarding the absence of wild animals in areas where their species had flourished in the preceding centuries are indicative of similar human interventions. For the region of Gujarat, the author of *Mi'rat-i Ahmadi* observed that sometime before 1761, wild elephants were no longer seen in the Rajpipla area because their 'forest route' that had comprised unbroken belt of forest linking Rajpipla with Malwa had been cut off by human settlements; this barred the entry of wild elephants into Gujarat from central India.[11]

The greater portion of new cultivation since the sixteenth century occurred in the ubiquitous frontiers of settlement. As settlement frontiers advanced and made inroads into forests, grasslands, and other habitats, human land-use intensified and productivity per square kilometre rose. Almost invariably such expansion caused a reduction in the quantity and diversity of vegetation or a reduction in biomass and biodiversity.[12] The pioneer cultivators cleared forests and woodlands to support themselves for their livelihood and to produce food and commercial crops according to the market demand. Settlement patterns from diverse regions illustrate gradually increasing modes of state control over the environment; the state encouraged human intervention and set the norms for it. For instance, prior to the sixteenth century, a large part of the Mughal *sarkar*[13] Gorakhpur in the *suba* (province) Awadh was thickly forested. The area between the *sarkar* Awadh and the *sarkar* Gorakhpur (both in the *suba* Awadh) was covered by *kans* grass and bamboo forests considered 'useless for man and beast'.[14] But soon afterwards, this tract was clear of forests, as shown in James Rennell's map, prepared in 1780.[15] What is also noticeable is a marked change in the land patterns of the *sarkar* since the sixteenth century – reclamation and cultivation of land with remarkable rapidity and its quick rehabilitation under the new name of Muazzamabad in the seventeenth century (coinciding with the reign of Mughal emperor Aurangzeb). The *sarkar* continued to be so designated in the later revenue lists. Intensified land use was marked by a process of improvement in the use of land and changed patterns of agricultural production. Fresh cultivable lands were cleared and brought under cultivation. The state encouraged peasants to experiment with new crops that enhanced productivity. Expanding cultivation moved further into the forest area towards the northern frontier of Gorakhpur into the Terai region. Frontiers of settlement marked a significant change in the way humans used land and consumed natural resources, signifying a change from one form of human exploitation of the natural world to another. The fact that human intervention and land use showed good performance was evidently noticed by the mid-eighteenth century, apparent by its significant rise in the *jama*.[16] According to an eighteenth-century revenue roll, the aggregate rise in *jama* of the *suba* Awadh was by over 85 per cent when compared to the figures of the late sixteenth century; the maximum increase of 267.37 per cent, for instance, was noticed in the *sarkar* Gorakhpur by 1755 in comparison with the figures recorded in the *Ain-i Akbari*.[17]

Variety of negotiations with nature, through the use of technology and processes of production, reflected the complexities and intricacies of human intervention in the environment.[18] Regions of urbanism, ethnicity, empire, literature, and territoriality made the land look very different in *c.* 1800 than what it did in *c.*1200. There was a qualitative change in the way people thought about the land. The slow, incremental processes of the thirteenth–fourteenth centuries laid the basis for dramatic trends that emerged after 1500; as agricultural expansion accelerated, the state extracted more and more revenue and mobility of people intensified. With regional formations of agrarian territory knitted together by urban networks, shifting patterns of social power, agricultural expansion, and cultural change characterized the early modernity.[19] The evolution, growth, and sustenance of the human settlements as well as the human–nature interaction in different ecological contexts were significantly established by the monsoon ecology and its erratic nature. Mayank Kumar applies the 'larger umbrella of monsoon ecology' to understand human–nature interactions and the peculiar identity of Rajasthan and its people.[20] Kathleen Morrison provides evidence from the Ganga and Indus river-basins and the Vijayanagara region to explain changing ecological contexts of forests, agriculture, and land property.

She argues that the environmental and cultural developments in the Western Ghats during the fifteenth through the seventeenth centuries witnessed forest-loss and regeneration, alterations in the composition and distribution of vegetation and soil movement, and also oscillating long-distance and local exchange involving forest products.[21]

Small, often unnoticed, innovations and changes gradually improved human life and productivity, as illustrated in the works of Richard Eaton, John Richards, and Chetan Singh.[22] In his contribution on the region of Punjab, Singh suggests the importance of the integration of ecological and historical developments in the seventeenth century.[23] There were long-established and fundamental relationships between society and its physical surroundings. No society could survive without them, making imperative the understanding of the socio-economic processes and the specific ecological environment within which these relationships operated. Jos Gommans, on the other hand, invokes the deployment of money and horsepower to argue that the period from the sixteenth through the eighteenth centuries achieved unprecedented agricultural, commercial, and political expansion. In terms of ideology and ritual too, the Mughal state reflected as much the 'world of the settled court as that of the nomadic war-band' during this period.[24] Constant variations and transformations were visible within the ecological perimeters of India's limits and inner frontiers. Most polities during the period emerged on the roads and crossroads of commercial and nomadic interactions.[25] Their ecological systems were transient, uncertain, and constantly changing, although all transmutations might not have been contributed by human beings; some modifications in nature could also have been sudden and cataclysmic.[26] The shift away from communal forest use towards increasing state intervention was strengthened by the Mughal state during the sixteenth and seventeenth centuries. It was further accelerated by the regional states in the eighteenth century, particularly on the west coast of India, where timber harvesting was most intensive. As early as the 1740s, the rulers of the Maratha Empire had found it expedient to acquire control over large tracts of coastal forest and set up plantations, for both shipbuilding and revenue. In Cochin and Travancore, similar state-monopoly controls over forests were initiated. The most extensive programmes for afforestation and forest protection were carried out between 1770 and 1840 by the Amirs of Sind. So, by the 1770s, throughout many regions of South Asia, there was widespread emergence of state-forest controls – something that was the culmination of processes that had heightened in the course of the sixteenth century. This phenomenon developed as relatively integrated forces of economic penetration began to respond to new levels of trade and demand, particularly in search for timber to meet the increasingly complex demands of the growing urban centres and that of European and indigenous naval systems.[27]

This heightened intensity with which humans transformed nature and modified land-use patterns was something that characterized the sixteenth through the eighteenth centuries, and hence needs to be recognized as one of the hallmarks of early modernity in South Asia. Human intervention established a new relationship between society and nature, with communities constantly attempting to mould the environment according to their own needs, notwithstanding the limits set by nature.

Shared Historical Processes and Ecological Change

In this section, I highlight another dimension of South Asian early modernity by investigating how the people who used the environment sought to define it, organized their relations with it, intervened in it, and modified natural conditions in that process. Using these discussions, I exemplify shared historical processes and how human societies were continuously engaged in defining and constructing the ambience around them, people's ecological pressures, and their responses to the changes during the period. It is difficult to establish whether these archetypes were present in the period prior to the sixteenth century in South Asian environment. At any rate, there were large stretches of land that abounded with dense forests at that time. These were identified as *mawas*, or 'difficult terrain', a 'natural fastness' for local chieftains outside the control of the sultans of Delhi and a barrier for the assertion of state authority.[28] Sunil Kumar defines *mawas* as 'disturbed, troubled territory' in the control of a rebel,[29] whereas Irfan Habib characterizes it as 'rebel territory', a term he says that was in use from the thirteenth century and had been derived from Hindustani *mahwas* – forest, wood, retreat. Regardless of the definition, the thirteenth and the fourteenth centuries saw a strong connection between *mawas* on the one hand and notions of disturbed and rebellious areas on the other.[30] The state, nevertheless, extracted revenue from the forests by imposing *bankar* (taxes) on forest produce and nourished wild elephants, a military asset to the state available only in the dense forests. To maintain the population of the wild elephants and prevent reduction in the number of captive elephants to be used in the wars, forests were not cut down. But as the forests, especially those surrounding the capital city of Delhi, became threatening to the residents as a result of the attack by the Meos who hid in these forests, Sultan Balban responded with military campaigns. Finding it difficult to traverse the dense forests, the Sultan deployed *tabarzan* (woodcutters) to clear the path for the army to march. It may have changed the character of the territory but it still remained an armed camp, a military cantonment, and the onslaught was felt by the pastoral, forest-dwelling people as well. What emerges from this description is that there was hardly any contact between the people of the forests and the settled population and that there was considerable antagonism between pastoralist and sedentary communities. This animosity became worse when Sultan Balban used state power to 'resettle' the lands through obtrusive tactics of sedentary societies against pastoral groups, defeated forest dwellers and pastoralists, and resettled and repopulated their lands with new personnel whom he gave *mafruzi* (rent-free lands) and for whose security he established military cantonments.[31] In all these processes of state-sponsored and state-controlled reclamation and resettlement, there were hardly any evidences of shared historical processes and interactions – tendencies that became remarkably noticeable from the sixteenth century as the markers of a new era.

The study of the interaction between humans and the environment – whether in the domain of the cultivated lands, forests, forest products, wildlife, or river courses – show vast changes that took place from the sixteenth through the eighteenth centuries. Man's natural environment and the relationship between man and nature demonstrate an interconnectedness and mutuality between different environmental elements during the period, something that was absent earlier.[32] Continuous interaction and shared experiences among communities of different ecological niches – riverine, forest, desert, and mountain areas – marked the period. Pastoralists and agriculturists emerged as dynamic categories that mutually participated in shared historical processes. Pastoralists traversed both the forests and the cultivated land, and the agriculturists did the same; forests too provided both resources and revenue.[33] Environmentalists today may consider sedentary cultivation and grazing as negative activities that lead to the erosion of the soil and may deem grazing as dangerous to the forests because as the sheep and the cattle eat the seedlings of trees, they damage their reproductive potential. However, the developments of this period reveal that the pastoralists did not reckon the replacement of forests by grasslands as degradation, even though the hooves of large number of cattle driven into a forest to graze may make the ground hard, compacted, and dry, rendering it less conducive for the seeds to germinate or plants to grow.[34] Similarly, farmers did not perceive the replacement of forests by agricultural lands as degradation despite the adverse changes in the soil and micro-climate[35] and logging that could restrain the new plant growth[36]. In fact, the farmers often preferred agriculture and the development of cultivation in the proximity of or within the ambit of a forested area so as to benefit from the springs, a high water-table, less-eroded soil, or even the new soil produced by the decayed leaf litter in these areas.[37] In several regions, the debris of burnt forest waste was considered a particularly good medium for seed growth. An abundant supply of such waste was considered well-suited for agriculture – a feature commonly noticed, for instance, in the forest tracts and wastelands (uncultivated and/or barren lands) of the Mughal *sarkar* Gorakhpur in the *suba* Awadh.[38]

So, while it would be prudent to consider how the impact of human activity on the fauna and flora might have changed the ecosystem, it would be equally pertinent to observe that nature's ability to reconcile competing human interests is not limitless, nor are all humans equally culpable of exploiting nature.[39] In this context, it may be mentioned that although nomadic pastoralists have sometimes been seen as predators to the sedentary agricultural societies, the two major forms of subsistence – pastoralism and agriculture – are neither totally separated nor fixed; they are, in fact, interchangeable and interactive.[40] There are occasions when specialized herding is often made possible only by a symbiotic relationship with agriculture. During the period under focus, agro-pastoralism prevailed in zones that could not exclusively support successful agriculture or pastoralism; those who earned their livelihood largely from herds spent less time and labour on fields and vice versa.[41] In the case of sixteenth- and seventeenth-century Punjab, the growth of commercialized agriculture under the Mughals encouraged and facilitated the absorption of pastoral people into the agrarian system. The contribution of the sedentary communities to the creation and consolidation of economy and society was not isolated or exclusive of the tribal pastoralist communities. In fact, there are several instances of interdependence between pastoral and sedentary life; one such example was the village communities in the Mughal Empire that subsisted at a reasonable proximity to pastoral societies. There was continued participation of pastoral population in the socio-economic processes and the stabilization of agrarian society and certain other social formations, although in many cases the sedentarized relied considerably on pastoralism. Even within the cultivated area, there existed not only variations of the agrarian system but also socio-economic systems that were remarkably different from it. There are innumerable examples from several regions that demonstrate the close relationship between tribal-pastoralism and sedentary-commercialized society. They were, in fact, so inextricably linked in their economic interests that any shift in the structure of any one of these societies would not leave the other unaffected. Singh argues that if tribal-pastoral population in other regions were as integral to the agrarian society as in sixteenth- or seventeenth-century Punjab, then ignoring them would mean risking an incomplete understanding of the agrarian system that early modernity signified in South Asia.[42] While many tribes were fairly dependent on pastoralism, they were also engaged in economic exchange with the adjoining agrarian society and were added as new social groups to the sedentarized agricultural population. The lives of the peasants and pastoralists were remarkably entwined. Their involvement in the mutual exchange of products was accompanied simultaneously with the scramble for encroachment on each other's space: the herdsmen who wandered on the fringes of productive areas re-appropriated the abandoned fields and habitations and the agriculturists treaded on the grazing grounds of the pastoralists; in yet other circumstances, *jhum* cultivators moved to settled cultivation and the cultivators escaped to the forests.[43]

As human settlements arose during the period, communities showed adaptation and accommodation to ecological interventions whereby nature was altered and landscape modified. Agriculture was certainly a major constituent in it and the single-most important means by which mankind changed the lands and the ecosystems. It represented a connecting point between the human powers that organize agriculture and the changing natural environment. It was a major element of ecological transformation in human history, for no occupation other than farming alters the land so much. However, without undermining the significance of agrarian landscape and arguing against the singularity of it in historical investigations and understanding environmental processes, it can be suggested, as David Ludden has observed, that 'farming landscapes are not defined by their physical or environmental qualities but rather by their long-term interaction of geography, culture, technology and social power'.[44] New cultivation occurred in the frontiers of settlement, when the pioneer settlers intruded upon the remote lands inhabited by shifting cultivators, hunter-gatherers, and pastoralists. Agrarianism includes not only farming but also animal husbandry, pastoralism, fishing, and harvesting the forest. It can thus be defined as a major source that produces organic material for human use, of which animal and forest products are an evidence of.[45]

Drastic changes in the landscape occurred during the period under focus as a result of newer sets of negotiations with climatic variability, as illustrated by Morrison for South India in general and the region of Vijayanagara during the sixteenth and seventeenth centuries in particular. She argues for continuous interactions between given landscape and social action, which modified and changed both – landscape as well as ways and means of social interactions. Examining the water systems in and around Vijayanagara during the period, she shows the nature of extension of agriculture into the marginal areas. Monsoon rains were increasingly captured to develop the agrarian potential of the areas on the fringes of agrarian landscape. It was the scarcity of water that had restricted agrarian production earlier, but with the channelization of monsoon rains for agricultural purposes, agrarian settlements could be expanded steadily.[46] Emphasizing the intertexture between different modes of livelihood and human–environment interaction, Singh raises the issue of the significance of environmental factors in determining the economic development of the Mughal Empire and understanding the evolution of state and society. Reiterating that agriculture cannot be seen exclusive of the other elements of environment, he argues that it has long been assumed that the prosperity of the Mughal state – a new form of early modern state apparatus – depended on its agrarian base. To the contrary, however, he suggests that it was in fact not upon the settled villages and the revenue-yielding lands that the stability of the Mughal society rested; there was much that lay beyond the agrarian economy. The Mughal ruling class did not possess absolute monopoly over geographical space or the natural resources even if they fell within the political limits of the empire. Ecological diversity – a mix of agricultural production, forests, and grasslands – prevailed in the empire. This fostered a variety of socio-economic systems that necessitated a relationship of sharing with other social organizations that used the environment in diverse ways. The extent of forested or uncultivated territory was considerable with several *qasba*s, towns, and adjoining agricultural fields lying amidst forests.[47]

The shared historical processes, congeniality, and harmony between the agrarian and other environmental forces are evident by the fact that while agriculture developed leading to a sedentary lifestyle, agricultural zones were interspersed with sizeable thick and impenetrable woods that not only had ecological significance but were also an important economic factor and a necessary requirement for agriculture. They provided pasture for cattle, as well as space for getting firewood, timber, and forest products like wild fruits, honey, and toddy. The extent and type of forests from the sixteenth through the eighteenth centuries can be inferred from the locations of hunting grounds and the habitats of wild animals. For example, while the presence of wild elephants would indicate the presence of a dense forest, that of the wild cheetahs would imply the existence of grasslands and scrubs in the vicinity. All these, Moosvi observes, can be ascertained by examining the statistics of area under cultivation for the different regions.[48] Her analysis of economic geography and natural environment clearly demonstrates close connections and interactions and a dialectical relationship that urge upon 'an *ecologicalism* that recognizes the inherent interdependence of all life-systems'.[49] It establishes that notwithstanding the vast agrarianism in early modern India, forests remained central to the lives of many of its inhabitants. It served as their home, a shelter, a source of fodder, firewood, and timber, even if the capital value of the latter was of no great importance to them. The *zamindar*s possessed proprietary, hereditary rights over the forests within their jurisdiction. Generally, they did not consent to the cutting of trees nor did they, as Buchanan Hamilton observed, 'agree to receive a pecuniary compensation for this sacrilege'.[50] Large parts of forest were home to large mammals, ungulates, and carnivores. These included lions and tigers, cheetahs and leopards, hyenas and wolves, elephants and ants. Some ant hills, for example in the Mughal *sarkar* Gorakhpur, were found to be at least ten feet high; many trees were coated with ant tunnels and a few points of ant nests were broken with large open galleries inside. However, irrespective of whether the forests were dense or subjected to the incursions of wild animals that made the passage through the forests dangerous and difficult, there was nothing to deter the local inhabitants from defining their relationship with the forests.[51] On several occasions, forests served as 'hideouts' and provided a haven for those peasants and *zamindar*s who wanted to avoid the payment of taxes to the Mughal state. Sujan Rai described the Lakhi jungle near the channels of the rivers Sutlej and Beas as an area of refuge for the recalcitrant in the late sixteenth century, while *Tuzuk-i Jahangiri* informs us that during the reign of Mughal emperor Jahangir, villagers in the vicinity of Mathura fled to the jungles on the other bank of river Yamuna to resist payment of land revenue. Forests served as an asylum too for the seriously ill and convalescents of infectious diseases, particularly smallpox, which was rampant in the eighteenth century in several areas. The disease was so dreaded that infected persons would be removed from their homes and sent to the forest until the disease was eradicated from the village or until they had recuperated.[52]

Land was also reclaimed; agro-forestry, pastoralism, and settlements could overwhelm the forests. There was constant fluctuation and fluidity between forests and cultivation, with shifting boundaries between the jungle and the arable. Fath Ullah Shirazi's observation regarding revenue matters for the reign of Mughal emperor Akbar substantiates the point. He stated, 'The fluctuations of civilization are apparent to everyone. If in a village some land falls out of cultivation, one endeavors to increase cultivation elsewhere.'[53] The rulers from the sixteenth century encouraged reclamation of forests by granting *nankari* rights to the landholders.[54] Connections between military campaigns, forests, and settlements are also evident during the seventeenth century. During the reign of the Mughal emperor Shahjahan, the Mughal army would be accompanied by *tabarzan* and ploughmen who would clear the land to make way for the army and establish new *zamindari*s. Asserting their political power, the *zamindar*s and the *jagirdar*s too hired professional woodcutters to clear the jungles and settle new villages.[55] In the late eighteenth century, the *zamindar*s of the Mughal *sarkar* Gorakhpur were the sole holders of timber rights. They planted *sal* (known as *sakhuya* in Gorakhpur) and allowed it to be cut and sold. With such incentives and entrepreneurship, many *zamindari*s emerged at the frontiers of cultivation consequent upon the clearings of forests.[56] While reclamation was carried out in some parts of this Mughal *sarkar* in 1801, there were tracts of jungles and wastelands that remained along the river Gandak and its numerous streamlets that were used as *dhab* lands (pasture lands) during cold and hot months.[57]

Community locations, thus, were rarely fixed during the early modern period when desertions and migrations were often the response to climatic or political factors (*asmani wa sultani*), resulting in situations where wanderers might settle, and the settled wander; forests be cleared, and forests be grown.[58]

The Advent of Colonial Modernity

Using environmental processes as exemplar to identify markers of early modern in South Asia, I uphold that in the period defined as early modern, the pace and magnitude of change had increased in human societies in every part of the world, including South Asia; it was marked by shared historical processes and long-term currents that not only accelerated in this period but also had a deep impact on the changes during the nineteenth and the twentieth centuries. Imbibing and invoking early modern Mughal patterns and yet remarkably at variance, colonial modernity showed paradigmatic shift in its concerns, strategies, and norms. Forests and forestry significantly figured on the agenda of the colonial government, though forest clearance, expansion of cultivation, and the commercial and strategic advantages of forests were known in the early modern period as well. The English East India Company inherited these patterns and began experiments within it. However, with its different vision on forests, the Company introduced a structure and framework, reinvented and reformulated in its form, and introduced notable changes. The objectives of the English East India Company were clear – an adequate and profitable supply of timber, regulated cutting of timber, and conservation of trees. Conservation, for the Company, was an act towards economic growth with huge promises of growing revenue from timber. It had no moral underpinnings. In fact, the Company had little concern for environmental ethics, even though some of its officials might have had personal convictions about the importance of ecological equilibrium and a balance in the ecosystem.[59]

By the mid-nineteenth century, as urban population grew and export markets developed for various crops, the prices of agricultural commodities moved upwards. Sedentary cultivation expanded. Expanding cultivation cut deeply into the forests. By 1830, the new regime actively encouraged forest-clearing and settlement. Its attention shifted from the more easily accessible and less heavily forested wastelands to the more forbidding forest areas. As forest products became a profitable and legitimate source of income, the Company asserted its exclusive rights on the forest products. In one instance, it declared in Gorakhpur through an *ishtihar* (advertisement) its right to forest products and invited proposals for farming them; it thus replaced the *zamindar*s whether in granting leases or gathering and propagating the forest product to the highest bidder.[60]

Forest clearance moved swiftly in the nineteenth century. The developments during this century and the attitude of the Company towards land – forests, grasslands, and wastelands – were influenced by the political and economic developments in Britain. The agricultural revolution in Britain had brought lessons that all processes of agrarian improvement and progress entailed cutting of trees and cultivation of wastelands.[61] Immediate clearing and cultivation of wastelands was placed in high priority on the agenda of the colonial government. The *zamindar*s, through the early modern period had possessed hereditary, proprietary rights over all lands, including wastelands, within their territorial limits. They were not divested of their powers and privileges by the Company. Instead, the Company depended on their ability to procure capital and labour for clearing and cultivating wastelands. The *zamindar*s were vested with the responsibility to improve the general condition of the estates. They, too, became aware of the inducements to extend cultivation as commercialism and material concerns penetrated into the villages. Changes in their attitudes gradually became visible. The *zamindar*s had, during the early modern period, adamantly stood by their trees and protected them from human harm, but now they succumbed to commercialism, cut trees, and even grew trees for the timber trade. More importantly, they also acquired access to revenue and the franchise to retain the entire surplus revenue after paying the government's share of the *jama*. If the *zamindar* defaulted or refused to cooperate, if the wastelands did not form a part of any *mahal*,[62] or if there were no claimants to the land, the Company resumed them as state property.[63] This was a most assured means of agrarian and commercial advancement.[64]

By the twentieth century, significant changes wrought throughout the world in the inter-relationship between man and his environment. This was caused by rapidly expanding urbanization and industrial growth. These systems threatened to irreversibly destroy natural ecosystems. There was also a constant engagement with the issues of striking a balance between human civilization and nature or establishing compatibility between growth and equilibrium; preserving spaces for nature even as the development continues and replacing fertile lands with industrial sites.[65] Growth, equity, and sustainability became major political issues. The question of sustainability raised serious questions about the kind of growth humans want, re-emphasizing the need for equity, both globally and locally.[66] Despite a global consensus on these matters, the Western industrialized nations, including the erstwhile colonial powers, have remained hesitant in their commitment to significant reductions, compensation for 'historical offences', or pledging costs for necessary improvements, pitting issues of the environment against historical legacies, historical justice, and a desire for development.[67]

Notes

1. Christopher A. Bayly, *The Birth of the Modern World, 1780–1914* (Oxford: Blackwell Publishing, 2004), 11. Modernity, Bayly argues, was not only a process but also a period which began at the end of the eighteenth century and has continued up to the present in various forms.
2. Harbans Mukhia, 'Subjective Modernities', NMML Occasional Paper, History and Society, New Series 13 (New Delhi: Nehru Memorial Museum and Library, 2013), 2–7.
3. Mukhia, 'Subjective Modernities', 8. Also see Prasannan Parthasarathi, *Why Europe Grew Rich and Asia Did Not: Global Economic Divergence, 1600–1850* (Cambridge: Cambridge University Press, 2011); Harbans Mukhia, 'Agricultural Technology in Medieval North India', in Harbans Mukhia, *Exploring India's Medieval Centuries: Essays in History, Society, Culture and Technology*, 277–306 (New Delhi: Aakar Books, 2010).
4. Environmental history is a dynamic and growing field; while it may be rooted in 'older questions' of medieval history, it takes advantage of new and exciting sources and methods and explores themes such as climate and ecological history, the history of agriculture and water, and landscape and religious studies, and it facilitates a look at the catalysts for human change. Defined as that which deals with the role and place of nature in human life, environmental history has been described as 'an unevenly spreading blob'. Formulations such as these reflect wide array of methods and approaches, and studies from different regions and periods. In fact, one of the significant features of environmental history is its competence to derive from the insights and techniques of several disciplines, and then to combine them in novel and often provocative ways of its own. See Ellen F. Arnold, 'An Introduction to Medieval Environmental History', *History Compass* 6, no. 3 (2008): 898–916, see in particular 898; Donald Worster, 'Doing Environmental History', in *The Ends of the Earth: Perspectives on Modern Environmental History*, ed. Donald Worster, 289–308 (Cambridge: Cambridge University Press, 1988); H. Ritvo, 'Discipline and Indiscipline', *Environmental History* 10, no. 1 (2005): 75–76. To understand various directions of environmental history, see Adam Rome, Michael Bess,

Tamara Giles-Vernick, Angela Gugliotta, Ramachandra Guha, Marcus Hall, David Igler et al., 'Anniversary Forum: What's Next for Environmental History', *Environmental History* 10, no. 1 (2005): 30–109; David Arnold and Ramachandra Guha, 'Introduction', in *Nature, Culture, Imperialism: Essays on Environmental History of South Asia*, ed. David Arnold and Ramachandra Guha, 1–20 (New Delhi: Oxford University Press, 1995), 4.

5. There were shared historical processes and long-term trends that accelerated during this period and deeply influenced human-induced environmental changes in a later period during the nineteenth and the twentieth centuries. In fact, it reflected profound continuities that linked the environmental history of the early modern and modern worlds. See John F. Richards, *The Unending Frontier: An Environmental History of the Early Modern World* (Berkeley: University of California Press, 2003), 1–3, 22.

6. *Pargana* was a piece of territory delimited by Mughal administration for revenue and administrative purposes.

7. Irfan Habib, *Man and Environment: The Ecological History of India*, A People's History of India 36 (New Delhi: Tulika Books, 2010), 88–89. Also see Shireen Moosvi, *The Economy of the Mughal Empire c. 1595: A Statistical Study* (New Delhi: Oxford University Press, 1987); Shireen Moosvi, *People, Taxation and Trade in Mughal India* (New Delhi: Oxford University Press), 2008.

8. Shireen Moosvi, 'Ecology, Population Distribution and Settlement Pattern in Mughal India', in Moosvi, *People, Taxation and Trade*, 89–102, see 89, 92–93.

9. Habib, *Man and Environment*, 94–95. Also see Moosvi, 'Ecology, Population Distribution and Settlement Pattern', 93; Tapan Raychaudhuri and Irfan Habib (eds.), *The Cambridge Economic History of India*, vol. 1: *c. 1200–c. 1750* (New Delhi: Orient Longman, 1984), 6.

10. Francisco Pelsaert, *Jahangir's India: The Remonstrantie of Francisco Pelsaert*, trans. W. H. Moreland and P. Geyl (Cambridge: W. Heffer & Sons, 1925), 48.

11. Ali Muhammad Khan, *Mi'rat-i Ahmadi*, vol. 1, ed. Nawab Ali (Baroda: Oriental Institute, 1927), 214. Also see Abdul Hamid Lahori, *Padshahnama*, vols. 1–2, ed. Kabiruddin Ahmad and Abdur Rahim (Calcutta: Bibliotheca Indica, 1867–1872).

12. Richards, *Unending Frontier*, 4–6. Also see John F. Richards, 'Only a World Perspective Is Significant: Settlement Frontiers and Property Rights in Early Modern World History', in *Earth, Air, Fire, Water: Humanistic Studies of the Environment*, ed. Jill Conway, Kenneth Keniston, and Leo Marx, 102–119 (Amherst: University of Massachusetts Press, 1999); Piers M. Blaikie and H. C. Brookfield, *Land Degradation and Society* (London: Methuen, 1987), 12; Meena Bhargava, *State, Society and Ecology: Gorakhpur in Transition, 1750–1830*, revised edition (New Delhi: Primus Books, 2014), 33–35.

13. *Sarkar* was a territorial subdivision of a *suba*, containing a group of usually contiguous *pargana*s.
14. Irfan Habib, *An Atlas of the Mughal Empire* (New Delhi: Oxford University Press, 1982), Map 8B, 29.
15. James Rennell, *Memoirs of a Map of Hindustan*, reprint (Patna: N.V. Publications, 1975).
16. *Jama* was the amount of revenue assessed on an individual, village, or larger area, or a standard estimate of net revenue for the purpose of *jagir* assignment.
17. Muzaffar Alam, *The Crisis of Empire in Mughal North India: Awadh and the Punjab, 1707-48* (New Delhi: Oxford University Press, 1986), 103. Also see Bhargava, *State, Society and Ecology*, xvi-xvii,
18. See Mayank Kumar, 'Ecology, Social Stratification and Agrarian Production in Medieval Rajasthan', in *Medieval India*, vol. 3: *Researches in the History of India*, ed. B. L. Bhadani, 257–270 (New Delhi: Manohar, 2012), see especially 258.
19. For more details, see David Ludden, *An Agrarian History of South Asia*, The New Cambridge History of India, vol. 4.4 (Cambridge: Cambridge University Press, 1999), 130–140, 148–150.
20. Mayank Kumar, *Monsoon Ecologies, Irrigation, Agriculture and Settlement Patterns in Rajasthan during the Pre-Colonial Period* (New Delhi: Manohar, 2013), 15–16.
21. Kathleen D. Morrison, 'Environmental History, the Spice Trade and the State in South India', in *India's Environmental History: From Ancient Times to the Colonial Period*, vol. 1, ed. Mahesh Rangarajan and K. Sivaramakrishnan, 296–326 (Ranikhet: Permanent Black, 2012); Kathleen D. Morrison, 'Conceiving Ecology and Stopping the Clock: Narratives of Balance, Loss and Degradation', in *Shifting Ground: People, Animals, and Mobility in India's Environmental History*, ed. Mahesh Rangarajan and K. Sivaramakrishnan, 39–64 (New Delhi: Oxford University Press, 2014).
22. Richard Eaton, *The Rise of Islam and the Bengal Frontier, 1204-1760* (New Delhi: Oxford University Press, 1997); Richards, *Unending Frontier*, 1–3; Chetan Singh, *Region and Empire: Punjab in the Seventeenth Century* (New Delhi: Oxford University Press, 1991).
23. Singh, *Region and Empire*; Chetan Singh, *Natural Premises: Ecology and Peasant Life in the Western Himalaya, 1800-1950* (New Delhi: Oxford University Press, 1998).
24. Jos Gommans, *Mughal Warfare, Indian Frontiers and High Roads to Empire, 1500-1700* (London and New York: Routledge, 2002), 202.
25. Gommans, *Mughal Warfare*, 201. Also see Rangarajan and Sivaramakrishnan (eds.), *Shifting Ground*, 10.

26. Rangarajan and Sivaramakrishnan (eds.), *India's Environmental History*, vol. 1, 1, 8.
27. Richard Grove, *Ecology, Climate and Empire: The Indian Legacy in Global Environmental History, 1400–1940*, (New Delhi: Oxford University Press, 1998), 56, 186.
28. S. H. Hodivala, *Studies in Indo-Muslim History: A Critical Commentary on Elliot and Dowson's History of India*, vol. 1 (Bombay: Popular Book Depot, 1957), 226–229.
29. Sunil Kumar, *The Emergence of the Delhi Sultanate* (Ranikhet: Permanent Black, 2007), 283–285.
30. Habib, *Man and Environment*, 95.
31. Kumar, *Emergence of the Delhi Sultanate*, 333–336.
32. Shireen Moosvi, 'Man and Nature in Mughal Era', Indian History Congress, 54th Session (Mysore, 1993), Thematic Symposium, *Symposia Papers 5* (New Delhi: Indian History Congress, 1993), 1–33.
33. Buchanan Hamilton, 'An Account of the Northern Part of the District of Gorakhpur', Book IV, MSS Eur D 91–93 (India Office Library, London), 91. Also see Abu Talib, *Tafzi'hul Ghafilin*, trans. William Hoey as *History of Asafu'd Daulah* (Lucknow: Pustak Kendra, 1971), p. 56.
34. Ghazala Shahabuddin, *Conservation at the Crossroads, Science, Society and the Future of India's Wildlife* (Ranikhet: Permanent Black, 2010), x; Laeeq Futehally, *Our Environment* (New Delhi: National Book Trust, 2004 [2000]), 33.
35. 'Micro-climate' refers to a set of climatic conditions, measured at a very local level, which directly affects the growth and reproduction of animals and plants. See Shahabuddin, *Conservation at the Crossroads*, x.
36. Shahabuddin, *Conservation at the Crossroads*, x.
37. Futehally, *Our Environment*, 33.
38. J. A. Voelcker, *Report on the Improvement of Agriculture* (London: Eyre and Spottiswoode, 1893), 109–110. Also see Bhargava, *State, Society and Ecology*, 34.
39. Gunnel Cederlof and Mahesh Rangarajan, 'Predicaments of Power and Nature in India: An Introduction', *Conservation and Society* 7, no. 4 (2009): 221–226, see 223.
40. Paul E. Little, 'Environments and Environmentalisms in Anthropological Research: Facing a New Millennium', *Annual Review of Anthropology* 28 (1999): 253–284, see particularly 262–263. Also see Xinru Liu, 'Migration and Settlement of the Yuezhi-Kushan, Interaction and Interdependence of Nomadic and Sedentary Society', in *India and Central Asia*, ed. Xinru Liu, 73–108 (Ranikhet: Permanent Black, 2012), 73, 102; Arun Agrawal and K. Sivaramakrishnan (eds.), *Social Nature: Resources, Representations, and Rule in India* (New Delhi: Oxford University Press, 2001), 5–6.

41. Shereen Ratnagar, *The Other Indians: Essays on Pastoralists and Prehistoric Tribal People* (New Delhi: Three Essays Collective, 2004), xi, 97–98.
42. Chetan Singh, 'Conformity and Conflict: Tribes and the "Agrarian System" of Mughal India', *Indian Economic and Social History Review* 23, no. 3 (1988): 319–340, reproduced in *Exploring Medieval India, Sixteenth to Eighteenth Centuries: Politics, Economy, Religion*, vol. 1, ed. Meena Bhargava, 259–286 (New Delhi: Orient Blackswan, 2010).
43. Chetan Singh, 'Forests, Pastoralists and Agrarian Society in Mughal India', in *Frontiers of Environment: Issues in Medieval and Early Modern India*, ed. Meena Bhargava, 71–97 (Hyderabad: Orient Blackswan, 2017), originally published in *Nature, Culture, Imperialism: Essays on the Environmental History of South Asia*, ed. David Arnold and Ramachandra Guha, 21–48 (New Delhi: Oxford University Press, 1995).
44. Ludden, *Agrarian History of South Asia*, 49.
45. See, Richards, 'Only a World Perspective Is Significant'; Richards, *Unending Frontier*, 4–10; Ludden, *Agrarian History of South Asia*, 16, 18, 49, 60.
46. Morrison, 'Environmental History, the Spice Trade and the State in South India', 296–325.
47. Singh, 'Forests, Pastoralists and Agrarian Society in Mughal India', 71–97
48. Moosvi, 'Man and Nature in Mughal Era'.
49. Daniel Esty and Marian Chertow (eds.), *Thinking Ecologically: The Next Generation of Environmental Policy* (New Haven: Yale University Press, 1997), 45.
50. Buchanan Hamilton, 'An Account of the Northern Part of the District of Gorakhpur', Book III, Mss Eur D 91–93 (India Office Library, London), 55. Also see David Hardiman, 'Power in the Forests: The Dangs, 1820–1940', in *Subaltern Studies* 8, ed. David Arnold and David Hardiman, 89–147 (New Delhi: Oxford University Press, 1994), 105.
51. 'Memorial Fragments of Azubah Clark' (Extracts from Her Diary and Letters), compiled by H. Clark, 1830, Mss Eur A 185 (India Office Library, London), 55. Also see Louisa Edwards, 'Illustrated Diary of a Journey to India', BM Add Mss, 43809–43813 (British Museum, London); Bhargava, *State, Society and Ecology*, 36–37; Bhargava 'Forests, People and State: Continuities and Changes', *Economic and Political Weekly* 37, no. 43 (26 October 2002): 4440–4446, also published in Bhargava (ed.), *Exploring Medieval India*, vol. 1, 287–306.
52. J. T. Brown to C. M. Rickets, 20 October 1803, Report on the Commerce and Customs of the Ceded Provinces, Board of Trade – Commercial Proceedings, vol. 172, 3–27 April 1804 (West Bengal State Archives, Kolkata). Also see Muzaffar Alam, 'Eastern India in the Early Eighteenth Century "Crisis": Some Evidence from Bihar', *Indian Economic and Social History Review*

28, no. 1 (1991): 43–71, see 66; Alam, *The Crisis of Empire*, 98; Moosvi, 'Man and Nature in Mughal Era', 13; Bhargava, 'Forests, People and State', 294–295.

53. See Singh, 'Forests, Pastoralists and Agrarian Society in Mughal India', 71–97.
54. *Nankari*, or *nankar*, was an allowance for *khidmat*, or service, performed by the *zamindars* in collecting and remitting land revenue. It was granted in the form of a deduction from the revenue paid or in the form of revenue-free land.
55. Alam, 'Eastern India in the Early Eighteenth Century "Crisis"', 66; Alam, *The Crisis of Empire*, 98; Satish Chandra, 'Role of the Local Community, the Zamindars and the State in Providing Capital Inputs for the Improvement and Expansion of Cultivation', in Satish Chandra, *Medieval India: Society, Jagirdari Crisis and the Village*, 166–183 (New Delhi: Macmillan, 1982), 175; Singh, 'Forests, Pastoralists and Agrarian Society in Mughal India'.
56. Buchanan Hamilton, 'An Account of the Northern Part of the District of Gorakhpur', Book III, Mss Eur D 91–93 (India Office Library, London), 55. Also see Bhargava, *State, Society and Ecology*, 36.
57. *Report on the Settlement of Goruckpore-Bustee District*, vol. 1 (Allahabad, 1871), 126, para 24. Also see Bhargava, *State, Society and Ecology*, 35–36.
58. Sumit Guha, *Environment and Ethnicity, 1200–1991* (Cambridge: Cambridge University Press, 1991), 28–29, 41–42, 55.
59. Secretary Sudder Board of Revenue to the Secretary to the Government NWP, 12 May 1868, Settlement of Jungle Tracts, Sl. No. 10, File No. 12, Box 3, Board of Revenue, NWP-Gorakhpur (Uttar Pradesh State Archives, Lucknow). Also see Bhargava, *State, Society and Ecology*, 33–51; Meena Bhargava and John F. Richards, 'Defining Property Rights in Land in Colonial India: Gorakhpur Region in the Indo-Gangetic Plain', in *Land, Property, and The Environment*, ed. John F. Richards, 235–262 (Oakland, CA: Institute for Contemporary Studies, 2002).
60. R. M. Bird to Officiating Member of the Sudder Board of Revenue, in-charge of unsettled divisions, 20 October 1829, Bengal Revenue Department, Right of Government to forest lands and their products in Gorakhpur, Board Collections, 1833–1834, vol. 1410, F/4/1410, 55691 (India Office Library, London). Also see Bhargava, *State, Society and Ecology*, 36–38.
61. Mahesh Rangarajan, 'Imperial Agendas and India's Forests: The Early History of Indian Forestry, 1800–78', *Indian Economic and Social History Review* 31, no. 2 (1994): 147–167, see in particular 152. Also see Bhargava, *State, Society and Ecology*, 45–48.
62. *Mahal* was a territorial unit for revenue purposes, identical with *pargana*.
63. Secretary to Government in the Department of Ceded Provinces to Thomas Graham, 11 October 1804, Proceedings Board of Revenue – Fort William,

vol. 9, September-October 1804 (Uttar Pradesh State Archives, Lucknow). Also see Deputy Secretary to Government, Revenue Department Fort William to Sudder Board of Revenue on deputation, 26 July 1831, Gorakhpur District, Settlement of Wastelands, Pre-Mutiny: Land Revenue Records, 1830–1837 (National Archives of India, New Delhi); Bhargava, *State, Society and Ecology*, 45–51.

64. R. M. Bird to Officiating Member of the Sudder Board of Revenue, in-charge of unsettled divisions, 20 October 1829, Bengal Revenue Department, Right of Government to forest lands and their products in Gorakhpur, Board Collections, 1833–1834, vol. 1410, F/4/1410, 55691 (India Office Library, London). Also see Bhargava, *State, Society and Ecology*, 45–51.
65. Cederlof and Rangarajan, 'Predicaments of Power and Nature in India', 222; Shahabuddin, *Conservation at the Crossroads*, xiv.
66. Anil Agrawal, 'An Indian Environmentalist's Credo', in *Social Ecology*, ed. Ramachandra Guha, 346–386 (New Delhi: Oxford University Press, 1994), 347.
67. Cederlof and Rangarajan, 'Predicaments of Power and Nature in India', 222.

8

The Early Modern Conundrum

Peninsular India and the Idea of Periodization in a 'Regional' Perspective

Ranjeeta Dutta

The idea of the sixteenth through eighteenth centuries comprising the early modern period has gradually and reluctantly acquired a certain currency in historical research. Nonetheless, it continues to remain an uncomfortable and nagging conundrum for 'medieval' Indian history, located conventionally between the thirteenth and eighteenth centuries. The condition of the early medieval, located approximately from the sixth to the twelfth centuries, was for a long time met with similar suspicion and uneasiness, though it is now a part of the historical canon.[1] While periodization has cognitively and conceptually structured time in history into the frames of ancient, medieval, and modern, it has also marginalized those areas and themes of historical investigation that do not conform to the categories of analysis comprising these time frames. This is what has given rise to newer categories for studying these marginalized subjects. However, notwithstanding the new challenges and excitement that these subjects have produced in historical research, they have often continued to remain marginal in university curriculum and classroom pedagogy. This chapter argues that the history of South India has conventionally appeared as the 'regional' exception within the frame of the medieval in Indian history. To address this, I emphasize the importance of alternate temporal frameworks like the early medieval and early modern to salvage the historical identity of South India and acknowledge its significance in academic research.

This chapter focuses on three issues. First, I discuss the idea of the medieval as a conceptual category and chronological construct in Indian history. Though there have been several writings in the recent past on the category of the medieval and its relevance in history writing, the emphasis here is on pointing out their implications.[2] I argue that the study of the medieval in Indian history, with its association with specific historical processes, is somewhat limited and exclusionary; this has in turn tended to influence pedagogical and research practices in Indian universities. Second, I argue that the chronological categories of the early medieval and the early modern provide frames of analysis that include a wide range of historical processes which till now have remained marginalized within the rubric of the medieval. Third, I focus on the historical processes in South Indian history from the fifteenth to the eighteenth centuries to argue that these comprise the early modern in the history of the region. While others have highlighted the role of shared experiences like the emergence of greater connections, global passageways, and transcontinental commerce in the rise of early modernity, there were also significant stimuli from within the subcontinent that contributed to the making of this historical condition during this period.[3] In this context, I will discuss the development of political and sacred geography, and the interactions between the two against the background of changing settlement patterns. I argue that these historical processes created a wider network of circulation and movement, which significantly influenced the idea of a region itself. At the same time, I emphasize that the onset of early modernity did not signify a total disjuncture from the medieval past; rather, there were elements of continuity. Colonial modernity was not completely disconnected from the medieval and early modern pasts of Indian history either. Their interactions were mediated by various historical processes, leading to different experiences of the modern, and in turn, producing subjective modernities.

Violence of Periodization in Indian History

Unlike the conceptual categories of the early medieval and the early modern, the medieval has hardly been problematized, debated, or discussed as a valid frame of periodization for Indian history. The chronological span of the medieval conventionally ranges from the thirteenth to the eighteenth centuries – a trend that began with the early nineteenth-century writings of James Mill and has continued into the present times.[4] The category of empire, the idea of political centralization influencing economic processes, religious developments mostly in terms of Sufism and Bhakti, and the notion of the ubiquitous use of the Persian language have dominated not only the research of this so-called medieval period but also its curriculum and pedagogy at universities. The establishment and decline of ruling dynasties – the Delhi Sultanate (early thirteenth to early sixteenth centuries) and the Mughal Empire (early sixteenth to mid-nineteenth centuries) – have traditionally determined the chronological limits and themes of various studies for this period in Indian history. The imperial framework dominated political history for a long time. Though state-formations were examined in terms of social and political processes, they were often reduced to a teleological analysis that would emphasize the indispensability of a centralized state. For a long time, any historical development or process that did not conform to this general framework remained neglected. The one important exception was a slim compendium published in 1970 on political formations in different regions in the centuries between the establishment and decline of the Delhi Sultanate.[5] Issues of social hierarchies – caste, *varna*, *jati*, and tribes – were rarely discussed for the longest time in the study of Indian history for the so-called medieval period, as if these issues were marginal to its understanding.

Roughly from the 1990s, certain shifts in historical research that were initiated almost three decades back emerged as the basis of several new themes. Sources in languages other than Persian, especially those in Rajasthani and Marathi, came to provide much-needed relief to the overwhelming domination of Persian as a source language. However, sources in these vernaculars were read around this time primarily within the hegemonic framework of Mughal history. They became important only as they were seen to be replicating the style of Mughal documents, and their histories were considered to be relevant only as a counterpoint or a complement to Mughal texts in Persian. Hence, while the Rajputs and Marathas dominated the histories of the regions of what we know today as Rajasthan and Maharashtra, other actors continued to remain marginalized.

As mentioned earlier, political processes that followed different trajectories outside the dominant Sultanate–Mughal imperial framework were treated as aberrations for a long time. Termed as 'regional', their historical importance remained marginal in history textbooks. In such a context, regional kingdoms emerged as counterpoints to the Delhi Sultanate and the Mughal Empire at particular moments in history, especially in the intervening period between the decline of the Sultanate and the advent of the Mughals. It was assumed until recently that since these regional kingdoms were not empires, they were not centralized; they were weak, short-lived, and their very existence – instead of the presence of a big empire – represented a phase of chaos and confusion. Thus, the phrase 'regional' came to denote a certain hierarchy of historical trajectories, and the history of southern India came to occupy a low position in this hierarchy.[6] Mohammad Habib and K. A. Nizami's edited volume, *A Comprehensive History of India*, reflects this understanding of history.

In many ways, some of the dominant historical trends that came to be characterized as medieval – the coming of Islam, ubiquitous presence of the Persian language, centralized states, the binary of empire and region, certain religious policies, and the selective relevance of some polities (especially the Mughal Empire) made the history of the peninsular region itself somewhat exceptional.[7] This exceptionalism was further highlighted when history-writing on the medieval period delineated a composite geographical space called 'South

India' with an ostensibly distinct homogeneous political and cultural identity. Such distinctiveness acquired legitimacy in the writings of history, which underlined a distinct trajectory called the 'History of South India'. In this historical imagination, South India was understood as 'a region characterized by a high degree of sharing of significant social, cultural and political elements and an order of interaction such as to constitute a viable unit for the study of certain problems'.[8] The kinship system based on cross-cousin and uncle–niece marriages, specific settlement patterns comprising the inimitable *nadu*s, the brahman villages called *brahmadeya*s, the ubiquitous temples, and, most significantly, specific languages and linguistic cultures – these came to be considered as the characteristics of this constructed image of South India.[9] Thus, in many ways, the South came to represent a challenge, especially in the medieval time frame, as its histories had repercussions in generating counter-categories that impeded the forging of cultural unity of the nation. Such a separate treatment by historiography is related to how a certain space was imagined in history and the process through which modern history-writing gradually became synonymous with a specific geographical and cultural construct of a region – both regarded as commensurable to each other.

K. A. Nilakantha Sastri pointed out that 'in general histories of India, the part of the country with which we are concerned figures in a small way ... on any view the history of South India is an integral and not the least interesting part of the history of India'.[10] It was against this backdrop that Sastri felt the need to write a separate history of the south, which according to him was 'all the land lying south of the Vindhyas'.[11] However, his treatment of the themes was always in conformity with the historiography of the general histories of India. In these histories, South India was shown to have centralized states with model institutions of local self-governance that were older than those in the 'North' and in many ways superior to them. For him, the periods that did not have 'stable' states did not merit any discussion. Thus, the phase following the decline of the Vijayanagara Empire (*c.* 1336–1672) in the sixteenth century and before the eighteenth went missing from the early history textbooks on South India, although this period was characterized by vibrant polities and cultures under various *nayaka* dispensations, especially those of Madurai, Tanjavur, and Ikkeri.[12]

This category of 'South India' in turn discursively produced certain regions with distinct cultural types within the space of peninsular India – one influenced by Sanskrit, Hinduism, and temples with a focus on the Tamil region; the other influenced by Islam, Persian, and the northern culture with a focus on the Deccan. The provenance of this regional binary can be traced to the formation of the Madras and Bombay Presidencies in the colonial period.[13] The history of the Vijayanagara

Empire and its territorial expanse stretching from Goa to Madurai for nearly three hundred years, the movement of various social groups from dry to wet regions integrating Tamil, Kannada, and Telugu linguistic regions, and the circulation of religious and intellectual ideas across boundaries – all challenging the simplistic notion of an ostensible 'clash of civilizations' between the 'Hindu South' and the 'Muslim Deccan' were virtually ignored in this historiography.[14]

Within the broad frame of South India, scholarly attention traditionally remained focused on certain areas, especially the Tamil region and its language. Indeed, the development of the Madras School of Orientalism and linguistic exercise under Francis Ellis at the College of Fort St George in the nineteenth century to produce a Dravidian proof underscoring the significance of the Dravidian language family set the tone for prioritizing Tamil over other southern languages.[15] In reality, however, there have always been distinct identities that have asserted themselves at different points in time – a fact that challenges the discursive homogeneity imposed by the overwhelming thrust on Tamil language and culture. This is exemplified in the historiography of the origins of the Vijayanagara state. N. Venkataramanyya argues for a Telugu origin of the Vijayanagara state and B. A. Saletore for a Kannada one.[16] Thus, even the idea of what comprises the space and history of the invented category of 'South India' has never been completely homogeneous, and this has continued to date.

Recent historiography has attempted to reduce the tyranny of the medieval time frame through research on the Vijayanagara Empire. But one cannot help one's cynicism about the existing histories of the Vijayanagara political formation. Guided by priorities set by the historiography of the Mughal Empire, the analytical focus here has remained largely on the *nayankara* system (a form of military tenure), the capital city at Hampi, the ruler Krishnadevaraya (*c.* 1509–1529), and the state's engagement with the Deccan Sultanates, especially the Bahamanis (*c.* 1347–1527).[17] In the process, various other themes like agrarian history, changing settlement patterns, demographic diversity and migrations, multiple political systems, shifting centres of political power, and forms of production and technology have been ignored.

Despite many discussions on periodization and the emergence of fresh analytical categories like the early medieval and the early modern, we still find the issue of periodization vexing. University departments continue to reflect the traditional tripartite division in their curriculum and teaching positions. The period of the early medieval has mostly been considered a part of early Indian historical scholarship and has usually been kept separate from the study of medieval Indian history. For instance, the history of the Cholas, considered a part of the early medieval in historical research, still appears in the curriculum of ancient Indian history in the functioning of most universities. The Chola state in addition has always been treated separately from the Vijayanagara kingdom, which is seen as a part of the medieval period. This has created many artificial separations in the historical processes of transition between the two political formations, considering that there were elements of continuity from the Chola period that influenced Vijayanagara state and society.

New Periodization, New Possibilities

Since the periodization of the medieval limits the range of historical analysis, the categories of early medieval and early modern – with their wider historiographical possibilities – have in many ways fostered new forms of historical writings. The category of the early medieval refers to the period between the beginning of the seventh century and the beginning of the thirteenth century. It has been described as a period of change or transition from the early historical (ancient) to the medieval. The historical processes that emerged during this period along with certain elements of continuity from the early period set the tone for historical tendencies since the thirteenth century. Developed as a reaction against the concept of disintegration and decline following the decline of the Guptas in the sixth century, the category of the early medieval focuses on the idea of historical processes as opposed to event-based histories. The proponents of this category feel that this period was significant in terms of regional histories, especially regional developments in economy and society. This regionalism, according to them, lent dynamism to Indian history in the subsequent period and was an expression of vibrant heterogeneous regional cultures. In recent years, these interventions have allowed historiographical discussions to be concentrated on the southern, eastern, and western parts of the subcontinent, as a move away from the traditional thrust on the northern parts, especially the Indo-Gangetic plains.[18] In many ways, the early medieval thus presents a historically sensitive schema that helps delineate complex historical processes like the expansion of state-society both horizontally and vertically, the evolution of polities 'from chiefdom to early kingdom to imperial kingdom', the growth of the regional societies simultaneous with the integration of tribal cults into the larger pantheon and 'peasantization of the tribal societies'.[19]

Over time, the analysis of state-formation in the early medieval period shifted from an overwhelming focus on dynastic changes, events, and stimuli from outside (invasions and wars) to social and economic dynamism from within. Historical research on the southern Indian polities could connect with this analytical framework because it provided analytical pathways to a complex gamut of historical processes in regions other than those in the Gangetic plains. For instance, the peasantization of tribes, agrarian expansion, social mobility, interactions between religious traditions, creation of hegemonic political ideologies, issues of legitimation, and the spread of state-societies – all identified with the study of the early medieval – could be applied to various regions including different parts of peninsular India. In this way, the emergence of the category of the early medieval has helped the cause of the historical analysis of South India.

Similarly, the category of the early modern has helped the analysis of fundamental and general historical processes that can further enrich the understanding of southern Indian history. The proponents of the category of early modernity argue that the Western world cannot be considered instrumental in ushering in modernity in South Asia. According to them, the historical processes between the sixteenth and eighteenth centuries exhibited indigenous characteristics of an early modernity that set them apart from the medieval. This early modernity emerged in conversation with India's interaction with the global world, which influenced its new indigenous processes. This set the tone for the emergence of colonial modernity in the nineteenth century, the nature of which was influenced by the Indian early modernity.[20] Since the advocates of the early modern have been mainly revisionists, the historians of medieval Indian history within the Indian academia have looked upon these new histories with suspicion and disdain. Further, according to some historians, there are limitations of early modern historiography which, while emphasizing 'various elements of modernity' in 'indigenous' cultural forms 'have often relied on the very tropes of the "medieval" that were once used to consign the Mughal empire to a backward 'medieval period'.[21] What can be said in response is that since the idea of historical transition is at the heart of periodization, it is expected that the concept of early modern will underscore the transition from the medieval. However, this does not mean that medieval times were backward and regressive. Rather, some of the historical processes of the medieval foreshadowed historical trajectories that characterized the early modern. In other words, the advent of early modernity did not engender a surgical break from the medieval. While a new-found global connectedness and its consequent influence on South Asian society indeed proved crucial in the production of early modernity, there were also significant pre-existent stimuli within the subcontinent that contributed eminently to this process.

The discussion in the following pages empirically demonstrates the meanings of the early modern in southern India through the changing historical processes that modified settlement patterns since the fourteenth century. The changes in these settlement patterns led to connections and interactions between the dry upland zones and fertile wet regions, with a simultaneous rise of warrior classes and newer agrarian elites who gradually challenged and replaced the older ruling elites. The socio-economic process generated the migration of various professional groups from one part of southern India to another, a phenomenon that was limited before the fourteenth century. The resultant opening of new areas of settlements and the rise of diverse social groups led to invigorated interactions between and integration of the Tamil, Kannada, and Telugu linguistic zones. All this formed the backdrop to the establishment of the Vijayanagara state in the fourteenth century.[22] This was accompanied by different imaginaries and practices of political and sacred geographies. On one hand, the older areas were *terra incognita* for the rising warrior groups. The conquest and occupation of these places created a 'geographic other' for them. On the other hand, new conceptions of political geographies occurred simultaneously with the development of sacred geographies reflected in the expanding pilgrimage networks and literature since the fifteenth century. Already present as a normative ideal in the textual traditions of the Shaiva and Srivaishnava communities, the pilgrimage was crucial in the circulation of the population through the creation of supra-local networks which gradually saw political consolidation. These developments marked the transition from the medieval to the early modern, a transition from local spheres of interaction to trans-local networks of transmission, movement, and distribution.

Settlement Patterns, Regional Configurations, and the Idea of a Region

Between the twelfth and fifteenth centuries, the Chola state policy of granting land to the brahmans and important officials eroded the traditional common rights over land and promoted individualistic landed relations resulting in an unprecedented rise in powerful individual landholders.[23] The growing number of landed titles – like *udaiyan, araiyan, nadalvan,* and *brahmanrayan* – bestowed by the Chola state indicate a rise in the number of powerful landed individuals. This affected the common holdings in villages, or *ur*s, where the population comprised the non-brahman Velalas. This led to a stratification of rural society, comprising a landed class, a class of cultivators, tenants, and landless peasants. Hill tribes, who had joined the Chola army, gradually also became a part of agrarian society by acquiring a landed base that transformed their social status from wandering martial groups to new sedentized *jati*s.

This change in the traditional agrarian landscape gradually ruined the erstwhile brahman landholders by the thirteenth century. Epigraphical evidence refers to the sale of land by the brahmans of the *brahmadeya*s to repay their debts. The decline of the traditional agrarian society led to tensions between the older and emerging landed classes. The focus of agrarian production gradually shifted to temples, which started emerging as central in the rural landscape as agrarian institutions expanded the agricultural base in the thirteenth century. Land grants to temples generated extensive agrarian activities. Controlled by rulers and rural elites, the temple cultivated the land through its religious functionaries. The returns from this form of agriculture were shared between the state, rural groups, and the temple in a certain proportion, decided by a prior agreement. Epigraphical records provide rich evidence on this matter.

Since the Kaveri delta – the core of the agrarian settlements – was already saturated and the *nadu*s, or the peasant ecotypes, had exhausted their capability, alternate areas of agricultural development emerged around this time with the spread of tank irrigation. This occurred not only in the dry areas of the Tamil region but also in the arid ecologically hostile areas of the Deccan. The expansion of agriculture in the core riverine areas of the Kaveri, Pennar, Tamraparani, and Krishna–Godavari led to competitive resource appropriation. The circulation of peasant groups and agricultural specialists like tank diggers accompanied this during this period. These groups had previously migrated from the Kannada and Telugu regions to the Tamil region. Further, there was a movement of warrior chieftains from areas of marginal resources to the wet riverine regions. The settlement of the migratory Telugu or the Vaduga groups in the central Deccan and the Tamil wet regions often displaced the older Tamil peasants and landholders, creating a new class of landed magnates with new groups of artisans and merchants. Consequently, the processes of migration integrated the dry upland areas and the river valleys of Kaveri and Tamraparani. These changes provided the context for the emergence of a warrior–peasant class, powerful both economically and politically, and primarily non-brahman and Telugu in composition. A new class of itinerant merchants and traders also emerged at the same time. Inscriptional references to the *pattanulkar* (silk weavers) from Saurashtra point to the development of brisk trade and increased craft production around this time.

Thus, changing settlement patterns, the rise of individual landed rights eroding collective ones, growing prominence of temples, migrations of various social groups, and circulation of resources together transformed the restricted areas of interactions in the Tamil region to create larger spaces and networks of integration across the entire peninsular region. The historical processes that led to the creation of these supra-local networks had already commenced in the thirteenth and fourteenth centuries with changing land rights and settlement patterns. The latter, in turn, set the tone for the fifteenth and sixteenth centuries in terms of the political consolidation across these supra-local networks. It is in this context that the Vijayanagara kingdom was established with its capital at Hampi in the north Karnataka region in the second half of the fourteenth century. The southward expansion and development of the state encompassing almost the entire peninsula occurred only by the end of the fourteenth century and the beginning of the fifteenth. This finally got consolidated and integrated in the sixteenth century under the Vijayanagara king, Krishnadevaraya.

Straddling different regions within the peninsula, these networks influenced political ideologies and constructed a certain kind of political geography for mapping the conquered areas. Defining the royal self, *prashasti*s (introductory portions) and political narratives articulated the imperial vision by metaphorically describing the lands to be conquered as a geographical 'other'. Moral decadence, the misery of the inhabitants, desolate temples with no festivals, and a tyrannical ruler would routinely be the characteristics ascribed to regions that were to be conquered. One of the earliest chronicles that in many ways set the tone was the *Madhuravijayam*, also called the *Kampanacharita*.[24] The text was composed in the fourteenth century by Gangadevi – the queen of the hero Kumara Kampana, the son of the king Bukka. It describes the southern campaigns, especially to Madurai, ruled by Alauddin Sikandar Shah. He was a descendant of Jalaluddin Ahsan Khan, the Khalji governor of Madurai who revolted around 1335 CE and established an independent sultanate. After the introductory portions, the text informs us that when prince Kampana grew up, his father Bukka advised him on his royal duties and pointed to the work that lay before him. Thereafter, Kampana marched southwards, subduing several forest chiefs and eliminating king Sambuvaraya of the Tondaimandalam region in a fierce battle. After describing this battle in considerable detail the narrative tells us that a goddess appeared before Kampana, describing the miserable plight of this southern country in the hands of the Turushkas or the Yavanas as a Dark Age, or Kaliyuga. She says: 'The Vedas have ended. Reason has disappeared. The voice of *dharma* is silent. Good conduct is gone. Noble birth is set aside.'[25] Thereafter, Kampana goes to Madurai, routs the Turkish (Turushka) forces, and beheads the Sultan. Gangadevi ends her narrative with Kampana being crowned and peace returning: 'With the Yavanas destroyed, the Dravida country shone again. It shone like a luster of forests when a forest fire has been put out. It shone like a bowl of the sky when an eclipse has just ended. It shone like the Yamuna river after Krishna killed the serpent demon Kaliya.'[26] Thus the defeat of the Sultan, undoubtedly a historic fact, was made honourable by creating an imagined geography of a region as the evil other to be urgently redeemed. Such narratives that collapsed the temporal–spatial idea with the social and cultural boundaries characterized early modernity in this part of the world. While the geographic vision created a political superior, it also delineated a distinct political identity in the pan-Indian conception of the Vijayanagara realms. Thus, our narratives tell us that their protagonists not only conquered the peninsular sites but also went up to the Himalayas and came back victorious to their kingdom. This imperial geographic ideal coincided with the Puranic cosmogony of 'the Lord of four Oceans' and became a significant statement of a great conqueror.

While the political chronicles of this period provided a conceptual template of the conquered regions, the inscriptions incorporated an epic Puranic vision of the extent of the royal territories and provided somewhat precise and concrete details of the kingdom. Almost all the inscriptions in their introductory portion introduce their patrons as the 'Lord of four Oceans' and 'he who ruled his kingdom on Earth'. Thankfully, for modern historians, in most cases, this is followed by concrete geographical details of the kingdom, including those about the territories, flora and fauna, precise regnal eras, and dynastic genealogies.

While the expansion of political geography involved a series of conquests, changes in the settlement patterns, and the circulation of various professional and social groups, it was also influenced by the simultaneous development of sacred geographies and increasing control over newly conquered areas. This is best illustrated by the visits the political elite paid to various temples along the route of conquests, their sojourns and donations in these areas, interactions with local social groups, and interventions in the temple administration. These indicated the desire for exercising political control over the religious resources of the region and its connections with sacred geography.

The descriptions of the geographical scope of conquests never missed an opportunity to mention the temples and sacred sites conquered, especially those that enjoyed great importance as centres of pilgrimage. There was already a vision of sacred geography between the fifth and tenth centuries among the Shaiva and Vaishnava communities, expressed through the hymns of their early saints – the *nayanmar*s and *alvar*s, respectively. The *nayanmar*s demarcated 274 sacred sites for the Shaiva community and the *alvar*s identified 108 sites for the Vaishnava community. These sites were not only confined to the southern parts but were present in the northern region also; this attributed a pan-subcontinental status to Shaivism and Vaishnavism.[27] However, the transition from an ideational norm, in which each site was sanctified and associated with divine action, specific divine presence, and physical descriptions of an area of active circulation in the fourteenth and fifteenth centuries made pilgrimage an important basis for religious identities. The actual practice of pilgrimage was reflected in the enactment of sacred performances in festivals and rituals involving various sections of the communities, enlarging the temple as an arena of public life. Besides, the journey to the sacred shrines within a well-defined area of circulation strengthened the spatial identity of the religious communities that encouraged not only the movement and interaction of people, but also the transmission, exchange, and circulation of ideas and beliefs.[28] This made the geographic imaginary of the sacred space relevant to a larger audience.

The concept of a *divyadesa*, or sacred space, emerged in the *guruparamparas*, or hagiographies, from the thirteenth century onwards. This was further developed in individual *sthalapurana*s, or temple texts, from the fifteenth century, against the backdrop of the development of the temple and its activities.[29] In these *guruparampara*s, the notion of pilgrimage had a special function. For the first time, pilgrimage emerged as a norm, enjoining devotees to physically visit the shrines to attain merit and salvation. The element of obligation implied that pilgrimage was equivalent to – and even more efficacious than – the exclusive brahmanical rituals and sacrifices. Eulogizing the sacred importance of a particular temple-centre within the pilgrimage network, the *sthalapurana*s often refashioned the epic and Puranic narratives to a specific geographical context. Their singular treatment of a particular site and a shrine was more to highlight the importance of the place. By considering themselves as a part of the Sanskrit *mahapurana*s, the composers of the *sthalapurana*s (mostly temple priests) linked the site to the larger pan-Indian sacred tradition.

Two ideas were introduced at the close of the thirteenth century. One was undertaking the actual journey to sacred places. Second, pilgrimage emerged as a sociocultural institution where each site with its individual history, legends, rituals, and deities came to be associated with the collective consciousness of the community and transcended the southern borders, thus fostering a pan-Indian identity. The pilgrimage network and its concurrent spatialization of the sacred sites thus created an interconnection between the local, supra-local, and subcontinental conceptualizations of space. For instance, in the case of the Srivaishnava community, the distribution of the formulaic 108 sites reflects this connection. The spatial distribution of the sites followed the traditional geographical divisions of the Tamil country and also included Ayodhya, Badrinath, Mathura, Dwarka, and other North Indian sites. The interconnections were further enhanced with the cosmic bonding of these sacred regions with two celestial sites – Vaikuntham, the Heavenly Abode of Visnu, and Tiruppadkadal, the Ocean of Milk.

However, the normative ideal of pilgrimage was not always fixed in the Shaiva and Srivaishnava communities. It was adopted, modified, and tacitly reconciled within the practical realm of community interactions in the fourteenth and fifteenth centuries. The pilgrimage process and its validation through mythical narratives in the *guruparamparas* and *sthalapuranas* represented a process by which the frontier was extended by the Vijayanagara Empire through the integrative ability of religion. This, in turn, had implications for the sustenance of kingship and the state. As a part of this process, those sites that had acquired political and religious relevance since the fourteenth century were incorporated within the frame of sacred geographies. An example of this is Melukote in Karnataka. With a focus on the Narayanasvami temple, it was not a part of the 108 sites in the Srivaisnava pilgrimage network. But both the site and the temple had become pilgrimage centres, more important than some of the 108 sites.

The interconnections within the sacred geographies were highlighted with the integration of diverse social groups with a particular temple site or several sites. For example, situated on a hilly tract in the Chandragiri area, Tirupati rose to prominence as a Srivaishnava centre in the fourteenth century. The establishment of the Vijayanagara political base in the Tondainadu area (close to Tirupati in the northern Tamil zone) and the consequent patronage made Tirupati a pre-eminent centre. Various local groups of the area, primarily comprising pastoral tribes like the Kodavars, Irulas, and Census were integrated through the temple and its ritual activities. The original myth of the Ahobila temple at Ahobilam (Kurnool district, Andhra Pradesh), recorded in its *sthalapurana*s, presented hunter chiefs as instrumental in the establishment of the site. An acknowledgement of their role by the myths justified and legitimized the patronage and participation of these groups in the administration of the Ahobilam temple.

One of the important motifs of integration was the divine marriage and the multiple consorts of Vishnu or Shiva. In this connection, the myths used the context of temples for projecting goddesses as spouses of the deity, where each goddess was situated in a particular local tradition. Since the temple was analogous to the cosmic world, the marriage between the god and the goddess was a re-enactment of the divine marriage that attempted to integrate and assimilate certain sites, their local folk populations, and religious beliefs.[30] The integration of the local population through this 'spousification' of the goddesses also consolidated the pilgrimage network. After all, it was the second bride who was a focus of the pilgrimage process. In all the temples, the marriage celebrations were an important part of the festivals and attracted numerous devotees. Very often, the process of spousification reflected the tensions that arose with the expansion of the religious network of the community. The tensions between the second bride and the brahmanical bride were palpable in such instances. The brahmanical bride would always be presented as 'golden complexioned', peaceful, and superior.[31] The second bride, who would be the autochthonous goddess and to whom the lord was attracted, would be dark and earthbound. For instance, one of the Puranic variants of the *Ahobilamahatmyu*, the *sthalapurana* of the Narasimhasvami temple at Ahobilam is as follows:

> Cencu princess being an expert huntress herself encountered lion in the forest who transformed into a man – i.e. Narasimhavami. They fell in love and after testing his prowess, sent him to her parents to get the consent. The parents had already heard the glory of Narasimha from the sage Narada who also informed them that their daughter was none other than Bhudevi herself. After their marriage, she was named Cenculaksmi. There were frequent quarrels between Laksmi and Cenculaksmi and ultimately, Laksmi deserted him and went away.[32]

This myth represented a process by which the frontier areas were extended by the Vijayanagara Empire through the integrative paradigm of religion, therefore having implications for the sustenance of kingship and state. Several such myths appear in the *sthalapurana*s of various temples. These temple texts represented a vision that combined the local and the pan-India, attributing the temple and its site with a sacrality that would make it significant both in the southern regions and in the larger pan-Indian pilgrimage network.

The conception of pilgrimage as the construction of a coherent sacred space was not without contestation. Further tensions and conflicts were evident when the sacred geographies and the pilgrimage networks were brought into the ambit of shared sacrality. Interestingly, two such temple centres were the ones at Srirangam and Tirupati, where Vaishnava and Shaiva communities clashed with each other, each trying to appropriate the other's sphere of control. The pilgrimage network evolved a hierarchy, both while projecting temple geography and also in the real sense. Some centres were of regional importance and hence enforced a regional identity. Some others promoted a supra-local identity and drew pilgrims from all over South India. Lastly, some pilgrimage sites became centres of religious activities and assumed a pan-Indian status. For example, Srirangam was a major Srivaishnava centre, and epigraphs refer to visits of the brahmans of 'Kasmiradesa' to it in the fourteenth century. Similarly, in the seventeenth century, Tirupati had emerged as the centre of Hathiram Jiyar *matha*, which was of North Indian origin.

Therefore, in many ways, the fourteenth, fifteenth, and sixteenth centuries were crucial in the circulation of populations through the creation of supra-local networks, especially pilgrimage networks. The pilgrimage networks mapped out a sacred geography that transcended the southern regions creating a pan-Indian identity. The resultant creation of a sacred geography of sub-continental proportions also provided a template for trade routes, political expansion, and movements of people. Paintings depicting temples and their respective plans become increasingly visible around this time, particularly in the seventeenth and eighteenth centuries. They represented pilgrimage maps. These pictorial depictions were not drawn on the scale and were heavy with cosmological symbolism, giving priority to the experience of the devotee, 'religious traditions of the place, forms of worship, the multitude of shrines, festivals, seasons, and often important political and social events (such as depictions of visits of royal or significant patrons, saints, processions, and pageants)'.[33] Topographic accuracy and topographic details of the actual site thus had no relevance in the process. In general, the 'pilgrimage maps are, to some extent, the first indigenous attempts to depict an abstract theology, a physical act of prayer and a sacred geography as physical representational space'.[34]

It is worthwhile to examine the interactions between the local and Portuguese geographic visions in the sixteenth and seventeenth centuries. It is possible that indigenous pictorial depictions of the region and the conceptualization of the process of spatialization influenced Portuguese cartography of the peninsular region. The advent of the Portuguese in the sixteenth century created another geographic vision as well as a concept of space and region through the introduction of European cartographic methods. Seas occupied an important place in this. It was an integral part of the geographical imaginary of South India. The passages through the seas created a space through which the Portuguese travellers Domingo Paes and Fernao Nuniz arrived at Vijayanagara in the fifteenth and sixteenth centuries, and wrote their well-known accounts of the region, city, kingship, festivals, and customs.[35]

Though influenced primarily by the new European tradition of cartography that emerged during the Renaissance, Portuguese map-making for the Indian subcontinent was an exercise that relied on the information and support of the Indians themselves. The Portuguese maps focused mainly on the coast, primarily the western coast, of India because of its economic and strategic significance. However, the advent of Portuguese cartography did not replace the cosmographic mappings from earlier times. It would be worthwhile to analyse whether the older and indigenous forms of spatial imaginations interacted with the new techniques of Portuguese map-making and if this produced new understandings of space. Interestingly, despite the presence of various European maps and the increasing knowledge about them, the peninsular region did not develop any indigenous maps as per European cartography during the period under focus. Rather, the people there continued with their own versions of visual representation of space, sacred geographies, and pilgrimage networks in response to the immediate needs of the society, polity, and economy.

Thus, there were multiple geographic visions of the peninsular region that influenced and contested each other. These varied and complex geographical imaginations produced an interconnected frame within which the ideas of the local and the cosmopolitan circulated, and generated contesting cultural and social identities. Edward Said's concept of 'imaginative geographies' becomes relevant here in identifying the intersections between geography and historical imagination of space and cultural identities during this period.[36] Imaginative geographies relate to the production of geographic knowledge in the imperial world while going beyond the techniques of cartographic mapping and focusing instead on the cultural and symbolic politics of space and place. In this sense, new spaces are constantly evolving and influencing not only the spatial orientation of the people but also the geopolitics of the region.

In our case, these pressures and conflicts were spatially reflected in varying perceptions and understandings of what constituted the 'South' in India. The dynamism and fluidity inherent in all these perceptions show that South India was never a static entity bounded by geopolitical and cultural specificities. Some ideas emerged at certain junctures and were handed down the generations, which within their respective sensitivities reworked or strengthened the received wisdom. Often described as a geographical space from the vantage point of one's existence, the idea of the South acquired multiple meanings. Thus, there was not one South but several such physical spaces that were considered the South, even within today's South India.[37]

Conclusion

Modernity has often been understood in terms of the creation of a sanitized secular sphere in which religion has no public role, its practice and ideas having been relegated to an individual's private life. It has been rightly argued that such an ideal of modernity is problematic for any culture, and the Indian case is no exception.[38] Recent writings have shown that religion and religious sectarianism were an integral part of early modernity and that indigenous factors significantly shaped the emergence of the public sphere that was informed by new ideas about individual identities, religion, and religious identities.[39] The idea of early modernity that I have outlined in this essay remained closely associated with religious processes. They marked at the same time a maturation of some of the tendencies of the preceding medieval period and the advent of novel tendencies that marked the emergence of modernity.

What also emerges is that the shift from the medieval to the early modern in peninsular India in course of the fifteenth through the eighteenth centuries needs to be understood in terms of changes in settlement patterns and circulatory networks from the local into the supra-local. Illustrated through political and sacred geographies and pilgrimage networks, these transformative processes challenged localism and insularities within the southern region. This went hand in hand with the emergence of global maritime networks, clearing of forests, rapid growth of agriculture, development of centralized states, connected world economies, and religious pluralism that characterized this period. Political and sacred geographies recast the idea of the local in this wider context, with localism being the defining characteristic of the pilgrimage sites. Connected through a supra-local network, specific local expressions of these sites acquired a cosmopolitan outlook during this period. It was at these interstices of the local and the global that we need to locate the emergence of the early modern condition.

Notes

1. Brajadulal Chattopadhyay, *The Making of Early Medieval India* (New Delhi: Oxford University Press, 2012).
2. Harbans Mukhia, '"Medieval India": An Alien Conceptual Hegemony?' *Medieval History Journal* 1, no. 1 (1998): 91–105; Daud Ali, 'The Idea of Medieval in the Writing of South Asian History', *Social History* 39, no. 3 (2014): 382–407. Also see *Medieval History Journal. Special Issue: Contextualizing the 'Medieval'* 1, no. 1 (1998): 3–164.
3. John F. Richards, 'Early Modern India and World History', *Journal of World History* 8, no. 2 (1997): 197–209; Sanjay Subrahmanyam, 'Connected Histories: Towards a Reconfiguration of Early Modern Eurasia', *Modern Asian Studies* 31, no. 3 (1997): 735–762; Sanjay Subrahmanyam, 'Hearing Voices: Vignettes of Early Modernity in South Asia, 1400–1750', *Daedalus* 127, no. 3 (1998): 75–104; Björn Wittrock, 'Early Modernities: Varieties and Transitions', *Daedalus* 127, no. 3 (1998): 19–40.
4. James Mill, *The History of British India*, vol. 1 (London: Baldwin, Cradock, and Joy, 1817).
5. Mohammad Habib and K. A. Nizami (eds.), *A Comprehensive History of India: The Delhi Sultanate (A.D. 1206–1526)*, vol. 5, part 2 (New Delhi: People's Publishing House, 1970).
6. Exceptions to this are the textbooks of Satish Chandra, Catherine Asher, and Cynthia Talbot. Satish Chandra, *History of Medieval India* (New Delhi: Orient Longman, 2007), 26–35, 138–161, 259–275; Catherine B. Asher and Cynthia

Talbot, *India Before Europe* (New Delhi: Cambridge University Press, 2008), 53–83, 186–224.
7. Janaki Nair, 'Beyond Exceptionalism: South India and the Modern Historical Imagination', *Indian Economic Social History Review* 43, no. 3 (2006): 323–347.
8. Burton Stein, *Peasant State and Society in Medieval South India* (New Delhi: Oxford University Press, 1980), 32.
9. Stein, *Peasant State and Society*; Noboru Karashima, *Ancient to Medieval: South Indian Society in Transition* (New Delhi: Oxford University Press, 2009); Noboru Karashima (ed.), *Concise History of South India: Issues and Interpretations* (New Delhi: Oxford University Press, 2014), 188–238; R. Champakalakshmi, 'Peasant State and Society in Medieval South India: A Review Article', *Indian Economic and Social History Review* 18, nos. 3–4 (1981): 411–426; Y. Subbarayulu, *Political Geography of the Chola Country* (Madras: Government of Tamil Nadu, Department of Archaeology, 1973); Kesavan Veluthat, *Political Structure of Early Medieval South India* (Delhi: Orient Longman, 1993).
10. K. A. Nilakantha Sastri, *A History of South India: From Prehistoric Times to the Fall of Vijayanagar* (Madras: Oxford University Press, 1975, Fourth Edition), 1–2.
11. Sastri, *A History of South India*, 3.
12. For an excellent study of the Nayaka period, see Velcheru Narayana Rao, David Shulman, and Sanjay Subrahmanyam, *Symbols of Substance: Court and State in Nayaka Period Tamilnadu* (New Delhi: Oxford University Press, 1992).
13. Thomas R. Trautmann, *The Madras School of Orientalism: Producing Knowledge in Colonial South India* (New Delhi, Oxford University Press, 2009).
14. Burton Stein, *Vijayanagara: The New Cambridge History of India*, vol. 1.2 (Cambridge: Cambridge University Press, 1989), 13–30; Asher and Talbot, *India Before Europe*, 53–83.
15. Thomas R. Trautmann, 'Inventing the History of South India', in *Invoking the Past: The Uses of History in South Asia*, ed. Daud Ali, 53–70 (New Delhi: Oxford University Press, 2000).
16. The arguments about the origin and nature of the Vijayanagara Empire were influenced by the rise of regional nationalism in the Madras Presidency amongst the Kannada and Telugu speakers in the 1930s. For details, see B. A. Saletore, *Social and Political Life in the Vijayanagara Empire: A.D 1346–1646* (Madras: Paul, 1934); N. Venkataramanayya, *Vijayanagara: Origin of the City and Empire* (New Delhi: Asia Educational Services, 1933 [1990]); Stein, *Vijayanagara*, 5–15.
17. Stein, *Vijayanagara*, 31–108; Noboru Karashima, *A Concordance of Nayakas: The Vijayanagar Inscriptions in South India* (New Delhi: Oxford University Press, 2002).

18. Hermann Kulke (ed.), *The State in India, 1000–1700* (New Delhi: Oxford University Press, 1995); Chattopadhyay, *Making of Early Medieval India*; Upinder Singh (ed.), *Rethinking Early Medieval India: A Reader* (New Delhi: Oxford University Press, 2012).
19. Chattopadhyay, *Making of Early Medieval India*.
20. Richards, 'Early Modern India and World History'; Subrahmanyam, 'Connected Histories'; Sanjay Subrahmanyam, 'Hearing Voices: Vignettes of Early Modernity in South Asia, 1400–1750', *Daedalus* 127, no. 3 (1998): 75–104; Wittrock, 'Early Modernities'; David Washbrook, 'Intimations of Modernity in South India', *South Asian History and Culture* 1, no. 1 (2009): 125–148.
21. Ali, 'The Idea of Medieval', 407.
22. For details, see Stein, *Vijayanagara*, 13–30; Karashima, *Ancient to Medieval*; Karashima (ed.), *A Concise History of South India*, 188–238; Ranjeeta Dutta, *From Hagiographies to Biographies: Ramanuja in Tradition and History* (New Delhi: Oxford University Press, 2014): 78–110.
23. Karashima, *Ancient to Medieval*.
24. Richard H. Davis, *Lives of Indian Images* (Princeton: Princeton University Press, 1997), 113–142; K. A. Nilakantha Sastri and N. Venkataramanayya, *Further Sources of the Vijayanagara History*, vol. 3: *Translations and Summaries* (Madras: University of Madras, 1946).
25. Davis, *Lives of Indian Images*, 117.
26. Davis, *Lives of Indian Images*, 119.
27. Friedhelm Hardy, *Viraha-Bhakti: The Early History of Krsna Devotion in South India* (New Delhi: Oxford University Press, 1983); Indira Viswanath Peterson, 'Lives of Wandering Singers: Pilgrimage and Poetry in Tamil Hagiography', *History of Religion* 22, nos. 3–4 (1983): 338–360; Indira Viswanath Peterson, *Poems to Siva: The Hymns of the Tamil Saints* (New Delhi: Motilal Banarsidass, 1991); Ranjeeta Dutta, 'Pilgrimage as a Religious Process: Some Reflections on the Identities of the Śrīvaiṣṇavas of South India', *Indian Historical Review* 37, no. 1 (2010): 17–38; Bharati Jagannathan, *Approaching the Divine. The Integration of Alvar Bhakti in Srivaisnavism* (New Delhi: Primus, 2015), 224–278.
28. Burton Stein, 'Circulation and the Historical Geography of Tamil Country', *Journal of Asian Studies* 37, no. 1 (1970): 7–26.
29. For a detailed study of the *sthalapurana*s, see David Dean Shulman, *Tamil Temple Myths: Sacrifice and Divine Marriage in South Indian Saiva Tradition* (Princeton: Princeton University Press, 1980).
30. Shulman, *Tamil Temple Myths*, 138–421.
31. Shulman, *Tamil Temple Myths*, 267–271.

32. Sri Govindacarya (ed.), *The Ahobilamahatmayu of Peddaru Aiyangar* (Madras, 1936): 45–92; M. L. K. Murty, 'The God Narasimha in the Folk Religion of Andhra Pradesha, South India', *South Asian Studies* 13, no. 1 (1997): 179–188.
33. Vivek Nanda and Alexander Johnson, *Cosmology to Cartography: A Cultural Journey of Indian Maps* (New Delhi: National Museum, 2015), 45.
34. Nanda and Johnson, *Cosmology to Cartography*, 31.
35. Vasundhara Filliozat (ed.), *Vijayanagar as Seen by Domingos Paes and Fernao Nuniz (16th Century Portuguese Chroniclers and Others)* (New Delhi: National Book Trust, 1996), 70–71.
36. Edward Said, *Orientalism* (New York: Vintage Books, 1979), 49–72.
37. The names of two groups within the Srivaisnava community tradition – Vatakalai and Tenkalai – can be cited as examples. Vatakalai meant north and refers to Kanchipuram (Chingelput district, Tamil Nadu) to the north of Srirangam (Tiruchchirapalli district, Tamil Nadu). Tenkalai means south and refers to Srirangam. It should be noted that both Kanchipuram and Srirangam are in south India.
38. For details, see Akeel Bilgrami, 'Secularism, Nationalism and Modernity', in *Secularism and Its Critics*, ed. Rajeev Bhargava, 380–417 (New Delhi: Oxford University Press, 1998); Peter van der Veer, *Imperial Encounters: Religion and Modernity in India and Britain* (New Delhi: Permanent Black, 2001), 3–54; Talal Asad, *Formations of the Secular: Christianity, Islam and Modernity* (Stanford: Stanford University Press, 2003), 1–20.
39. Elaine M. Fisher, *Hindu Pluralism: Religion and the Public Sphere in Early Modern South India* (Berkeley: University of California Press, 2017), 1–31.

PART III
POLITICS, LAW, WAR

9

Fidalgos, Soldados, Arrenegados
Portuguese Adventurers in Hugli and Early Modern Politics

Radhika Chadha

This chapter is a reflection on the political economy of South Asia in the sixteenth and seventeenth centuries, a period that often carries the epithet 'early modern'. It seeks to interrogate the processes of state formation in this period and asks whether the peculiarities and specificities of these allow a useful invocation of the term 'early modern'. I investigate this through the prism of a small region, Hugli, during the period *c.* 1580–1633 and approach the theme through the somewhat unusual case of a South Asian empire.

The Portuguese Estado da India is mostly regarded as a pre-modern European empire, akin to other contemporary pre-capitalist Iberian imperialisms, and distinct from its North European colonial successors. Correspondingly, contemporary Asian empires such as the Ottoman, Safavid, and Mughal have traditionally been studied as distinct species of the same genus, namely medieval South Asian empires. I suggest that there existed important similarities between the Portuguese and Mughal states, which allow us to contemplate certain political processes and features in the centuries immediately preceding the arrival of colonial modernity in South Asia. I argue that while they originated in entirely different worlds, these states shared broad 'family resemblances'.[1] These commonalities can be seen through an unusual point of contact: freelancing adventurers who moved between well-defined imperial spaces.[2]

One of the key formulations of early modernity – as it has been defined in recent years – in South Asia has been the emergence of large and stable empires unprecedented since ancient times.[3] It is sometimes regarded as an 'age of empire' between ages without empire – the unsettled fifteenth and the long eighteenth centuries. Some scholars have emphasized the assertion of regional identities as a conjunctural development of the second millennium.[4] This leads us to a picture in which empires of impressive size and strength loomed large over discernibly strong regions. In the sphere of political economy, early modernity has been characterized by regional players having a great say in determining imperial structures – something that vastly diminished in times to come. This becomes especially visible in peripheral areas, far removed from the core imperial zones.[5] Here, we find a political scene crowded with numerous political players whose activities shaped empires from the margins.

This chapter focuses specifically on coastal and deltaic Bengal in the sixteenth and seventeenth centuries. This was a region where Portuguese officials and freebooters jostled to carve out a space for themselves within a fiercely competitive political milieu. They formed a small component of more than one enormous imperial spread, involving the Estado da India, the Mughal Empire, the kingdom of Arakan, and the regional principalities of Bengali warlords. The ways in which the Portuguese related to each of these powers cast light on the nature of early modern political systems. Their pursuit of private fortunes serves as a frame that allows us to explore a political world composed of states that were ethnically and culturally entirely foreign to each other, yet structurally akin. This world was porous, accommodating, and not very 'tightly ruled'.[6] The political actors who operated in this zone successfully navigated spaces as far removed as Portuguese Goa and Cochin and the deltaic folds of Mughal Bengal.

These Portuguese adventurers operated within a complex political and cultural landscape, in which regions were amorphous. Linguistic skills and cultural osmosis were crucial for individual success. This was relevant at the upper end of the political scale as well. It was equally compelling for rulers to imaginatively reinvent notions of sovereignty, to suit multi-ethnic populations encompassing several cultural spheres.[7] Through the operations of merchants and adventurers, the coastal folds of the Bengal delta came to be yoked loosely to the Portuguese imperial arm while still forming a part of Asian empires. Portuguese settlements and enclaves lay, variously and simultaneously, in the domains of Afghan rulers, the Mughal emperor, and the king of Arakan. Their territories came to form a significant component of all these kingdoms.

One important characteristic of the early modern condition for South Asian polities was their imperfect control and indistinct boundaries. Frontiers did not represent hard boundaries to be defended but, rather, signified contact zones, merging spaces for negotiations and mediations, exchanges, and crossings.[8] Frontiers were also viewed as gateways, to be sized up for opportunities and knocked on for alliances. The incorporation of new territories was often merely indicated through imperial markers of sovereignty.[9] In terms of imperial formations, we can hence imagine early modernity in terms of the existence of sprawling webs of control radiating from foci of power at nodal points. The Mughal web spreading from towns and rural fortresses along well-maintained roads and efficient communication networks was a particularly successful example.[10] We can perceive a similarity with the Portuguese Estado da India, an empire floating on a seaborne web of oceanic and coastal routes linking its nodal points of power located in port cities.

Nevertheless, it is important to recognize that neither empire confined itself to its ostensible zone of strength. The historiographic divide created between Portuguese (read European) concerns at sea and Mughal (read Asian) limits on land is artificial.[11] I would like to argue that developments in these two vastly different ecological zones were closely linked through political actors on each side, displaying a close concern with events on the other.[12] This led to a linking of hitherto far-flung spaces in a new way. Individuals and states displayed unprecedented capacities to reach out beyond the predictable and familiar. The keen understanding displayed by political players of developments in seemingly unrelated regions is indicative of the early modern condition.

With multiple players straddling a variety of ethnic, cultural, and geographical worlds, working established channels and conduits of authority, and seeping through borderlands that lay all around, much that was crucial to early modern states often developed outside of state initiative and control. It is not that such processes occurred *despite* state directives and checks; rather, they took place *with* state endorsement of this 'joint enterprise'. The looseness of the weave in the fabric of early modern states gave ample scope for individual initiatives. Multiple players operating on the edges of empires were an integral part of the political economy of South Asia during the period under focus. In Bengal, where the web of state power – both Portuguese and Mughal imperial control – was especially thin, the fluidity, impermanence, and constant regenerative nature of rule in the hands of a number of actors are thrown into sharp relief. Bengal thus offers a particularly good site for analysing the dynamics of early modernity in the sphere of politics.

In this chapter, I first argue that Bengal was, and remained, peripheral to the Portuguese Empire in Asia, in terms of the Estado da India's core concerns and zones of activity. Second, I show how Portuguese personnel settling or moving on these margins formed the penumbra of Portuguese society in Asia. Finally, through a focus on the premier settlement at Hugli, I separate out the tangles that held together the imperial spread in the Bay of Bengal. A port that had seen a meteoric rise in the early seventeenth century, Hugli represents the nodal point of this world, drawing together individuals, communities, places, and regions in newly fashioned affiliations. It thus encapsulates the complex economic and political entanglements that were defining features of early modernity.

The Regional Setting

From the outset, the Portuguese knew that Bengal offered neither the Christians nor the spices that had originally brought them to Asia. Consequently, the Portuguese Crown did not evince much interest in the region during the first two decades of the sixteenth century. Yet, in its efforts to acquire spices for the European market via the Cape route, it soon realized that it had to get involved in the intra-Asian trade. It could pick up cotton and silk textiles from Coromandel and Bengal, gold and precious stones from Pegu, and silver from Bengal, and exchange these for spices in the Moluccas and Malabar. Further, many of its most important outposts, including Goa, Malacca, and Hormuz, were mostly dependent for their basic supplies of foodstuffs on overseas sources. In this scenario, the reputation of Bengal and Pegu as food-surplus areas flush with supplies held special promise. Yet another reason for the growing official interest in the region was its flourishing ship-building industry, reputation of which soon reached the officials at Cochin and Malacca. Given the intense maritime activity that they had to undertake for their vast, pan-Asian seaborne empire, not to speak of the great fleet that sailed from Lisbon to Goa and back each year, the Portuguese rapidly became keen to establish contact. Moreover, Bengal was the largest Asiatic producer of saltpetre – the main ingredient of gunpowder, which in turn was a vital instrument and component of Portuguese firepower in the Indian Ocean region.

As the Portuguese Empire was being laid out in Asia, closely supervised by the Crown to safeguard its primary interests, alternative constituencies were developing within.[13] These were as powerful in giving shape to the enterprise as the priorities and concerns of the court itself. Private interests of the highest-ranking *fidalgo*s (nobles) and coteries of *casado*s (settlers) reared up almost immediately – 'regional' interests carrying their weight in the corridors of high power and prevailing in momentous matters. It was this 'region within' that was instrumental in replacing a centrist like Afonso de Albuquerque with a regionalist like Lopo Soares de Albegaria for the top job of governor general itself. It was able to project sharply its own spaces in the 'imperial' enterprise, in terms of territories and operations. Such private determinants of state concerns grew visibly under the momentum of their own success. As they blotted out regions like Bengal from direct operations of the king, they sucked large numbers out of these operations themselves, tempting *soldado*s (soldiers) to jump ship and turn *arrenegado* (renegade) with the promise of opportunity. Such developments allow us to question the idea that the Portuguese Empire in Asia was centrally driven, as many crucial turns taken were directed by back seat concerns.

Clearly, private interests could press hard enough to frame state policies of consequence. Even after the centre fought back to regain the reins of control, the 'region within' prevailed in having *carreira*s (trading voyages) instituted to areas it had already identified as its own. Arguably, this is how the Portuguese presence in Bengal–Arakan–Pegu came to develop differently from the way it did in the western Indian Ocean. In turn, this region provides a filter through which to view the overall Portuguese imperial enterprise in Asia.

Men on the Move: Greener Pastures, Newer Horizons

In 1548, one of the officers serving in the Estado da India wrote from Goa to D. Joao III, the king of Portugal, that in 'Pegu and Bengal and the whole coast of Coromandel … are settled a quarter of the people that come (to Asia) from the Kingdom [of Portugal]'.[14] Clearly, in terms of manpower alone, such regions had come to form a major part of the Portuguese presence in Asia.

The significance of regions ringing the Bay of Bengal has long been belittled, classified as the 'shadow' of the Portuguese Empire in Asia. But a closer investigation reveals that the activities of Portuguese 'renegades' in the east did not develop as an aberration of 'normal' activity under the aegis of empire. Rather, their activities help us understand the Portuguese presence in Asia in a more holistic manner. These were collaborative and creative rather than controlled and dictated centrally. If a quarter of the Portuguese personnel who landed on the west coast of India left for Bengal aboard ships owned or sponsored by the Crown, armed with artillery taken from the royal stores, with the active help of the monarch's own caretakers and storekeepers, it is difficult to see them as fleeing the shores of empire rather than leading a joint enterprise into unchartered waters.[15]

The host of small – and not-so-small – settlements that sprang up around the Bay of Bengal most often were, in fact, not seen by contemporaries as lying 'in the shadow' of empire. Many were set up with the knowledge, and sometimes even the tacit assent, of imperial authorities in the west. In every case, the Estado da India showed itself eager to embrace a success story in the east. Sanjay Subrahmanyam points out that as Portuguese 'official' settlements were being hammered out along the west coast, so was *fidalgo* corsair activity taking place elsewhere. The privately initiated settlements formed a part of the Portuguese presence in Asia – a different part no doubt than those with an alternate origin story, but a large enough part to qualify in our understanding of the nature of the Portuguese Empire. As we shall see, boundaries were not so well drawn, and the formation and maintenance of states remained fluid and processual throughout this period. References to them reveal that settlements created by personnel operating outside Crown directives continued to occupy the interest of the Estado da India as much as the Estado constantly remained on the fringes of the vision of these adventurers, fluctuating between hesitation and embrace.[16]

The significant numbers of personnel that chose to venture forth did so for a variety of reasons. Very early in the history of the Portuguese in Asia, we find references to the corruption of the king's officers and the ill-paid and neglected state of the soldiers and lower officials in the Estado da India, forcing them to desert in large numbers.[17] This complaint was echoed through the sixteenth century and came to be recognized in all quarters as a real problem facing the Portuguese establishment. Yet not everyone fled under pain of starvation; some sought to test new waters in search of better prospects. The accusation *foy a Bengala sem liçenca* ('unauthorizedly left for Bengal') is endlessly repeated in the letters of the 1540s, with the implicit understanding that the captain and other officials at Cochin received handsome payoffs and protected the thieves.[18] The Bay of Bengal soon acquired the reputation of a region of much opportunity; even senior *fidalgos* were tempted to make a brief sojourn in the area to try their hand at making some money on the side.

Most of these deserters from the Estado da India left, burning their bridges behind them, to seek better fortunes elsewhere. They attempted to settle in regions of their choice and establish good relations with local polities. As early as 1521, we have settlers like Martim de Lucena at Gaur, well-blended into local society and culture, speaking fluent Persian, clad in 'Moorish' attire, in the employ of and on excellent terms with the Sultan. We are told that he wielded so much influence that he could single-handedly make or break the fate of the governor of Goa's embassy to the court at Gaur.[19] He was not a stray example either; there were already several Portuguese settled in Bengal by this time. Many discovered that they could find fruitful employment as mercenaries in the armies of local rulers and warlords. Most also carried their own artillery. At least one account of their activities in the seventeenth century preferred to count the strength of these warring bands of Portuguese roaming the area, not in terms of the number of persons but in terms of the number of carbines.[20] In this deltaic and coastal terrain, their naval skills offered enormous advantages.

There are several words associated with persons settled in areas beyond the reaches of empire in contemporary official Portuguese correspondence. These include *alevantado* (rebel), *arrenegado* (renegade), *chatim* (deserter), and *homiziado* (refugee or fugitive). The distinctions are interesting in themselves and indicate various shades of official attitudes. The Estado da India seems to have maintained a register of runaways. Classifying them in this manner served the purpose of negotiating passages of return for them along with their acquisitions. Significantly, we have no references to punitive plans on the part of the state to rein them in or to prevent such an exodus. Rather, the Estado contemplated seriously, and in a sustained manner over a century, various ways of reclaiming such persons for the official fold. The names of dozens of such adventurers pepper contemporary accounts. In the description of their actions, the sheer enterprise, daring, gall, and bravado of these adventurers are striking. Such interest-governed action in the pursuit of profit points to the emergence of a new kind of political actor around this time, who were not bound by customary loyalties and typified the early modern political milieu.

Hugli: The Jewel Evading the Crown

The story of Hugli – by far the largest, longest-lived, and best-entrenched Portuguese enclave in the region of Bengal – allows us to examine the Portuguese Empire as an example of an early modern polity in Asia. I argue that Portuguese Hugli was also a crucial element in Mughal Bengal – a valued economic presence and a transformative force in military matters.

Unlike several Portuguese settlements in the region, Hugli was not associated with the career of a particular adventurer. In that sense, its own history was not limited to the capacities, vision, and fortunes of any single individual. Located 'sixty leagues inland from the sea', it was originally only a salt market.[21] Portuguese traders arrived there to conduct seasonal trade from temporary straw-and-thatch settlements, something that formed the norm of their mercantile activity in the western Gangetic delta.[22] It seems to have gradually taken over from Satgaon, which was situated slightly upriver and was earlier the chief port of Bengal in the western delta. This was the *porto pequeno* (small port) of the Portuguese sources till about 1565. In course of the sixteenth century, the harbour of Satgaon began to silt up, so that already in 1532 João de Barros found it 'not ... so convenient for the entrance and departure of ships'.[23] By 1565, larger ships had stopped going there and instead anchored downstream at Betor.[24] The shifting of Portuguese trade further downstream to Hugli appears to have been a fallout of these general developments.

Despite the impression of the rudimentary nature of the trade conducted from Satgaon in these travel accounts, it seems to have been quite substantial in scale in terms of money, manpower, and shipping. Ironically, the stakes involved only become clear to us when the system broke down. The ramifications of this trade figured prominently in the complaints filed before the Portuguese Crown in 1563. At a time when the harbour at Satgaon was presumably proving prohibitive to furthering trade, Antonio Furtado, the captain major of the voyage from Cochin to Porto Pequeno, reported that a crackdown on the port by the Bengal Sultan the previous year had led to

> ... losses in terms of money and goods [which] amounted to over 300,000 gold *pardaos* and between Portuguese and other Christians some hundred people were killed and over three hundred captured, and thirty large and small ships captured and burnt, together with much artillery, and many muskets, and many other arms....[25]

Several questions and implications linger in the wake of such an incident. Why did the ruler of Bengal destroy a long-standing trade in this brutal and decisive manner? The Estado da India had had a customs house in Satgaon since 1536, and Portuguese traders had been frequenting the port since much earlier. Interestingly, local trading interests seemed keen to repair the rupture almost immediately, because on the heels of the Captain Major there arrived at Cochin envoys from Bengal, with the promise to have the captives and ships released. Trade with the Portuguese was obviously too valuable to lose in the heat of the moment. The Portuguese seem to have returned to their usual practice of seasonal trade soon afterward as we have references to this even a decade later. Yet this kind of vulnerability made them keen to acquire a more secure foothold where they had some protection. This became a factor in their move to Hugli when the opportunity presented itself.

Testing a Knot: New Possibilities

Most of the Persian accounts pertaining to the origin of the Portuguese settlement at Hugli are ambiguous and generic in nature. We know from Friar Manrique that it was founded based on an imperial *farman* from the Mughal emperor Akbar. He clearly indicates that Akbar's interest in these Portuguese merchants who came to Hugli every year from all over Asia and chiefly from Goa, Malacca, Ceylon, and China stemmed from their reputation as formidable maritime merchants who commanded a very profitable trade. In fact, the Mughal *shiqdar* of the district apparently had long since been trying to befriend them and persuade them to settle there. The vast scale of their trading activities, which were still conducted in a seasonal manner from temporary installations, can be gauged from the fact that they had given out money advances amounting to over two hundred thousand rupees to local merchants in 1577 to acquire goods prior to their return the following season.[26]

It was in this context that Akbar sent word, summoning the Portuguese merchants from Hugli to his court. The Portuguese deputation to Fatehpur Sikri was led by one Pedro Tavares, the recipient of the Crown voyage from Goa

Fidalgos, Soldados, Arrenegados

to Satgaon in 1578. Subsequently, the emperor issued a *farman*, allowing the Portuguese to choose the site of construction of their proposed settlement at Hugli and granting them adjoining lands to support their establishment.[27] The Portuguese settlement at Hugli was, thus, formally founded around 1579–1580 with imperial sanction. The viceroy at Goa and the bishop at Cochin were immediately informed.[28]

The early settlers at Hugli were described in Portuguese official circles as 'highway robbers and men of loose lives', who then actively encouraged others like themselves to come and settle there.[29] The 'captain' of the settlement, presumably the same Pedro Tavares, 'assisted everyone; to some he gave gifts of money, to some he made loans, while he stood security for others. All started trading and soon raised Ugulim [Hugli] to the position of one of the richest towns in the East'.[30] In addition, the plentiful availability of foodstuff in Bengal proved very attractive to *casado*s (married settlers) from various parts of the Estado da India. They moved with their families in increasing numbers, year after year, to escape the food shortages that the Estado settlements often faced elsewhere.[31]

Hugli soon became the premier settlement of the Portuguese in Bengal. While it is difficult to determine the exact strength of its population, we do get the sense that it was numerically much larger than any other in the region. Writing in 1603–1604, Fr Fernão Guerreiro reckoned that Hugli had a population of five thousand, of which two and a half thousand were Portuguese, both pure and of mixed blood.[32] Fr Joseph de Castro, in a letter from Agra in 1638, said that there were twelve thousand Christians at Hugli before the siege of 1632.[33] Augustinian records place the figure at seven thousand Christian residents of Hugli, plus a large number of foreign merchants who were at the port at the time.[34] Taking into account the Indian mercantile communities and, above all, the huge assortment of artisans and working groups, the actual size of the composite population of the town would have been much larger.

Riding Bareback: Estado on Lasso, Mughals in Arms

Based in Hugli, Portuguese merchants operated an enormous and widespread trade throughout the Bay of Bengal and beyond. Possibly the most lucrative part of their trade was in the commodities forbidden to private trade in Asian waters by the Portuguese Crown: cloves, nutmeg, and mace from the Molucca Islands and Banda, camphor from Borneo, and cinnamon from Ceylon.[35] The trade circuit between Bengal and Cochin was another large and important component, in which the *casado*s of Cochin participated with as much enthusiasm as the Portuguese merchants of Hugli.[36] The main item of trade was Malabar pepper in exchange for Bengal textiles, sugar, and rice. Though this trade was in principle illegal, it was highly profitable. From Hugli, pepper was shipped to the Red Sea by Gujarati merchants, thus circumventing the blockade of direct linkage of the ports of the Red Sea with the Malabar Coast.[37] It is this kind of trans-regional trade, with its truly global reach, that John Richards highlighted as a defining feature of early modernity.[38]

Apparently, Hugli pulled its weight with the Estado and Mughals alike. State policies were bent to accommodate its operations that yielded rich dividends. In 1632, the sudden rupture of trade from Hugli following the Mughal attack provided an occasion for the Council of State in Goa to deliberate on its significance. Clearly, Hugli figured high in the Estado's priorities. The restoration of trade there was so imperative that the viceroy reported gladly to the king that 'the Council decided (and I concurred) that since it was an occasion in which this trade *of which we have such need* was being offered to us [emphasis added]', rules otherwise to be strictly enforced were relaxed.[39] Thus, a ship of Asaf Khan – one of the most senior Mughal nobles, the father-in-law of Shah Jahan, and a trading partner-cum-ally of the Portuguese – caught in violation of the Estado's prohibition of trade directly with the Maldives was to be released for the greater good of restoring trade at Hugli. This is more astonishing when we recall that its inception and growth was a private enterprise that flourished outside state concerns, and even in defiance of them.

Mughal jealousy provides indirect testimony to the prosperity of Hugli. It has been suggested that this was because Shah Jahan was the most mercantile of the Mughal emperors.[40] The bustling trade conducted by the Portuguese, from which the Mughal Empire benefitted somewhat disproportionately less, irked him enough to intervene in these arrangements. This is captured well in the official account of these matters – the *Padshahnama* of his court historian, Abdul Hamid Lahori. The Mughal court conveniently chose to gloss over the fact that the right to trade and settle at Hugli had been granted to the Portuguese by an imperial *farman*. The perception that the Mughal Empire had been short-changed in the arrangements from which the Portuguese had profited enormously left Shah Jahan bristling. Ultimately, it led to a Mughal attack on the port and its obliteration in 1632. This avarice of the 'Great Mughal' points to the growing allure of Portuguese Hugli in seventeenth-century Bengal.

Among other contemporaries, too, Hugli was widely reputed to have been a rich and prosperous settlement. Fr Cabral noted in 1632, 'the Bandel was exceedingly rich'.[41] It was these 'immense riches, riches far exceeding anything … [one] could imagine' that Martim Afonso de Melo, the Portuguese resident of Hugli who betrayed the town to the Mughal armies in 1632, pointed out to the Mughal administration. He elaborated that the Casa de Misericordia was the depository of more than 14 lakh *tanga*s (*tanka*s) which was the money of the residents who had died at Hugli. There were also very rich individual merchants, both Portuguese and 12–13 native merchants, 'in possession of large capital'.[42] During the siege of Hugli by the Mughal forces in 1632, the Portuguese paid out a hundred thousand *tanka*s, with the promise of two hundred thousand more, to bring an end to the hostilities.[43] One Portuguese ship that went down was loaded with over three hundred thousand *tanka*s of private property.[44] Among the survivors at Sagor Island was a rich Portuguese lady, who left large amounts of money to the Jesuit fathers of Bengal, as well as to several other good works, and to the rector of Hugli to create a college in Bengal. Some of this money was used by the Jesuits to repair the damages caused by the siege.[45]

Local merchants seem to have shared a close and profitable relationship with the Portuguese at Hugli. Significantly, their supporters included highly placed and influential officials in the Mughal administration. Thus, while the Mughal emperor Shah Jahan commanded Qasim Khan, the governor of Bengal, 'to march upon the Bandel of Hugli and put it to fire and sword', the governor showed himself to be very reluctant; he hesitated and postponed the attack several times for as long as he could.[46] The Portuguese were, in the meantime, forewarned of the impending attack by 'a Moorish captain' – a nephew of Muqarrab Khan, then the governor of Surat and one of the high-ranking officials of the Mughal court – and by 'some friendly Moors'.[47] In the negotiations conducted before the attack, there were merchants – both Muslim and Hindu – 'who had for many years been trading at Hugli', and who were willing to 'prove ... by ... authoritative evidence' that the Portuguese were not guilty of any of the misbehaviour and lawlessness that the Mughal administration was accusing them of.[48]

After the fall of Hugli, Shah Jahan ordered the execution of four priests who were among the prisoners at his court in Agra. The order was stayed on the intervention of Asaf Khan and other nobles, who pointed to the likely retaliation by the Portuguese state at Goa and the loss of life and trade that it could cause all along the coast. Meanwhile, 'some merchants who were in correspondence with the City of Goa' negotiated with the emperor to secure their freedom. Finally, several of the prisoners escaped from Agra with the assistance of local Muslim merchants, who even advanced them three thousand rupees in return for a letter of exchange drawn on the Portuguese captains in Bengal.[49] Clearly, even after the capture of their premier settlement in the region, the Portuguese had enough supporters and allies who facilitated their return to Bengal.

Hugli, which occupied a space in between empires, was much valued across the frontiers. The Estado da India had been reaching out to its residents for years, even making exception to accommodate their concerns. Mughal merchants and elites alike had their fortunes closely tied to Hugli and were keen to ensure it a long lease of life. Thus, in the wake of the wrath of the Mughal emperor, a part of the Mughal nobility dared to press on and restore Hugli back to its previous condition and status a year later. In an important reversal of a decisive imperial show of strength, the town was rebuilt in 1633. Clearly, the settlers could well afford to be independent minded on the strength of these closely cultivated political constituencies.

The Portuguese at Hugli had generally enjoyed a good relationship with the Mughal emperors from Akbar to Shah Jahan. Thus, 'they were in possession of a document confirmed by Jahangir and his son, Sultan Parvez, to the effect that the settlers would never be held responsible, as a body, for the misdemeanors of particular individuals'.[50] The Portuguese had also rendered valuable mercenary service to the Mughal armies in Bengal. In Jahangir's reign, one Miguel Rodriguez, who was the captain of Hugli in 1632, commanded a band of Portuguese mercenaries who had such an impressive reputation in the region that they were on the payroll of the Mughal emperor. They were used by prince Parvez in his Bengal campaign against Khurram, the rebel prince. The Portuguese contingent contributed in an important way to the defeat of the rebel prince by the imperial forces. Significantly, prince Khurram too had tried to persuade them to join his forces before the battle, but they had turned down the offer.

Portuguese Hugli represents a social and political fragment through which we can reconstruct broad processes. It was located at the interstices of empires, a space in which crucial aspects of state-formation were forged. A characteristic geographical and political fluidity allowed frequent 'break-ins' by people from outside.[51] The activities and concerns of such groups on the fringes could become central in directing processes of state-formation and the making of imperial centres.

Straddling Worlds

The engagement of the Mughal emperors with the Portuguese settled in the Mughal provinces seems to have been deeper than what appears at first glance. There is evidence that by 1610, Jahangir was contemplating taking Chittagong from Arakan. Chittagong was an even larger hub of Portuguese trade – the *porto grande* (big port) of Bengal. By taking control of it, Mughal frontiers could be extended to the eastern end of the delta. Shah Jahan's attack on Hugli in 1632 may have been a run-up to the real prize. Chittagong was finally taken in 1666. In Mughal understanding, the Portuguese were an important part of the political economy of Bengal. Their trade, conducted from Hugli and Chittagong, generated enormous revenue. This included traffic in slaves, which left a great trail of devastation in its wake.

The active presence of Portuguese freebooters in the region became an important factor that urged the Mughals into pushing the limits of their empire. Crucial to the success in this campaign was the ability to 'manage' them to Mughal advantage. Arguably, the attack on Hugli in 1632 was merely a form of severe disciplinary action. It is in the context of such an interpretation that the restoration of the settlement within a year by an imperial *farman* becomes comprehensible. The sack of 1632 might have been intended to warn the Portuguese in Bengal rather than to make them an enemy of the Mughal Empire. The Mughal emperors probably understood well that the Portuguese settlers could prove useful in the wresting of Chittagong from the Arakan kingdom finally. Jahangir had already tried, though in vain, to win them over on two occasions – in 1619 and 1623. A Portuguese observer had noted that 'had it not, indeed, been for the seven hundred and fifty Portuguese whom the Magh ruler had in his pay the Mogores would on both occasions have seized Chatigan'.[52] If these calculations were made, they seemed to have paid off. When Shaista Khan, Aurangzeb's governor of Bengal, sought military alliance with the Portuguese of Chittagong in 1666, they finally decided to relent. The memory of the blow suffered at Hugli in 1632 may have played a part. The significance of this was not lost on the Mughal chronicler who provided details of the whole episode and commended Shaista Khan, who 'regarded the coming over of the *Feringis* as the commencement of the victory' and attacked immediately.[53] Thus, in 1666, after nearly half a century of vain attempts, the Mughals were successful in capturing Chittagong. Contemporary Mughal texts indicate that the contribution of the Portuguese was gratefully acknowledged and 'wealth beyond measure was given to the *Feringi* pirates'.[54] Such political entanglements by anonymous players operating on the margins, representing 'regions within' both political and territorial spaces, are the hallmark of processes of early modern state formation.

A Twilight Zone

Hugli had shared an uncertain relationship with the Portuguese authorities at Goa almost from the beginning. Consequently, the Portuguese authorities tried that 'in the ports of Bengal ... be maintained a normal trade with this *Estado*', while fully recognizing that the personnel settled there were largely outside its control. Most of them 'had created families outside the Portuguese law and maintained a lifestyle proper to the region'.[55]

At the end of the sixteenth century, Hugli lay in a twilight zone, oscillating between being counted amongst the official ports and maintaining a largely independent identity. The Estado continued to appoint its own representative to the post of the *ouvidor* (magistrate) of *porto pequeuo* (Satgaon or Hugli).[56] At the same time, it recognized the right of the settlers to elect from among themselves candidates to offices that were considered important state appointments in other Estado outposts. These included the *juiz dos orfãos* (judge of the orphans), the *procurador dos ausentes* (administrator of the property of absent persons), and the *escrivão* (scrivener) of Hugli.[57] Whatever might have been the official perception concerning the status of Hugli, it was commonly understood that the settlement was an autonomous haven for the Portuguese based at Cochin, Malacca, or Goa, who were deserting the Estado even at the end of the sixteenth century.[58]

Indeed, the Portuguese king and the viceroy constantly sought to prevent such an exodus of manpower. They explored channels to communicate to deserters a royal pardon and pave the way for their return to the official fold.[59] In 1599, the Estado sought to reinforce its control; a contemporary document records: '... hence the lord Viceroy is seasonally trying to reduce all the bandels in which the Portuguese are scattered [in the region] and to make only two, viz, this great port of Dianga or Citigā and the smaller port which they call Gulim'.[60]

Perhaps the most telling indication of its position in the Portuguese Empire came at a moment of crisis, when the authorities at Goa received credible intelligence that the Mughals were preparing to attack Hugli. Confronted by this challenge, the viceroy had no choice but to wash his hands of it. He wrote in reply to Shah Jahan's complaints of slave trade that 'he had nothing to do with them',[61] indicating that Hugli was outside the purview of the Estado da India. The viceroy and the establishment, who had been involved partly in promoting this trade, left Hugli to its fate.

The Portuguese settlers at Hugli, like the rest of their brethren in the region, maintained a relationship of convenience with the Estado da India. After the fall of the settlement in 1632, the survivors who had taken refuge on Sagor Island decided to make a new beginning. In this, as in all new and shaky enterprises in the region, they found it useful to invoke authorization in the name of the king of Portugal. Fr Cabral, who was there, reported that 'it was decided to convert the pagoda [on Sagor Island] into a strong fortress *for His Majesty* [emphasis added]'.[62] In the meantime, they sought help from all quarters to this end. In a gesture telling of their affiliations, church fathers were sent as envoys both to the viceroy at Goa as well as to the king of Arakan, who evinced keen interest in this matter. He sent 27 galleons manned by Portuguese sailors in his employ, commanded by one Manoel Palmeiro. They were an untamed set of marauders who came eagerly to Sagor Island, ever on the lookout for the opportunity to grab the loot that was the inevitable fallout of any war. They seized 'an enormous booty' from some Muslim vessels that they encountered on the way and arrived expecting to find an ongoing struggle. Discovering that the Portuguese loss of Hugli was final, they moved on – true to the spirit of their enterprise, looking for new opportunities for more plunder. Fr Cabral could not resist quipping: 'seeing that the past was beyond cure, as true Christians and Portuguese they offered their services for the future'. A few remained behind, but most of them sailed upriver 'with the intention of privateering on Moorish vessels'.[63]

Conclusion

The idea of the early modern posits that specific pre-colonial historical contexts were not just parochial and specific, but displayed visibly cross-regional trends and patterns of linkages. These included not only long-distance commercial relations – as John Richards points out – but also close political involvement of outsiders as well as linguistic and cultural intermixing and hybridity. Thus, historical developments can be seen to be taking place 'laterally', connected with the outside, along with 'vertically' aligned developments of patterns or institutions that took place in various regions.[64]

The Portuguese entrepreneurs placed their eggs in more than one basket. If they understood the Estado da India well, they also learnt rapidly about the political world of local powers and how to operate within it. Significantly, they always had friends in high places amongst the regional powers with whom they had profitable dealings. These ranged from highly placed elites at the court of the Bengal Sultan and the local chieftains in Bengal to the top tier of the Mughal nobility itself. They culled profits from all sorts of trade, made valuable additions to the military labour market, carved out privileges, administrative commands, and governorships in local polities. In one case, they even secured a kingship on the Arakan coast early in the seventeenth century. In each case, they played an important role in the region's evolving political economy.

Particularly striking is their resilience and flexibility of operation, a feature not allowed to more formal structures of empire. As the example of Hugli shows, the settlers on the ground were enormously invested in their commercial ventures buttressed by shreds of political power. They rose to meet challenges and provided instinctive, experimental, and innovative solutions with spontaneity of action and flexibility. This could not have been offered by the sheer power of the leviathan that was the Estado da India and its slow procedures and heavy operations. The Hugli settlers succeeded in returning within a year of being swept off the map by one swipe of the Mughal paw. This, despite the refusal of the viceroy of Goa to assist in any manner and the treachery of the rescue party from Arakan sent supposedly to bail them out.

This study thus affirms the polyvocality of structures like the Portuguese Empire in Asia. It highlights the fluidity of some Asian political systems in this period, which stretched themselves as they accommodated new arrivals and negotiated collaborations. My study echoes others' in confirming that imperial centres were not free to impose their will on early modern political systems in an unrestrained manner. These impressively large empires were not driven simply by the ambitions and whims of emperors, no matter how absolutist we may imagine them to have been. Yet the many drivers of their historical development were not symptoms of weakness. Rather, they lent to the early modern state a tensile flexibility that explains its palpable strength and longevity. This would go far in developing a typology of early modern politics in Asia, of which the Portuguese adventurers formed an important component.

Notes

1. C. A. Bayly, *The Birth of the Modern World, 1780–1914: Global Connections and Comparisons* (Oxford: Blackwell, 2004), 30.
2. Richard M. Eaton, *A Social History of the Deccan, 1300–1761: Eight Indian Lives* (Cambridge: Cambridge University Press, 2005), especially the chapter on Malik Ambar, 105–128.
3. John F. Richards, 'Early Modern India and World History', *Journal of World History* 8, no. 2 (1997): 197–209; Sanjay Subrahmanyam, 'Connected Histories: Towards a Reconfiguration of Early Modern Eurasia', *Modern Asian Studies* 31, no. 3 (1997): 735–762.
4. Rosalind O'Hanlon, *At the Edges of Empire: Essays in the Social and Intellectual History of India* (Ranikhet: Permanent Black, 2014); Sheldon Pollock, 'India in the Vernacular Millennium: Literary Culture and Polity, 1000–1500', *Daedelus* 127, no. 3 (1998): 41–74.
5. Subrahmanyam, 'Connected Histories', 758.
6. Bayly, *The Birth of the Modern World*, 30.
7. Eclectic religious and ethnic policies are regarded as a crucial reason behind the remarkable success of Akbar and his successors in creating an empire of unprecedented size and stability.
8. Jos Gommans, *Mughal Warfare: Indian Frontiers and the High Roads to Empire, 1500–1700* (London and New York: Routledge, 2002); Jorge Flores, *Unwanted Neighbours: The Mughals, the Portuguese and Their Frontier Zones* (New Delhi: Oxford University Press, 2018); Pratyay Nath, *Climate of Conquest:*

Fidalgos, Soldados, Arrenegados

War, Environment, and Empire in Mughal North India (New Delhi: Oxford University Press, 2019).

9. The Mughals were willing to share sovereignty, as they did with Rajput kings in the imperial *suba* Ajmer and with the Portuguese in Diu. See R. C. Hallissey, *The Rajput Rebellion Against Aurangzeb: A Study of the Mughal Empire in the Seventeenth Century* (Columbia and London: University of Missouri Press, 1977); Flores, *Unwanted Neighbours*, 22–23.

10. Gommans, *Mughal Warfare*.

11. C. R. Boxer, *The Portuguese Seaborne Empire, 1415–1825* (London: Hutchinson & Co., 1969). For a different perspective, see Sanjay Subrahmanyam, *The Portuguese Empire in Asia, 1500–1700: A Political and Economic History* (London and New York: Longman, 1993). The lack of Mughal oceanic perspective has been highlighted by the following works: M. N. Pearson, *Merchants and Rulers in Gujarat: The Response to the Portuguese in the Sixteenth Century* (New Delhi: Munshiram Manoharlal, 1976); K. N. Chaudhuri, *Trade and Civilisation in the Indian Ocean* (London: Cambridge University Press, 1985); Ashin Das Gupta, 'The Maritime Merchant of India', in *The World of the Indian Ocean Merchant, 1500–1800: Collected Essays of Ashin Das Gupta*, compiled by Uma Das Gupta, 88–101 (New Delhi: Oxford University Press, 2001).

12. For keen Mughal interest in lands and seas far beyond their dominions, see 'The Deccan Frontier and Mughal Expansion, c. 1600', in Muzaffar Alam and Sanjay Subrahmanyam, *Writing the Mughal World* (New York: Columbia University Press, 2012), 165–203. For the close watch that the Portuguese kept on fluctuating relations between the Mughals and Safavids over Qandahar and its implication for the Estado da India, see Flores, *Unwanted Neighbours*, 32–73.

13. Radhika Chadha, *Merchants, Renegades, Padres: Portuguese Presence in Early Modern Bengal and Arakan* (New Delhi: Primus Books, forthcoming).

14. 'Cristandade de Goa, Goa, 13 de Outubro de 1548', in *Documentação para a historia das Missoês de Padroado Português de Oriente: India (1548-1550)*, ed. A. da Silva Rego, vol. 4 (Lisbon: Fundacao Oriente, 1991), document 17, 66–72.

15. See documents cited in R. O. W Goertz, 'The Portuguese in Cochin in the mid-sixteenth century', *Indica* 23, no. 3 (1986): 63–78.

16. In research related to the Portuguese presence in Brazil and West Africa, Jorge Pedreidro has suggested that distance from the imperial centre at Lisbon gave merchants more autonomy, wealth, and status. Colonial merchants and officials found freedom of agency and operated whole networks of their own. See *Commercial Networks in the Early Modern World*, ed. Diogo Ramado Curto and Anthony Molho (Florence: European University Institute, 2002), 13.

17. 'Letter from Antonio da Fonseca to the King, Goa, 18.10.1523', in *Documentos sobre os Portugueses em Moçambique e na Africa Central, 1497–1840*, vol. 4 (1519–1537) (Lisbon: Centro dos Estudos Historicos Ultramarinos, 1962), 181–237.
18. R. O. W. Goertz, 'The Portuguese in Cochin', 67.
19. G. Bouchon and L. F. F. R. Thomaz (eds.), *Voyage dans les Deltas du Gange et de l'Irraouaddy (1521)* (Paris: Fundação Calouste Gulbenkian, 1988), para 32, 35, and passim.
20. Manuel de Abreu Mouzinho, *Breve discurso em que se conta conquista do reino de Pegu na India Oriental* (Lisbon: Tipographia Rollandiana, 1829), trans. A. McGregor, *Journal of the Burma Research Society* 16, no. 2 (1926): 124–125.
21. Fr John Cabral, S. J., 'The Fall of Hugli', Appendix to *The Travels of Fray Sebastien Manrique (1629–1643)*, vols. 1–2, trans. C. E. Luard and H. Hosten (Oxford: Hakluyt Society, 1927), vol. 2, 391–422.
22. *Fray Sebastien Manrique*, vol. 1, 27–8.
23. Cited in Sushil Chaudhury, 'The Rise and Decline of Hugli: A Port in Medieval Bengal', *Bengal Past and Present* 86, no. 1 (1967): 33–67, see 35.
24. 'Extracts of Master Caesar Frederike His Eighteene Yeers Indian Observations', in *Hakluytus Posthumus or Purchas His Pilgrims*, vols. 1–20, trans. Samuel Purchas (Glasgow: Hakluyt Society, 1905) vol. 10, 113–114.
25. 'Letter of Antonio Mendes de Castro in the ship Sao Vicente to the Queen, 1.8.1563, cited in "Persianisation and Mercantilism" in Bay of Bengal History, 1400–1700', in Sanjay Subrahmanyam, *Explorations in Connected History: From the Tagus to the Ganges* (New Delhi: Oxford University Press, 2004), 45–78, in particular see 66.
26. *Fray Sebastien Manrique*, vol. 1, 28–29.
27. *Fray Sebastien Manrique*, vol. 1, 34–38; Manrique's account is corroborated by *Akbar Nama* in which Partab Tar Feringhi's audience with the emperor is recorded under the 23rd regnal year (1579), while he is noticed as the Portuguese governor of Hugli in the 25th regnal year (1581). Abul Fazl, *Akbar Nama*, vols. 1–3, trans. H. Beveridge (New Delhi: Ess Ess Publications, 1979), vol. 3, 349–350, 469.
28. *Fray Sebastien Manrique*, vol. 1, 37–38.
29. *Fray Sebastien Manrique*, vol. 1, 40–41.
30. *Fray Sebastien Manrique*, vol. 1, 40–41.
31. Cabral, 'The Fall of Hugli', 393.
32. Relacao Anual, *Catholic Herald of India*, 8 January 1919, 35; Fr Fernão Guereiro's Annual Relation for 1604–05, Hosten Collection, Vidyajyoti Library, New Delhi, 'Bengal XVI, XVII', Mss. 9.

33. Cited in Agnelo P. Fernandes, 'Hugli under the Portuguese prior to Its Destruction by Shah Jahan', *Purabhilekha-Puratatva* 2, no. 2 (1984): 39–44, in particular see 39.
34. Fernandes, 'Hugli under the Portuguese', 40.
35. *Fray Sebastien Manrique*, vol. 1, 29–32.
36. 'Letter of Fr Mestre Belchior to the Bothers of the Company in Portugal, Cochin, 25.1.1559', in *Documentação para a historia das Missoês de Padroado Português de Oriente: India (1548–1550)*, ed. A. da Silva Rego, vol. 7 (Lisbon: Fundacao Oriente, 1991), document 54, 243–261, see 243.
37. 'Jorge Cabral to the King, Cochin, 21.2.1550', in *Documentacao para a historia dos Missoes*, ed. A. da Silva Rego, vol. 4, document 84, 488–499, see especially 488–489.
38. Richards, 'Early Modern India', 198–199, 206
39. 'Letter of the Viceroy to the King, 2.12.1636', cited in '"Persianisation and Mercantilism" in Bay of Bengal History', in Subrahmanyam, *Explorations in Connected History*, 68–69.
40. 'On Indian Views of the Portuguese in Asia, 1500–1700', in Subrahmanyam, *Explorations in Connected History*, 17–42, in particular see 41.
41. Cabral, 'The Fall of Hugli', 418.
42. Cabral, 'The Fall of Hugli', 397.
43. Cabral, 'The Fall of Hugli', 410.
44. Cabral, 'The Fall of Hugli', 415.
45. Rev. H. Josson, S. J., *Histoire de la Mission du Bengale*, cited in H. Hosten, 'A Week at the Bandel Convent, Hughli', *Bengal Past and Present* 10, no. 1 (1915): 36–120, in particular see fn. 46.
46. Cabral, 'The Fall of Hugli', 396.
47. Cabral, 'The Fall of Hugli', 395–396.
48. Cabral, 'The Fall of Hugli', 400.
49. Manrique, *Catholic Herald of India*, trans. H. Hosten, June 12, 1918, 455.
50. Cabral, 'The Fall of Hugli', 400.
51. Bayly, *The Birth of the Modern World*, 59.
52. *Fray Sebastien Manrique*, vol. 1, 285.
53. Shihabuddin Talish, *Fathiyya-i Ibriyya*, trans. Jadunath Sarkar, *Journal of the Asiatic Society of Bengal* 3, no. 6 (1907): 405–425, in particular see 416.
54. Talish, *Fathiyya-i Ibriyya*, 416.
55. 'Letter of the King to the Viceroy, Lisbon, 5.2.1597', in J. H. da Cunha Rivara, *Archivo Portuguez Oriental (APO)* (New Delhi: Asian Educational Services, 1992 [1857–1876]), Fasciculo 3, Document 239, 668–679.
56. 'Alvara of the Viceroy, Goa, 1593', in da Cunha Rivara, *APO*, Fasciculo 3, Document 133, 408–409; da Cunha Rivara, *APO*, Fasciculo 5, Part 3, Document 998, 1324; Cabral, 'The Fall of Hugli', 397.

57. da Cunha Rivara, *APO*, Fasciculo 6, Document 591, 1278–1279.
58. 'Alvara of the Viceroy, Goa, 9.8.1597', in da Cunha Rivara, *APO*, Fasciculo 3, Document 281, 773–774; 'Alvara of the Viceroy, Goa, 22.4.1598', in da Cunha Rivara, *APO*, Fasciculo 3, Document 353, 901–902.
59. 'Alvara of the Viceroy, Goa, 1593', in da Cunha Rivara, *APO*, Fasciculo 3, Document 133, 408–409; 'Letter of the King to the Viceroy, Lisbon, 5.2.1597', in da Cunha Rivara, *APO*, Fasciculo 3, Document 239, 668–679; 'Letter of the King to the Viceroy, Lisbon 17.1.1618', in da Cunha Rivara, *APO*, Fasciculo 6, Document 440, 1131; da Cunha Rivara, *APO*, Fasciculo 6, Supplements 1 and 2, Document 893, 17.6.1597, 720–722; Letter of the King to the Viceroy, 12.2.1603, Historical Archives of Goa, Livros das Monçoes do Reino (M.R.) 7, folios 164–164v; Letter of the King to the Viceroy, 6.1.1602, M.R.8, folios 47–51.
60. Letter of Fr Andrew Boves, S. J. to the General of the Society of Jesus in Rome, Chittagong, November 25, 1599, Hosten Collection, Vidyajyoti Library, New Delhi, 'Bengal XVI, XVII'.
61. Manrique, *Catholic Herald of India*, trans. H. Hosten, May 22, 1918, 395.
62. Cabral, 'The Fall of Hugli', 419.
63. Cabral, 'The Fall of Hugli', 420.
64. Bayly, *The Birth of the Modern World*, 4

10

Law, Empire, and the New Julfan Armenians
The Early Modern in the Indian Ocean World

Santanu Sengupta

The category of the early modern for the period between the fifteenth and nineteenth centuries has worked as a crucial tool to reclaim pre-colonial South Asian history from the elusive gap between the medieval – a product of Eurocentrism – and the modern, which is conventionally associated with the advent of European colonialism. This chapter intends to navigate this divide and revisit the utility of the category for this phase of South Asian history by analysing what distinguished this period from the nineteenth century in terms of historical tendencies. It intends to do so by looking at the period through the lens of the New Julfan Armenian diaspora and their agency in the shaping of the legal culture of the eighteenth century.

In his pioneering work, John Richards lists six major processes that characterized early modernity. The rise of the global oceanic routes and circulation across long distances was one of these processes. This was facilitated by the formation of networks like that of the New Julfan Armenians.[1] Reviewing the era through the eyes of stateless, transoceanic, and cross-cultural actors like the Armenians is useful in understanding the idea of the global connectivity and cross-cultural exchange that developed during this period.[2]

The chapter is divided into three main sections. The first looks at the customary legal culture of the New Julfans and how that became the basis of both their diasporic culture and activities. The second section looks at the impact of the early colonial legal regime on the maritime trade that became a crucial area of Anglo-Armenian interaction. Building upon this idea of interaction, the third section looks more specifically at their experience and dialogue with the Mayor's Court of Madras. I argue that the early colonial regime that had evolved by the end of the eighteenth century was a product of the deliberations between the colonial state and the various indigenous elements that emerged in the period from the fifteenth to the eighteenth centuries. In course of the nineteenth century, however, the flexibility of this early colonial regime was transformed into a state of much more stringent colonial authority.

New Julfans and Their Legal Culture

The New Julfan Armenian network was formed during the course of the Safavid–Ottoman contests in the seventeenth century. In 1604, Shah Abbas resettled the merchants from the town of Julfa in a conclave near Isfahan, in a place that came to be called New Julfa.[3] Their operations expanded into the Indian Ocean world through the Eurasian land route from Narva to India. They were also active on the maritime route from the eastern coast of Africa to the Philippines, giving the network an amphibious geographical character.[4] The network followed a specific social and legal culture that distinguished it from its respective host societies and allowed its members mobility across distant zones by reducing risk.[5] Historians have considered intra-community trust as the key to the success of the New Julfan Armenians as itinerant traders.

In the existing literature, the aspect of trust in the Armenian network has been seen from two main analytical perspectives. One group of scholars has seen the existence of an ethos or culture of trust. This, in turn, was based on a sense of familiarity, which developed around principles of kinship, marriage, and common point of origin.[6] Sebouh Aslanian, on the other hand, looks at the functioning of trust as a product of exclusive institutional arrangements, elaborate contract-writing, and well-organized systems of self-regulation and dispute management. *Commenda* partnership, the merchants' assembly (Vacharakanats Zhoghov) in New Julfa, the Armenian Church, and the local courts (*jumiat*s) in the diasporic settlements formed an elaborate system that regulated this intra-network trust.[7]

Bhaswati Bhattacharya questions the real agency of such exclusive legal culture and suggests that in distant stations, formal contracts made under the aegis of colonial courts of law were what really worked.[8] The actual efficacy of an exclusive concept of trust certainly needs to be reviewed, but it is also important to see whether the pre-colonial milieu offered conditions that promoted the agency and the importance of the diasporic identity in negotiating with the emerging colonial regime.

Dispersed over a massive geopolitical expanse, the Armenians showcased fascinating examples of negotiation with various states and legal regimes. According to Edmund Herzig, the New Julfan legal experience not only formed the basis of the unity of the network but also provided the rhetoric of negotiating with their host states.[9] The history of the compilation of the *Datastanagirk Astrakhani Hayots*, or the Astrakhan Law book, reaffirms this idea. The law book was compiled to assist the activities of the Astrakhanski Asobi Armiyanski Sud (Armenian Court of Astrakhan), just as they intended to preserve the codes for the unity of the larger network.[10]

However, Armenian legal culture was not as insulated as it has been conventionally perceived. Rather, due to the demands of cross-cultural trade, the Armenians needed to make the contracts comprehensible to their associates from other communities.[11] *Datastanagirk* also underlined the utility of flexibility, dialogue and adaptation in a plural legal atmosphere for adapting to local conditions, while successfully maintaining a core cultural identity.[12]

The experience of the Armenian legal culture as it evolved across multiple empires highlighted the conditions that developed during this period. According to Lauren Benton, the period between the fifteenth and the early nineteenth centuries was a time of various forms of legal pluralism, characterized by multiculturalism, negotiation, and flexibility. In this milieu, it signified the existence of multiple, overlapping, parallel, or hierarchical ideas and centres of providing justice within a political regime. It also indicated the porosity between legal regimes that could be utilized by individuals or groups by jockeying to gain maximum benefit from what was offered. In other words, it allowed actors like the Armenians to engage in forum-shopping to suit their interests. This could also allow the actors to act as a bridge between two disparate legal systems. It has been further argued that although the pluralistic scenario waned with the ascendance of a stronger and more composed colonial regime, this transformation was neither automated nor pre-determined. Benton's vantage point of looking at this legal culture is the agency of the colonized that actually performed this act of negotiation.[13]

However, there are those who have questioned the actual limits of this agency. In her case study of Surat, Lakshmi Subramanian suggests that there was a constant supremacy of the colonial institution even when indulging in legal pluralism.[14] Aparna Balachandran applies this logic for early colonial Madras and asserts that within the apparent heterogeneous legal environment, the paramountcy of the English court had already been established. What actually happened in the course of the legal encounters was a quick appropriation of the indigenous norms into the codes of the colonial legal corpus and a reduction in the utility of forum-shopping.[15] I draw upon Benton to argue that while the nineteenth century did witness the establishment of a clear supremacy of the colonial legal culture, the agency of the indigenous and hybrid legal discourses that developed through the various encounters at courts of law in the early days of the Company rule cannot be discounted; nor can they be divorced from the pluralistic character of the period between the fifteenth and the early nineteenth centuries.

The rise in the political importance of the European companies in the Indian Ocean littoral in course of this period produced a complicated scenario. The growing marine presence of the Europeans began to regulate the character of trade.

This was accompanied by the increasing importance of colonial legal institutions. All this had the potential of altering the conditions that had earlier helped the New Julfan Armenians to flourish. However, I suggest that the Armenians continued to be relevant in the era of increasing European influence during the late eighteenth and early nineteenth centuries. In fact, their dialogue with the English East India Company was a part of their strategy of reorganization around regional nodes after the fall of New Julfa. I also investigate how interactions between the New Julfan customs and the growing English legal dispensation generated a process of negotiations and adjustments. This assisted the Armenians in developing a hybrid self-representation which, in turn, helped them to maintain their diasporic identity, while also managing to utilize the tools of colonial governance. The following section examines the Anglo-Armenian legal encounters and hybridity of the system by studying the impact of the colonial legal culture in the arena of maritime trade.

The Laws of the Sea

It has been widely believed that the backward Asians were swiftly put out of business once the Europeans arrived and established their superior naval control on the sea passages.[16] However, several historians have questioned the actual viability and scale of such naval control.[17] While accepting the limitations of the actual execution of sea domination, Elizabeth Mancke suggests that the Indian Ocean was nevertheless politicized to an unprecedented degree by the arrival of the Europeans during this period. European imperial aspirations altered both the political and commercial dynamics of the ocean by the end of the eighteenth century.[18]

European ascent in the sea was further bolstered by the pervasiveness of colonial legal culture among mercantile groups in the littoral societies of the Indian Ocean. Subramanian notes that even in the period of European ascent, indigenous maritime traders and their auxiliary groups remained extremely vital. They got involved in the complex structure of trade that emerged in colonial towns through the interaction of conflicting power, law, and regulation.[19] The Armenians also quickly entered the colonial institutional framework to safeguard their interest. They used their bargaining power as a significant trading community to influence the system, producing a constantly changing and rather mixed legal narrative out of the colonial court at least till the end of the eighteenth century. The first case study of this section involves the capture of a ship called *Santa Catharina*. It shows how the option of using multiple legal regimes could produce an interesting commentary on the correlation of the political situation and the legal systems.

The Santa Catharina *Incident*

Till the middle of the eighteenth century, there were still possibilities of challenging European authority using the parallel domain of the indigenous states. The Armenians tried to utilize the opportunities of the new legal culture, while also making an attempt to hold on to the potentialities of settling issues outside the colonial courts. The capture and the ensuing trial of the ship *Santa Catharina* in the 1740s provides an entry point into understanding Armenian encounters with British maritime regulations. *Santa Catharina* was a freight ship hired in 1746 by a group of Armenians from Calcutta to conduct a voyage to Basra and back. In spite of hoisting the Armenian flag, it was stopped near Nagapatnam by a British squadron as a fallout of the ongoing Anglo–French War on Austrian Succession. The pretext was the presence of Frenchmen on board the Armenian ship.[20]

The trial regarding the salvage rights of *Santa Catharina* at the High Court of Admiralty in London has been analysed by Sebouh Aslanian.[21] This trial was undoubtedly a major battle waged by one of the most important trading networks of the Indian Ocean against the control mechanism of the English colonial regime. Philip C. Webb, the legal solicitor of Admiral Griffin, successfully proved that the power of attorney of the ship given to Stephen Cogigian, an Armenian merchant operating from Amsterdam, was forged. The authenticity of such documents had to be ratified by the Merchants' Assembly. The fact that New Julfa had faced a decline in the 1740s, following Nadir Shah's ascent in Iran, meant that the assembly was no longer functional.[22] The case demonstrated the outcomes of the colonial–local exchange of information that had equipped the state with considerable knowledge to find loopholes in the existing customs of the locals.

It also showed an attempt by the Armenians to utilize the overlapping claims and counterclaims of jurisdiction over maritime space to challenge the attempts of hegemony by the English East India Company. The Armenians in Bengal used their position in Murshidabad to cajole Nawab Alivardi Khan to pressurize the English East India Company officials to provide redress in the *Santa Catharina* case.[23] While they did not see much success in London, their tactics yielded better results in Bengal as English ships were banned from operating in the province. Following this, Company officials had to break the ice with the Armenians with the promise of providing various mercantile favours.[24]

A different perspective on this issue appears in the accounts of the Armenian nationalist adventurer Emin Joseph Emin. Emin's narrative pointed towards the aspiration of the Armenians regarding the colonial legal system, especially in a later period, when extracting restitution from parallel centres of authority like the Nawab was no longer possible. Emin, who was present during the *Santa Catharina* legal proceedings in London, had a rather sympathetic view of the role of the Company officials in the affair, even as he held the British imperial navy to be the culprit.[25] Emin's take on them position was influenced by his sympathetic disposition towards the Company. Yet it is difficult to overlook the variation between his observations regarding the legal politics of the period in London and Calcutta, respectively. Emin expressed his anguish at the nature of proceedings in London and asserted that the process and the outcome would have been fair had it taken place in the Supreme Court of Judicature in Calcutta.[26]

The Supreme Court of Judicature in Calcutta had been formed by the time Emin published his memoirs in 1792. Incidentally, 43 members of the Armenian community had expressed their support towards the institution on the eve of its establishment in 1775.[27] This trust on the colonial judicial system probably grew out of the long experience of the Armenians at the municipal courts of Calcutta, Madras, and Bombay, the proceedings of which had represented considerable flexibility. This also indicates that early colonial legal institutions were more of a product of the pluralistic legal milieu associated with early modernity than of more rigid legal institutions of the mid-nineteenth century that distinctively mirrored the imperialist vision of the metropole. While *Santa Catharina* was a specific and spectacular event, the colonial maritime legal culture began to make more mundane but significant impact through the regulations that were introduced in the sphere of finance and insurances. But the question remains whether the narrative of the court itself had become streamlined and paramount before the nineteenth century or if it remained hybrid.

Maritime Finance: Respondentia *and Insurance*

The money market in Mughal India had sophisticated credit arrangements like *hundi* and *avog*.[28] While *hundi*s represented bills of exchange, *avog* was the term used for a speculative form of investment in merchant cargo. The investors would lend money to purchase the goods to be taken on the voyage that would have to be repaid on the successful return of the ship.[29] Similar instruments of mortgage used by the New Julfan merchants were called *avak* or *jukami avak* in the New Julfan documents.[30] These instruments were critical for both risk sharing and raising capital for maritime trade.

In addition to this, *respondentia* had emerged as a major form of financial arrangement in the eighteenth century. Scholars hold different opinions regarding the extent and timing of the impact of the colonial regime on this financial arrangement. Sinnappah Arasaratnam suggests that in Coromandel of the seventeenth and early eighteenth centuries, both indigenous customary norms and European law worked abreast.[31] Kanaklatha Mukund, on the other hand, argues that European influences were rather limited till the middle of the eighteenth century, after which the shift of power equations in the Coromandel Coast exerted a strong European influence on trading customs, particularly through the courts of law.[32]

Respondentia loans were mortgaged upon the goods and merchandise and were given at a higher rate of interest; a clause of no return was included in case of failure of the voyage or loss of the cargo.[33] Disputes were rather common in *respondentia* as the interest of the lender and the borrower stood opposed to each other. The frequency and gravity of such disputation pushed the Mayor's Court authorities to place several regulations on the practice of *respondentia*.[34] According to the prevalent customs, a number of underwriters collectively decided the terms and premium of a *respondentia*. In case of a dispute, the decision of the majority of the underwriters or lenders would be upheld. In some cases, the major investors involved in the deal would take a decision that would be binding on the others.[35]

However, by the mid-eighteenth century, there was a greater acceptance of the colonial courts among the indigenous merchants. This was catalysed by an appreciation for the Company's judicial institutions and the attraction of an unambiguous tariff system and provisions of naval protection.[36] In a study of the *respondentia* cases brought to the Bombay Mayor's Court during this period, Subramanian demonstrates that the indigenous norms of conflict resolution on *respondentia* deals were significantly challenged, as the rhetoric of individual interest gained supremacy over the convention of collective decision-making.[37] Although this was not a complete abrogation of the indigenous legal culture, it was certainly a portent of an emerging dialogue.

Shifts such as these, along with more structural changes such as the rise of new colonial port centres like Bombay replacing older ones like Surat, further altered the equation between the indigenous and the colonial regimes.[38] The increasing tendency of the indigenous merchants to rely on English courts rather than work around older conventions of trust and reciprocity suggests a shift from the earlier scenario. But as the next case study demonstrates, the shift did not accomplish a complete transformation of the language of legal deliberation. The legal discourse in the court would often involve both indigenous and colonial norms, that too in a way that complicated the expected positions of the colonizer and the colonized. The Armenians in the eighteenth-century Indian Ocean arena were well-integrated in this system. Not only were they affected by the emerging culture of commerce, but as the following case study suggests, their deliberations over trade and finance in the English law courts also helped in the development of the multiplex legal language that signified the character of this period.

Let us proceed to look closely at this case. In 1771, Jacob Pimer, an Armenian merchant from Madras, filed a case against Edmund Whatmough, an English merchant and owner of the ship *Morning Star*, for the recovery of an amount of 487 *pagoda*s due on *respondentia*.[39] Whatmough had passed away before the completion of the voyage; Pimer hence placed his demands in front of Reynold Adams and John Groslin, the executors of the estate. They, however, refused to pay, saying that by accepted conventions, repayments could be executed only after the disposal of the effects on the basis of collective decision of the stakeholders. The English party in this case rested their argument on the prevalent custom of collective decision-making, while the Armenian based his claim on the imported notions of the sanctity of private property and individual interest. More interestingly, the court in its verdict held on to the sanctity of the conventional collective interest.[40]

This was characteristic of the period – a complex legal culture formed by the coexistence of indigenous and English legal norms imported along with the British legal institution of the Mayor's Court. The possibility of appropriation of the rhetoric of the other was perhaps most symptomatic of the dialogic culture of the era. The legal culture that had emerged was based on rationalization, exchange, and a shared experience between the colonial state and the merchants. The emerging milieu was no doubt complicated by the increasing intervention from metropole of the Empire. Control over maritime financing was bolstered by a series of regulations introduced by the British Parliament regarding the finance business, especially pertaining to the general development in maritime insurances.[41] The impact of these measures was expected to be felt in the colonial enclaves like Madras.

Mukund suggests that although insuring ships for overseas trade was a common practice in the Coromandel, not much of it is reflected in the Mayor's Court records.[42] The stark absence of insurance disputes in the court records indicates that the indigenous mechanisms were functioning successfully until a significant shift occurred in the second half of the eighteenth century. As the volumes of disputes grew, the state repeatedly sought ways to intervene and regulate the arena. While this resurrects the concept of a colonial takeover of a flexible realm of legal pluralism, a closer reading of the insurance-related court cases suggests that the pattern of participation of the merchants and languages adopted by them did not represent a simple acceptance of the colonial hegemony but a very calculated response of reaping the maximum benefit possible within the perimeter of an emerging system.

In the late eighteenth century, various European insurance organizations like the Madras Insurance Company, New Madras Insurance Company, Madras Equitable Insurance Company, and Society of Madras Insurers became significant in the insurance sector.[43] While it would not be right to suggest that these companies had ousted all indigenous forms of insurance, it is also difficult to deny their increasing pre-eminence. The consultations of the Madras Equitable Insurance Company reveals a sense of the regulations followed by the British insurance providers in Madras in the late eighteenth and early nineteenth centuries In general, the board members of the Company decided to strictly adhere to the insurance-related legislations of the British Parliament and the recent rulings of the Madras Mayor's Court and deny any policies which might bear political risks.[44]

This signalled towards pressure operating from the imperial metropole on the existing mercantile system in South Asia. However, numerous disputes that appeared in the last two decades of the eighteenth century show that the mutation of Madras trading culture under the English insurance regulations was not simple or unilateral. The law court became a site of dialogue between the existing and the emerging systems. The nature of colonial assertion on the sea and the coastal enclaves along with the indigenous reaction is exemplified by a lawsuit filed by two Armenian merchants, Anna Seth Aviet and Philipus Jacob Peltum, against Madras Insurance Company. They intended to secure the payment for the insurance on a *respondentia* loan on a ship called Wallajah for its voyage from Madras to Manila and back.[45] The plaintiffs argued that the ship had been lost while returning due to a mutiny on board by a section of the crew and had returned to Madras after the expiration of the stipulated time. When the Madras Insurance Company declined to pay the money, the complainants moved the Mayor's Court and secured a verdict in their favour. The central debate in the case revolved around the definition of barratry and the idea of 'hostility by belligerent nationals'.[46] The insurers pointed out that the mutineers were French – people of an enemy state. Hence, they argued, that the mutiny should be considered as an act of political hostility, which would render the policy null and void.[47] The Armenians convinced the Mayor's Court that the act was not one of political hostility but of barratry – an act of causing harm to a ship without the consent or knowledge of the owner.

The insurers then approached the Court of Appeals and asserted that mutiny on board by men of an enemy state could not be termed as barratry according to

British law. They also argued that there was no provision of paying the insured amount in such cases. The Armenians tacitly accepted the notion of political hostility in their rebuttal but claimed that there was a custom of applying for an extra premium during such extraordinary conditions. They cited the precedence of a case between Nazar Jacob Shamier and Madras Insurance Company at the Supreme Court of Judicature in Bengal, where the insurers had been instructed to pay in spite of the loss of the ship due to French and Spanish hostilities.[48] However, the insurers claimed that this was not applicable in Wallajah's case as such a warranty had to be inserted only on the basis of a consensus between all concerned parties.[49] The idea of a consensus in terms of altering the originally accepted notions of risk in a voyage was not very different from the idea of the collective decision-making of the underwriters traditionally prevalent in the indigenous *respondentia* sector. On the basis of these arguments, the Court of Appeals overturned the decision of the Mayor's Court. The case underlines the primacy of the colonial institution in deciding commercial disputes.

One of the most intriguing inferences from this case pertains to how the enemy state of the colonizer and the colonized became one due to the imposition of the Court of Appeals. But this shift in the trend need not be equated with a diminution of the heterogeneous narrative. On the contrary, commercial adjudication remained fluid and accommodated notions like that of the consensus, clearly demonstrating how emerging colonial law was not entirely averse to the validity of pre-existing customs.

These narratives from the long eighteenth century reveal the role of exchange and hybrid language in the process of the formation of mercantile culture as well as that of the legal sphere. The Armenians invoked local and pre-existing conventions as well as British law and legal precedents to support their arguments, as was seen in their usage of the idea of barratry. It was not a case of simple colonial hegemony but that of dialogue between local merchants like the Armenians and the newer and increasingly powerful British regime. What underpinned the dialogue was a multiplicity of languages that drew from diverse sources and experiences, trying to influence the sphere of hegemony.

This dialogue, however, was not without its own caveats. While the previous section dealt with the shifts in the broader cross-cultural mercantile affairs of the Indian Ocean, the following looks at a more intimate space where the members of the community engaged with each other in the Mayor's Court. It explores the long-term impact of the various negotiations and adjustments on indigenous groups like the Armenians as well as the hybrid self-representation that developed through the process.

The Madras Experience

Madras was one of the earliest centres of the English East India Company government. In the eighteenth century, it had a significant Armenian presence. Notable individuals like Petrus Uscan or Shahmir Shahmiryan, along with various others, acted as traders, *respondentia* dealers, moneylenders, and freighters. They had also established themselves as an important factor in running the everyday administration of the government of English East India Company.[50]

The Mayor's Court played a crucial role as a site of interactions and negotiations.[51] It was an important contact zone for various groups in Madras to assert their individuality and self-representation, while also engaging with the new regime.[52] It has been questioned whether participation in the Mayor's Court led to a definite rupture of the pre-existing legal system, or if the process was more complex. The indigenous participation in the court has been rationalized by considering the lack of formality in its structure. Inclusiveness in its proceedings made the court hybrid and it allowed a greater scope of individualization of legal practices there. This gave the Armenians an opportunity to expand their options without drastically altering themselves from the network's judicial culture. At least initially, the court allowed the incorporation of indigenous norms along with English standards without much centralization.[53]

Aside from this, the claim of delivering justice on the basis of equity also attracted participation. The Mayor's Court gained importance particularly in situations where the structural limitations of the indigenous merchant courts failed to guarantee impartiality and effectiveness in cross-cultural conflicts.[54] The coercive and executive arrangements of the court were also a cause of attraction.[55]

It has also been argued that it was easy for the Armenians to adapt to the practices of the Mayor's Court, as their diaspora actually lacked any distinct legal binding. This claim challenges what had been considered as one of the most important parameters of the functioning of the network. The altercations between the New Julfan *kalanthar* (mayor) and Sultan David (a New Julfan merchant settled in Madras) have been used as an example to show how the exposure to the new colonial legal institutions allowed evasion from the moral authority of the core of the diaspora – New Julfa. Bhaswati Bhattacharya makes a valid case for this by highlighting Sultan David's claim that he could not be held accountable to the *kalanthar*, since the Julfan merchants generally adopted the law of their respective host states.[56] But with the spotlight on this statement of Sultan David, the portion of his intention to clear the debts of his father-in-law in New Julfa to prove that he was a trustworthy person has been overlooked.[57] This portion shows David's intentions of gaining reputation among the members of the network.

Here, it needs to be asked whether the self-regulating structures of the network could continue to be pertinent even when external agencies or authorities could potentially intervene.

The apparent leap of faith in the early colonial legal culture did not necessarily turn the mercantile groups into collaborators of the colonial regime. Rather, they acknowledged the colonial legal culture and the indigenous regimes of law concurrently.[58] It has to be accepted that the scope of forum-shopping and the flexibility of legal pluralism, as highlighted by Benton, got reduced eventually when legal conversations were buttressed by military and coercive power. But at the same time the extent to which homogenization and standardization occurred under the Mayor's Court also needs to be reviewed. The Armenians, through their regular negotiations with colonial institutions, underwent a degree of metamorphosis themselves. But as the narrative of the Mayor's Court suggests, there was always an enduring inclination to preserve their community agency and identity.[59]

The litigations among the Armenians in the Mayor's Court during the first half of the eighteenth century were not particularly troubled, as drastic measures were not yet enforced to subvert customary practices. In cases involving community members, the court generally upheld prevalent norms. A body of referees from the community was summoned to handle the arbitration.[60] Mutual understanding and trust invested in the group and established customs were the basis of such arbitrations. This could be seen as a marker of a mutated continuation of the New Julfan *jumiat* tradition, even when they were formed under the tacit direction of the colonial court.

Examples of such litigations also show that New Julfan customs were generally referred to in the proceedings as the basis of arbitration.[61] Reports of the tribunals used language assertive of the self-representation and customary norms of the community.[62] During this period, the court generally upheld the decision taken by these tribunals. Therefore, the integration of the Armenians with the Mayor's Court in Madras in the early eighteenth century could be seen as a mixed process of preservation and adjustments that had marked their negotiations with other regimes during this period.

But the crossover of the two modes of legal arbitration was not as smooth as it appeared. In the second half of the eighteenth century, the court began to assume a much more dominating tone. In a significant departure from the earlier practice, it began to scrutinize the decisions made by the tribunals closely before concurring to it. Sometimes it even overruled these decisions.[63]

The tensions and fissures in the Anglo-Armenian interactions of the late eighteenth century began to appear rather evidently in cases that dealt with

Armenian wills and inheritances. The wills generally spoke for the unity of Armenian diasporic identity. For one, the wills represented the connectedness of the diaspora. Armenian merchants continued to leave donations for the institutions of their homeland or their community.[64] The wills also reflected the connection between individuals and families across the globe. As the wills determined the inheritance and control over property, they were pivotal in the functioning of the family firm-based commerce of the Armenian merchants. The Armenian wills generally designated administrators and executors from within the community. Exposure to the rationale of the Mayor's Court, however, began to introduce certain apprehensions. The practice of the court selecting the administrator for estates left intestate led to instances of intervention into the well-guarded space of the community.[65]

Consequently, the initial pragmatism characterizing the Armenian tendency to abide by their customs gradually gave way to a more considered appreciation of English law. In time, this impacted their own conventions, organization, and identity. Both the tension as well as the coping mechanism to survive within the emerging system was reflected in the following case study involving an Armenian widow. Although the women found some rights in the New Julfan wills, their actual agency was rather limited.[66] The Mayor's Court provided an opportunity to these women to exert their rights. But at the same time, this created a sense of anxiety that was met by a collective reaction from the community, which represented attempts to hold on to a group identity.

A case from 1785, relating to the inheritance of the property of Grigor Miqaelian, an Armenian merchant, reflects a similar crisis that the community faced. Magdalena, the widow of Miqaelian, filed a petition at the Mayor's Court against Sett Aviet and Sanad Coja Maul, the administrators appointed for the estate. She claimed that her share in the estate had been denied on the accusation that she had eloped. The court appointed a five-member community tribunal to decide the issue of inheritance.[67] The rhetoric used by the tribunal continued to show the balance that the Armenians sought to establish between the pragmatic usage of the court and the preservation of the symbolic capital of the Armenian identity.[68] The scope of executing the customary norms was, however, becoming limited by this time. The traditionally autonomous Armenian portable court had to accept the status of a subordinate institution when it was compelled to accept the directions of the Mayor's Court and accept Magdalena as a lawful heir.[69] However, in the course of the proceedings, the administrators and the members of the tribunal continued to assert that the situation was caused by Magdalena and her attorney's ignorance regarding the community's customs.[70] This suggests that the community constantly looked for rhetoric to balance their diasporic self-representation with the new socio-legal conditions produced at the Mayor's Court. The court was therefore able to impose its sensibilities on the community. The community in turn resisted by crafting the narrative of a distinct cultural identity even when it did not always translate successfully into the outcome of the case. But this scope of highlighting the idea of a distinct self-representation assisted the preservation of heterogeneity and a specific form of self-representation.

Thus, by the late-eighteenth century, the hegemony of the colonial regime was increasingly limiting the scope of pluralism and forum-shopping that the early modern legal sphere provided. But at the same time, it is difficult to discount the complex and accommodating language which developed within the institutional structure of the early colonial courts. The scope of dialogue and adjustment, along with a sense of flexible ambiguity in the verdicts, were what really distinguished the period from the historical trajectories of the nineteenth century, when the British colonial apparatus had become much more hegemonic.

Conclusion: Towards Colonial Modernity

The experiences of New Julfan merchants in the legal sphere in South Asia, Persia, and Russia in course of the seventeenth and eighteenth centuries showcase a picture of negotiation and adaptation that was symptomatic of this period. This history shows that certain core ideas, like the notion of the community, remained constant throughout this period. Constant cultural dialogue led to the development of new nomenclatures or rhetorics of self-representation almost mirroring the balancing act between being an Armenian merchant and British subject. Nazar Hakob Shamier's petitions sent to the Councils of Fort William and Prince of Wales Island provided a fascinating prototype of this, that is, of *an Armenian subject of the British Nation*.[71]

The key to understand the making of this hybrid identity could be found in the complex legal culture that sustained till the early nineteenth century. The trend of jockeying between indigenous customs and British law suggests that the emerging system was composite, formed not by a unilateral imposition but through a long process of exchanges. In this way, the initial Company state did not quite represent a departure from the multicultural exchanges signified by the early modern condition; rather, it was a part of this condition.[72] Even with the narrowing of the utility of forum-shopping, the heterogeneity of the legal discourse shows that the idea of legal pluralism was not yet redundant. We have seen repeatedly in this chapter that it was this early modern condition of multiplicity and flexibility that allowed a diasporic trading community like the Armenians to sustain a distinct self-identity through negotiations and adjustments in the courts of law.

However, by the second quarter of the nineteenth century, increasing imperial interest and subsequent control of the colonies in South Asia caused a profound shift in legal culture.[73] This shift could be seen in the context of the establishment of cultural paramountcy of the West. This is what ultimately paved the way for the derailment of the hybrid early modern condition and the emergence of colonial modernity in the legal sphere of South Asia.[74]

The transformation was clearly visible in the sheer change in the rhetoric of Armenian self-representation that had been a crucial key to understanding the scope of dialogue and hybridity in the legal sphere. In a petition submitted to the Governor General in 1833, the Armenians in Calcutta appealed to be placed solely under English law that was applicable in the King's Court.[75] They complained that in the earlier Company courts, there had been no set standard of pronouncing a verdict. While a few judges had applied English law, others had either worked on the basis of the notion of equity or had chosen to look towards Armenian customs. Interestingly, the Armenians endorsing this petition suggested that since Armenia had ceased to be a nation long back in the fourteenth century, the concept of Armenian customs or norms was a false idea. While this sudden inversion from their long-standing narrative of cultural identity and heritage might come as a surprise, this act of surrendering their legal agency should be understood in the broader context in which the petition was submitted. The imposition of the English Alien law by two Acts of 1826 and 1832 of the Supreme Court of Calcutta had unsettled the rights of the Armenians over the properties and inheritances that they owned in the Bengal province. By the introduction of the English Alien law passed earlier in the British Parliament in 1793, properties belonging to the Armenians (or any other groups marked out as foreigners) could be claimed by the Crown. The only way of cementing their rights was to acquire the full-fledged status as subjects of the British Empire by surrendering claims to any other identity. Therefore, the political, military, and financial ascendancy of Company rule along with the increasing involvement of the British imperial government into the affairs of its South Asian colonies pushed out the last remnants of the hybrid legal culture that had been one of the signifiers of early modernity.

Notes

1. John F. Richards, 'Early Modern India and World History', *Journal of World History* 8, no. 2 (1997): 197–209.
2. Philip D. Curtin, *Cross-Cultural Trade in World History* (New York: Cambridge University Press, 1984), 3; Charles H. Parker, *Global Interactions in the Early Modern Age* (Cambridge: Cambridge University Press, 2010), 2–3.

3. Ina Baghdiantz McCabe, 'Global Trading Ambitions in Diaspora: The Armenians and Their Eurasian Silk Trade 1530–1750', in *Diaspora Entrepreneurial Networks: Four Centuries in History*, ed. Ina Baghdiantz McCabe, Gelina Harlafti, and Ienna Pepelasis Minoglou, 27–48 (Oxford: Berg, 2005), 27–28.
4. Sushil Chaudhury, 'Introduction', in *Armenians in Asian Trade in the Early Modern Era*, ed. Sushil Chaudhury and Keram Kevonian, 3–18 (Delhi: Manohar, 2014), 8.
5. Vahe Baladouni and Margaret Makepeace (eds.), *Armenian Merchants of the Seventeenth and Early Eighteenth Centuries: English East India Company Sources* (Philadelphia: American Philosophical Society, 1998), 11–12.
6. Chaudhury, 'Introduction', 10.
7. Sebouh David Aslanian, *From the Indian Ocean to the Mediterranean: The Global Trade Networks of Armenian Merchants from New Julfa* (California: University of California Press, 2011), 166–201.
8. Bhaswati Bhattacharya, 'The Book of Will of Petrus Woskan (1680–1751): Some Insights into the Global Commercial Network of the Armenians in the Indian Ocean', *Journal of the Economic and Social History of the Orient* 51, no. 1 (2008): 67–98, see 74–75.
9. Edmund Herzig, 'The Commercial Law of the New Julfa Armenians', in *Armenians in Asian Trade*, ed. Chaudhury and Kevonian, 69–70; William Floor, 'The Secular Judicial System in Safavid Persia', *Studia Iranica* 29, no.1 (2000): 9–60, see 10.
10. F. G. Poghosyan (ed.), *Datastanagirk Astrakhani Hayots* '(Yerevan: Haykakanssh Gitutyunneri Akadimiyai Hratarakchutyun, 1967), 6. 'Since the Armenian community lacked a country or King, they should organise their business and other activities through information, understanding and consensus within the community.' Herzig, 'Commercial Law of the New Julfa Armenians', 66; Sebouh David Aslanian, 'The Salt in a Merchant's Letter: The Culture of Julfan Correspondence in the Indian Ocean and the Mediterranean', *Journal of World History* 19 no. 2 (2008): 127–188, see 145.
11. Herzig, 'Commercial Law of the New Julfa Armenians', 73–76.
12. The last passage of the *Datastanagirk* established the concern regarding the applicability and acceptability of the law book in various legal regimes that their compatriots encountered across the span of the network. It insisted on holding on to a distinct Armenian identity through the legal culture and ethics described in the book. It also took a pragmatic stance to accept the need of negotiating and adapting to the host states and accepted the necessity of readjustments of legal culture in that process. Poghosyan (ed.), *Datastanagirk*, 232.

13. Lauren Benton, *Law and Colonial Cultures: Legal Regimes in World History, 1400–1900* (Cambridge: Cambridge University Press, 2011), 6–12.
14. Lakshmi Subramanian, 'A Trial in Transition: Courts, Merchants and Identities in Western India, circa 1800', *Indian Economic and Social History Review* 41, no. 3 (2004): 269–292.
15. Aparna Balachandran, 'Petition Town: Law, Custom and Urban Space in Colonial South India', in *Iterations of Law: Legal Histories from India*, ed. Aparna Balachandran, Rashmi Pant, and Bhavani Raman, 147–167 (New Delhi: Oxford University Press, 2018).
16. See, for instance, K. M. Panikkar, *Asia and Western Dominance: A Survey of the Vasco Da Gama Epoch of Asian History, 1498–1945* (London: George Allen & Unwin Ltd., 1953).
17. Ashin Das Gupta, *Indian Merchants and the Decline of Surat: c. 1700–1750* (Wiesbaden: Franz Steiner Verlag, 1979).
18. Elizabeth Mancke, 'Early Modern Expansion and the Politicization of the Oceanic Space', *Geographical Review* 89, no. 2 (1999): 225–236; R. P. Anand, *Origin and Development of the Law of the Sea* (The Hague: Mrtinus Nijhoff Publishers, 1983), 99.
19. Lakshmi Subramanian, 'Reaping the Risks of Transition: Merchants and Trade in Western India, 1750–1818', in *History of Science, Philosophy and Culture in Indian Civilization*, vol. 3, part 7: *The Trading World of the Indian Ocean, 1500–1800*, ed. O. Prakash, 285–307 (Delhi: Pearson India Education, 2012), 286.
20. Bruce P. Lenman, 'Colonial Wars and Imperial Instability, 1688–1793', in *The Oxford History of the British Empire*, ed. P. J. Marshall, vol. 2: *The Eighteenth Century*, 151–168 (Oxford: Oxford University Press, 1998); Gagan D. S. Sood, *India and the Islamic Heartlands: An Eighteenth Century World of Circulation and Exchange* (Cambridge: Cambridge University Press, 2016), 23.
21. Sebouh Aslanian, 'Trade Diaspora versus Colonial State: Armenian Merchants, the English East India Company, and the High Court of Admiralty in London, 1748–1752', *Diaspora: A Journal of Transnational Studies* 13, no. 1 (2004): 37–100.
22. Aslanian, 'Trade Diaspora versus Colonial State', 76–83.
23. Kali K. Dutta (ed.), *Fort William–India House Correspondence, 1748–1756*, vol. 1 (New Delhi: National Archives of India, 1958), 310.
24. Dutta (ed.), *Fort William–India House Correspondence*, vol. 1, 310.
25. Amy Apcar (ed.), *The Life and Adventures of Joseph Emin: 1726–1809* (Calcutta: Baptist Mission Press, 1918), 16.
26. Apcar (ed.), *Life and Adventures of Joseph Emin*, 17.

27. R. P. Patwardhan (ed.), *Fort William–India House Correspondences 1773–1776*, vol. 7 (New Delhi: National Archives of India, 1971), lxii.
28. Irfan Habib, 'Potentialities of Capitalistic Development in the Economy of Mughal India', in Irfan Habib, *Essays in Indian History: Towards a Marxist Perception*, 180–232 (New Delhi: Tulika Books, 1995), see 227.
29. Irfan Habib, 'Merchant Communities in Pre-colonial India', in *The Rise of Merchant Empires: Long Distance Trade in the Early Modern World, 1350–1750*, ed. James D. Tracy, 371–399 (Cambridge: Cambridge University Press, 1990), see 395–396.
30. Shushanik Khachikian, 'The Bill of Exchange in the Milieu of New Julfan Armenian Merchants', in *Armenians in Asian Trade*, ed. Chaudhury and Kevonian, 277–282 (Delhi: Manohar, 2014), see 277–279.
31. Subramanian, 'Reaping the Risks of Transition', 289; Sinnappah Arasaratnam, *Merchants, Companies and Commerce on the Coromandel Coast 1650–1740* (Delhi: Oxford University Press, 1987), 274, 280; Kanaklatha Mukund, *The Trading World of the Tamil Merchant: Evolution of Merchant Capitalism in the Coromandel* (Chennai: Orient Longman, 1999), 172–174.
32. Mukund, *Trading World of the Tamil Merchant*, 175–177.
33. Alexander Annesley, *A Compendium of the Law of Marine Insurances, Bottomry, Insurances on Lives and of Insurance Against Fire* (Middletown: I. Riley, 1808), 173–174.
34. Arasaratnam, *Merchants, Companies and Commerce*, 280.
35. Lakshmi Subramanian, 'Seths and Sahibs: Negotiated Relationships between Indigenous Capital and the East India Company', in *Britain's Oceanic Empire: Atlantic and Indian Ocean Worlds, c. 1550–1850*, ed. H. V. Bowen, Elizabeth Mancke, and John G. Reid, 311–339 (Cambridge: Cambridge University Press, 2012), see 324.
36. Subramanian, 'Reaping the Risks of Transition', 287–288.
37. Subramanian, 'Seths and Sahibs', 324–327.
38. Ashin Das Gupta, 'Trade and Politics in Eighteenth-century India', in Ashin Das Gupta, *The World of the Indian Ocean Merchant 1500–1800*, compiled by Uma Das Gupta, 141–179 (New Delhi: Oxford University Press, 2004), 141, 168–169.
39. Tamil Nadu State Archives (TNSA), *Mayor's Court Records: Pleadings in the Mayor's Court*, vol. 25, General no. 12020, 401–403.
40. TNSA, Pleadings in the Mayor's Court, vol. 25, 406–408.
41. *A Collection of Statutes relating to the East India Company: With an Appendix Containing Acts and Parts of Acts, Relating to Shipping, Duties, Regulations for Export and Import, &c. &c. which in General Do Not Solely Relate to the East India Company…* (London: G. Eyre and A. Strahan, 1810), 97.

42. Mukund, *Trading World of the Tamil Merchant*, 174–175. Just one case has been located in 1744, where the court went in favour of the insurer on the basis of prevalent conventions.
43. TNSA, *Mayor's Court Records: Series XII-C*, Private Papers (MISC), Marine Insurance Book.
44. TNSA, Series XII-C, Marine Insurance Book.
45. TNSA, *Mayor's Court Records: Appeals against the Mayor's Court*, vol. 36, General no. 12096. Case entry dated 12th June 1797–17th November 1798, 543–770.
46. TNSA, Appeals against the Mayor's Court, vol. 36, 580.
47. TNSA, Appeals against the Mayor's Court, vol. 36, 565. The clauses of the policy had mentioned that political aggression would not be held as a valid risk. For an evolution of the definition of barratry in British insurance law, see Chief Justice Daly, *Barratry: Its Origin, History and Meaning in the Maritime Laws* (New York: Baker and Godwin Printers, 1872).
48. TNSA, Appeals against the Mayor's Court, vol. 36, 767.
49. TNSA, Appeals against the Mayor's Court, vol. 36, 753.
50. Records of Fort Saint George (RFSG), *Diary and Consultation Book of 1707* (Madras: Madras Record Office, Superintendent Government Press, 1929), 61; Henry Davison Love, *Vestiges of Old Madras: 1640–1800* (London: John Murray, 1913), vol. 1, 559–560; vol. 2, 25–28.
51. Mary L. Pratt, *Imperial Eyes: Travel Writing and Transculturation* (London: Routledge, 1992), 6–7. Contact zone is a junction where disparate groups came into contact with each other and often interacted within a milieu of unequal relation of power that led to the exchange of information in moments of colonial encounters.
52. Mattison Mines, 'Courts of Law and Styles of Self in Eighteenth Century Madras: From Hybrid to Colonial Self', *Modern Asian Studies* 35, no. 1 (2001): 33–74, see 34, 41.
53. Mines, 'Courts of Law and Styles', 37, 40–46; John J. Paul, *The Legal Profession in Colonial South India* (Bombay: Oxford University Press, 1991), 12.
54. TNSA, *Mayor's Court Records: Pleadings in Mayor's Court*, vol. 24, General no. 12019, 23. For instance, Khachik Pogos, or Catchik Pogos [*sic*], an Armenian Merchant, had proposed to resolve his disputes with Cammo Caul Chitty and Adapamum Chitty, in any of the merchant courts, other than the 'Malabarese'.
55. TNSA, Public Department Sundries, vol. 8, Form and Method of Proceedings in All Civil Suits (1726), 41–45.
56. Bhattacharya, 'The Book of Will', 79.
57. RFSG, *Diary and Consultation Book of 1745* (Madras: Madras Record Office, Superintendent Government Press, 1931), 118.

58. Benton, *Law and Colonial Cultures*, 257–258.
59. There has been a considerable debate as to what added up to a New Julfan or Armenian identity. In spite of the differences between the Orthodox (Apostolic Church) and Catholic New Julfans, a common identity probably emerged for the sake of the trade in South and South-East Asia. See Bhaswati Bhattacharya, *Ashtadash Shatake Bharater Armani Samaj o Banijya: Kichu Prasangik Alochana* (Kolkata: Paschimbanga Itihas Sangsad, 2018), 15. The construction of a common Armenian identity was also seen in the nationalist articulations of Shahmir Shahamirian. In *Tetrak vor Kochi Nshavak* (Booklet of Aim), published in 1783, he attempted to write a constitution for the Armenians in Madras. His concern was to devise a more rounded and political identity of the community. See Sergey Arutiunov, 'Triple Laws and Quasi-states in the Caucasus', in *State and Legal Practice in the Caucasus: Anthropological Perspectives on Law and Politics*, ed. Stephane Voell and Iwona Kaliszewska, 25–30 (New York: Routledge, 2015), see 26–27.
60. TNSA, *Mayor's Court Records: Pleadings in the Mayor's Court*, vol. 1, General no. 11996, 154. For example, in a suit filed in 1731 by Khwaja Zachariah against Khwaja Amouner, the court admitted that the matter was exclusively related to Armenian customs. '[I]t appearing [*sic*] that the matters in question between the plaintiff and the defendant depended on the customs of the Armenian merchants ... it is therefore ordered the several matters and accounts ... are hereby referred to Coja Pacedon, Coja David and Coja Gregoris ... award made by the arbitrators be final.'
61. RFSG, *Pleadings at the Mayor's Court, 1745*, vol. 5 (Madras: Madras Record Office, Superintendent Government Press, 1939), 49–73.
62. RFSG, *Pleadings at the Mayor's Court*, vol. 5, 62. The tribunal's report opened with the statement: 'We whose names are hereunto subscribed do hereby certify and declare that it is the custom among us Armenians.'
63. TNSA, *Mayor's Court Records: Pleadings in the Mayor's Court*, vol. 23, General no. 12018, 128–145.
64. TNSA, *Pleadings in the Mayor's Court*, vol. 23, 138–139. For example, the will of Joseph, the son of Maruth stated, '... five hundred rupees are to be sent to Holy Egmiasun (Edjmiatzin) and five hundred rupees to the convent at Holy Jerusalem, three hundred rupees to the convent at Aminapurkich at our Julpha, two hundred rupees to the convent of the Numse at our Julpha, two hundred rupees to our church at Purtvee'.
65. TNSA, *Public Department Sundries*, vol. 8, 125–126.
66. Houri Berberian, 'Unequivocal Sole Ruler: The Lives of New Julfan Armenian Women and Early Modern Laws', *Journal of the Society for Armenian Studies* 23 (2014): 82–112.

67. TNSA, *Mayor's Court Records, Wills, Probates and Letters of Administration*, vol. 35, General no. 12129 (1787), 193–194.
68. TNSA, *Wills, Probates and Letters of Administration*, vol. 35, 194. '… therefore we proceed to our determination that the said Gregorio Miguel dying intestated [*sic*], Seth Ter Avieth and Sanad Coja Maul the son of Coja Maul relations of the said Gregorio Miguel deceased of Madras merchants by terms agreeable to the customs of Armenian merchants and agreeable to the noble use of Great Britain was granted by the Mayor's Court at Madras with letters of administration for the estate of the said deceased Gregorio Miguel.'
69. TNSA, *Wills, Probates and Letters of Administration*, vol. 35, 194.
70. TNSA, *Wills, Probates and Letters of Administration*, vol. 35, 308. 'That they wanted the said Miguel Johannes to give them a receipt or discharge in the Armenian language in like manner as the said Joseph Maroot had given on the part and behalf of the said Zeptha Stephan to which the said Miguel Johannes replied that as he did not fully understand the form that would be necessary in the Armenian language and did not know what kind of receipt or discharge had been given by the said Joseph Maroot.'
71. National Archives of India, Home-Public Proceedings, 1805, 66–67.
72. Mahmood Kooria and Sanne Ravensbergen, 'The Indian Ocean of Law: Hybridity and Space', *Itinerario* 42, no. 2 (2018): 164–167.
73. H. V. Bowen, 'British India, 1765–1813: The Metropolitan Context', in *Oxford History of the British Empire*, vol. 2: The *Eighteenth Century*, ed. P. J. Marshall, 530–551 (Oxford: Oxford University Press, 1998). Also see Lakshmi Subramanian, *History of India, 1707–1857* (New Delhi: Orient Blackswan, 2010), 89–92.
74. Anthony D. King, 'The Time and Spaces of Modernity', in *Global Modernities*, ed. Mike Featherstone, Scott Lash, and Roland Robertson, 108–123 (London: SAGE Publications, 1997).
75. A copy of the appeal was printed in the October issue of the *Calcutta Monthly Journal and General Register* (Calcutta, 1836), 465–467.

11

Was Mughal Warfare Early Modern?

Pratyay Nath

It has become increasingly commonplace in the last two decades to refer to the Mughal Empire as an early modern polity. By extension, Mughal warfare too gets designated as early modern. But what does it really mean for Mughal warfare to be early modern? Is it simply because it is associated with a certain historical period that has now been re-categorized and redefined? Or did this warfare exhibit certain features that actually set it apart from those of earlier and later times, thereby necessitating the use of a new temporal category? If that indeed is the case, then what features might these be? The present chapter addresses these questions.

The first section discusses how historians have looked at Mughal warfare in relation with the historical evolution of military processes in the Indian subcontinent. These discussions have been dominated by an emphasis on the role of a single technology – gunpowder weaponry – and a single explanatory framework – the Military Revolution hypothesis. I argue that much of this has been a Eurocentric exercise, whereby historians have assessed South Asian warfare using parameters drawn from the European historical experience. For some, this has created the problematic impression of drastic change – a historical break – brought about by the proliferation of gunpowder weaponry in the sixteenth century. For others, it has created an equally debatable notion of military changelessness between the eleventh century and the eighteenth. Moving away from both these interpretations, the present chapter analyses Mughal warfare on its own terms and in the specific historical context of South Asia. I explore four major facets of Mughal warfare in four subsequent sections – military adaptation, army organization, management of war, and culture of war. I argue that in all these fields, Mughal warfare ushered in a new paradigm that should be called early modern because of the considerable shift it marked away from its antecedents. It was only since the mid-eighteenth century that this military early modernity was derailed in a large measure by the onset of colonial modernity.[1]

Warfare, Revolutions, and the Search for a Military Early Modernity

There are two strands of thought that see the rise of Mughal power as a major military shift in South Asia. First, one idea that emerged in course of the 1970s and 1980s was that of the Mughal polity being a 'gunpowder empire'. Marshall Hodgson and, following him, William McNeill argued that the emergence and consolidation of Mughal imperial power owed primarily to its effective use of gunpowder technology.[2] The second argument emerged by challenging this gunpowder empire hypothesis. In 1989, Douglas Streusand offered a more nuanced argument that continued to see the rise of the Mughals as a watershed in South Asian military history but did not ascribe primacy for this to any one technology. Instead, he said that the military shift owed to the introduction of a 'new military system' in the subcontinent, one that 'supplanted the existing elephant-based system and remained dominant until the appearance of infantry armies on the European model in the eighteenth century'.[3] This new form of warfare, he argued, gave the Mughals 'a definite but limited margin of military superiority' over their opponents, one that emanated from their 'sole possession of a complete array of artillery, infantry armed with firearms, and an army of mounted archers'.[4]

More recently, these ideas of a break in South Asian military history with the advent of the Mughals in the early sixteenth century has come under fire from Jos Gommans, who has deployed the Military Revolution framework to analyse this history.[5] Gommans argues that while the advent of gunpowder weaponry triggered a Military Revolution in Europe in the sixteenth and seventeenth centuries, the Indian subcontinent experienced only a 'false dawn of the gunpowder' during this period.[6] According to him, this resulted from the failure of gunpowder artillery to make an impact on South Asian forts, owing to their strong build and inaccessible locations. Because of this, there never arose the need for the major transformations in fort architecture and the concomitant tactical and strategic changes that transpired in Europe. In battles, Gommans explains the tactical marginality of firearms in terms of the underdeveloped nature of infantry tactics. He also underlines the inefficiency of field artillery, owing to its lack of mobility and standardization, as well as the relatively poor quality of gunpowder. According to Gommans, the lack of interest of Indian states in developing drilled and disciplined infantry units of musketeers emanated from the abundance of warhorses. The highly skilled cavalrymen – especially the mounted archers – who operated in the subcontinent held a distinct tactical advantage over the Indian musketeers. The latter – in contrast to their European counterparts – were poorly clad, ragtag bands of part-time mercenary soldiers using slow-firing matchlock guns even after the spread of more efficient flintlocks in the seventeenth century. Hence, although gunpowder weaponry saw widespread dissemination in South Asia since the fifteenth century, Gommans suggests that they failed to propel musketeers and artillery into tactical centrality; instead, cavalry continued to dominate the military stage.[7] He argues that it was only between the mid-eighteenth and mid-nineteenth centuries that the subcontinent saw a gunpowder revolution owing to the rise of British colonial power and the simultaneous Europeanization of the armies of the various post-Mughal regional states of the subcontinent.[8]

Gommans' analysis is a sophisticated one. It helps us situate Mughal warfare in a wider military context. Yet, because he applies the Military Revolution hypothesis in the South Asian context, he effectively assesses this part of the world in terms of parameters derived from the European historical experience. Here, however, he is not an exception. Since the late twentieth century, an increasing number of historians working on different non-European parts of the world have engaged with the ideas of Michael Roberts and Geoffrey Parker.[9] Many of them use the Military Revolution hypothesis as a convenient analytical framework to interpret military changes in non-European regions during the sixteenth through eighteenth centuries. The result is that processes similar to the European Military Revolution have started being spotted in different non-European parts of the world. Certain aspects of the framework – as developed by Roberts and Parker in the context of western Europe – have started featuring in these discussions repeatedly.[10] In juxtaposing the parameters of the European Military Revolution onto South Asia, these concerns also dominate Gommans' analysis. Unlike other similar exercises that have resulted in the discovery of the Military Revolution in regions like Russia, Japan, and Korea, Gommans' study reveals a lack of analogous changes in the Indian subcontinent. This prompts him to argue against the incidence of the Military Revolution in this part of the world and to counter the idea of Mughal warfare heralding any paradigmatic shift in military matters.

In effect, these exercises – not only of Gommans but also of other scholars who have discovered parallels to the European Military Revolution in various non-European parts of the world – prioritize the European historical experience over others. In this approach, European military processes become the yardstick against which military changes in other regions are understood and assessed. In some cases, the intentions are entirely noble – to show that various parts of the world were at par with Europe in terms of technology, tactics, strategy, and army organization during the sixteenth through eighteenth centuries. Quite rightly, some historians argue against a form of Eurocentrism that projects backward in time the nineteenth-century European military supremacy over the rest of the world.[11] Yet, as a means of arguing, this takes the form of an attempt to show that various non-European regions experienced roughly the same changes as Europe did. Consequently, military histories of these regions often end up being cast in the mould of European history. Through this discursive universalization of the European experience, a new form of Eurocentrism makes way for the older one. The continued focus on the Military Revolution hypothesis also obscures various military aspects that did not appear in Europe but characterized the historical experiences of various other parts of the world. Discussions around these processes get relegated to the margins of the historical discourse as the European experience occupies the mainstream of global scholarship on the subject. As the primary set of shifts to have engulfed the domain of warfare in the sixteenth through the eighteenth centuries, the Military Revolution becomes synonymous with what can be called a military early modernity.

All this has profound implications for South Asian history. According to Gommans, the Mughals did not bring about any paradigmatic military shift in the subcontinent, mainly because they did not inaugurate a Military Revolution in the subcontinent. Owing to this, he argues that they largely fitted into and continued the historical tendencies established by the horse-warrior revolution in the eleventh and twelfth centuries, and the fortress revolution in the thirteenth and fourteenth centuries.[12] Gommans' work thus foregrounds long-term historical continuities in the field of warfare between the eleventh century and the eighteenth, thereby denying South Asia of a military early modernity.[13] For him, the one enduring feature of South Asian warfare through these centuries was the overwhelming centrality of the warhorse. This also contributed, he argues, to an ostensible lack of emphasis on siege warfare in the Mughal case, because 'they had opted for the mobility of the horse and not for the stability of the walls, for ruling India from the camp and not from the fort'.[14]

It is true that South Asia did not experience most of the military processes that characterized the European Military Revolution. However, the very fact that Gommans makes this European framework his parameter for investigating change and continuity in South Asian warfare renders his methodology problematic. I am also sceptical of his arguments about the enduring tactical centrality of the warhorse in South Asian warfare.[15] It is my contention that Mughal warfare *did* herald a new military paradigm in South Asia. The category of early modernity helps us conceptualize these changes that emerged in the sixteenth and seventeenth centuries. However, they get obscured when one studies Mughal warfare using the framework of the Military Revolution and focuses only on the elements that characterized the European military transformation – the use of gunpowder weaponry, transformation of positional warfare, and rise of massed infantry formations. In order to trace the important shifts that characterized the rise of Mughal warfare, it is necessary to look beyond this analytical framework altogether.[16] At the same time, it is also vital to move beyond primacy that historians like Hodgson ascribe to the role of technology – especially gunpowder weaponry – in heralding military change in the fifteenth to sixteenth centuries. Instead of focusing only on military techniques or the dynamics of combat, one needs to adopt the more inclusive 'war and society' approach. Doing this enables us to understand the nature of Mughal warfare on its own terms within the historical context of the subcontinent and in relation with the dynamics of the state, culture, and society. This is the exercise I undertake in the following sections by focusing on four themes one by one – military adaptations, army organization, management of war, and culture of war.

Military Adaptation

At the most fundamental level, the so-called Military Revolution was a set of military adaptations. A few years back, Jeremy Black pointed out that while the category of revolution suggests something with a certain degree of intention in bringing about change, adaptation is more open-ended. According to Black, this makes the category of adaptation more helpful in capturing the variety of military changes that states and armies went through between the sixteenth and eighteenth centuries in creatively responding to various challenges.[17] More recently, Richard Eaton and Philip Wagoner have applied Black's suggestions in the context of the sixteenth-century Deccan Plateau. They argue that the changes that accompanied the so-called Military Revolution were largely absent among the Deccan polities. Hence, the category of revolution does not prove to be helpful in interpreting the other sorts of military changes that *did* occur. It is here that the category of military adaptation renders itself useful. It helps us understand and analyse the myriad changes in military techniques and architecture that the spread of gunpowder weaponry triggered, even as these changes did not conform to the tendencies visible in western Europe.[18]

In light of these interventions, it is possible to revise the implicit equivalence between the Military Revolution and a military early modernity. I argue that it is better to conceptualize the latter in terms of heightened military adaptations. As large empires vied with each other to control the fate of the continents during this period, each of them faced certain challenges that their predecessors had not. These included financial, environmental, technological, political, and cultural hurdles related to rapid imperial expansion in terms of human, material, and territorial resources. As these empires negotiated these hurdles, they constantly adapted to changing circumstances to fight wars more efficiently. Since the sixteenth through the eighteenth centuries witnessed heightened state- and empire-building activities across the world, it can be argued that this engendered heightened military adaptations as well. Instead of positing the path of western Europe as the standard and all the others as aberrations, it is more historically accurate to look at the entire set of these escalating adaptations as being one of the features of a military early modernity. While some of the characteristics of this condition – like the necessity of engaging with new technologies like gunpowder weaponry – were globally shared, some others were specific to the cultural, political, and environmental contexts of individual political formations.

Seen in this light, Mughal warfare was certainly early modern. Babur (r. 1526–1530) and his followers arrived in North India in 1526 with military techniques thoroughly rooted in the post-Timurid, post-nomadic traditions of Central Eurasia. As Streusand points out, Babur's victories at Panipat (1526) and Khanua (1527) rested squarely on his ability to deploy together heavy cavalry, mounted archers, field artillery, and musketeers, all around the wagon laager.[19] This combination itself was a product of Ottoman military adaptation in the late fifteenth century, whereby the central European defensive formation of the wagon laager, the post-nomadic traditions of cavalry warfare, and the new technology of gunpowder weaponry were fused together into a cogent battle tactic.[20] It is from the Ottomans that Babur received the knowledge of this tactic in the early sixteenth century, and deployed it to great effect at Panipat and Khanua. In all big battles since then, Mughal armies used this composite tactic.

Gommans sees this as a subversion of firearms by the traditional tactical importance of cavalry. However, I am more inclined to interpret this as an adaptive response to a question that almost all armies of the sixteenth century faced – how to protect one's own matchlock-bearing infantry from attacks by the enemy forces in a battle? Western European armies used pikemen to shield their matchlockmen. Armies of imperial Russia positioned their matchlockmen behind temporary field fortifications called *guliai gorod*. In 1575, Oda Nobunaga (r. 1534–1582) positioned his Japanese matchlockmen behind stockades in the battle of Nagashino. The Ottomans made use of a line of defensively arranged wagons to the same end. Moving away from the idea that the western European adaptation – the combination of pike and shot – was the standard and all the rest were aberrations, it is more worthwhile to look at all these as different – but equally resourceful – examples of military adaptation, produced by the specific set of material and cultural conditions each polity was operating under. Even the Mughal appropriation of the Ottoman tactic was shaped by their specific historical trajectories thereafter. I have argued elsewhere that under Akbar (r. 1556–1605), Mughal battle tactics went through a shift that could perhaps be conceptualized as a form of sedentarization. Even as the wagon laager retained its value, mounted archery got gradually marginalized; in contrast, heavy cavalry, war-elephants, and the common infantry assumed greater tactical importance.[21] These were a result of the specific military, political, and cultural processes that Mughal empire-building went through at this time. The shifts in battle tactics comprised adaptive responses of Mughal armies to these processes.

Mughal military adaptability also manifested itself in how armies learnt to subjugate the massive stone forts of South Asia through arduous sieges. Imperial expansion into Central India and the Deccan Plateau in particular entailed a large number of sieges. These ranged from the likes of Chitor (1567–1568), Ranthambhor (1569), Ahmadnagar (1600), and Asirgarh (1600–1601) under Akbar to Bijapur (1685), Golconda (1687), and Gingee (1698) under Aurangzeb (r. 1658–1707). The winning combination of firearms, cavalry, and the wagon laager in battles had to be set aside here for the slow game of positional warfare. However, the lack of rivers in these regions prevented imperial armies from transporting artillery to many of these sieges, while the inaccessible locations of fortresses restricted the successful deployment of artillery even when they were successfully transported. Instead, Mughal adaptation entailed the use of more traditional methods of siegecraft, like mining and sapping, as well as efforts to win over garrisons through negotiations.[22]

A completely different sort of conditions presented itself as Mughal armies entered Sind and Bengal in the 1570s and Assam in the 1610s. Rivers dominated the landscape of these regions. Every year, monsoon rains would cause extensive floods, making it quite difficult for cavalry or infantry to move around freely. Here, Mughal military adaptation took the form of learning to wage amphibious campaigns. Although imperial armies fought some amphibious wars in Sind in the 1570s and 1590s, they came to experience their seriousness in Bengal only by the close of the sixteenth century. From extremely meagre resources in terms of boats, they were forced to gradually build up a huge flotilla by the early years of the seventeenth century. This comprised partly the imperial flotilla under the command of *mansabdar*s and partly the war-fleets of co-opted local *zamindar*s. Imperial armies also learnt to mount artillery pieces onto boats, possibly from Portuguese military professionals and renegades who abounded the region around this time. It was these military adaptations that enabled imperial forces to conquer most of Bengal by 1612. However, the ability to adapt reached its limits in the face of Portuguese–Arakanese naval raids in southeastern Bengal between the early 1620s and the mid-1660s. It also failed to bring many military victories in Assam, where imperial armies fought four wars – much of them amphibious – between 1613 and 1682.[23]

These examples indicate that Mughal war-making in South Asia entailed a constant process of military adaptation. Some of them were responses to challenges faced by almost all polities globally, like the need to raise more and more money to make war. Some of the adaptations, however, were brought by military specificities of the subcontinent – like the peculiarities of its terrain, climate, and ecology – and hence were specific to the Mughal case. If a military early modernity can be conceptualized in terms of heightened military adaptations, then the Mughals were integral to that shared early modernity. Admittedly, there are many instances of military adaptations in South Asia even before the Mughals.[24] However, what marks a paradigmatic shift in the sixteenth century was both the remarkable extent of Mughal military adaptations and the way these changes helped the dynasty to eventually create a truly subcontinental empire. Also, it was this heightened adaptability that enabled them to fight wars in extremely diverse environmental zones, ranging from the Himalayan foothills to the forested delta of the Ganga and the Brahmaputra, from the arid lands of Balkh and Qandahar to the broken hills and plateaus of the Deccan. In this, they were assisted by new centralizing tendencies of military organization. This is what we turn to next.

Army Organization

One of the hallmarks of medieval warfare in Islamicate polities was the institution of military slavery. Developed in the Abbasid caliphate in the later centuries of the first millennium CE, this institution was one of the pillars of military organization and statecraft in medieval Islamicate polities from North Africa to South Asia. Aside from comprising a major component of the army and the ruling elite, the *mamluk* (military slaves) also ruled in their own right as sovereigns in many cases.[25] Some of the Islamicate polities – like the Ottomans, Safavids, and Deccan Sultanates – continued this medieval practice through the sixteenth and seventeenth centuries as well.[26] The Mughal Empire, however, did not make use of this institution. While Mughal commanders prided in calling themselves *banda* (slave) – a term also used for a military slave – in relation to the emperor, this was meant in a figurative rather than juridical sense. It was invoked to express one's complete loyalty and devotion to the emperor.[27] Instead of using the institution of military slavery that served as one of the cornerstones of the armies of the Delhi

Sultanate, Mughal emperors filled their ranks with free men. This was a big change in terms of the nature of military personnel.

There was also a major shift between the medieval sultanates and the Mughal Empire in matters of fiscal-military administration and organization. In the Islamicate world, one of the traditional mechanisms of linking army organization with the collection and distribution of the resources of the realm was *iqtadari*. *Iqta* was a revenue assignment given to individual military commanders by the sultan. In return, the commander had to maintain troops and make them available to the sultan in times of war. The economic resources the *iqtadar* was supposed to collect was meant for the maintenance of his household and his troops. This fiscal-military institution arrived in North India from West Asia in the early thirteenth century. The institution had a checkered history under the sultans of Delhi between the thirteenth and the fifteenth centuries. In order to centralize power in their hands, sultans repeatedly tried to make *iqta*s transferrable, get the commanders to maintain a fixed number of troops, have them surrender any revenue collected in excess of the stipulated amount, and prevent sub-infeudation and inheritance of *iqta*s. However, they encountered stiff resistance in all these matters from the *iqtadar*s, who preferred a more decentralized administrative structure. Overall, fiscal-military administration under the Delhi sultans remained rather decentralized notwithstanding periodic centralizing drives launched by sultans like Alauddin Khalji and Muhammad bin Tughlaq.[28]

This kind of fiscal-military administration saw a reversal under the Mughals in the sixteenth century. Iqtidar Alam Khan argues that since the mid-sixteenth century, there was an increasing drive to centralize the administration of revenue assignments. He conjectures that this might have been a maturation of the administrative reforms of the Afghan ruler Sher Shah (r. 1540–1545) as well.[29] Athar Ali too points out that Sher Shah – and in his footsteps Islam Shah (r. 1545–1553) – introduced the *zabt* arrangement of assessing land-revenue and re-imposed the practice of branding of horses as a measure towards centralizing his administration and imposing his authority over the commanders.[30] His revenue reforms were complemented by his introduction of the pure silver *rupaya* (rupee) in addition to pure gold and copper currency.[31]

The third Mughal emperor, Akbar, built on these measures and brought about further centralization since 1561. Khan argues that this was a part of a 'new concept of assignment, which, in the post-1561 period, was increasingly perceived as pre-sanctioned income determined in accordance with the status and obligations of the assignee'.[32] This began the practice of fragmenting the land assignment given out to military commanders.[33] Thereby, land assignments were decoupled from territorial jurisdiction under individual military commanders. Instead, their land assignments increasingly came to be conceptualized in terms of the sanctioned income of the commander. This acted against the tendency of commanders to control compact territorial units. Mughal drive for administrative centralization thus began to hold sway over something that had been the essence of *iqtadari* in the immediate pre-Mughal period – the tendency of political fragmentation of authority and governance. Finally, the fiscal jurisdiction of the holder of the revenue assignment was increasingly separated from the conduct of routine administration of the area. Khan argues that these changes between 1561 and 1567 introduced the first elements of Mughal administrative centralization, something that was finally implemented by Akbar's decisive administrative reforms in 1574–1575.[34] These reforms introduced sophisticated mechanisms for assessing and collecting land revenue. This was linked with the military ranks (*mansab*) that were instituted for Mughal commanders in 1573–1574. Every commander was ascribed a single number to denote their salary, the size of their cavalry contingent, and the number of horses, elephants, carts, and beasts of burden they were expected to maintain.

This format underwent a further modification in 1596–1597, when the *mansab* was broken down into two numbers – *zat* and *sawar*. The first denoted the position of an individual commander in the official hierarchy of the Mughal state. It also determined his salary. The second denoted the number of horsemen and horses he was supposed to maintain. Most *mansabdar*s were paid by transferrable revenue assignments called *jagir*. The allotment of both *mansab* and *jagir* was centralized. All the military commanders reported directly to the emperor. There was no scope for sub-infeudation or inheritance of them. Assignment, promotion, and cancellation could only be done by the emperor.[35] Instituted by Akbar, this arrangement underwent several changes in course of the seventeenth century in response to changing circumstances, making *mansabdari* a dynamic practice rather than a static system.[36] As a part of this centralization of military organization, the Mughal state also kept forts under its direct control by assigning them to commanders (*qaladar*) appointed by and answerable to the emperor.[37]

It is true that this military organizational centralization was not an unqualified one. Several historians have pointed out that the *mansabdari* and *jagirdari* practices might not have worked in the strong centralized fashion in which it was envisioned at the imperial level. In fact, at the operational level, the state had to accommodate strong local interests and bend to the ambitions of powerful *mansabdar*s.[38] Even the regulations regarding branding of horses were not enforced in some cases.[39] Akbar's increasing measures to centralize political and military powers precipitated a major revolt by several of his commanders in 1580–1581. The result of the clash between Akbar's desire to centralize and the ruling class' desire for autonomy was what Streusand calls 'the Akbari compromise'. This entailed ceding some autonomy to his commanders while retaining the central control of the new military organization in his own hands.[40] We also need to remember that the fiscal-military reforms of Akbar and his descendants did not appear out of the blue; rather, they represented the maturation of older efforts at achieving greater efficiency and centralization – something that spanned across the Delhi Sultanate and the Sur interregnum. Akbar's decimal system of ranking military commanders was also inspired by Turko-Mongol practices of military organization.

Yet, seen in a comparative perspective, what the Mughals were able to achieve since the late sixteenth century was remarkable. Various limitations notwithstanding, the state was able to attain an unprecedented level of centralization in comparison with earlier polities.[41] The practice of organizing the military commanders through centralized ranking system (*mansab*) and paying most of them through transferrable, non-hereditary revenue assignments (*jagir*) lasted through the seventeenth century, well into the period of imperial fragmentation in the eighteenth. While Akbar's descendants had to repeatedly make concessions and adjustments to the measures he introduced, Mughal fiscal-military administration in the empire's heyday never devolved into the rampant sub-infeudation, hereditary ownership, or community dominance that land assignments had seen under the sultans of Delhi. In this sense, Mughal military organization since the reign of Akbar represented a definitive shift away from its antecedents.

Management of War

Mughal military success in South Asia was based not only on changing military techniques and an efficient, centralizing fiscal-military administration, but also on the meticulous management of military labour, supply, and logistics. This section discusses the myriad facets of this excellent military management, which – as I have argued in greater detail elsewhere – substantially contributed to imperial territorial expansion. The empire emerged against the backdrop of a teeming military labour market in North India. Dirk Kolff and Jos Gommans have shown that between the mid-fifteenth and mid-nineteenth centuries, the Indian subcontinent had a vast pool of different sorts of soldiers. This was a large and heterogeneous body, comprising peasant-soldiers, armed ascetics, military slaves, indigenous chieftains, foreign adventurers, and military professionals of all description. One important group among them were the part-time peasant-soldiers, who initially served as foot-archers but gradually switched to using muskets in course of the sixteenth century. A big challenge for the Mughal state was to negotiate this teeming labour market and harness its manpower to expand its own armies. Gommans' work indicates that the Mughal state met with considerable success in this direction. Its employment of thousands of peasant-soldiers in its own ranks neutralized a part of the potential military threat that they might have posed otherwise and channelized their military resources towards the pursuit of the empire's own ambitions.[42]

However, managing combat labour was only a part of the task. Aside from the skills of soldiers, military campaigns also depended majorly on a whole range of logistical operations. To this end, Mughal armies employed very large numbers of labourers and animals of diverse descriptions. In forested regions like the Aravallis, armies on the march would be led by corps of woodcutters and pioneers, who would cut down trees to create a path of the army to proceed. Similarly, on the rugged terrain of Kashmir or the Afghan region, pioneers and workmen would advance ahead of the main army. They would level the ground and, in some cases, remove snow to create a passable road for the soldiers, animals, and transport. In Bengal and Assam, the imperial flotilla required thousands of boatmen and labourers to row and man the vessels as well as to manoeuvre artillery pieces mounted on some of them. In sieges, carpenters, stonecutters, and other workers were of prime importance for constructing mines, saps, and siege towers. Contemporary sources suggest that most of these logistical labourers were raised seasonally for individual campaigns. Aside from them, a very large number of workers remained perennially employed by the state for taking care of war-animals, manufacturing weapons, managing the operation of military camps, and so on. Another equally important part of Mughal military management was the gathering of war-animals, used in both combat and logistics. Mughal military success owed a great deal to the ability of the state to recruit labourers and mobilize animals in extremely large numbers and channelize their labour into making expansionist wars.[43]

Supplying armies in course of campaigns was complex business. Mughal military logistics was based first and foremost on a command over routes of communication. Across the length and breadth of the empire, the state maintained control over these routes through a network of forts. The important ones among these forts were kept under the direct watch of the emperor through the appointment of imperial fort commanders. Taking over the control of routes and building new ones, if necessary, lay at the heart of military campaigns. The logistical labourers mentioned earlier played a vital role in this regard. In cases where imperial armies failed to keep routes under their control (as in the Afghan or Bengal regions) or failed to create new ones (as in the Aravalli forests), the course of imperial expansion and consolidation faltered.[44]

In the field of supply, Mughal armies relied heavily on the itinerant grain merchants of South Asia, who were designated by the generic name of the Banjara. To satiate the need for water, armies usually followed the courses of available water bodies. Imperial forces also invested heavily towards the production of military infrastructure like boats and bridges, which enabled them to wage wars in negotiation with the natural environment. The state also needed to maintain a steady flow of military information in course of campaigns between its different armies as well as with the major centres of military mobilization.[45]

In the realm of military finance, the state benefitted from the existence of a thriving cash nexus and extensive banking networks in South Asia. Irfan Habib argues that this cash nexus had emerged in North India by early fourteenth century under the Delhi Sultanate. The Mughals developed this further by collecting land revenue in cash across large portions of their empire. The centralizing fiscal apparatus, a robust currency system, and the pouring in of New World precious metals also contributed to this process. Finally, all this benefitted from the presence of a sophisticated network of transfer and remittance of credit, operated by specialized moneylending and money-changing communities like the Sarrafs.[46]

In all these fields of military management, Mughal armies showed remarkable dexterity. Doubtless this military management reached its limits in certain cases. But on the whole, it served as one of the main factors that enabled the Mughals to create an empire of truly subcontinental scale – the first one since the Mauryan Empire (fourth to second centuries BCE). Unfortunately, the lack of historical research on military management and logistics for the period before the sixteenth century makes it difficult for us to compare the Mughal case with its antecedents. Hence, for the time being, the suggestion that the rise of Mughal power marked a paradigmatic shift in terms of military management must remain a conjecture to some extent.

However, there is enough circumstantial evidence to indicate that fundamental shifts came about in this field in the sixteenth century. To mention one example, Abhimanyu Singh Arha points out that the close association of the Rajputs with the Mughal state created for them new managerial needs of raising large cavalry armies. In turn, this pushed the Rathor state of Marwar towards better ecological management in the seventeenth century. Driven by the anxiety of creating a robust equestrian economy, the state closely intervened in the local management of fodder by bringing in new regulations and appointing officials.[47] This serves to indicate the new circumstances that the rise of the Mughal Empire produced in South Asia, and the novel infrastructural and managerial demands this generated, which I contend made the sixteenth century a watershed in the history of much of the subcontinent.

Culture of War

Alongside the various material changes discussed so far, profound shifts appeared in the realms of military culture and ideology with the rise of Mughal power in the sixteenth century. In the Delhi Sultanate as well as the various regional sultanates, Islam played an important role in shaping the broad ideological framework of kingship and authority. The sultanate of Delhi itself was a product of a major wave of Islamicate expansion under Turkish dynasties that rose to prominence around the eleventh century. During much of this phase of expansion, Turkish rulers – who were relatively new converts to Islam – derived their authority as Muslim rulers from the Abbasid caliph in Baghdad. Major sultans like Shamsuddin Iltutmish, Muhammad bin Tughlaq, and Firuz Shah Tughlaq obtained investiture from the Abbasid caliph to legitimize their royal authority. Since the early thirteenth century, Islam faced a major civilizational and confessional crisis in the face of the violent expansion of the Mongol Empire. Following the assassination of the caliph al-Musta'sim by Mongol forces in the mid-thirteenth century, many of the Turkish sultanates emerged as the new havens of political Islam. During most of the thirteenth and fourteenth centuries, the Delhi Sultanate embraced this role as one of the centres of the Islamicate civilization in the east. Although it never became a theocracy, Islam played an important role as one of the main points of reference in formulating norms of kingship and governance. Many intellectuals and chroniclers used the examples of the Prophet and Sufi *shyakh*s to create models of royal authority. Caliphal authority also remained a major source of political power. In all, Islam served as the most important ideological framework for conceptualizing sultanic authority and power during the thirteenth through the fifteenth centuries.[48]

The Mughal Empire marked a profound change of direction in this domain. Although Sunni Islam remained the religion of the rulers, Islam increasingly came to be substituted by the ideology of universal sovereignty in course of the sixteenth century as the overarching ideological framework of kingship and governance. The Mughals were the inheritors of the universalist ideologies of the Turko-Mongol tradition. The empire was founded with Babur's vision of inaugurating a Timurid renaissance. Subsequent Mughal emperors drew upon this ideology alongside others to fashion their own versions of universalist claims. As Azfar Moin shows, these claims often elevated emperors to the status of the *mahdi*, or the reviver of Islamic religious faith, due to arrive around the completion of the first Islamic millennium in 1591.[49] An even more dominant ideological framework for defining kingship and governance was a Persianate normative tradition of political theology, championed by the thirteenth-century philosopher Nasiruddin Tusi. Muzaffar Alam points out that Tusi's *Akhlaq-i Nasiri* and commentaries on it were widely read in the empire. Especially since the reign of Akbar, they formed the bedrock of Mughal political philosophy and the major political framework of the empire.[50] While Islam came to hold a more prominent role in courtly culture under Shah Jahan (r. 1628–1658) and Aurangzeb in the seventeenth century, this did not challenge the universalist ideals established primarily by Humayun (r. 1530–1540, 1555–1556) and Akbar in the sixteenth.

This shift had three major implications for the domain of warfare. First, this political universalism made the Mughal diplomatic outlook extremely flexible and accommodative. Since the state did not align itself with the interests of any particular religion, community, or race most of the time, it remained open to allying with anyone and everyone, as long as they would accept Mughal suzerainty and dutifully undertake the concomitant responsibilities. Recent research indicates that the Mughal Empire expanded more by absorbing and co-opting the various powers of South Asia than by eliminating them outright.[51] This accommodative politics reflected in the extremely composite nature of the political aristocracy and the army, both in terms of race and religion.

Second, this political universalism allowed the Mughals to justify war and military violence not in the name of any sectarian interest or identity; rather, this was done using the abstract notion of justice, at least since the late sixteenth century. This the Mughals borrowed mainly from Nasirean *akhlaq*. In Akbar's official biography, Abul Fazl borrowed Tusi's ideas about kingship to fashion a theology of kingship for the Mughal Empire. In the process, he fused Tusi's ideas with a variety of other inspirations – Sufi ideals, Turko-Mongol motifs, Brahmanical symbols, and medieval Persian *ishraqi* ideas – to create a sophisticated political theology that became hallmark of the state. In this framework, war and military violence were portrayed as unavoidable means for spreading justice across the world. In Mughal imperial chronicles produced since the late sixteenth century, most military invasions were justified as a means to eradicate the suffering of the common people, bring them under the just and benevolent rule of the Mughal sovereign, and punish evil, misguided, or lackadaisical rulers whose reigns bring misery to their subjects.[52]

Finally, the ideology of universal sovereignty helped the Mughals from Akbar onward to build a vast and disparate military aristocracy into one composite body bound together by a corporate ethos around the figure of the sovereign. Rosalind O'Hanlon points out that in this milieu, the emperor was projected as a paternalist sovereign, whose watchful eyes monitored the behaviour of his officialdom and the subjects alike. *Mansabdar*s serving the empire for multiple generations were given the epithet of *khana-zad* (son of the house). Court etiquettes inculcated certain bodily disciplines among the *mansabdar*s to render the disparate elements of the nobility into one ideal prototype of the loyal imperial servant.[53] The *mansabdar*s were also bound with the emperor by a strong reciprocal relationship of gift exchange.[54] As a part of their duties, they had to attend to the emperor in the court as an expression of their subordination to imperial authority. They were expected to ride into battle fearlessly to forward the military agenda of the empire. They would also be expected to dutifully honour the responsibilities that accompanied the rewards of ranks and remunerations by the emperor. Loyalty and servitude to the emperor were hailed as the highest forms of virtue in Mughal court society. Even in the absence of institutional military slavery, *mansabdar*s prided in referring to themselves as *banda* (slave) as a mark of their devotion. John Richards argues that the unifying corporate identity created around the figure of the emperor contributed greatly to the centralization that characterized the imperial military aristocracy.[55]

In its thrust on universal sovereignty as the basis of how kingship was conceptualized and military violence was legitimized in the official imperial discourse since the late sixteenth century, the Mughal Empire marked a fundamental shift from earlier – especially Islamicate – polities. It fostered the development of arguably a more accommodative and cosmopolitan politico-military elite than South Asia had seen so far.

Conclusion

What emerges from this discussion is that the Mughal world of war exhibited certain features that *did* set it apart from its antecedents. Remarkable adaptability in waging military campaigns across different environmental zones, centralizing military organization and fiscal administration, increasingly efficient management of military resources, and integrative and cosmopolitan military culture framed by a universalist political ideology were some of the features that made Mughal warfare distinctly different from what South Asia had witnessed till the fifteenth century. As indicated earlier, these shifts were a result of both global processes and local conditions. All this necessitates the use of a different analytical category that differentiates Mughal warfare from military processes of the earlier centuries. This is where the category of early modernity proves useful. It distinguishes Mughal warfare, on the one hand, from its antecedents, which we can continue to designate as medieval, and, on the other, from what emerged with the advent of colonial modernity in the late eighteenth century.

It is possible to see this novelty of the Mughal world of war only by discarding the category of the Military Revolution in studying change and continuity in the domain of warfare. In this sense, this chapter represents a methodological shift away from the earlier approach of historians like Gommans. It affirms the utility of using more flexible categories like military adaptation. At the same time, it represents a move away from the technology-centrism that prompted earlier historians like Hodgson to argue in favour of a historical break in military matters in the sixteenth century. Rather, I have arrived at the idea of a similar historical break in very different terms, by adopting the more inclusive war and society approach. This has helped identify the military changes not in isolation but in their wider connections with state, culture, and empire-building.

It was since the mid-eighteenth century that this military early modernity was gradually derailed. On the one hand, the new post-Mughal regional polities of this time embarked on a drive to Europeanize their armies under the guidance of European military professionals. On the other hand, British and French armies fought to outdo each other as the dominant European power in the Indian subcontinent – a struggle from which the British emerged victorious. Through these processes, there was another paradigm shift in military matters. Under the increasing influence of European military techniques and culture, South Asian armies were introduced to European models of drill, discipline, and uniform. On the battlefield, the centrality of the cavalry finally saw a demise with the rise of flintlock-equipped massed infantry formations. The introduction of lighter and more mobile artillery also brought about profound changes in military techniques.[56] All this comprised a decisive shift away from the military early modernity that the emergence of Mughal power in South Asia had ushered in.

These changes in terms of military techniques complemented the shifts in the four domains discussed in this chapter. As Kaushik Roy argues, British victories were made possible by heightened forms of military adaptation, which he calls 'military synthesis'.[57] Army organization and fiscal-military administration were completely overhauled to introduce greater centralization and better chain of command. In terms of military management, the work of Randolph Cooper shows that the rise of British power introduced new and more efficient methods of supply, logistics, and labour deployment.[58] Finally, in contrast to the cosmopolitan and accommodative ideological paradigm of Mughal rule, the rise of British power ushered in the emergence of colonialist and imperialist political framework that legitimized both rule and violence using very different – often civilizational – parameters.[59] By the mid-nineteenth century, the process of derailment of the military early modernity that Mughal warfare represented and its substitution with its colonial modern counterpart was complete.

Notes

1. In these discussions in this chapter, one major point of comparison is the Delhi Sultanate, arguably the most important Islamicate polity of North India before the advent of the Mughals.
2. Marshall G. S. Hodgson, *The Venture of Islam: Conscience and History in a World Civilization*, vol. 3: *The Gunpowder Empires and Modern Times* (Chicago and London: University of Chicago Press, 1977 [1974]), 18; William H. McNeill, *The Pursuit of Power: Technology, Armed Forces, and Society since A.D. 1000* (Chicago: University of Chicago Press, 1982), 95–98.
3. Douglas E. Streusand, *The Formation of the Mughal Empire* (New Delhi: Oxford University Press, 1989), 65.
4. Streusand, *Formation of the Mughal Empire*, 65–67.
5. The Military Revolution hypothesis was first propounded by Michael Roberts in 1955. He identified four major changes in the domain of war in Europe between 1560 and 1660. These comprised the rise of handgun-equipped, drilled, and disciplined infantry armies; emergence of a new strategic consciousness; rapid growth of army size; and a general rise in the impact of war on society. Roberts argued that these shifts comprised a Military Revolution that transformed the face of European warfare. Since the 1970s, this framework has been revised and expanded by Geoffrey Parker, among others. Roberts argues that the motor of much of these changes was the rise of gunpowder artillery, which in turn precipitated a revolution in fortress architecture. In the face of the threat that the new siege artillery posed to medieval fortifications, fort architects developed the new *trace italienne* design of artillery fortresses around the close of the sixteenth century. This neutralized the initial tactical advantage siege artillery bestowed on besiegers. Instead, it forced besiegers to once again fall back upon more traditional techniques of siegecraft like blockading, mining, and sapping. It was this, according to Parker, that led to the dramatic rise in army size in Europe. Michael Roberts, *The Military Revolution 1560–1660* (Belfast: Marjory Boyd, 1956); Geoffrey Parker, *The Military Revolution: Military Innovation and the Rise of the West* (Cambridge: Cambridge University Press, 1988), 6–44.
6. Jos Gommans, 'Warhorse and Gunpowder in India, c. 1000–1850', in *War in the Early Modern World, 1450–1815*, ed. Jeremy Black, 105–127 (London and New York: Routledge, 1999).
7. Gommans, 'Warhorse and Gunpowder in India', 117.
8. Gommans, 'Warhorse and Gunpowder in India', 117–119. Since the publication of Gommans' monograph on Mughal warfare in 2002, several other historians have arrived at similar conclusions, partly owing to their use of Gommans' work in their own analyses. Kenneth Chase, *Firearms: A Global History to 1700*

(Cambridge: Cambridge University Press, 2003), 131–134; Peter Lorge, *The Asian Military Revolution: From Gunpowder to the Bomb* (Cambridge and New York: Cambridge University Press, 2008), 112–131; Geoffrey Parker and Sanjay Subrahmanyam, 'Arms and the Asian: Revisiting European Firearms and Their Place in Early Modern Asia,' *Revistade Cultura* 26 (2008): 12–42, see 14–24.

9. This globalization of the Military Revolution hypothesis occurred even as it was repeatedly challenged as an explanatory framework for European history itself. For a collection of important essays of this debate, see Clifford J. Rogers, *The Military Revolution Debate: Readings on the Military Transformations in Early Modern Europe* (London and New York: Routledge, 1995).

10. For examples of histories spotting the Military Revolution in different parts of the world using these parameters, see Michael Paul, 'The Military Revolution in Russia, 1550–1682', *Journal of Military History* 68, no. 1 (2004): 9–45; Matthew Stavros, 'Military Revolution in Early Modern Japan', *Japanese Studies* 33, no. 3 (2013): 243–261; Tonio Andrade, Hyeok Hweon Kang, and Kirsten Cooper, 'A Korean Military Revolution? Parallel Military Innovations in East Asia and Europe', *Journal of World History* 25, no. 1 (2014): 51–84.

11. See, for example, Günhan Börekçi, 'A Contribution to the Military Revolution Debate: The Janissaries Use of Volley Fire during the Long Ottoman–Habsburg War of 1593–1606 and the Problem of Origins', *Acta Orientalia Academiae Scientiarum Hung* 59, no. 4 (2006): 407–438. Here, the discovery of Ottoman volley fire during the Long War (1593–1606) against Habsburgs becomes a way for the author to argue in favour of Ottoman equality with European armies in matters of infantry tactics and the use of technology in the sixteenth and seventeenth centuries.

12. Gommans, 'Warhorse and Gunpowder in India'.

13. This is also indicated by the fact that he takes roughly this time period as a temporal unit of analysis in many of his essays.

14. Jos Gommans, *Mughal Warfare: Indian Frontiers and Highroads to Empire* (London and New York: Routledge, 2002), 141.

15. I have argued elsewhere that Gommans' ascription of this overwhelming importance to the warhorse is a result of his conceptualization of post-nomadism as a relatively static condition. In my view, Mughal post-nomadism was dynamic; it was decisively moulded by the dynasty's long habitation within the South Asian landmass. As a result, the role of the warhorse in Mughal warfare seems to have been much more heterogeneous across both space and time than what Gommans concedes. Pratyay Nath, *Climate of Conquest: War, Environment, and Empire in Mughal North India* (New Delhi: Oxford University Press, 2019), 53, 108–111, 273–274, 278–279.

16. I have argued this in greater detail elsewhere. Pratyay Nath, 'Looking beyond the Military Revolution: Variations in Early Modern Warfare and the Mughal Case', *Journal of Military History*, forthcoming.
17. Jeremy Black, *Beyond the Military Revolution: War in the Seventeenth-Century World* (Basingstoke and New York: Palgrave Macmillan, 2011), 5.
18. Richard M. Eaton and Philip B. Wagoner, 'Warfare on the Deccan Plateau, 1450–1600: A Military Revolution in Early Modern India?' *Journal of World History* 25, no. 1 (2014): 5–50, especially 48.
19. Streusand, *Formation of the Mughal Empire*, 52–57.
20. Rhoads Murphey, *Ottoman Warfare: 1500–1700* (New York: Routledge, 1999), 107–108; Brian Davies, 'Guliai-gorod, Wagenburg, and Tabor, "Tactics in 16th–17th Century Muscovy and Eastern Europe"', in *Warfare in Eastern Europe, 1500–1800*, ed. Brian Davies, 93–108 (Leiden and Boston: Brill, 2012), 100–102; Chase, *Firearms*, 86.
21. Nath, *Climate of Conquest*, 32–38.
22. Streusand, *Formation of the Mughal Empire*, 57–64; Nath, *Climate of Conquest*, 38–43; Gommans, *Mughal Warfare*, 187–197; John F. Richards, *The New Cambridge History of India*, vol. 1.5: *The Mughal Empire* (Cambridge: Cambridge University Press, 2001), 220–222, 229–230.
23. Nath, *Climate of Conquest*, 57–74.
24. In a recent article, Philip Wagoner has shown myriad forms of such adaptations in the period between c. 1000 and c. 1500. Using the examples of polities like the Delhi Sultanate and the Vijayanagar kingdom, Wagoner shows how this manifested in battle tactics, army organization, fiscal-military administration, defensive architecture, and military culture. Phillip B. Wagoner, 'India, c. 1200–c. 1500', in *The Cambridge History of War*, vol. 2: *War and the Medieval World*, ed. Anne Curry and David A. Graff, 470–506 (Cambridge: Cambridge University Press, 2020).
25. Peter Jackson, 'Turkish Slaves on Islam's Indian Frontier', in *Slavery and South Asian History*, ed. Indrani Chatterjee and Richard M. Eaton, 63–82 (Bloomington and Indianapolis: Indiana University Press, 2006); Sunil Kumar, 'When Slaves Were Nobles: The Shamsi Bandagan in the Early Delhi Sultanate', *Studies in History* 10, no. 1 (1994): 23–52.
26. David Nicolle and Christa Hook, *The Janissaries*, Osprey Elite Series (London: Osprey Publishing, 1997); Sussan Babaie, Kathryn Babayan, Ina Baghdiantz-McCabe, and Massumeh Farhad, *Slaves of the Shah: New Elites of Safavid Iran* (London and New York: I.B. Tauris, 2004); Richard M. Eaton, 'The Rise and Fall of Military Slavery in the Deccan, 1450–1650', in *Slavery and South Asian History*, ed. Chatterjee and Eaton, 115–135.

27. John F. Richards, 'Norms of Comportment among Imperial Mughal Officers', in *Moral Conduct and Authority: The Place of* Adab *in South Asian Islam*, ed. Barbara Daly Metcalf, 255–289 (London, Berkeley, and Los Angeles: University of California Press, 1984), 264–267.
28. Irfan Habib, 'Agrarian Economy', in *The Cambridge Economic History of India*, ed. Tapan Raychaudhuri and Irfan Habib, vol. 1: *c. 1200–c. 1750*, 48–75 (Cambridge: Cambridge University Press, 1987 [1982]), 68–74.
29. Iqtidar Alam Khan, 'The Mughal Assignment System during Akbar's Early Years, 1556–1575', in Iqtidar Alam Khan, *India's Polity in the Age of Akbar*, 19–92 (Ranikhet: Permanent Black, 2016), 26.
30. M. Athar Ali, 'Towards an Interpretation of the Mughal Empire', in M. Athar Ali, *Mughal India: Studies in Polity, Ideas, Society, and* Culture, 59–73 (New Delhi: Oxford University Press, 2008 [2006]), 60–61. Also see Irfan Habib, 'Agrarian Relations and Land Revenue: North India', in *Cambridge Economic History of India*, ed. Raychaudhuri and Habib, vol. 1, 235–249, see 236.
31. Irfan Habib, 'The Monetary System and Prices', in *The Cambridge Economic History of India*, ed. Raychaudhuri and Habib, vol. 1, 360–381, see 360.
32. Khan, 'Mughal Assignment System', 35.
33. Khan, 'Mughal Assignment System', 35–39.
34. Khan, 'Mughal Assignment System', 39–41.
35. M. Athar Ali, *The Mughal Nobility under Aurangzeb* (New Delhi: Oxford University Press, 2015 [1966]), 38–94; Shireen Moosvi, 'The Evolution of the *Mansab* System under Akbar until 1596-7', *Journal of the Royal Asiatic Society of Great Britain and Ireland* 113, no. 2 (1981): 173–185.
36. Ali, *Mughal Nobility under Aurangzeb*, 42–49.
37. Streusand, *Formation of the Mughal Empire*, 65–66.
38. Chetan Singh, 'Centre and Periphery in the Mughal State: The Case of Seventeenth Century Punjab', *Modern Asian Studies* 22, no. 2 (1988): 299–318.
39. R. A. Alavi, 'New Light on Mughal Cavalry', in R. A. Alavi, *Studies in the History of Medieval Deccan* (Delhi: Idarah-i Adabiyat-i Delli, 1977), 20–62, see 20–22.
40. Streusand also points to the various constraints that prevented the Mughals from developing a central army under the direct command of an imperial bureaucracy. These included a general inclination of Mughal commanders for autonomy, the armed nature of the North Indian peasantry, the strong local bases of *zamindar*s, and the difficulties of collecting and redistributing land revenue among the ruling class. Streusand, *Formation of the Mughal Empire*, 154–172, 178.
41. This is something Streusand also points out. Streusand, *Formation of the Mughal Empire*, 176.

42. Streusand, *Formation of the Mughal Empire*, 70–72; Dirk H. A. Kolff, *Naukar, Rajput and Sepoys: The Ethnohistory of the Military Labour Market in Hindustan, 1450–1850* (Cambridge: Cambridge University Press, 1991); Gommans, *Mughal Warfare*, 67–98; Pratyay Nath, 'Towards a People's History of the Mughal Empire: War and the Non-Elite', *Medieval History Journal*, forthcoming.
43. Nath, *Climate of Conquest*, 120–167; Nath, 'Towards a People's History of the Mughal Empire'; Pratyay Nath, 'What Is Military Labour? War, Logistics, and the Mughals in Early Modern South Asia', *War in History* 28, no. 4 (2021), DOI: https://doi.org/10.1177/0968344520918615.
44. I have shown elsewhere that a failure to exert control over existing routes of communication or create new ones, contributed to limiting the ambit of Mughal imperial authority and, in turn, creating frontiers of the empire. Nath, *Climate of Conquest*, 172–176.
45. Nath, *Climate of Conquest*, 148–167.
46. John F. Richards, 'Mughal State Finance and Premodern World Economy', *Comparative Studies in Society and History* 23, no. 2 (1981): 285–308; Irfan Habib, 'The System of Bills of Exchange ("Hundis") in the Mughal Empire', *Proceedings of the Indian History Congress* 33 (1971): 290–303.
47. Abhimanyu Singh Arha, 'Hoofprint of Empire: An Environmental History of Fodder in Mughal India (1650–1850)', *Studies in History* 32, no. 2 (2016): 186–208. Similar changes are discussed by Mayank Kumar in his chapter in this volume.
48. Blain H. Auer, *Symbols of Authority in Medieval Islam: History, Religion and Muslim Legitimacy in the Delhi Sultanate* (London: I.B. Tauris, 2012).
49. A. Azfar Moin, *The Millennial Sovereign: Sacred Kingship and Sainthood in Islam* (New York: Columbia University Press, 2012).
50. Muzaffar Alam, *The Languages of Political Islam in India, c. 1200–1800* (New Delhi: Permanent Black, 2004), 61–64.
51. Farhat Hasan, *State and Locality in Mughal India: Power Relations in Western India, c. 1572–1730* (New Delhi: Cambridge University Press, 2006); Nath, *Climate of Conquest*, 279–281.
52. Nath, *Climate of Conquest*, 235–252.
53. Rosalind O'Hanlon, 'Kingdom, Household and Body: History, Gender and Imperial Service under Akbar', *Modern Asian Studies* 41, no. 5 (2007): 889–923.
54. Streusand, *Formation of the Mughal Empire*, 139–145.
55. Rosalind O'Hanlon, 'Manliness and Imperial Service in Mughal North India', *Journal of the Economic and Social History of the Orient* 42, no. 1 (1999): 47–93; Richards, 'Norms of Comportment'.

56. Gommans, 'Warhorse and Gunpowder in India', 117–119; Kaushik Roy, *War, Culture and Society in Early Modern South Asia, 1740–1849* (Oxon and New York: Routledge, 2011).
57. Kaushik Roy, 'Military Synthesis in South Asia: Armies, Warfare and Indian Society, c. 1740–1849', *Journal of Military History* 69, no. 3 (2005): 651–690.
58. Randolf G. S. Cooper, 'Beyond Beasts and Bullion: Economic Considerations in Bombay's Military Logistics, 1803', *Modern Asian Studies* 33, no. 1 (1999): 159–183.
59. Thomas R. Metcalf, *The New Cambridge History of India*, vol. 3.4: *Ideologies of the Raj* (Cambridge: Cambridge University Press, 2001).

About the Contributors

Meena Bhargava teaches History at Indraprastha College for Women, University of Delhi. She is the author of *State, Society and Ecology, Gorakhpur in Transition, 1750–1830*, Revised Edition (2014 [1999]) and *Understanding Mughal India: Sixteenth to Eighteenth Centuries* (2020); the co-author of *Women, Education and Politics: The Women's Movement and Delhi's Indraprastha College* (2015 [2005]); and the editor of anthologies on Mughal history and environmental history. She specializes in the medieval and early modern Indian history. Her research interests include social and economic history of India, especially agrarian history, environmental history, and history of drugs and narcotics. She has also published several research articles in peer-reviewed national and international journals and edited volumes.

Radhika Chadha is Associate Professor of History, Miranda House, University of Delhi. She is the author of *Merchants, Renegades, Padres: Portuguese Presence in Bengal and Arakan, 16th and 17th Centuries* (forthcoming). She received her PhD in History from Jawaharlal Nehru University, New Delhi. She has been Fellow, Fundacao Oriente, Lisbon. Her academic interests include medieval Islamic empires, the history of early modern India, the visual culture of medieval and early modern South Asia, and gender.

Rajat Datta retired as Professor of History from Jawaharlal Nehru University, New Delhi. He was the author of *Society, Economy and the Market. Commercialization in Rural Bengal, ca. 1760–1800* (2000) and the editor of *Rethinking a Millennium: Perspectives on Indian History from the Eighth to the Eighteenth Century* (2008). He published widely in journals and edited volumes on economic history of early modern India, the eighteenth century in Indian history, comparative trajectories of early modern economic development in an Asian perspective, and the nature of globalization in the early modern world with special reference to India in the world economy.

Ranjeeta Dutta teaches at the Centre for Historical Studies, Jawaharlal Nehru University, New Delhi. She is the author of *From Hagiographies to Biographies: Ramanuja in Tradition and History* (2014), the editor of a special issue of *Summerhill* (Shimla) titled 'Regions, Identities and Entangled Geographies', and the co-editor of *Negotiating Religion: Perspectives from Indian History* (2012). Her areas of interest are the history of religion, and ideas of region and space in medieval and early modern India. She has been a fellow at Max Weber Kolleg, University of Erfurt, Germany, and the Indian Institute of Advanced Studies, Shimla. She is one of the editors of *Medieval History Journal*.

Kashshaf Ghani is Assistant Professor of History at Nalanda University, Rajgir, Bihar. He is the author of *Sufi Rituals and Practices: Experiences from South Asia 1200–1450* (forthcoming). He specializes in premodern South Asian history between 1000 and 1800, with a focus on the history of Sufism, and its practices, interactions, networks, and regional experiences. He is also interested in Indo-Persian history, cosmopolitan cultures, and Asian interconnections. He has previously held research positions at the Asiatic Society, Kolkata; Universite Sorbonne Nouvelle, Paris; and Zentrum Moderner Orient, Berlin. His co-edited volumes include *Exploring the Global South: Voices, Ideas, Histories* (2013) and *Imagining Asia(s): Networks, Actors, Sites* (2019).

Shalin Jain is Professor of History, University of Delhi. He is the author of *Identity, Community and State: The Jains under the Mughals* (2017). His research and teaching interests include social history of the Jain community, religious thought and practices, gender and society, identity formation, environment and society, popular culture, and resistance in medieval and early modern South Asia. He has published several research papers in journals like the *Indian Historical Review*, *Studies in History*, and *Social Scientist*. A two-time winner of Professor J. S. Grewal award for the best research paper in Medieval Indian History at Indian History Congress (2004 and 2013), he has also been a recipient of UGC (University Grants Commission) Raman Fellowship award for Post-Doctoral Research in the United States of America (2013–2014) and honorary fellow at the Centre for South Asia at the University of Wisconsin-Madison, USA (2013).

About the Contributors

Mayank Kumar is Associate Professor of History, School of Social Sciences, Indira Gandhi National Open University, New Delhi. He is the author of *Monsoon Ecologies: Irrigation, Agriculture and Settlement Patterns in Rajasthan during the Pre-Colonial Period* (2013) and the co-editor of *Revisiting the History of Medieval Rajasthan: Essays for Professor Dilbagh Singh* (2017). His research focuses on human-nature interactions in pre-colonial India. He was associated with the Decision Centre for Desert City, Arizona State University, as a Fulbright fellow. He was a fellow at Nehru Memorial Museum and Library, New Delhi, before availing the UGC (University Grants Commission) National Research Award.

Pratyay Nath is Assistant Professor of History, Ashoka University, Sonipat. He is the author of *Climate of Conquest: War, Environment, and Empire in Mughal North India* (2019). His research lies at the intersection of environmental history, military history, and imperial history, with a focus on the Mughal Empire. His research articles have been published in the *Journal of the Royal Asiatic Society*, *War in History*, the *Journal of Military History*, and *South Asia: Journal of South Asian Studies*, as well as several edited volumes. He is one of the editors of the *Medieval History Journal*. He writes in English and Bangla.

Charles M. Ramsey teaches history of South Asia at Baylor University, Texas. He is the author of *God's Word, Spoken and Otherwise* (2021), co-translator and editor of *The Gospel according to Sayyid Ahmad Khan* (2020), and editor of *South Asian Sufis: Devotion, Deviation, and Destiny* (2012). He is also the editor of the South Asia section of the *Brill Encyclopedia of Christian–Muslim Relations* (CMR 1500–1900). He has been awarded grants from the British Library's Endangered Archives Program, United States Institute of Peace, and the American Institute for Pakistan Studies.

Santanu Sengupta is Assistant Professor of History, Polba Mahavidyalaya, University of Burdwan, West Bengal. He earned his PhD from Jadavpur University, Kolkata, in 2021. His thesis was titled 'The Empire's Network: Formation of the British Empire in the Eastern Indian Ocean and the Armenian Agency (From Mid-18th to 19th Century)'. His articles on the legal and cultural history of the Armenian merchants of eighteenth-century Madras have been published in the *Journal of the Asiatic Society* and *Global Networks* respectively.

Index

administrative, 19, 59n8, 124, 136, 232
   centralization, 233
   commands, 197
   documents, 125
   interventions, 130–132
   manuals, 126–127
   regulation, 133
   stability, 109
agency(ies), 9, 27, 29, 64, 76, 85, 87, 203–205, 215, 217
   external, 98n20, 214
   individual, 89–93
agriculture/agricultural/agrarian, 9, 19, 21, 106–107, 113, 116–118, 125–126, 131–134, 136, 141–142, 144–145, 147–150, 153, 154n4, 165, 168–169, 177
   aristocracy, 30
   European, 105
   expansion, 130–132, 167
   frontier, 30, 51
   land–labour ratio, 110
   productivity, 114, 128, 130
   revolution in Britain, 153
   settlements, 143, 169
   specialists, 169
   surplus, 110
ancient, 5–11, 21, 24, 34n24, 88, 108, 124, 161, 166, 183
anthropogenic, 21, 30, 141

Ardhakathanak, 89–93
*arhsatta*s, 126, 134
*arzdasht*s, 126, 130–131
Astrakhan, 204

Banarsidas, 29, 85–86, 89–94, 96, 98n20
Bay of Bengal, 185, 187–188, 191
Bhakti, 162
biotic factors, 142
Bottomry, 220n33

cartography, 22, 38n91, 72, 175–176
Chishti, 45, 48, 51–54, 56–57
   saints avoids association with temporal authority, 44
   Sabiri, 50
   Salim, 45–47
   sama and *dhikr* (practices of), 49
climatic factors, 142
colonial/colonialism, 2–4, 8–11, 17, 22, 25–28, 31–32, 36n68, 39n111, 58, 64–66, 83, 93–95, 107, 110–111, 118, 124, 142, 152–154, 162, 164, 167, 183, 199, 203–214, 216–217, 224, 226, 239–240
Commenda, 204
commercialization, 107, 113, 115–116, 118

Index

conservation, 152
court/Mayor's court, 203, 209–216
cross-cultural, 21
    actors, 203
    conflicts, 213
    mercantile affairs of Indian Ocean, 212
    trade, 205
cultural, 1–3, 5, 8–9, 18, 23, 29, 37n75, 43–44, 49, 51–52, 57, 83, 86, 94–95, 104, 106, 118–119, 130, 164, 167, 176, 184–185, 197, 216–217, 228–230
    adaptation, 48
    boundaries, 171
    change, 144
    cosmopolitanism, 11
    developments in Western Ghats, 145
    expression, 56
    hegemony, 15
    pluralism, 109
    sensibilities, 20
    synthesis, 48
curriculum, 161–162, 165–166
custom/customary, 46, 53, 105, 175, 189–190, 203, 206–207, 209–210, 212, 214–217, 222n60, 222n62, 223n68

Dakhni, 49–50
dark age, 5, 7, 9–10, 170
    Mohammedan, 8
decolonization, 11, 24, 27, 32
demography, 27, 115–117, 142, 165
diaspora/diasporic communities, 16, 31, 109, 203–204, 206, 213, 215–216
documenting geography, 126–128
dominant, 6, 10, 18–19, 24–25, 55, 84, 86, 89–90, 93–94, 130, 163, 225, 237, 240

early medieval, 11–12, 27, 32, 161–162, 165–167
early modern/early modernity, 3–4, 12–13, 28–32, 35n46, 36n68, 36n69, 37n75, 39n111, 43, 49, 53, 56, 58, 64, 66, 71, 76, 104, 107–109, 113–118, 124–126, 128, 130, 136, 141–142, 144, 146, 148, 150, 152–153, 155n5, 161–162, 165–168, 171, 176–177, 183–186, 189, 195, 197–198, 203, 208, 216–217, 224, 239
    defence, 23–27
    defined, 17–23, 105
    and individualism, 83–89
    in Jain tradition, 93–97
    military, 225–229, 231, 240
East India Company/Company, 1, 141, 152–153, 205–209, 213, 216–217
ecology/ecological/ecosystems, 21, 30, 105, 118, 125–127, 132, 141–142, 144–150, 152–153, 169, 185, 231, 236
environment/environmental, 4, 21–22, 29–31, 64, 71–72, 76, 94–95, 109, 118, 125, 127, 132, 136, 141–147, 149–150, 152–154, 205, 228–229, 236
    history, 154n4
    human-induced changes, 155n5
    zones, 231, 239
epigraphical evidence/records, 168–169
Eurocentrism, 15, 105, 203, 226–227

fiscal, 103, 111, 118, 131, 232–234, 236, 239–240, 243n24
    intermediation, 107
    -military state apparatuses, 109

refinements, 112
transactions, 110
forest(s), 51, 108, 133, 142–147–153, 170, 174, 177, 231, 235
frontier(s), 19, 30, 51, 104, 112, 132, 142–145, 149, 152, 173–174, 184, 193–194, 245n44

gaccha, 86, 89, 91, 94
global growth models, 115

hagiography, 70, 86, 172
heterodoxy, 11, 56, 84–86, 93–94, 97
history, 3–13, 15, 17, 19–20, 23, 26–27, 29, 31, 36n69, 39n111, 43, 56, 64–67, 71, 83–85, 92, 97, 103–104, 106–108, 114, 117–118, 124, 141, 149, 161–162, 167, 172, 188–189, 203–204, 216, 225, 227, 232, 236
   agrarian, 125
   comparative, 32
   connected, 32
   environmental, 154n4, 155n5
   evolution of western Europe, 20
   global, 32
   intellectual, 25
   temporalization of, 18, 23, 37n75
Hugli, 183, 185, 189–197, 200n27
human–environment relationships, 141–142, 150

Ibn Sina, 67, 69–70, 72–73
identity, 29, 37, 144, 161, 164–165, 171–172, 196, 205, 214, 217, 238
   Armenian, 218n12, 222n59
   civilizational, 107
   corporate, 239
   cosmopolitan, 96

   diasporic, 204, 206, 215
   hybrid, 216
   individual, 75, 84, 96
   regional, 19, 174, 183
   religious, 20, 91, 96, 171, 176
   sectarian, 91, 95–96
   segregation, 91
imagination, 10, 20, 35n36, 66, 73–74, 164, 175–176
imperial, 46, 92, 109, 112, 118, 187, 194, 198, 211, 217, 229–230, 236, 238–240
   army, 59n8, 230–231, 235
   cities, 49
   directives, 126
   elite, 47, 57
   enterprise, 186–187
   farman, 190, 192, 195
   formations, 184
   framework, 162–163
   household, 44, 57
   servants, 44
   spaces, 183
   suba, 199
   zones, 184
individual(s), 4, 18, 20, 29, 46, 66, 75, 83, 89–93, 105, 134–136, 168–169, 176, 184–185, 189, 193–194, 205, 209–210, 215, 229, 232–233, 235
   and early modernity, 83–89
   liberty, 13
   *sthalapurana*s, 172
insurance, 208–212
Islam/Islamic/Islamist, 7, 10–12, 27, 31, 46, 50–51, 53, 55, 56–58, 75, 77n4, 87–88, 95, 107, 109, 163–164, 231–232, 238
   anthropology of, 99n31
   millenarianism, 71

Index

modernity a western malady, 66
philosophy, 43
political, 29
radical, 5
role in shaping framework of kingship and authority, 237

jama, 144, 153, 156*n*16
Jain/Jainism, 29, 83–97, 99*n*31
judicial process, 134–136, 208–209, 213

kinship system, 164, 204

land-use pattern, 30, 108, 142–146
law, 1, 4, 30, 55–56, 71, 195, 204–205
    civil, 105
    of sea, 206
legal, 14, 30, 69, 134–136, 218*n*12
    arbitration, 214
    culture of Indian Ocean, 31
    deliberation, 209
    New Julfan culture, 204–206
    pluralism, 31, 210, 214, 216
    procedures, 30
    treatises, 55
    verdicts, 65
logistics, 208–212

Madras, 164, 205, 208, 210–211, 213–216, 222*n*59, 223*n*68
margins, 52, 84, 112, 149, 184–185, 195, 225, 227
maritime, 30–31, 107, 177, 186, 190, 203–204, 206–212
massive investments, 128–130
mawas, 146
medieval, 17–18, 24, 27–28, 31–32, 34*n*24, 44, 52, 56, 83–84, 87, 90–93, 96, 103–104, 107, 109, 117, 119, 124, 161–168, 176–177, 183, 203, 231–232, 238–239, 241*n*5
    European origins of, 4–6
    late, 64
    outside Europe, 6–8
    politics of, 8–12
    South Asian, 3–4, 97, 141
merchant, 29, 85–86, 89–90, 94, 109–111, 113–114, 133, 169, 184, 190–194, 199*n*16, 204, 207–213, 215–216, 221*n*54, 223*n*68, 236
military, 2, 22, 59*n*8, 105, 146–147, 165, 195, 197, 214, 217, 224
    adaptation, 224, 228–231
    changelessness, 224
    fiscalism, 30, 109
    mobilization, 236
    modernity, 225–228
    organization, 31, 231–234
    power, 1
    professionals, 19
    revolution, 224
    violence, 30
millennial sovereign, 59*n*6, 60*n*20
modern/modernity/modernization, 1, 6, 8–11, 36*n*69, 66, 68, 70, 93, 124–127, 130, 136, 176–177
    anterior, 106
    Bengal Renaissance, 2
    bourgeois, 2
    civilization, 7
    early, 3–4, 17–23, 28–32, 39*n*111, 43, 49, 53, 56, 58, 64, 76, 83, 107–109, 113–119, 141–142, 146, 148, 150, 152, 161–162, 165–168, 183–189, 195, 197–198, 208, 216–217, 224, 239–240

category of, 203
defence of, 23–27
defined, 104
and individualism, 83–89
in Jain tradition, 93–97
origin of, 104
European nationalism, 65
idea of, 12–17
indigenous, 75
late, 37n69
multiple, 105
reawakening, 5
secular, 71
singular, 141
subjective, 141
universal, 2
monetization, 110, 116–118
Mughal warfare, 31, 240
army organization, 231–234
culture of war, 237–239
management of war, 234–236
military early modernity, search for, 225–228
military adaptation, 228–231
military revolutions in, 225–228, 239

nadus, 164, 169
Naqshbandis, 45–50, 53–54, 56–57, 62n38, 69
naval, 22, 146, 188, 206, 209, 231
nayaka, 164
nayankara, 165
neo-Malthusian, 107
network, 57, 85, 94, 106, 110, 114, 118, 126, 132, 162, 203–204, 207, 213–214, 218n12, 235–236
expansion of, 49–53
of integration, 169
pilgrimage, 172–177

of power, 14
regional, 44
supra-local, 168–169, 177
trans-local, 168
urban, 144
New Julfa Armenian diaspora, 203, 215, 222n59
decline in 1740s, 207
jumiat tradition, 214
kalanthar, 213
legal culture, 204–206
merchants as *avak* or *jukami avak*, 208, 216
New World, 107–108, 110–111, 117, 236
normative, 84, 86, 90, 96, 98n20, 126–128, 134, 168, 172, 237

other
European, 85
geographic, 168, 170
majoritarian, 94

pastoral/pastoralists/pastoralism/
agro-pastoralism, 19, 104, 118, 125–126, 132, 147–149, 151, 173
pedagogy classroom, 161
peninsular region, 30, 163–164, 167, 169, 171, 175–177
periodization, 8–9, 25, 28, 32, 70, 103–105, 108–110, 124, 161, 165
historical, 4–6, 23–24, 26
new, 166–168
politics of, 3
tripartite, 83
violence in Indian history, 162–166
periphery, 184–185
Persian, 51–54, 56, 59n8, 60n25, 64–67, 69, 76, 80n35, 92, 109, 125, 162–164, 188, 190, 216,

Index

ishraqi ideas, 238
philosophy, 21
tradition, 43
waterwheels, 71
pilgrimage, 45–46, 91, 168, 171–177
political, 1–2, 8, 15, 18, 27, 84–85, 105–106, 110, 118, 127, 143, 145, 150–153, 162–167, 177, 197–198, 205–206, 217, 228–230, 233, 238–240
   actors, 184–185, 189
   application of technology, 68
   aristocracy, 238
   authority, 43, 128, 131–132
   baggage, 9
   consolidation, 168, 170
   culture, 71
   dynasties, 43
   economy, 9, 11, 30, 104, 110, 124, 132, 183, 194
   entanglements, 185, 195
   hostility, 211–212
   ideology of universal sovereignty, 22
   Islam, 29, 237
   orders, 43
   regimes, 11, 106
   right, 10
   superior, 171
   tribal kin-based formations, 124
population, 19, 22, 30, 48, 51, 57, 105, 108, 110, 115–117, 125, 129, 141–142, 146–149, 152, 168, 173–174, 184, 191
Portuguese Empire, 185–187, 189, 196, 198
privateering, 197

Qadiri, 46–47, 50, 52, 54, 56–57, 61n32
qasba, 69, 113–114, 150

Rahman, Fazlur, 66, 69, 73
reclamation, 144, 147, 151–152
reformism, 56
region(s)/regional, 1, 7, 11, 16, 19, 21–22, 24, 26, 30, 36n69, 43–45, 49, 51–53, 64–72, 76, 85, 87–88, 105–111, 114–116, 118, 125–130, 132–135, 141–145, 147–150, 154n4, 161–167, 177, 184–185, 188–189, 191, 193–196, 206, 227, 230, 235, 237, 240
   configurations, 168–176
   identities, 183
   military revolutions in, 226
   setting, 186–187
regulating the domestic and social lives, 125, 134–136
religion/religious developments, 4, 8, 13, 18, 20, 22, 29, 48, 57, 85–86, 88, 94–96, 109, 162, 173–174, 176, 237–238
respondentia, 208–213
roti sata, 136
rural production systems, 110, 112
rurban settlements, 113

sacred geography, 162, 168, 171, 173–177
Sadra, Mulla, 29, 31, 66–75, 79n23, 80n30, 81n47, 82n65,
Sanad Parwana Bahi, 135
sectarian, 20, 87
   interest or identities, 91, 95–96
   Jain, 86
   Shwetambar–Digambar, 91
sedentary cultivation, 142, 147, 152
self, 2, 93
   -assigned custodians, 12
   -expanding existence, 69

-governance, 164
-interest, 105
-praise, 72
-representation, 206, 212–214, 216
royal, 170
settlement patterns, 142–143, 162, 164–165, 167–177
Shah, Lonka, 29, 85–89, 93–94, 96, 98*n*20
shared historical processes, 21, 146–152, 155*n*5
Sirhindi, 31, 46, 53–55, 62*n*49, 66–67, 69–75, 79*n*29, *n*32, 81*n*47
social hierarchies, 93, 163
social use of natural resources, taxation on, 132–133
society(ies), 1–2, 7, 10, 25, 27, 29, 32, 43, 56, 70, 84–85, 89–90, 98*n*20, 103–104, 106–107, 109, 115–117, 124–125, 127–128, 132, 134–136, 142, 145–146, 148, 152, 166–169, 176, 188, 204, 206, 228, 239–240
  civil, 14
  coastal, 12
  contemporary, 17
  court, 48
  indigenous, 8
  medieval, 93
  modern, 14, 16, 26
  non-European, 15, 23
  Pashtun, 52
  pastoral, 19, 148
  Portuguese, 185
  profit-oriented, 35*n*46
  sedentary, 19, 147–148
South Asia, 2–4, 8, 13, 17, 19–20, 22, 24–32, 39*n*111, 48–49, 51–53, 56, 65–66, 69, 85, 90, 92–93, 103–104, 106–108, 113–114, 116–118, 124–126, 145, 167, 183, 203, 211, 216–217, 224–225, 227, 230–231, 239–240
  early modern of, 43, 83, 85, 94, 96, 141, 146, 148, 152
  engaged with European technological advancements, 76
  environmental processes in, 142
  gunpowder weaponry dissemination in, 226
  Jainism, 84, 94, 96
  medieval in, 97, 141
  Military Revolution hypothesis in, 226
  military success of Mughals in, 234–236
  political economy of, 183–185
  and politics of Medieval in twentieth-century, 8–12
  Sufism in, 43–44, 47
  and western Europe, difference between, 20–21
South India, 12, 30, 149, 165, 174, 176
  early modernity in, 20
  geographical imaginary of, 175
  history, 20, 161–162, 164, 167
South Indian vernaculars, 20
state formation, 183, 194–195
  cycles of, 103
  in early medieval period, 166
  reduced to teleological analysis, 162
Sufi, 29, 43, 55
  customs and practices as innovations, 53
  Islam, 31, 51
  masters, 43
  network, 44, 49–53, 57
  orders, 43–49, 51, 54–57

personalities, 50
premakhyan, 51
rituals, 50
romantic tales, 51
saints, 43
sama, 51
shrines, 56
spiritual discourse, 51
suborders, 49
treatises, 50
writings, 52
Sufism, 29, 49–50, 53, 55, 69, 162
    Chishti, 46–47
    colonial modernity for, 58
    history of, 43, 56
    South Asian, 44
sustainability, 153

trade, 114–115, 118, 141, 145, 153, 169, 175, 186, 189–191, 194–197, 204, 208, 222n59
    cross-cultural, 205
    global networks, 106
    interregional, 116
    maritime, 203, 206
    overseas, 111–112, 210
    and politics, 220n38
    transoceanic, 126
    transregional, 28, 192
trust, 46, 208–209, 214
    intra-community, 204

text, 20–21, 28, 51–53, 55, 70, 85–93, 95, 98n20, 125, 130, 135–136, 142, 163, 170, 172, 174, 195
tashkik, 69, 71
tashkik al-wujud, 69, 73

vernacular, 22, 29, 126, 130, 163
    culture, rise of, 37n75, 90
    languages, 49–53, 57, 19
    literary, 109, 125
    modernities, 84
    South Indian, 20
violence, 4, 15, 22, 240
    against women, 35n36
    caste system, 35n36
    of idea of modernity, 32
    legitimation of, 31
    military, 30, 238–239
    of periodization in Indian history, 162–166

warfare, 4, 29, 133. *See also* Mughal warfare
    interstate, 31, 106
wahdat al-wujud, 48, 54, 57, 59n9, 61n35, 62n40, 72
war and society approach, 228, 240

zamindar(s), 122n38, 142, 150–153, 159n54, 230, 244n40